Advance Praise for *Real World XML W*

Collected from reader comments on advance chapters
posted at www.learnxmlws.com.

"Of all the Web services development documents I have read, this material gives me the best sense of how to create a Web service with VS .NET."
   —Mark Conde, Systems Architect, Centers for Disease Control

"The book is very well written with complete and well structured examples. Good work!"
   —Henk ten Bos

"This book is very well written. It explains in simple terms the whole confusing technical web that has been constructed behind Web services."
   —Tanu Malik

"Very good. Clear and well structured! Actually gets to the point rather than regurgitating the hype."
   —Adam Ward, referring to Chapter 1—Introduction to Web Services

"Excellent—a good top-down approach. It touches on all aspects surrounding Web services."
   —Pankaj Chawla, referring to Chapter 1—Introduction to Web Services

"Excellent review of Web services. I have been using VB .NET and thinking about deploying Web services. This chapter helped me make up my mind to move forward."
   —Ben Park, MD, referring to Chapter 1—Introduction to Web Services

"Terrific coverage of a fairly complex range of topics. Very clear and lucid writing style."

—Marc Fairorth, President, Helpdesk Response, Inc.,
referring to Chapter 2—XSD: The Web Services Type System

"As a beginner to XML/XSD, I think this chapter is excellent. The explanation/examples become increasingly more complex as you read the chapter. I think this is great teaching. It is how I, personally, learn best."

—Doug Rowe, referring to Chapter 2—XSD: The Web Services Type System

"Intense subjects, presented well."

—Mitchell Rivera, referring to Chapter 2—XSD: The Web Services Type System

"This is the best information I have read. Such an eye-opener. Great job!"

—Anith Sen, referring to Chapter 2—XSD: The Web Services Type System

"Gives a very good overview of SOAP. Many developers have no clear picture about xml-messaging and xml-rpc. This chapter gives a very clear explanation. After reading it, one should be able to use the tools around SOAP much better."

—Josef Flatscher, software developer, referring to Chapter 3—SOAP: Invoking Web Services

"It's great to read an explanation of SOAP that goes past the trivial level."

—Paul Madsen, Web Services Product Manager, Entrust, referring to Chapter 3—SOAP: Invoking Web Services

"This chapter explains .NET XML Web service fundamentals. I cannot find these details in any book or online."

—Harenda Kumar, referring to Chapter 6—.NET Web Services

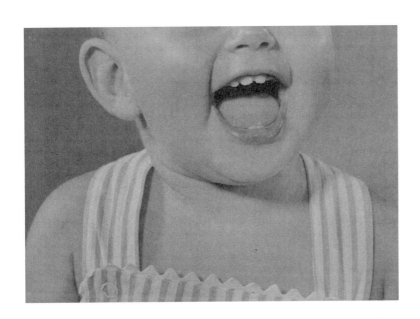

The DevelopMentor Series

Don Box, Series Editor

Addison-Wesley has joined forces with DevelopMentor, a premiere developer resources company, to produce a series of technical books written by developers for developers. DevelopMentor boasts a prestigious technical staff that includes some of the world's best-known computer-science professionals.

*"Works in **The DevelopMentor Series** are practical and informative sources on the tools and techniques for applying component-based technologies to real-world, large-scale distributed systems."*
    —Don Box, Architect, Microsoft Corporation

Titles in the Series:

Bob Beauchemin, *Essential ADO.NET*, 0-201-75866-0

Don Box, *Essential COM*, 0-201-63446-5

Don Box, Aaron Skonnard, and John Lam, *Essential XML: Beyond Markup*, 0-201-70914-7

Keith Brown, *Programming Windows Security*, 0-201-60442-6

Matthew Curland, *Advanced Visual Basic 6: Power Techniques for Everyday Programs*, 0-201-70712-8

Doug Dunn, *Java™ Rules*, 0-201-70916-3

Tim Ewald, *Transactional COM+L: Building Scalable Applications*, 0-201-61594-0

Jon Flanders, *ASP Internals*, 0-201-61618-1

Richard Grimes, *Developing Applications with Visual Studio.NET*, 0-201-70852-3

Martin Gudgin, *Essential IDL: Interface Design for COM*, 0-201-61595-9

Stuart Halloway, *Component Development for the Java™ Platform*, 0-201-75306-5

Joe Hummel, Ted Pattison, Justin Gehtland, Doug Turnure, and Brian A. Randell, *Effective Visual Basic: How to Improve Your VB/COM+ Applications*, 0-201-70476-5

Stanley B. Lippman, *C# Primer: A Practical Approach*, 0-201-72955-5

Everett N. McKay and Mike Woodring, *Debugging Windows Programs: Strategies, Tools, and Techniques for Visual C++ Programmers*, 0-201-70238-X

Aaron Skonnard and Martin Gudgin, *Essential XML Quick Reference: A Programmer's Reference to XML, XPath, XSLT, XML Schema, SOAP, and More*, 0-201-74095-8

Watch for future titles in The DevelopMentor Series.

Real World XML Web Services

For VB and VB .NET Developers

Yasser Shohoud

✦ Addison-Wesley

Boston • San Francisco • New York • Toronto • Montreal
London • Munich • Paris • Madrid
Capetown • Sydney • Tokyo • Singapore • Mexico City

The publisher offers discounts on this book when ordered in quantity for special sales. For more information, please contact:

Pearson Education Corporate Sales Division
201 W. 103rd Street
Indianapolis, IN 46290
(800) 428-5331
corpsales@pearsoned.com

Visit Addison-Wesley on the Web: www.awprofessional.com

Library of Congress Cataloging-in-Publication Data

Shohoud, Yasser.
    Real world XML Web services : for VB and VB .NET developers / Yasser Shohoud.
        p.   cm.
    Includes bibliographical references and index.
    ISBN 0-201-77425-9
    1. Internet programming. 2. XML (Document markup language) 3. Microsoft Visual
    BASIC. 4. Microsoft .NET Framework. I. Title.

    QA76.625 .S52 2002
    005.2'76—dc21

                                                    2002074700

ISBN: 0-201-77425-9
Text printed on recycled paper
1 2 3 4 5 6 7 8 9 10—CRS—0605040302
First printing, September 2002

To S, O, A, and P.

Contents

Foreword by Keith Ballinger

You are holding in your hands my favorite book on Web services and .NET. Yasser has done an outstanding job of pulling together an intelligent and well-thought-out book that provides you with tons of practical information about Web services.

One of the things that always used to frustrate me when I read a Web services book that cost more than five dollars was the apparent inexperience of the author, which became clear after a month of trying to implement his suggestions. You know what I'm talking about: wrong information about APIs, boneheaded architectural recommendations that would never perform well, and sample code that is a security hole. All that's the hard stuff.

With Yasser's book, I don't think you'll spend much time being frustrated; Yasser's covering the hard stuff and is also setting you up for success with this book. He's thought hard, written hard, and listened hard. Listened to whom? Well, to you. He's an active member of the developer community. He's also listened hard to me and the other members of Microsoft's development team.

What else can I say? Read his book, and be prepared for a new way of coding!

Keith Ballinger
Program Manager, XML Messaging
Microsoft
http://keithba.com

Foreword by Aaron Skonnard

There definitely isn't a shortage of XML or Web services-related titles today. What's missing from most of these books, however, is a focus on the true "Web services platform," which consists of the core XML technologies most authors prefer to brush over or avoid altogether.

You can't blame authors alone for this dilemma since most developers who purchase their books want to avoid XML technologies at all costs and they demand the same focus from publishers. Developers who feel this way about Web services typically want tool vendors to hide the XML details and make every Web service look like a method on an object. These developers are missing the point.

Yasser has written the first Web services book to break this trend. His book focuses on the Web services platform from the ground up. The book starts by introducing the fundamental Web services architecture and its core technology underpinnings, including XML 1.0, XML Schema, SOAP, WSDL, and UDDI. Yasser does a great job explaining not only how these technologies work, but also why they matter to a Web services developer grappling to understand the platform. Each chapter spotlights a core Web services technology centered on clear explanations, compelling examples, and most importantly, code.

Yasser's approach clarifies some common misconceptions about Web services design and helps to promote best practices that will prepare you for long-term success. As an example, he emphasizes that the Web services "interface" is the XML message on the wire, not the class definition one may work with to process the message in VB. Understanding this key distinction is crucial to understanding the rest of the Web services platform.

Not only is the book conceptually solid, it is also practical. The book is chock-full of examples illustrating how Microsoft's Web services implementations work in both the VB 6 (Microsoft SOAP Toolkit) and .NET environments. As you read through the prose and parse through the accompanying sample code, you're bound to experience the breakthrough epiphanies that make reading a technical book worthwhile.

If you've been searching for a book that goes beyond the Web services hype and distills the benefits of the actual platform; look no further, you've found the right one.

Aaron Skonnard
Instructor and Author, DevelopMentor
http://skonnard.com

Preface

There's no doubt that the Web was a catalyst for a revolution that changed the lives of software developers and end users alike. Web services provide the foundation for another profound revolution in the way we build and use applications. It is up to developers like you and me to take this foundation and make the revolution happen. In this book, I aim to give you the information and insight you need to design and build next-generation, distributed interoperable applications with Web services.

The book is divided into two sections: Chapters 1 through 4 explain the architectural foundation on which Web services are built. Chapters 5 through 13 explain the tools you use to build Web services, including the SOAP Toolkit and the .NET Framework.

Intended Audience

This book is intended for experienced developers who have little or no experience with Web services. The book assumes you have programmed with VB 6, classic ASP, and VB .NET. It assumes you understand the fundamentals of Web application development and have a basic understanding of XML documents and the XML Document Object Model (XML DOM). This book is not intended for developers who have no .NET knowledge or experience.

A Live Book

The world of Web services is changing rapidly. There are new standards being defined every month and new implementations of those standards being released on a hectic schedule. It is impossible for a traditional printed book to keep up with this rapid pace of change. When I set out to write this book, I decided to combine the print version with an online version that will be maintained and kept up-to-date with the evolving standards.

As an owner of the printed book, you have access to the online version, including all the new content being added as standards emerge and tools change. Please make sure you take a look at what's new online at http://www.LearnXml ws.com/book.

Chapter 1 Introduction to Web Services

To start things off I explain what Web services are and the scenarios where they prove useful. I also show you how to create Web services with .NET and with the SOAP Toolkit. The idea is to give you a head start on creating and invoking Web services before digging into the details.

Chapter 2 XSD: The Web Services Type System

This is the first of three chapters that covers the fundamentals of Web services. Chapter 2 explains the syntax and usage of XML Schemas and shows examples of validating schemas using VB .NET and VB 6. The chapter also covers XML Serialization and shows examples of shaping the XML generated by the .NET XML Serializer.

Chapter 3 SOAP: Invoking Web Services

Having understood schemas, this chapter explains SOAP, the Web services protocol. It explains how you can use SOAP for messaging and Remote Procedure Calls (RPC). It also shows you how to communicate error information to SOAP clients and the built-in mechanism for extending SOAP.

Chapter 4 WSDL: Describing Web Services

Chapter 4 completes the fundamentals by explaining the Web Services Description Languages (WSDL). The chapter begins with an overview then goes into the details of WSDL documents. It shows you practical examples of writing and reading WSDL documents. While it's unlikely that you'll need to create WSDL documents from scratch, it's likely that you'll need to read them and possibly modify them.

Chapter 5 The Microsoft SOAP Toolkit

Chapter 5 is the first of a series of chapters that covers the tools you use to build Web services. This entire chapter is dedicated to building Web services with the SOAP Toolkit. It shows you how to expose an existing COM component as a Web service using both the high-level and low-level APIs. It also explains how to handle SOAP headers and SOAP faults.

Chapter 6 .NET Web Services

After learning the SOAP Toolkit, this chapter explains how to create and invoke Web services using the .NET Framework. Beyond the basics, this chapter shows you the various features provided by the .NET Framework, such as output caching, data caching, and SOAP message shaping. The last section of this chapter dives into the details of Web service clients explaining how Web service proxies work and how you can customize them.

Chapter 7 SOAP Header and Fault

This chapter builds on what you learned in Chapters 3 and 6 and shows you how to implement SOAP headers with the .NET Framework. It explains how to create SOAP headers that are understood by the Web service and how to process headers on the service. It also shows you how to use SOAP Fault to communicate rich error information between service and client.

Chapter 8 Interface-Based Web Service Development

This chapter explains the process of interface-based Web services development that is necessary for large-scale projects and useful for smaller projects. The chapter goes through the steps of defining and implementing an interface, and then covers implementing multiple interfaces on one Web service.

Chapter 9 Handling Data In .NET Web Services

When building real-world Web services, most of the problems you'll encounter will center on data. Whether you are sending or receiving data, you'll almost always need to decide the optimum format for the data and how to achieve it. This chapter focuses on the mechanics of handling data in .NET Web services. The chapter is divided into sections covering ADO.NET DataSets, XML documents, custom objects, and object arrays.

Chapter 10 Reusable Infrastructure with SOAP Extensions

.NET provides an architecture for performing custom request/response processing at the SOAP message level via SOAP extensions. Chapter 10 explains how SOAP extensions work and shows you three example SOAP extensions, including one for compressing/decompressing SOAP messages.

Chapter 11 UDDI: A Web Service

This chapter explains the Universal Description, Discovery, and Integration standards and demonstrates scenarios where UDDI is useful. The objective of this chapter is to open your mind to design patterns and usage scenarios that leverage Web services registries. Such registries will become commonplace within the intranet with future versions of Windows server.

Chapter 12 Other SOAP Toolkits

Throughout the process of building and maintaining Web services you're likely to run into interoperability issues with other SOAP implementations. This chapter explains some of the more common SOAP toolkits including Apache SOAP and PocketSoap and shows you how they interoperate with .NET Web services.

Chapter 13 A Web Service Walkthrough

To wrap things up, Chapter 13 walks you through the steps of building a .NET Web service with .NET and VB 6 clients. The chapter also covers registering the service with UDDI.

Acknowledgments

I always thought authors exaggerated when they said a book wouldn't have been possible without the help of dozens of folks. Now I know it is an understatement. There are so many people who directly or indirectly helped make this book a reality that I don't even know where to start, but I am sure I will unintentially omit some of them. So if you contributed to this project and your name is not mentioned here, I apologize for that.

First, I would like to thank the folks at Microsoft for their help. Especially Mike Iem for all his ongoing support, Karsten Januszewski, Keith Ballinger, and Jeffery Schlimmer for their valuable suggestions and comments.

A special thanks to the Addison-Wesley team for their focus and dedication to quality. Thanks to Stephane Thomas for working with me through this project and being patient when some deadlines went whizzing by. Thanks also to Kathy Cantwell, Patrick Cash-Peterson, Curt Johnson, Chanda Leary-Coutu, and Simone Payment.

Thanks to Ethan Roberts, Colin Bowern, and Robert Kobenter for providing useful and insightful feedback.

For the dozens of people who have reviewed my book online: Thank you for taking the time to read drafts and volunteer your feedback.

Thanks to my wife Paky, for believing in me and being patient while I worked on this and many other projects. Finally, thanks to my children—Sara, Omar, and Amro for enduring my absence and providing much needed encouragement through the highs and lows of completing this book.

Chapter 1

Introduction to Web Services

Imagination is more important than knowledge. —Albert Einstein

You've probably heard and read about Web services. It seems like every trade publication, book, and Web site mentions Web services. Unfortunately, most of the current coverage does not clearly explain what Web services are really all about. It just trumpets how wonderful they are; which comes across as hype. Chapter 1 focuses on two things: explaining what Web services are really all about and showing you scenarios where you should use Web services and scenarios where you shouldn't.

1.1 Distributed Applications and the Browser

If you look around at today's application development, you'll find a definite shift toward thin, browser-based clients. Obviously this is not because thin clients offer a richer user experience; it's because such clients eliminate the high costs of deploying an application to the desktop. Desktop applications are costly to deploy, partly due to the issues of installing and configuring the application and partly due to the issues of communicating between the client and the server.

Traditionally, a rich Windows client uses Distributed Component Object Model (DCOM) to communicate with the server and to invoke remote objects. Configuring DCOM to work properly in a large network is usually a challenge that most IT professionals dread. In fact, most IT professionals would rather put up with the limited functionality of a browser than the issues of running DCOM over an intranet. The result, in my opinion, is an application that is easy to deploy, but difficult to develop, and severely limited in its user interface. Ultimately, this means you spend more time and money developing what is, from a user's standpoint, a less-functional application. To understand exactly what I mean, ask accountants what they think about the new Web-based accounting application that replaced the older Windows version. Most business application users would rather have the rich Windows user interface.

An ideal solution to the client-server communications problem is to use HTTP as the communications protocol.[1] HTTP is a good choice because any machine that can use a Web browser is by definition running HTTP. Also, many firewalls today are configured to allow only HTTP traffic.

1.2 Interoperability

Another issue that many business applications face is that of interoperability with other applications. It would be great if all applications were written in COM- or .NET-aware languages running on Windows. However, the fact is most business data is still kept on mainframes in non-relational databases (such as Virtual Storage Access Method) files and accessed by mainframe applications written in COBOL. (There are also many business applications being developed every day in C++, Java, Visual Basic, and a variety of other languages.) Today, all but the simplest applications need to integrate and exchange data with other applications running on heterogeneous platforms. Integrating such applications is typically done on a case-by-case basis via file transfer and parsing, message queuing, or possibly proprietary APIs like IBM's Advanced Program to Program Communication (APPC). There were no standards that enabled two applications to communicate regardless of their platform, component model, and programming language. Through Web services standards, clients and servers can communicate over HTTP regardless of platform or programming language.

1.3 What Are Web Services?

There are at least two answers to the question "What are Web services?" On the surface, a Web service is simply an application that exposes a Web-accessible

---

[1]To make Windows clients a viable alternative, the deployment problem must also be solved. Fortunately, .NET Windows Forms provide a solution to this problem. Now the problem becomes getting the .NET Framework on every desktop!

API. That means you can invoke this application programmatically over the Web. Applications invoking this Web service are referred to as clients. For example, if you wanted to build a Web service that returns current weather information, you could build an ASP page that accepts a zip code in the query string and returns a comma-delimited string containing the current temperature and weather condition. To invoke this ASP page, the client sends an HTTP GET request with a URL that looks like this:

```
http://host.company.com/weather.asp?zipcode=20171
```

and the returned data might look like this:

```
86,sunny
```

This simple ASP page is a legitimate Web service because it exposes a Web-accessible API based on HTTP GET requests. But there is a lot more to Web services than this. A more accurate explanation of Web services is: *Web services are a new, standard platform for building interoperable distributed applications.* As a Windows developer, you've probably built component-based distributed applications using COM and DCOM. While COM is an excellent component technology, there are certain scenarios where it doesn't work well.

The Web services platform is a set of standards that applications follow to achieve interoperability via the Web. You write your Web services in whatever language and on any platform you like, as long as those Web services can be viewed and accessed according to the Web services standards.

1.4   The New Platform

The Web services platform needs a minimum set of features to enable building distributed applications. Any platform must have a data representation format and a type system. To enable interoperability, the Web services platform must provide a *standard* type system that bridges today's differences among type systems of different platforms, programming languages, and component models.

Traditionally, interface-based platforms for distributed systems have provided some means of formally describing interfaces, methods, and parameters.

Similarly, the Web services platform must provide a means for describing a Web service and for providing the information others need to invoke this Web service.

Finally, there must be a mechanism for invoking Web services remotely, similar to a Remote Procedure Call (RPC) protocol. To promote interoperability, this RPC-like protocol must be platform- and programming-language independent. The following sections briefly describe the technologies that make up the Web services platform.

1.4.1 XML and XSD

Extensible Markup Language (XML) is the basic format for representing data on the Web services platform. In addition to being simple to create and parse, XML was chosen because it is neither platform- nor vendor-specific. Being neutral is more important than being technically superior: Software vendors are much more likely to adopt a neutral technology than one that was invented by a competitor.

XML provides a simple way of representing data, but it says nothing about the standard set of data types available and how to extend that set. For example, what exactly is an integer? Is it 16, 32, or 64 bits? Such details are important to enable interoperability. The W3C XML Schema (XSD) is a standard that specifies some built-in types and a language to define additional types. The Web services platform uses XSD as its type system. When you build Web services in your programming language (for example, VB .NET or C#), the data types you use must be translated to XSD types to conform to the Web services standards. The tools you use might automate this translation for you, but you are likely to have to tweak the result to meet your needs. Chapter 2 explains XSD and how to translate custom types (for example, classes) to XSD types.

1.4.2 SOAP

Once you've built a Web service, you and/or others will want to invoke it. The Simple Object Access Protocol provides the standard RPC mechanism used for invoking Web services. A clever acronym, SOAP is actually a bit of a misnomer: It implies that the underlying Web service representation is an object when in fact it doesn't have to be. You can write your Web service as a series of functions in C and still invoke it using SOAP. The SOAP specification provides standards for the format of a SOAP message and how SOAP should be used over HTTP. SOAP also builds on XML and XSD to provide standard rules for encoding data as XML. Chapter 3 discusses SOAP and explains the components of SOAP messages.

1.4.3 WSDL

How do you explain to others the functions that your Web service exposes and the parameters each function accepts? You might do it informally by writing a document that provides this information or you might simply verbalize it to someone who needs to invoke your Web service. The informal approach has at least one serious problem: When a developer sits down to build a client for your Web service, his development tool (for example, Visual Studio) cannot offer him any help because that tool has no idea about the Web service's functions and parameters. Providing a formal description in a machine-readable format solves this problem.

The Web Service Description Language (WSDL) is an XML-based grammar for describing Web services, their functions, parameters, and return values. Being XML-based, WSDL is both machine- and human-readable, which is a big plus. Some modern development tools can generate a WSDL document describing your Web service as well as consume a WSDL document and generate the necessary code to invoke the Web service. Chapter 4 explains the WSDL grammar and shows you examples of WSDL documents generated by various tools.

1.5 Typical Web Service Architecture

Regardless of the tools or programming languages you use to build Web services, the high-level architecture shown in Figure 1.1, is typical, assuming you are using SOAP over HTTP to invoke the Web service. Typically, you'll build your Web service using your favorite programming language (for example, VB 6 or VB .NET) then expose it using the SOAP Toolkit or .NET's built-in support for Web services. A client written in any language and running on any platform can invoke your Web service by processing the WSDL document that describes your service. The client then formulates a SOAP request message based on the

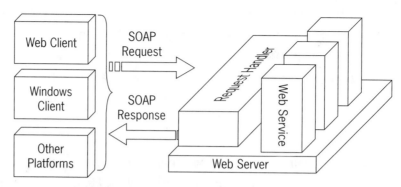

Figure 1.1   Typical Web service architecture

service description. Your Web service will sit behind a Web server, typically Internet Information Server (IIS), which receives the SOAP request message as part of an HTTP POST request. The Web server forwards these requests to a Web service request handler for processing. For VB 6 Web services, the request handler is either an ASP page or an ISAPI extension working together with the SOAP Toolkit components. For VB .NET, the request handler is part of the .NET Framework. The request handler is responsible for parsing the SOAP request, invoking your Web service, and creating the proper SOAP response. The Web server then takes this SOAP response and sends it back to the client as part of the HTTP response.

1.6   Remote Procedure Calls versus Messaging

Web services are all about applications communicating. There are two common ways that applications communicate today: RPC (Remote Procedure Calls) and Messaging. The difference between the two is largely a matter of approach and architecture rather than hard-core technical differences. SOAP supports both RPC and messaging and most of today's tools, including the Microsoft SOAP Toolkit and .NET Web services support both formats. Which one you use depends on how you perceive your application's architecture.

When using RPC, the client thinks in terms of invoking a remote procedure on the server. This usually means instantiating a remote object and invoking its methods. Thinking is centered on the remote object and its interface, that is, the properties and methods that it exposes and their parameters. DCOM and .NET remoting are examples of RPC mechanisms.

Messaging is typically associated with more loosely coupled systems. A messaging client thinks in terms of sending a message to a server and, possibly, receiving a response message. Thinking in messaging systems is centered on the request and response message format rather than the remote object's interface. By focusing only on message formats, and by designing extensible messages, the client and server are less tightly coupled than in the case of RPC.

Some RPC systems try to provide location transparency: They expose the remote object's interface as if it were local and hide what's being sent on the wire so the client does not need to worry about the fact that the server object is on another machine. For example, when you use VB 6 to invoke a remote object via DCOM, your code can look identical to that when invoking a local object. On the other hand, messaging systems let you control what's on the wire (that is, the message payload) and hide what's on the other end. The client has no idea how the server is implemented or how it processes the message.

That said, you can create a messaging server that dispatches calls to objects based on the messages it receives. This effectively implements RPC via two-way messaging. If the client still thinks and operates in terms of messages, you call it messaging. If the client thinks and operates in terms of instantiating and invoking a remote object, you call it RPC.

When you implement XML-based messaging, most of your focus will be on the XML request and response messages. Tools for building Web services in VB .NET do much of the work involved in XML messaging. VB 6 tools (the SOAP Toolkit) also handles a great deal of the work, but you have to do a little more work yourself compared with .NET. Therefore in many cases, you'll need to do some message manipulation yourself. Understanding XML and XML Schemas is essential to implement XML messaging systems effectively.

Throughout this book, you'll find recommendations to use messaging over RPC whenever possible. This is because messaging relies on XML Schemas to describe the data being transmitted. This close relationship with the standard XML type system means messaging can be far more effective at interoperability.

1.7 Creating Web Services

By now you are probably anxious to get your hands dirty with some coding and to see Web services in action. This section introduces you to the mechanics of creating and invoking Web services in VB 6 and VB .NET. The intent is to expose you to the tools rather than to provide detailed coverage of how Web services work. The remainder of this book focuses on the inner workings of Web services and the tools you use, including the Microsoft SOAP Toolkit and .NET. See Chapters 5 and 6 for details on building Web services with the SOAP Toolkit and .NET respectively.

1.7.1 Using the SOAP Toolkit

Microsoft's SOAP Toolkit lets you expose COM components as Web services. There are three major components of the toolkit: `SoapClient` is a COM component that COM-enabled clients use to invoke Web services. `SoapServer` is a COM component responsible for processing incoming SOAP requests and returning the SOAP response. The WSDL Wizard reads your component's type library and generates a WSDL document that describes the methods you want to expose.

Assume you have a COM component that exposes a `GetTemperature` method:

```
Public Function GetTemperature(ByVal zipcode As String, _
                          ByVal celsius As Boolean) As Single
```

To make this component into a Web service, you start by running the WSDL Wizard and pointing it to the component's binary (the .DLL). The Wizard will then ask you to choose the methods you want to expose, the URL of the Web service (for example, http://VBWSServer/VBWSBook/Chapter1/Temperature/), and whether you want an ASP or ISAPI listener (Figure 1.2). The wizard will then ask for the folder where the generated WSDL (and possibly ASP) file should be saved.

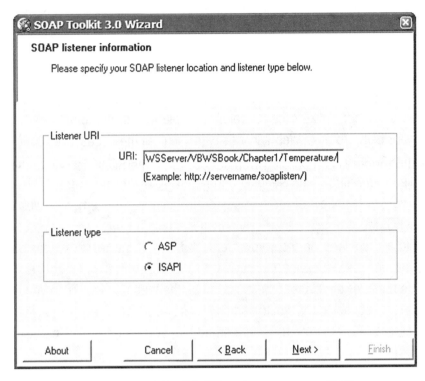

Figure 1.2 Using the SOAP Toolkit Wizard to expose a COM component

To invoke this Web service, you use the `SoapClient` component from VB or any other COM-enabled client. The following code snippet invokes the Web service's `GetTemperature` method:

```
Dim soap As MSSOAPLib.SoapClient
Set soap = New MSSOAPLib.SoapClient
soap.mssoapinit _
"http://VBWSServer/VBWSBook/Chapter1/Temperature/
➥Temperature.wsdl"
MsgBox ("Temperature is: " & _
soap.GetTemperature("20171", False))
```

First, you initialize the SoapClient by calling `mssoapinit` and passing it the URL of the WSDL document. The WSDL document's URL is made up of the URL that you specified when you ran the wizard with the *ServiceName*.wsdl appended to it. Once the `SoapClient` is initialized, you can call the Web service methods as if they were `SoapClient` methods.

1.7.2 Using .NET

The .NET platform provides built-in support for building and consuming standards-based Web services. Unlike other development platforms, you don't need additional tools or SDKs to build Web services with .NET. All the necessary support is built into the .NET Framework itself, including the server-side request handlers and the client-side support for sending and receiving SOAP messages. This section gives you an overview of the steps used to build and implement a Web service with .NET. More details will be discussed starting in Chapter 6.

To build a .NET Web service, you create a file with the .asmx extension. In this file, you put a WebService directive with the programming language you'll use and the name of the class to be exposed as the Web service. Then you write your class as you normally would, adding a `System.Web.Services.Web-MethodAttribute` attribute to each method that you want to expose as shown in Listing 1.1.

Listing 1.1 Creating a Web service with VB .NET (VBWSBook\Chapter1\myService\calc_vb.asmx)

```
<%@WebService Language="VB" class="Calc" %>
'a WebService in VB .NET (calc_vb.asmx)
Imports System.Web.Services
Public Class Calc
    <WebMethod()> _
    Public Function Add(ByVal a As Double, _
                        ByVal b As Double) As Double
        Return a + b
    End Function
End Class
```

You can view a test page for this Web service by using a browser and navigating to the .asmx file. For example, if you placed the calc_vb.asmx file in a folder called myService under the VBWSBook virtual directory, the corresponding URL would be:

```
http://vbwsserver/vbwsbook/chapter1/myService/calc_vb.asmx
```

Navigating to this URL brings up the Web service test page shown in Figure 1.3. This auto-generated page shows you the service name at the top, followed by a list of methods exposed by this service. Below this list of methods, there's a long essay explaining that you are using the default namespace `http://tempuri.org/` and that you should pick a different and unique namespace for your Web service when you publish it. I'll discuss XML namespaces in Chapter 2. In Chapter 6, I will show you how to specify your Web service namespace and otherwise customize the service using CLR attributes.

If you click on the link to the Add method, you will get an HTML form that you can use to test that method (see Figure 1.4). On this form, there's an HTML input

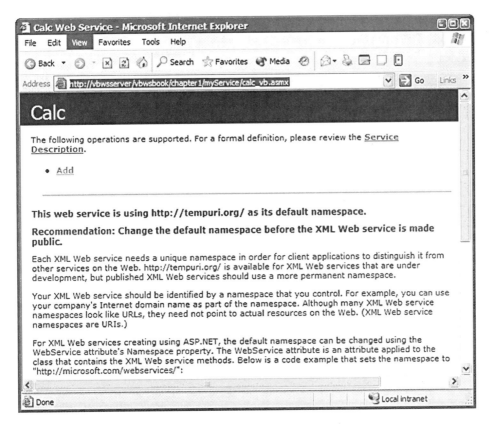

Figure 1.3 The auto-generated Web service test page

field for each parameter the method accepts. When you enter the parameter values and click Invoke, the form is submitted to the Web server. This is essentially invoking the Web service via an HTTP GET request. You get back the result in a simple XML document that looks like this:

```
<double xmlns="http://tempuri.org/">158</double>
```

Alternatively, you can invoke the Add method directly by navigating to the following URL:

```
http://vbwsserver/vbwsbook/chapter1/myService/calc_vb.asmx/
➡Add?a=123&b=3
```

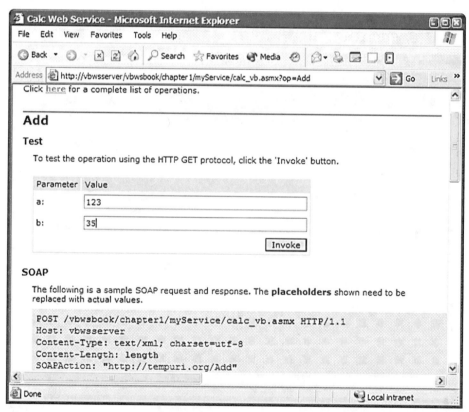

Figure 1.4 The auto-generated HTML form for testing a Web method

As you can see, the method name becomes the actual resource you are requesting (it is case sensitive) and each method parameter becomes a parameter in the query string. This test form is very convenient for quickly testing a Web service. However, because it uses HTTP GET, it has some limitations on the data types and parameter directions it supports.

If you go back to the Web service test page and click on the service description link at the top of the page, you can view the WSDL document describing this Web service as shown in Figure 1.5. You can also go directly to this WSDL document by adding a query string with `wsdl` at the end of the URL:

```
http://vbwsserver/vbwsbook/chapter1/myService/calc_vb.asmx?wsdl
```

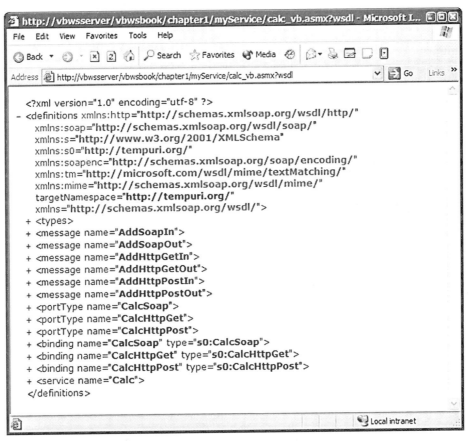

Figure 1.5 The WSDL document for the Calc service. Note that XML elements are collapsed to show you more of the document.

To invoke this Web service using a .NET client, you must create a class that acts as a proxy for the Web service. Clients then invoke methods on this class and the class handles invoking the Web service.

While you can manually create such a class, there's a .NET tool called wsdl.exe that will automatically generate the proxy class for you. This tool reads the WSDL describing your Web service and generates a proxy class that can be used to invoke that Web service. For example, to generate a proxy class for the Calc service, type the following at a command prompt:

```
wsdl.exe /language:VB http://vbwsserver/vbwsbook/chapter1/
➥myService /calc_vb.asmx?wsdl
```

Listing 1.2 shows a snippet of the proxy class generated for the calculator service in VB. The generated proxy class inherits from `System.Web.Services.Protocols.SoapHttpClientProtocol` and exposes a method called `Add` that takes in two doubles and returns a double.

Listing 1.2   Snippet of the Web service proxy generated by wsdl.exe

```
Imports System.Web.Services.Protocols
'Other code omitted
Public Class Calc
 Inherits SoapHttpClientProtocol
 'Other code omitted
 <System.Web.Services.Protocols.SoapDocumentMethodAttribute( _
"http://tempuri.org/Add", _
RequestNamespace:="http://tempuri.org/", _
ResponseNamespace:="http://tempuri.org/", _
Use:=System.Web.Services.Description.SoapBindingUse.Literal, _
ParameterStyle:= SoapParameterStyle.Wrapped)> _
    Public Function Add(ByVal a As Double, ByVal b As Double) _
         As Double
           Dim results() As Object = Me.Invoke("Add", _
                                     New Object() {a, b})
           Return CType(results(0), Double)
    End Function
        'Other code omitted
 End Class
```

Calling the Web service from a VB .NET client is as easy as creating an object from the `Calc` proxy class and invoking its `Add` method.

```
Dim ws As New Calc()
Dim result As Double = ws.Add(20.5, 10.9)
MessageBox.Show("Result is: " & result.ToString)
```

The proxy's `Add` method simply invokes the Web service using the .NET Framework's `SoapHttpClientProtocol` class. It then returns the result that it gets back from invoking the Web service.

Of course there's a lot more to creating and invoking .NET Web services than what I just showed you. But before we can dig into those details, you need to understand the underlying technologies that make Web services work, namely XSD, SOAP, and WSDL. The next three chapters explain the foundation for Web services; then, starting in Chapter 5, we dig deeply into the tools and mechanics for building Web services.

1.8   When to Use Web Services

Now I'll explain some scenarios where you can realize significant benefits by using Web services. After that, I'll explain scenarios where it makes no sense to use them.

1.8.1   Communicating through a Firewall

When you build a distributed application with hundreds or thousands of users spread over many locations, there's always the problem of communicating between the client and the server because of firewalls and proxy servers. You cannot easily use DCOM in this scenario and you don't want to deploy a client to the thousands of users out there, so you end up building a browser-based client and writing a facade of Active Server Pages (ASPs) to expose the middle tier to the user interface. The resulting architecture is at best difficult to develop in, and at worst impossible to maintain.

Consider what you have to do to add a new screen to your application: First, you must create the user interface (the Web page) and the corresponding middle-tier components that represent the business logic behind the new screen. But you must also build at least one active server page that receives input from the user interface, invokes the middle tier components, formats the result as HTML, and sends a new "results page" to the browser with the results. Wouldn't it be great if the client were easier to build with less dependence on HTML forms and the extra step of building the ASP could be avoided?

You can avoid this step by exposing your middle tier components as Web services and invoking them directly from a Windows user interface running on client machines. To invoke the Web service, you can use either a generic SOAP client like the Microsoft SOAP Toolkit or .NET, or you can build your own SOAP client and roll it out with the application. Not only does this save on development time compared to Web applications, but it also reduces the code complexity and improves overall maintainability. In addition, your application no longer has to navigate to a results page each time it invokes a middle-tier component. While using Windows clients requires that you deploy those clients, such deployment is becoming easier with .NET.

From experience, I can tell you that in an application with intensive interaction between the user interface and middle tier, this architecture can easily save 20 percent of the time spent on developing the user interface. As an added bonus, you end up with a layer of Web services that can be reused for any other purpose, such as application integration. Ultimately, exposing your application's logic and data via Web services provides a foundation for reusing your application from any client running on any platform.[2]

1.8.2 Application Integration

Corporate developers know that a good portion of development effort is spent on integrating applications written in various languages and running on disparate systems. Typically you need to get data into your application from a legacy application running on an IBM mainframe, or you need to send data from your application to a mainframe or Unix-based application. Even on the same platform, applications from different vendors often need to be integrated. By exposing some of its functionality and data via a Web service, an application provides a standard mechanism for other applications to integrate with it.

---

[2]There are two .NET technologies that let you expose components to remote clients via Web services: ASP.NET Web services and .NET Remoting. ASP.NET Web services is messaging oriented (by default) while Remoting is RPC oriented.

For example, you might have an order-entry application that's used to enter new orders, including customer information, shipping addresses, quantities, prices, and payment information. You might also have an order fulfillment application from another vendor. When a new order is entered, the order-entry application must notify the fulfillment application to ship the order. By adding a Web service layer on top of the fulfillment application, the "AddOrder" function can be exposed as a Web service. As shown in Figure 1.6, the order-entry application invokes this function each time a new order is placed.

1.8.3 Business-to-Business Integration

By using Web services to integrate applications, you can better automate business processes within a company. But what happens when the business processes cross company boundaries to span your company's suppliers and/or customers? Integrating business processes across multiple businesses is commonly referred to as business-to-business integration.

Web services are an enabling technology for B2B integration. By using Web services, your business can expose vital business processes to authorized

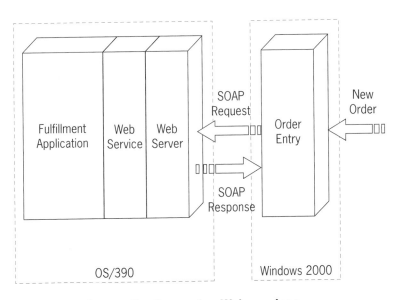

Figure 1.6 Integrating applications using Web services

suppliers and customers. For example, you can expose electronic ordering and invoicing, thereby enabling your customers to send you purchase orders and your suppliers to send you invoices electronically. This is not a new concept: Electronic Document Interchange (EDI) has been around for a while. Today the key difference is that Web services are much easier to implement than EDI and operate over the Internet, which is widely available to businesses globally, at a relatively low cost. However, Web services do not provide a complete solution for document interchange or B2B integration as EDI attempts to do. Instead, Web services are a key enabling component in B2B integration, with many other components typically needed to complete the picture.

The key advantage to using Web services for B2B integration is low-cost interoperability. By exposing your business functions as Web services, you are enabling any authorized party to invoke these services easily regardless of the platform and programming language they use. This reduces the time and effort it takes to integrate a business process across company boundaries and ultimately, leads to time and money savings. The low cost of integration opens the playing field for smaller companies that in the past found implementing EDI cost-prohibitive.

1.8.4 Software Reuse

Software reuse can take place in various forms and at different levels. The most basic form of code reuse is through reuse of source code modules or classes. Another form of code reuse is binary component-based reuse. Today there is a significant market for reusable software components such as grids and other user interface widgets. But software reuse has always been limited by one key factor: You can reuse the code but not the data behind it. The reason for this is that you can easily distribute components or source code, but you cannot easily distribute data unless it's fairly static data not expected to change much.

Web services let you reuse code along with its necessary data. Instead of buying and installing a third-party component and calling it from your application, your application calls a remote Web service. For example, if your application's user enters a mailing address that you want to validate, you can send it to an address verification Web service. This service can look up the street address, city, state, and zip code to make sure the address exists and is located in the specified zip code area. The service provider might charge you a periodic or per-use fee for using the service. A service like this is impossible with component reuse; you need to have the current database of street addresses, cities, states, and zip codes.

Another scenario for software reuse is when you are building an application that aggregates the functionality of several other applications. For example, you might build an intranet portal application that lets the user check on the status of a FedEx package, verify a stock quote, view their calendar, or purchase movie tickets. Today, all these functions can be performed on the Web using individual, separate applications. As those applications begin to expose their functionality through Web services, you can easily write a portal application that combines all their functionalities into one, consistent, easily-accessible user interface as shown in Figure 1.7.[3]

Many applications will take advantage of Web services to extend today's component-based architectures to become hybrids of component-based and service-based architectures. You will build applications that use one or more third-party Web services to perform their function. You might also expose your own Web services for use by others. In all these cases, you are reusing code and the data behind it. This is an extremely powerful form of software reuse.

1.9   When Not to Use Web Services

This introduction would be incomplete without explaining the situations where you should *not* use Web services. It is clear that Web services offer the most benefit in cases where interoperability and/or remoting over the Web are desired. That said, there are many scenarios where you do not benefit from using Web services.

---

[3]The OASIS Web Services for Remote Portals Technical Committee (WSRP) is working on defining an XML and Web services standard that will allow the plug and play of Web services that emit user interface rather than raw data. For more information see http://www.oasis-open.org/committees/wsrp.

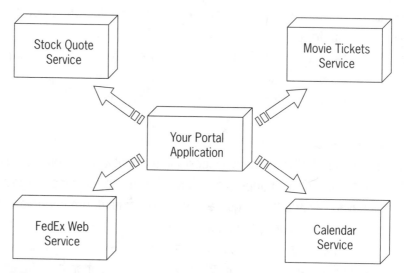

Figure 1.7 Using Web services to aggregate functionality from many applications into one, consistent user interface

1.9.1 Single Machine Applications

There are still many desktop applications for business and personal use. Some of those applications might need to communicate with others running on the same machine. In this case, it is almost always better to use a native API rather than a Web service. Software component technologies such as COM and .NET components are very effective in this scenario because using such components requires relatively little overhead. The same applies to server applications running on the same server: Use COM or some other native API to invoke one application from the other. While it's possible to use a Web service in this scenario, it is considered suboptimum with no added value.

1.9.2 Homogeneous Applications on a LAN

In many cases, you'll have applications developed using Visual Basic and/or Visual C++ and COM running on Windows platforms on the same Local Area Network (LAN). For example, you might have two server applications that want to communicate with each other or, more commonly, a Win32 or Windows Forms client that wants to communicate with its server counterpart on the same LAN. It's much more efficient for two such applications to communicate using DCOM rather than SOAP/HTTP. Similarly, if you have .NET applications that need to communicate with each other over a LAN, you can use .NET remoting. Interestingly, .NET remoting offers the option of using SOAP over HTTP, essentially acting as a Web service. But .NET remoting can also utilize a binary format, instead of SOAP, for RPC calls. This binary format is supposedly more efficient than using SOAP due to lower serialization/deserialization overhead. You can use remoting with the binary formatter over HTTP or directly over Transmission Control Protocol (TCP). Using HTTP as the transport allows you to use remoting through firewalls, while using TCP is supposed to yield better performance. Again, you would not use Web services in a scenario where you have other viable options that are more efficient or sensible from an application architecture viewpoint. This means if you have a scenario where it's feasible to use .NET remoting with the binary formatter over TCP, that's what you should use.

1.10 Summary

Web services are a new, standard platform for building interoperable distributed applications. The main thrust behind Web services is cross-platform interoperability. To achieve this, the Web services platform relies heavily on vendor and platform-neutral standards such as XML and XSD.

Web services offer tremendous value in scenarios that involve applications communicating across platform boundaries and over the Internet. Web service applications include application integration, business-to-business integration, code and data reuse, and the facilitation of communication between client and server over the Web.

Web services however, are no silver bullet and you shouldn't use them just because you can. There are certain scenarios where using Web services will cost you performance without buying you anything. For example, homogeneous applications running on the same machine or on different machines on the same LAN should not use Web services to communicate with each other.

The following chapters explore the technologies that make up the Web services platform beginning with the Web service type system based on XML and XSD.

Chapter 2

XSD: The Web Services Type System

If you open an empty cupboard and don't find an elephant inside, are
the contents of the cupboard different from opening it and not finding a
bicycle? —Andrew Layman, commenting on reification of NULLs.

Web services are all about data exchange between heterogeneous applications.
This data exchange cannot be accomplished without a common, agreed-upon
type system that provides standard types and enables you to define your own.
Chapter 2 is designed to get you up and running with XSD, the Web services
type system, and to show you how XSD is used to specify message formats and
validate data exchanged between client and service. This chapter is not intended
as a rigorous explanation of XSD—that would require another book. Rather, it explains those aspects of XSD that are commonly used in Web services.

2.1 Why a Type System?

Imagine a scenario where a VB 6 application needs to invoke a Java application.
The Java application is exposed as a Web service with one method called get-
Data. You are writing the VB application and you are told that the Java method
getData returns an integer. So you write your VB code to invoke the Web service
using SOAP, which I'll cover in the next chapter. When you run your application,
you can invoke the Web service, but sometimes you get runtime error 6 over-
flow! You get this error because a Java integer is a 32-bit number while a VB 6 integer is a 16-bit number.

What just happened was a problem due to the mismatch between the service and client type systems. To solve this problem, the client and service developer must agree on a common type system. Such a type system must provide a set of built-in types similar to the intrinsic types you get with any development language, like integer and double.

In addition, the type system must also provide a means for creating your own data types. This capability is analogous to creating your own classes or User Defined Types (Structures) in your favorite programming language. This is an extremely important requirement for the type system because in most cases applications will want to exchange structured data rather than simple, scalar values. For example, your VB .NET application might contain a method called SubmitInvoice that looks like this:

```
Public Function SubmitInvoice(ByVal theInvoice As Invoice) _
              As Integer
    . . .
  End Function
```

where the Invoice type is a class that you created. As you learned in Chapter 1, you can easily expose this as a Web method by adding the WebMethod attribute to it. Before a client can invoke this method, it needs to know exactly what this Invoice class looks like. What properties does the Invoice have? Because the client can be written in any language, it needs a language-independent definition of the Invoice class. This is why the Web services type system must allow you to extend it by creating your own types. In this case, you would define a new type that represents your Invoice class and the Web service clients would read and understand this type definition in order to invoke your Web service.

2.2   What Is XSD?

On May 2, 2001, the W3C finalized a standard for an XML-based type system known as XML Schema. The language used to define a schema is an XML grammar known as XML Schema Definition (XSD) language. Web services use XML as the underlying format for representing messages and data; this made XSD a natural choice as the Web services type system.

The W3C XML Schema standard is logically two things: a set of predefined or built-in types like int and string and an XML language for defining new types and for describing the structure of a class of XML documents like an invoice or a purchase order. To help you understand the role of XSD in the world of XML, consider this analogy to your favorite programming language (Figure 2.1): The programming language you use to define application classes (for example, VB 6 or VB .NET) is analogous to XSD. When you define a class named CCustomer, this corresponds to a type definition for a CCustomer type in XSD. Finally, when you instantiate an object from the CCustomer class, this object instance is analogous to an XML document that represents a customer—an XML instance document.

To show you a quick example, assume we have the following Customer class:

```
'In VB
Public Class Customer
    Public CustomerID As Integer
    Public ContactName As String
    Public Telephone As String
End Class
```

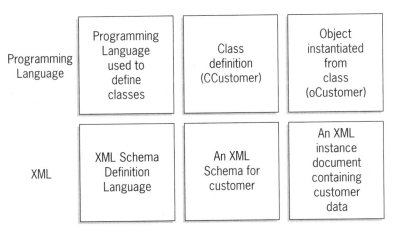

Figure 2.1 Analogy between XSD and a programming language

The corresponding XSD type definition is[1]:

```xml
<complexType name="CustomerType">
  <sequence>
    <element name="CustomerID" type="int" />
    <element name="ContactName" type="string" />
    <element name="Telephone" type="string" />
  </sequence>
</complexType>
```

This schema defines a new type called `CustomerType`. This type contains three XML elements: `CustomerID`, `ContactName`, and `Telephone` in that sequence. Notice the use of the XSD element `<complexType>` to define the `CustomerType` type. Also note that `int` and `string` are both XSD built-in types.

If you have an XML document that claims to adhere to a specific schema, you can use a validating parser to validate the document against that schema. If the document adheres to the schema, it is called a **valid XML document**. This ability to validate a document against a schema means that schemas are not only used to specify the structure of an XML document or a message, but also to enforce that structure through validation. Later in this chapter you will see an example of validating an invoice document against the invoice schema.

2.3 The XSD Type System

In this section, I'll explain the essential concepts of the XSD type system to prepare you for creating your own schemas. XSD's type system is comprised of simple and complex types. Simple types represent non-structured or scalar values. (For example, int, date, and string are all simple types.) Complex types represent structured data as you saw earlier in the Customer class example. A VB class or UDT (Structure), can be represented as an element that contains child elements or attributes. Such an element would be of a complex type because it represents a non-scalar type. In general, XML elements may have attributes and may contain simple text and/or child elements. If an element has attributes and/

---

[1]All schema examples in this chapter assume the default namespace is set to the XML Schema namespace: http://www.w3.org/2001/XMLSchema unless otherwise noted.

or contains child elements, it is of a complex type. However, an element that has no attributes and contains text only is of a simple type because it represents a scalar value. XML attributes, on the other hand, always contain text only, so they always contain scalar values and are of simple types. To help clarify the difference between simple and complex types, consider the following example XML document:

```
<examples>
<!-- this element is of a complex type because it has
attributes-->
<example anAttrib="7">some text</example>

<!-- this element is of a complex type because it has child
elements -->
<example>
  <elem1>some text</elem1>
  <elem2>more text</elem2>
</example>

<!-- this element is of a simple type -->
<example>some text content</example>
</examples>
```

The XSD type system is similar to the .NET type system in that every type derives from some other base type. In .NET, System.Object is at the root of the type system. Similarly, the XSD type system is a hierarchy of types with the built-in type called anyType at its root. Every type, whether built-in or user-defined, derives from some other type. Therefore the type hierarchy of all built-in types forms a tree as shown in Figure 2.2. This hierarchy diagram is taken from the W3C Recommendation XML Schema Part 2: Datatypes (http://www.w3.org/TR/xmlschema-2/).

In Figure 2.2, types that derive directly from anySimpleType are known as **primitive** types. All others are called **derived** types. There are three ways to derive from a base type: restriction, extension, and list. Derivation by restriction is when a type derives from a base type to restrict the base type's definition. For example, the type int derives from long by restricting permissible values to the range –2147483648 to 2147483647. The NMTOKENS type derives from

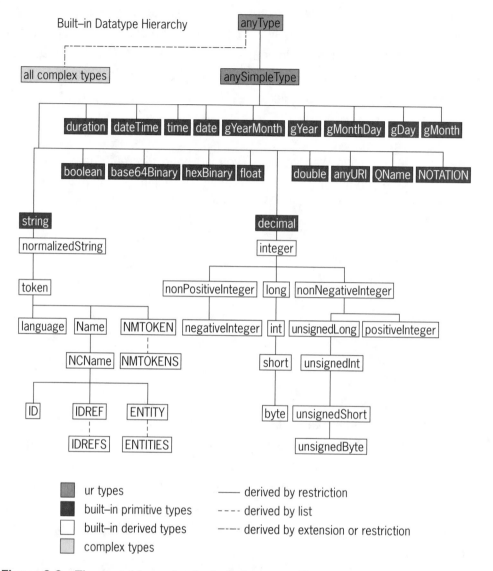

Figure 2.2   The type hierarchy for built-in types. Note that anyType is at the root of this type hierarchy. All built-in types are simple types based (directly or indirectly) on anySimpleType.

Copyright © May 2, 2001, World Wide Web Consortium, (Massachusetts Institute of Technology, Institut National de Recherche en Informatique et en Automatique, Keio University). All Rights Reserved. http://www.w3.org/Consortium/Legal/.

NMTOKEN by list: this means a value of type NMTOKENS is a list of space-delimited values of type NMTOKEN. The built-in types do not contain any types derived by extension. In practice, however, you might need to define a new type that extends the base type. There are examples of type derivation later in this chapter.

2.4 Authoring XSD Schemas

When building and using Web services, you will need to create new XSD schemas and/or read and understand existing ones. Occasionally, you might need to tweak an XSD schema that was auto-generated by your development tool. This section builds on the concepts of the XSD type system to show you how to create XSD schemas.

Typically, there are two steps to create XSD schemas: define new data types and declare elements and attributes using your defined types and the built-in ones. The order of these steps doesn't matter—you can declare elements first or define types first or mix the two.

2.4.1 Declaring Elements

When you declare an element you specify the element's name and its type. For example, if your XML document contains an element called quantity that is an integer, you would declare it like this:

```
<element name="quantity" type="int"/>
```

Essentially, the XML document must contain exactly one element called quantity. You can use the minOccurs and maxOccurs attributes to change the number of occurrences of the <quantity> element. The default is minOccurs=maxOccurs=1. For example, to indicate that <quantity> is optional (may or may not be in the XML document):

```
<element name="quantity" type="int" minOccurs="0"/>
```

Or, if the <quantity> element has to appear between one and five times:

```
<element name="quantity" type="int" minOccurs="1" maxOccurs="5"/>
```

In many cases, you don't want to put an upper bound on the number of occurrences of an element; in this case you can use `maxOccurs="unbounded"`.

```
<element name="quantity" type="int" minOccurs="1"
maxOccurs="unbounded"/>
```

The element's type can be one of the built-in types or a type that you define. When the built-in types do not meet your needs, you will need to define new simple or complex types.

2.4.2 Defining Simple Types

Although there are many built-in simple types, often you will need to define new simple types. For example, as in the method:

```
Public Sub GetCustomerByName (ByVal custName As String)
```

where, based on the application's database schema, `custName` is a string with a maximum length of 50 characters. In this case it is not sufficient to use the built-in XSD `string` as the data type for `custName` because that says nothing about its maximum length. Instead, you define a new type that derives from `string` and restricts its maximum length to 50:

```
<simpleType name="LimitedLenString">
  <restriction base="string">
    <maxLength value="50"/>
  </restriction>
</simpleType>
```

The `<restriction>` element indicates that this simple type derives from `string` and restricts it. The `<restriction>` element contains one or more child elements called **facets,** which are used to restrict the base type. In this case, we use the `maxLength` facet to specify a maximum length of 50. You can also indicate the minimum length:

```
<simpleType name="LimitedLenString">
  <restriction base="string">
    <maxLength value="50"/>
    <minLength value="2"/>
  </restriction>
</simpleType>
```

Another useful facet is `enumeration`. Consider the case where you want to represent the following enumerated type in XSD:

```
Public Enum OrderStatus
    Pending = 3
    Processed = 4
    Shipped = 5
End Enum
```

The XSD equivalent would be:

```
<simpleType name="OrderStatus">
<restriction base="int">
  <enumeration value="3"/>
  <enumeration value="4"/>
  <enumeration value="5"/>
</restriction>
</simpleType>
```

The problem with this type definition is that it exposes the underlying enumerated values rather than their names. To expose the names instead of the actual values, you can create a new simple type that derives from `string` instead of `int` and use the `enum` names: `Pending`, `Processed`, and `Shipped` as the values of the enumeration facets:

```
<simpleType name="OrderStatus">
<restriction base="string">
  <enumeration value="Pending"/>
  <enumeration value="Processed"/>
  <enumeration value="Shipped"/>
</restriction>
</simpleType>
```

An extremely useful facet is the `pattern`, which lets you use regular expressions to specify a pattern that values must follow. For example, if you want to create a type that limits values to a valid U.S. zip code, you can use the `pattern` facet with this pattern:

```
<simpleType name="zipType">
  <restriction base="string">
    <pattern value="\d{5}(-\d{4})?"/>
  </restriction>
</simpleType>
```

Here we use the pattern `"\d{5}(-\d{4})?"` to indicate that the string must contain five digits followed by an optional dash and four digits.

Table 2.1 shows a list of available facets and a brief description of each. You can find more information on facets in the .NET documentation under the topic Data Type Facets (http://msdn.microsoft.com/library/en-us/cpgenref/html/xsdrefdatatypefacets.asp) or in the W3C XML Schema Part 2: Datatypes (http://www.w3.org/TR/xmlschema-2/).

Table 2.1   List of XSD facets that may be applied to simple types

Facet	Description
enumeration	Specifies a set of allowable values.
fractionDigits	The maximum number of digits in the fractional part. Applies to datatypes derived from decimal. (Therefore, it does not apply to double or float).
length	The fixed length of values of this type. Note that the unit of length depends on the base type: For strings, the unit is characters. For hexBinary and base64Binary, the unit is an octet (a byte). Finally for types derived by list, length is the number of items in that list.
maxExclusive	Is the exclusive allowable upper bound, that is, values must be less than this upper bound.
maxInclusive	Is the inclusive allowable upper bound, that is, values must be less than or equal to this upper bound.
maxLength	The maximum allowable length. The unit of maxLength depends on the datatype; see length above.
minExclusive	Is the exclusive allowable lower bound, that is, values must be greater than this lower bound.
minInclusive	Is the inclusive allowable lower bound, that is, values must be greater than or equal to this lower bound.
minLength	The minimum allowable length. The unit of minLength depends on the datatype; see length above.

Table 2.1   (continued) List of XSD facets that may be applied to simple types

Facet	Description
`pattern`	A regular expression that restricts values to the specified pattern.
`totalDigits`	The maximum number of digits. Applies to types derived from decimal.
`whiteSpace`	Must be preserve, replace, or collapse. Specifies how white space (tab, carriage return, line feed, and space) in string types is treated. preserve indicates that all white space should be left as is. replace indicates that each tab, carriage return, and line feed is replaced by a space. collapse indicates that first white space is replaced as in replace, then contiguous spaces are replaced by one space and leading and trailing spaces are removed.

2.4.3 Defining Complex Types

Complex types are used to represent classes, structures, arrays, and other data structures. To define a complex type, you use the `<complexType>` XSD element. For example, assume you want to create a type definition for the following XML fragment:

```
<!-- an example XML fragment -->
<example>
  <elem1>some text</elem1>
  <elem2>more text</elem2>
</example>
```

The corresponding type definition would begin with the `<complexType>` XSD element that has a name attribute that indicates the type's name. You then specify the **content model** for this new type. For example, the type definition below uses the XSD `<sequence>` element to indicate that elements of this type must contain a sequence of `<elem1>` followed by `<elem2>`. All elements declared within the `<sequence>` element must appear in the same order in which they are declared. In this example, if the order of `<elem1>` and `<elem2>` were reversed, the XML fragment would be considered invalid.

```
<!-- the corresponding type definition -->
<complexType name="exampleType">
  <sequence>
    <element name="elem1" type="string"/>
    <element name="elem2" type="string"/>
  </sequence>
</complexType>
```

The XSD `<sequence>` element defines what is known as an element **model group**. Basically, you are saying "the following group of elements must appear in this sequence." Besides `<sequence>`, you can also use `<choice>` and `<all>` to define element model groups. `<choice>` indicates that only one of the elements may appear in the XML document. `<all>` indicates that either zero or one instance of each of the elements may appear in the XML document in any order.

If an element declaration appears in more than one place in your schema, you can declare the element as a **global element,** that is make its declaration a direct child of the `<schema>` element. You can then reference this declaration by name within a type definition:

```
<schema ...>
<!-- global declaration -->
<element name="AnElement" type="string"/>

  <complexType name="someType">
   <sequence>
    <element name="AnotherElement" type="int"/>
    <!-- local declaration references
    the global declaration by name -->
    <element ref="AnElement" maxOccurs="4"/>
   </sequence>
  </complexType>
</schema>
```

Note that you cannot use `minOccurs` or `maxOccurs` on a global element declaration; instead, you use them on the local declaration that references the global declaration.

2.4.4 Declaring Attributes

Attributes are declared as part of the complex type definition after the model group. For example, assume we modify the previous XML fragment by adding two attributes to the example element:

```
<!-- an example XML fragment -->
<example quant="3" size="big" >
  <elem1>some text</elem1>
  <elem2>more text</elem2>
</example>
```

We would need to modify the XSD type definition to declare the two attributes:

```
<!-- the corresponding type definition -->
<complexType name="exampleType">
  <sequence>
    <element name="elem1" type="string"/>
    <element name="elem2" type="string"/>
  </sequence>
 <attribute name="quant" type="int" use="required"/>
 <attribute name="size" type="string" use="optional"/>
</complexType>
```

For each attribute, we add an `<attribute>` element and specify the attribute's name, data type, and use. The allowable attribute `use` values are `optional`, `required`, or `prohibited`. By default, attributes are optional. Specifying `prohibited` means the attribute should not appear in an XML document. This is useful if you are creating a new version of the schema where some older attributes are no longer supported and you want to cause all older documents to be invalidated according to your new schema. You can also specify a default value using the `default` attribute. For example, the following attribute declaration states that if the `size` attribute is missing, its value defaults to "small":

```
<attribute name="size" type="string"
          use="optional" default="small"/>
```

2.4.5 Simple Content

Up to this point, I have focused on type definitions for complex types that contain child elements. Remember that a type is complex if it has attributes and/or contains child elements. If a complex type contains child elements, it is said to have **complex content**. However, if a complex type has attributes but contains only text, it is said to be a complex type with simple content. For example, the following element `<example>` is of a complex type with simple content:

```
<example size="Large">test</example>
```

The corresponding complex type definition would use the `<simpleContent>` child of `<complexType>` like this:

```
<complexType name="exampleType">
 <simpleContent>
   <extension base="string">
     <attribute name="size" type="string" use="required"/>
   </extension>
 </simpleContent>
</complexType>
```

This type definition says that elements of the `exampleType` will contain only `string` values (no child elements) and will have an attribute called `size` of type `string`.

2.4.6 Mixed Content

An XML element is said to have mixed content if it contains text and child elements. The `<examples>` element in the following XML fragment has mixed content:

```
<examples>
  This is text content
  <elem1>some text</elem1>
  <elem2>some text</elem2>
</examples>
```

To represent mixed content in an XSD complex type definition, you set the mixed attribute to true (it is false by default):

```
<!-- the corresponding type definition -->
<complexType name="exampleType" mixed="true">
  <sequence>
    <element name="elem1" type="string"/>
    <element name="elem2" type="string"/>
  </sequence>
</complexType>
```

Mixed content is commonly used for document publishing applications but has little use in data processing applications. In a document publishing markup language, such as HTML, element tags are used to format text. For example, HTML defines the paragraph tag (element) `<p>` which may contain text mixed with other markup tags such as the bold tag `<b>`:

```
<p>This is an HTML paragraph with some <b>BOLD</b> text</p>
```

In data processing applications, however, each element represents a data field or a member of a class so it makes no sense for such an element to have a value (text content) and at the same time contain child elements. To illustrate this, reconsider the example customer class repeated here with an added member called `Numbers`:

```
'the Customer class
Public Class Customer
    Public CustomerID As Integer
    Public ContactName As String
    Public Telephone As String
    Public Numbers() As Integer
End Class
```

Assuming you have an object instance of the above class and you want to serialize it to XML, you might end up with an XML fragment like this:

```
<ACustomer>
  <CustomerID>1234</CustomerID>
  <ContactName>John Smith</ContactName>
  <Telephone>123-123-7183</Telephone>
  <Numbers>
    <item>4</item>
    <item>7</item>
    <item>2</item>
  </Numbers>
</ACustomer>
```

Each of `CustomerID`, `ContactName`, and `Telephone` is represented by an XML element that contains only text. These elements are all of simple types. The `Numbers` array is represented by a `<Numbers>` element that contains only child elements, that is, the `<Numbers>` element does not itself contain text.

Each item in the array is represented by an `<item>` element that has text content only. Therefore, members that contain simple values are represented by elements that contain only text, while members that contain arrays (or collections) are represented by elements that contain only child elements. As you can see, there is no place for mixed content in this scenario. While this is a simple example, the point it makes holds true for more complex scenarios. Generally, mixed content models are not (or at least *should* not be) used in data processing applications.

2.4.7 Empty Elements

An element doesn't need to have content; it may be empty. An empty element is an element that has no text content and no child elements. Would such an element be of a complex or a simple type? It depends; if the element has attributes it is of a complex type. Note that attributes are not considered part of an element's content, therefore whether or not an element has attributes has nothing to do with whether or not the element is empty: An empty element may or may not have attributes. An example of an empty element and the corresponding type definition follows:

```
<!-- This is an empty element -->
<emptyElem attrib1="some string value" attrib2="50.02"/>

<!-- This is the corresponding type definition -->
<complexType name="emptyType">
  <attribute name="attrib1" type="string"/>
  <attribute name="attrib2" type="float"/>
</complexType>
```

Note that this complex type definition has no model group, therefore elements of this type must be empty.

2.4.8 Anonymous Types

In all the previous examples, each defined type had its own unique name. However, it is not always necessary to name types. If you include the type definition as part of an element declaration, then you do not need to name that type. For example, if you have an element called `<zipCode>` that contains a U.S.

zip code, you can combine the element declaration and the corresponding type definition:

```
<element name="zipCode">
 <simpleType>
  <restriction base="string">
    <pattern value="\d{5}(-\d{4})?"/>
  </restriction>
 </simpleType>
</element>
```

Note that the element declaration does not have a `type` attribute (that is, no `type=""` in `<element>`) and the type definition does not have a `name` attribute. This is an anonymous type definition and is quite common when there's only one element declaration that needs to use that type.

Complex types may also be defined anonymously in the same way:

```
<element name="example">
 <complexType>
  <sequence>
    <element name="elem1" type="string"/>
    <element name="elem2" type="string"/>
  </sequence>
 </complexType>
</element>
```

2.5 XSD and XML Namespaces

2.5.1 A Quick Introduction to XML Namespaces

As simple as XML namespaces are, they are so pervasive in Web services technologies that they warrant an explanation.

The purpose of XML namespaces is to prevent naming collisions in element and attribute names. An XML namespace is identified by a unique string that is used as a prefix to element and attribute names. [2]

For example, if you are building a project management application, you might use a `<schedule>` element to represent the project's schedule. An accounting

---

[2]Do not confuse XML namespaces and .NET namespaces. They are similar in that both are used to prevent name collisions, but they come from different worlds and work differently.

application might also use `<schedule>` to represent an accounting schedule. If for some reason an XML document contains information about the project's schedule *and* the accounting schedule, how do you tell which is which? Even if you could infer which is which based on context and other information, how would an application reading this document understand which is the accounting schedule and which is the project management schedule? By prefixing each `<schedule>` element with a unique string that corresponds to either the project management application or the accounting application, you can distinguish between schedule elements simply based on this new, fully qualified name. For example, the project management application might use the namespace "projManage" and the accounting application might use the namespace "accountingApp" making the fully qualified `<schedule>` names `<projManage:schedule>` and `<accountingApp:schedule>`.

This solves our problem as far as these two applications go. However, `projManage` and `accountingApp` are fairly common names and could themselves be used by different people to mean different things that would again lead to the naming conflict problem. XML namespaces are actually required to be Uniform Resource Identifiers (URIs). A Uniform Resource Locator (URL) is a form of a URI. So, the URL `http://schemas.devxpert.com/projectManage` can be used as a namespace URI. *When used as a namespace, a URL is nothing more than a unique string.* It doesn't need to point to anything on the Web, and you should not try to use it as a hyperlink. It is just a unique string. URLs are particularly useful as namespaces because Internet domain names are already guaranteed to be unique. So if each company uses its Internet domain name in the namespace, then we already have a system for getting unique namespace strings.

But you do not have to use URLs for your namespaces. Here is a valid namespace URI that is not a URL:

```
urn:devxpert-com:schemas
```

This example namespace uses a Uniform Resource Name (URN) which is a form of URI. Whether you use URLs or URNs, your namespaces will tend to be rather long. Therefore, instead of prefixing every element in your document with a long namespace, you can give that namespace a short nickname and use that nickname to refer to the namespace. For example, the following XML snippet declares dx as the prefix (nickname) for the namespace `urn:devxpert-com:schemas`. It then uses `dx` as the prefix for elements and attributes.

```
<dx:example
 xmlns:dx="urn:devxpert-com:schemas">
  <dx:example1 dx:name="test"/>
  <dx:example2>test</dx:example2>
</dx:example>
```

The special syntax `xmlns:prefix="namespace-uri"` is used as if it were an attribute and declares a **namespace prefix**. The scope of this prefix declaration starts at the element on which the prefix was declared (in this case `<example>`) and extends to all its descendants. In this example, a namespace-aware parser would understand that all elements and attributes whose names are prefixed with `dx` belong to the namespace `urn:devxpert-com:schemas`.

Let's define the terms commonly used for documents that contain namespaces so that you'll know what they mean as you encounter them throughout this book. First, the term fully qualified name refers to an element's name including the namespace or the namespace prefix. For example, `dx:example1` is a fully qualified name. A **fully qualified name** is made up of two parts: a namespace prefix and a **local name**. For example, `dx` is the namespace prefix and `example1` is the local name. Finally, an element's or attribute's **namespace URI** is simply the namespace that the element belongs to. In the above example, the namespace URI for `<dx:example1>` is `urn:devxpert-com:schemas`.

It's quite common for all (or at least most) elements in an XML document to belong to the same namespace, which makes prefixing each element name a tedious task. As a matter of convenience, you can define a default namespace that applies to all elements that do not have an explicit namespace prefix on them. The syntax for declaring a default namespace is: `xmlns ="namespace-uri"`.

For example, this code snippet defines a default namespace which means `<example>`, `<example1>`, and `<example2>` all belong to that default namespace:

```
<example
 xmlns="urn:devxpert-com:schemas">
  <example1 name="test"/>
  <example2>test</ example2>
</example>
```

Note that unprefixed attributes do not belong to the default namespace. Therefore, the `name` attribute on `<example1>` does not belong to any namespace. If you wanted the `name` attribute to belong to the same namespace as `<example1>`, you would have to prefix it like this:

```
<example
 xmlns="urn:devxpert-com:schemas"
 xmlns:dx="urn:devxpert-com:schemas">
  <example1 dx:name="test"/>
  <example2>test</example2>
</example>
```

Here, the namespace `urn:devxpert-com:schemas` is mapped to the `dx` prefix and is also the default namespace, which is perfectly acceptable.

Throughout the rest of this book, most of the examples will use URLs as namespaces. That said, you should keep in mind that XML namespaces are nothing but unique strings. Therefore, all the URLs you see used as namespaces need not point to anything on the Web. So do not be surprised or confused to get an error if you try to use your browser to navigate to one of those URLs.

2.5.2 Namespaces in Instance Documents

In most cases, the XML documents you work with will use namespaces. For example, a document may be using a default namespace like this:

```
<!-- XML document using a default namespace -->
<example xmlns="http://schemas.devxpert.com/examples">
  <elem1>some text</elem1>
  <elem2>more text</elem2>
</example>
```

In this case, all elements in the document are qualified and belong to the `http://schemas.devxpert.com/examples` namespace. When you declare these elements in an XSD schema, you must specify that they will be qualified in instance documents. The easiest way to do this is to set the `elementFormDefault` attribute of the `<schema>` element to `"qualified"`:

```
<schema elementFormDefault="qualified"
  ... other namespace declaration omitted ... >
  ... type definition and element declarations omitted ...
</schema>
```

If you are declaring attributes in your schema, you can also specify `attributeFormDefault`. `elementFormDefault` and `attributeFormDefault` are by default set to `"unqualified"`, which means that elements and attributes in your instance document will not belong to any namespace. In most (but not all) cases, this is not what you want for elements but is what you want for attributes. You can also override the `elementFormDefault` and `attributeFormDefault` setting by using the form attribute on the element or attribute declaration, respectively.

2.5.3 XSD Types and Namespaces

You've seen how each type you define has a name (unless it's an anonymous type). As developers create schemas with type definitions, it is likely that different types will end up using the same name. This can lead to naming collisions and would make it difficult for applications using different types with the same names to interoperate. This is similar to the problem that arose with XML element and attribute names and was solved by applying XML namespaces: prefixing each element and attribute name with a unique namespace string. XSD uses the same solution for data types: Each type may belong to a namespace.

All built-in types belong to the XSD namespace `http://www.w3.org/2001/XMLSchema`. It just so happens that all XSD elements such as `<complexType>` also belong to the same namespace, which makes authoring schemas a bit more convenient because you need to deal with one namespace for all XSD elements and built-in types. Take a look at a complete schema example that uses a namespace prefix for the XSD namespace instead of using it as the default namespace:

```
<xsd:schema
  xmlns:xsd="http://www.w3.org/2001/XMLSchema">
  <xsd:element name="example">
    <xsd:complexType>
      <xsd:sequence>
        <xsd:element name="elem1" type="xsd:string"/>
        <xsd:element name="elem2" type="xsd:string"/>
      </xsd:sequence>
    </xsd:complexType>
  </xsd:element>
</xsd:schema>
```

Note that references to built-in types such as string are prefixed with the same namespace prefix used for XSD elements such as `<complexType>` and `<sequence>`. I chose to use `xsd` as the prefix here, but it could have been anything. In fact, different Web services tools that generate schemas use different prefixes. Don't let that fool you, it's okay as long as the prefix corresponds to the XSD namespace `http://www.w3.org/2001/XMLSchema`.

So, the built-in types belong to the XSD namespace, but what about types that you define? What namespace do they belong to? You get to determine that by specifying the `targetNamespace` attribute on the `<schema>` element:

```
<xsd:schema   targetNamespace=
"http://schemas.devxpert.com/examples"
  xmlns:xsd="http://www.w3.org/2001/XMLSchema"
  elementFormDefault="qualified">
    <xsd:complexType name="exampleType">
      <xsd:sequence>
        <xsd:element name="elem1" type="xsd:string"/>
        <xsd:element name="elem2" type="xsd:string"/>
      </xsd:sequence>
    </xsd:complexType>
</xsd:schema>
```

Here I define the target namespace for new types to be `http://schemas.devxpert.com/examples`. Therefore, the type called `exampleType` now belongs to this namespace. When you want to reference this type, you must now specify its fully qualified name including the namespace:

```
<xsd:schema  targetNamespace=
"http://schemas.devxpert.com/examples"
  xmlns:dx="http://schemas.devxpert.com/examples"
  xmlns:xsd="http://www.w3.org/2001/XMLSchema"
  elementFormDefault="qualified">
    <xsd:complexType name="exampleType">
      <xsd:sequence>
        <xsd:element name="elem1" type="xsd:string"/>
        <xsd:element name="elem2" type="xsd:string"/>
      </xsd:sequence>
    </xsd:complexType>
    <xsd:element name="example" type="dx:exampleType"/>
</xsd:schema>
```

To reference types using their fully qualified names, first you declare a namespace prefix (dx in the above example) for the target namespace, then you use this prefix with the type name when you declare elements of that type. In this example, the element declaration for the <example> element references the exampleType using the type's fully qualified name dx:exampleType.

In this example, we use two namespaces http://schemas.devxpert. com/examples and http://www.w3.org/2001/XMLSchema and we declare a prefix for each of them. We can make the schema more readable by making one of the namespaces the default namespace. For example, if we make the XSD namespace the default, the schema becomes:

```
<schema targetNamespace="http://schemas.devxpert.com/examples"
  xmlns:dx="http://schemas.devxpert.com/examples"
  xmlns="http://www.w3.org/2001/XMLSchema"
  elementFormDefault="qualified">
    <complexType name="exampleType">
      <sequence>
        <element name="elem1" type="string"/>
        <element name="elem2" type="string"/>
      </sequence>
    </complexType>
    <element name="example" type="dx:exampleType"/>
</schema>
```

Note that the default namespace applies to type names as well as elements. That's why the `string` type is no longer prefixed in this example: it belongs to the default namespace. Whether or not you make the XSD namespace the default is up to you. It is only a matter of readability and has no effect on the meaning of the schema.

2.6 Validating with XSD

In addition to acting as a specification for a class of XML documents, an XSD schema can also be used to validate XML documents. To do this, you need to use a validation program, which is capable of checking an XML document against a schema and reporting validation errors. In general, there are two categories of such programs: parsers and XML/XSD editors. When building your application and designing your XML documents and schemas, you typically use a schema editor. When your application is running, it might programmatically validate XML documents using a validating parser. Figure 2.3 shows how a validating program (parser or editor) validates an XML document using a schema.

The validating program must somehow know which schema to use to validate the document. There's a standard way for an XML document to point to its

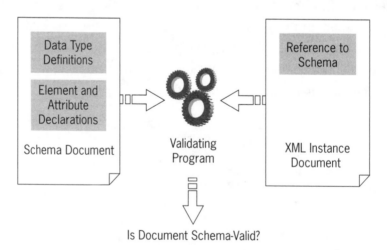

Figure 2.3 Validating an XML document using a schema

schema. There are two attributes depending on whether or not you are using namespaces in the instance document. The attributes are called `schemaLocation` and `noNamespaceSchemaLocation`. Both attributes belong to the XML Schema Instance namespace: `http://www.w3.org/2001/XMLSchema-instance`. If the elements or attributes you are validating do not belong to any namespace, you use the `noNamespaceSchemaLocation` attribute to specify the physical location of the schema document. The `schemaLocation` attribute lets you specify the physical location of a schema in order to validate elements and attributes in a given namespace. For example, if the schema for the examples document is located in `C:\schemas\examples.xsd` you could write:

```
<!-- using schemaLocation to specify the schema -->
<example xmlns="http://schemas.devxpert.com/examples"
    xmlns:xsi=" http://www.w3.org/2001/XMLSchema-instance"
    xsi:schemaLocation="http://schemas.devxpert.com/examples
file:///C:\schemas\examples.xsd">
  <elem1>some text</elem1>
  <elem2>more text</elem2>
</example>
```

Note that the default namespace (to which all elements in this document belong) is the same as the target namespace used in the schema itself (see previous examples). Also note that the `schemaLocation` attribute belongs to the XML Schema Instance namespace. The value of `schemaLocation` is a white space delimited list of namespace and schema locations. It's like saying "validate elements that belong to the `http://schemas.devxpert.com/examples` namespace using the schema at `C:\schemas\examples.xsd`." Here's what it would look like if you had elements from two different namespaces in your document:

```
<!-- using schemaLocation with multiple namespaces -->
<example xmlns="http://schemas.devxpert.com/examples"
    xmlns:bk="http://schemas.devxpert.com/books"
    xmlns:xsi=" http://www.w3.org/2001/XMLSchema-instance"
    xsi:schemaLocation="http://schemas.devxpert.com/examples
file:///C:\schemas\examples.xsd http://schemas.devxpert.com/books
file:///C:\schemas\books.xsd">
  <elem1>some text</elem1>
```

```
<elem2>more text</elem2>
<bk:another>This element belongs to another namespace
</bk:another>
</example>
```

Note that the element `<another>` belongs to the namespace `http://schemas.devxpert.com/books` and that schemaLocation associates that namespace with the schema document `C:\schemas\books.xsd`. The schema location is actually a URL, so you could have your schema out on the Web somewhere and point to it by its URL:

```
<!-- schema Location on the Web -->
<example xmlns="http://schemas.devxpert.com/examples"
    xmlns:xsi=" http://www.w3.org/2001/XMLSchema-instance"
    xsi:schemaLocation="http://schemas.devxpert.com/examples
http://myserver.mydomain.com/examples.xsd">
  <elem1>some text</elem1>
  <elem2>more text</elem2>
</example>
```

The above example maps the namespace `http://schemas.devxpert.com/examples` to the schema at `http://myserver.mydomain.com/examples.xsd`. Note that although both are URLs, `http://schemas.devxpert.com/examples` is simply a namespace (a unique string) while `http://myserver.mydomain.com/examples.xsd` is a URL that points to the XSD document.

2.6.1 Programmatic Validation

Your Web service methods may receive data as XML documents. For example, your Web service may expose a method for submitting an XML invoice document:

```
Public Function SubmitInvoice(ByVal invoice As _
      System.Xml.XmlNode) As Integer
         . . .
   End Function
```

Of course you'll want to programmatically validate the input invoice document before you actually process it. To do this you use a validating parser. VB 6 applications can use the MSXML 4.0 parser that supports XSD validation. .NET applications use the `System.Xml.XmlValidatingReader` that is a streaming parser that supports XSD-based validation.

There are two example applications that show you how to do XML validation: XMLValidator6 and XMLValidator. XMLValidator6, shown in Listing 2.1, uses the MSXML 4.0 parser to load the specified XML document and validate it.

**Listing 2.1 Validating with MSXML 4.0
(VBWSClientCode\Chapter2\XmlValidator6\frmMain.frm)**

```
Private Sub GetNamespace()

'tries to guess the namespace URI
'it uses the document element's namespace
    Dim doc As New MSXML2.DOMDocument
    If Not doc.Load(txtXML.Text) Then
        MsgBox "Could not load XML document: " _
                &doc.parseError.reason
        Exit Sub
    End If
    'use document element's namespaceURI by default
    txtNS = doc.documentElement.namespaceURI
End Sub
'   _____
'validate document
Private Sub cmdValidate_Click()
    Dim schemaCache As MSXML2.XMLSchemaCache40
    Dim doc As MSXML2.DOMDocument40
    'schema cache to hold the schema and namespace
    Set schemaCache = New MSXML2.XMLSchemaCache40
    On Error Resume Next
    schemaCache.Add txtNS.Text, txtXSD.Text
    If Err.Number <> 0 Then
        MsgBox "Error in schema: " & _
            Err.Description, vbCritical, "XSD Validator"
        Exit Sub
    End If
    'the document to load the XML
    Set doc = New MSXML2.DOMDocument40
    Set doc.schemas = schemaCache
    doc.async = False
    If Not doc.Load(txtXML.Text) Then
```

```
                Dim PErr As IXMLDOMParseError
                Set PErr = doc.parseError
                MsgBox "Error loading XML document: " & _
                        PErr.reason & vbCrLf & _
                        "Text: " & PErr.srcText & _
                        " Line " & PErr.Line & " Col " & PErr.linepos, _
                        vbCritical, "XSD Validator"
        Else
                lblStatus.Caption = "Validation succeeded. No errors."
        End If
End Sub
```

When you browse for an XML document, the application tries to be helpful by guessing the namespace you want to validate. GetNamespace does this by loading the document and getting the document element's namespace. The document element is the outermost element in the document.

When you click on the validate button, the application creates an XMLSchemaCache40 object and uses it to add the XML Schema document and the associated namespace. You need this schema cache because, as you have seen earlier, an XML document may contain elements and attributes that belong to different namespaces and need to be validated against different schemas. The schema cache lets you specify which schemas to use and the namespace to which each schema applies. The application then creates a DOMDocument40 and sets its Schemas property to the schema collection.

Next, the application loads the specified XML document, which causes it to be validated against the schema. Any validation errors will cause DOMDocument40.Load to return false. You can then get the error details using the DOMDocument40.parseError property, which returns an object that implements IXMLDOMParseError. You can get detailed error information from this object including the line number and character position that caused the validation error.

The .NET XMLValidator application demonstrates the use of XmlValidatingReader to programmatically validate an XML document. When you click on the Validate button, the program will load the specified XML document and validate it by running the ValidateDocument function in Listing 2.2.

Listing 2.2 Validating with XmlValidatingReader (VBWSClientCode\XmlValidator\Form1.vb)

```vb
Private Sub ValidateDocument(ByVal docPath As String, _
            ByVal xsdPath As String, ByVal ns As String)
    txtStatus.Text = ""
    Dim tr As XmlTextReader = Nothing
    Dim vr As XmlValidatingReader = Nothing
    isValid = True
    Try
        tr = New XmlTextReader(docPath)
        vr = New XmlValidatingReader(tr)
        vr.ValidationType = ValidationType.Schema
        Dim xsc As XmlSchemaCollection = New XmlSchemaCollection()
        'add the schema to the collection
        xsc.Add(ns, xsdPath)
        'add the schema collection
        vr.Schemas.Add(xsc)
        If (chkContinue.Checked) Then
            AddHandler vr.ValidationEventHandler, _
            New ValidationEventHandler(AddressOf
                Me.ValidationError)
        End If
        Do While (vr.Read())

        Loop
        If (isValid) Then
            txtStatus.Text = "The document is valid."
        End If

    Catch ex As XmlSchemaException
        txtStatus.Text = "Validation error on line " & _
                        ex.LineNumber & " col " & _
                        ex.LinePosition & vbCrLf & _
                        ex.Message
    Finally
        If Not (vr Is Nothing) Then
            vr.Close()
        End If
        If Not (tr Is Nothing) Then
            tr.Close()
        End If
    End Try
End Sub
```

```
'The ValidationEventHandler delegate
Public Sub ValidationError(ByVal sender As Object, _
                           ByVal args As ValidationEventArgs)
    Dim ex As XmlSchemaException = args.Exception
    txtStatus.Text &= "Validation error on line " & _
            ex.LineNumber & " col " & _
            ex.LinePosition & vbCrLf & _
            ex.Message & vbCrLf & _
            " ... Continuing Validation ..." & vbclf
    isValid = False
End Sub
```

The `XmlValidatingReader` can read a document from a stream, a string, or an `XmlReader`. In this example, I use an `XmlTextReader` (which inherits from `XmlReader`) to open the document. I then pass the new `XmlTextReader` to the `XmlValidatingReader`'s constructor. I create an `XmlSchemaCollection` and add to it the XSD document path and the namespace. The schema collection lets you map the element and attribute namespace to the corresponding schema. The actual validation starts when you call `XmlValidatingReader.Read()`. If it encounters a validation error, the `XmlValidatingReader` will, by default, throw a `System.Xml.Schema.XmlSchemaException` exception and stop processing the XML document. However, you could hook up a delegate to the `ValidationEventHandler`. The reader will call this delegate when it encounters a validation error and will continue processing the document. The example XMLValidator application lets you choose to use the `ValidationEventHandler` by checking the "Continue on errors?" box.

You've seen how to load the XML into a DOM document when using MSXML 4.0. The XmlValidator example application demonstrates validating XML using VB .NET and the `XmlDocument` object. Basically, you create the `XmlValidatingReader` and add a schema collection to it, which maps namespaces to schema documents. Then you create a `System.Xml.XmlDocument` object and call its `Load` method passing it the validating reader. The `XmlDocument` will use `XmlValidatingReader.Read` to read the underlying XML document. So while the `XmlDocument` is loading the XML, the validating reader is validating it.

2.7 Type Substitution

You've seen how XSD supports type derivation through restriction, extension, and list. XSD also supports type substitution: the ability to substitute an element of a derived type in a place where an element of the base type is expected. This maps nicely to how you use interface implementation in VB 6/COM (limited to one interface) and inheritance in VB .NET. For example, consider two VB .NET classes called `IceCream` and `Cake`, which both inherit from `Dessert` as shown in Listing 2.3. The `DessertMenu` class in Listing 2.3 contains three fields named `Item1`, `Item2`, and `Item3`, each of type `Dessert`. At runtime, DessertMenu's constructor puts `IceCream` objects in both `Item1` and `Item2` and a `Cake` object in `Item3`.

**Listing 2.3   An example class hierarchy in VB .NET
(VBWSClientCode\Chapter2\Dessert.vb)**

```vb
Public Class Dessert
    Public Calories As Long
End Class

'IceCream inherits from Dessert
Public Class IceCream
    Inherits Dessert
    Public Flavor As String
End Class

'Cake inherits from Dessert
Public Class Cake
    Inherits Dessert
    Public IsChocolate As Boolean
End Class

'DessertMenu contains Dessert items
Public Class DessertMenu
    Public Item1 As Dessert
    Public Item2 As Dessert
    Public Item3 As Dessert
    Public Sub New()
        Dim ice As New IceCream()
        ice.Calories = 1000
        ice.Flavor = "Cherry-Vanilla"
        Item1 = ice
```

```
                ice.Calories = 3000
                ice.Flavor = "Oreo cookie"
                Item2 = ice

                Dim ACake As New Cake()
                ACake.Calories = 4000
                ACake.IsChocolate = True
                Item3 = ACake
        End Sub
    End Class
```

The XSD schema that represents the `DessertMenu` with the `Dessert` class hierarchy is shown in Listing 2.4.

Listing 2.4   Schema representing the DessertMenu (VBWSClientCode\Chapter2\XmlDocuments\DessertMenu.xsd)

```
<schema
 elementFormDefault="qualified"
 targetNamespace="http://schemas.devxpert.com/examples"
 xmlns:dx="http://schemas.devxpert.com/examples"
 xmlns="http://www.w3.org/2001/XMLSchema">

<!-- the DessertMenu -->
 <element name="DessertMenu">
    <complexType>
      <sequence>
        <element name="Item1" type="dx:Dessert" />
        <element name="Item2" type="dx:Dessert" />
        <element name="Item3" type="dx:Dessert" />
      </sequence>
    </complexType>
 </element>

<!-- the Dessert base type -->
 <complexType name="Dessert">
   <sequence>
     <element name="Calories" type="long" />
   </sequence>
 </complexType>

<!-- the IceCream type derives from Dessert -->
 <complexType name="IceCream">
    <complexContent mixed="false">
```

```xml
      <extension base="dx:Dessert">
        <sequence>
          <element name="calories" type="long"/>
          <element name="Flavor" type="string" />
        </sequence>
      </extension>
    </complexContent>
  </complexType>

  <!-- the Cake type derives from Dessert -->
  <complexType name="Cake">
    <complexContent mixed="false">
      <extension base="dx:Dessert">
        <sequence>
          <element name="calories" type="long"/>
          <element name="IsChocolate" type="boolean" />
        </sequence>
      </extension>
    </complexContent>
  </complexType>
</schema>
```

To represent this class hierarchy in XSD, I define a complex type called `Dessert` and two complex types that derive from `Dessert` by extension. Let's take a closer look at how this works. In the `IceCream` type definition, the `<complexContent>` element means that this complex type will contain elements (recall that a complex type is said to have complex content if it contains child elements). The `<extension>` element specifies `Dessert` as the base type and contains a `<sequence>` that contains a `<Flavor>` element. The `IceCream` type definition is like saying: "`IceCream` inherits the definition of `Dessert` and adds to it the `<Flavor>` element." Comparing this to the VB `IceCream` class declaration, you can see that they are functionally equivalent. Similarly, the `Cake` type definition extends `Dessert` and adds the `IsChocoloate` element.

I declared the `DessertMenu` element itself using an anonymous type that contains `Item1`, `Item2`, and `Item3` elements, each of type `Dessert`. Going back to the `DessertMenu` class example in Listing 2.3, you see that `Item1` and `Item2` contain `IceCream` while `Item3` contains `Cake`. Therefore, in the XML instance document, `<Item1>` and `<Item2>` will contain `IceCream`, and `<Item3>` will contain `Cake`. But the schema declares all three items of type

`Dessert`, so the question is: Given the schema and an instance XML document, how can an application know what each item really contains? This question has to do more with the item elements in the XML instance than with the type definitions or element declarations in the schema. Therefore, it is answered by introducing an attribute called `type` that belongs to the XML Schema Instance namespace. Adding this attribute on elements in the XML instance document lets you specify the exact type of those elements.

Listing 2.5 shows an example XML instance document that corresponds to the `DessertMenu` with `xsi:type` added to each item on the menu.

Listing 2.5   Example instance document representing the DessertMenu (VBWSClientCode\XmlDocuments\DessertMenu.xml)

```
<DessertMenu
 xmlns:xsi="http://www.w3.org/2001/XMLSchema-instance"
 xmlns="http://schemas.devxpert.com/examples"
 xmlns:dx="http://schemas.devxpert.com/examples">
  <Item1 xsi:type="dx:IceCream">
    <Calories>3000</Calories>
    <Flavor>Oreo cookie</Flavor>
  </Item1>
  <Item2 xsi:type="dx:IceCream">
    <Calories>3000</Calories>
    <Flavor>Oreo cookie</Flavor>
  </Item2>
  <Item3 xsi:type="dx:Cake">
    <Calories>4000</Calories>
    <IsChocolate>true</IsChocolate>
  </Item3>
</DessertMenu>
```

XSD also supports the concept of abstract base types. In the above example, if `Dessert` was a `MustInherit` (abstract) class, the corresponding XSD type would be the same as shown before with the `abstract` attribute set to `true`:

```
<!-- the Dessert base type made abstract -->
<complexType name="Dessert" abstract="true">
  <sequence>
    <element name="Calories" type="long" />
  </sequence>
</complexType>
```

Just like you cannot instantiate an object from a `MustInherit` class, you also cannot have an element of an abstract type in an XML document. Therefore by making `Dessert` abstract, you require that all `<Item>` elements in the `DessertMenu` be of `IceCream` or `Cake` type, that is, it is now illegal for an `<Item>` element to *not* have the `xsi:type` attribute.

2.8 Nil Values

XSD lets you indicate explicitly that an element is nil (`Nothing` in VB) as opposed to empty (that is, no content). For example, if you were out of chocolate cake and the `DessertMenu` object had only two items, you'd expect `Item3` to be `Nothing`. To express this in the schema and instance document, you perform two steps. First, modify the schema so that the item elements are nillable:

```
<!-- the DessertMenu -->
<element name="DessertMenu">
  <complexType>
    <sequence>
      <element name="Item1" type="dx:Dessert" nillable="true" />
      <element name="Item2" type="dx:Dessert" nillable="true"/>
      <element name="Item3" type="dx:Dessert" nillable="true"/>
    </sequence>
  </complexType>
</element>
```

then modify the XML instance document by adding `xsi:nil="true"` to `<Item3>` thereby indicating that it is nil:

```
<Item3 xsi:nil="true"></Item3>
```

Notice that I removed the `xsi:type` attribute from `<Item3>`. I did this because if an object reference is `Nothing`, do I know or care what type it really is? See the chapter's opening quote for a humorous analogy on this topic.

2.9 Uniqueness and Keys

When you use XML to represent your application's data, you'll want the ability to specify uniqueness constraints similar to the concept of a primary key common in database technologies. XSD provides the `<unique>` element, which you can use to define uniqueness constraints on element or attribute values. The

`<unique>` element contains a `<selector>` element that lets you specify a restricted XPath expression to indicate the scope of the uniqueness constraint. In the relational database analogy, this is similar to indicating the table on which you are defining the primary key. The `<unique>` element also contains one or more `<field>` elements that indicate which fields form the primary key. As in a relational database, the primary key can be made up of multiple fields. XSD also lets you specify more than one `<field>` element within a `<unique>` constraint. Listing 2.6 shows an example schema fragment that defines a uniqueness constraint on the invoiceID attribute of `<invoice>` elements.

Listing 2.6   Defining a uniqueness constraint for the invoiceID (VBWSClientCode\Chapter2\XmlDocuments\unique.xsd)

```
<xsd:element name="invoices">
 <xsd:complexType>
   <xsd:sequence>
     <xsd:element name="invoice" maxOccurs="unbounded">
       <xsd:complexType>
         <xsd:sequence>
           <!-- invoiceID must be unique -->
           <xsd:element name="invoiceID" type="xsd:int" />
           <xsd:element name="invoiceNumber" type="xsd:string" />
           <xsd:element name="supplierID" type="xsd:int" />
           <xsd:element name="invoiceDate" type="xsd:dateTime" />
           <xsd:element name="amtDue" type="xsd:decimal" />
         </xsd:sequence>
       </xsd:complexType>
     </xsd:element>
   <xsd:sequence>
 </xsd:complexType>
 <!-- a uniqueness constraint -->
 <xsd:unique name="PKInvoice">
    <!-- applies to invoice elements -->
   <xsd:selector xpath="./invoice" />
   <!-- invoiceID is the element
   whose value must be unique -->
   <xsd:field xpath="invoiceID" />
 </xsd:unique>
</xsd:element>
```

Note that the uniqueness constraint for `<invoice>` is defined within the `<invoices>` element declaration, which is the container for `<invoice>` elements.

You can also define key-based relations similar to the foreign-key primary-key relations found in relational databases. Defining relations is a two-step process: first define the key using a `<key>` element, and then reference that key using a `<keyref>` element. Listing 2.7 shows an example of defining a relation between the part number in an invoice item and the part number of a product.

Listing 2.7   Defining relations with key and keyref
(VBWSClientCode\Chapter2\key.xsd)

```
<xsd:schema targetNamespace="http://schemas.devxpert.com/
➥examples"
elementFormDefault="qualified"
xmlns="http://schemas.devxpert.com/examples"
xmlns:dx="http://schemas.devxpert.com/examples"
xmlns:xsd="http://www.w3.org/2001/XMLSchema">
    <xsd:element name="invoices">
        <xsd:complexType>
            <xsd:sequence>
                <xsd:element ref="products" />
                <xsd:element ref="invoice" />
            </xsd:sequence>
        </xsd:complexType>
        <!--
          a key on the product element
          this say> that the prodNum attribute on
          product must be unique
          -->
        <xsd:key name="prodKey">
            <xsd:selector xpath=".//dx:product" />
            <xsd:field xpath="@prodNum" />
        </xsd:key>
        <!--
          a reference to the product key
          this is the equivalent of a foreign key
          -->
        <xsd:keyref name="productRef" refer="prodKey">
            <xsd:selector xpath=".//dx:item" />
            <xsd:field xpath="dx:partNum" />
        </xsd:keyref>
    </xsd:element>
```

```xsd
<xsd:element name="products">
    <xsd:complexType>
        <xsd:sequence>
            <!-- the product element -->
            <xsd:element name="product"
                        maxOccur cf2 ="unbounded">
                <xsd:complexType>
                    <xsd:sequence>
                        <xsd:element
                        name="description" type="xsd:string"
➡/>
                    </xsd:sequence>
                    <xsd:attribute name="prodNum"
                        type="xsd:string" use="required" />
                </xsd:complexType>
            </xsd:element>
        </xsd:sequence>
    </xsd:complexType>
</xsd:element>
<xsd:element name="invoice">
    <xsd:complexType>
        <xsd:sequence>
            <!-- item element -->
            <xsd:element name="item" maxOccur cf2 ="unbounded">
                <xsd:complexType>
                    <xsd:sequence>
                        <xsd:element
                            name="partNum" type="xsd:string" />
                        <xsd:element
                            name="quant" type="xsd:int" />
                    </xsd:sequence>
                </xsd:complexType>
            </xsd:element>
        </xsd:sequence>
    </xsd:complexType>
</xsd:element>
</xsd:schema>
```

The `<products>` element declaration contains one or more `<product>` elements, each with a `prodNum` attribute. The key, `prodKey`, is defined on the `prodNum` attribute of `<product>`. This is the equivalent of a primary key and means the products element cannot have two product elements with the same prodNum. The invoice element declaration contains one or more `<item>` elements, each with a `<partNum>` child element. The `<keyref>` element defines the value of `<partNum>` as a foreign key that refers to prodKey. The result is a one-to-many relation between products and invoice items based on the part number, exactly as you would have in a relational database.

So far we have discussed the XSD type system and how to use XSD for defining your application's type. The remainder of this chapter focuses on mapping object instances to XML based on an existing XSD schema. This process is called **serialization**.

2.10 Object Serialization

As you build Web services, you will find that XML messaging is a more natural fit compared to RPC. This means you'll find yourself designing Web services that send your data back and forth as XML documents. For example, the Sub- mitInvoice method you saw earlier accepts an invoice document, like that shown in Listing 2.8, in a `String` parameter. To process the invoice, the Sub- mitInvoice method needs to parse the invoice document (using a DOM parser for example), then read the data out of the document and use it to set the properties of an object from the Invoice class shown in Listing 2.9. This is called **deserializing** an object from XML. Similarly, if a client is trying to invoke the SubmitInvoice method, it might internally create the invoice in an Invoice object then read its properties one at a time and generate the XML document to send to SubmitInvoice. This process is known as **serializing** an object to XML.

Listing 2.8   Example invoice document sent to SubmitInvoice

```
<Invoice>
  <invoiceItems>
    <InvoiceItem>
      <partNum>58</partNum>
      <quant>50</quant>
      <unitPrice>13.25</unitPrice>
      <total>662.5</total>
    </InvoiceItem>
  </invoiceItems>
```

```
<invoiceNumber>123-JFD-0923</invoiceNumber>
<supplierID>27</supplierID>
<invoiceDate>2001-07-23T00:00:00.0000000-04:00</invoiceDate>
<poNumber>AX0192</poNumber>
<subTotal>662.5</subTotal>
<salesTax>29.81</salesTax>
<paymentReceived>0</paymentReceived>
<amtDue>692.31</amtDue>
<terms>Net 30 days</terms>
<contactName>John Smith</contactName>
<contactNumber>(123) 456-7890</contactNumber>
<promotion>10% discount on items purchased this month
                </promotion>
</Invoice>
```

Listing 2.9   Example invoice and InvoiceItem classes
(VBWSClientCode\Chapter2\Serialize\Invoice.vb)

```vb
Public Class Invoice
    Public invoiceItems(2) As InvoiceItem
    Public Sub AddItem(ByVal invItem As invoiceItem)
        'code omitted
    End Sub
    Public Function ComputeTotal(ByVal SalesTaxPercent _
                As Single) As Double
        'code omitted
    End Function

    Public invoiceNumber As String
    Public supplierID As Integer
    Public invoiceDate As Date
    Public poNumber As String
    Public subTotal As Double
    Public salesTax As Double
    Public paymentReceived As Double
    Public amtDue As Double
    Public terms As String
    Public contactName As String
    Public contactNumber As String
    Public promotion As String
End Class

Public Class InvoiceItem
    Public partNum As String
```

```
        Public quant As Integer
        Public unitPrice As Double
        Public total As Double
    End Class
```

The SOAP Toolkit V3.0 includes a default serializer/deserializer that can handle serializing public fields and properties of your VB 6 objects. I'll cover the SOAP Toolkit in Chapter 5. .NET also provides excellent support for automatic object serialization and deserialization. To demonstrate how easy serialization is with .NET, Listing 2.10 shows an example of creating an invoice object, setting its properties, then serializing it to XML. The few lines of code in Listing 2.10 result in the XML document in Listing 2.8.

Listing 2.10 Serializing an invoice object to XML. The code setting invoice properties has been omitted (VBWSClientCode\Chapter2\Serialize\Form1.vb).

```
Private Sub btnSerialize_Click(ByVal sender As System.Object, _
            ByVal e As System.EventArgs) _
            Handles txtSerialize.Click
    Dim inv As SellerInvoice = CreateInvoice()
    Dim serializer As New XmlSerializer(inv.GetType)
    Dim file As String = Environment.CurrentDirectory _
                    & "\Invoice.xml"
    Dim writer As New StreamWriter(file)
    serializer.Serialize(writer, inv)
    writer.Close()
    MessageBox.Show("Serialized invoice to: " & file)
End Sub
```

2.10.1 How Serialization Works

The .NET class library includes a framework for XML serialization under the `System.Xml.Serialization` namespace. Figure 2.4 shows the classes involved in a simple serialization process; shaded classes are part of the XML serialization framework.

Assuming you have an object from the Invoice class that you want to serialize, you use the `System.Xml.Serialization.XmlSerializer` class. You call the `Serialize` method on this class by passing it the `Invoice` object and one of the following: `Stream`, `TextWriter`, or `XmlWriter`. The `XmlSerializer` uses reflection to read public properties and fields of the `Invoice` object

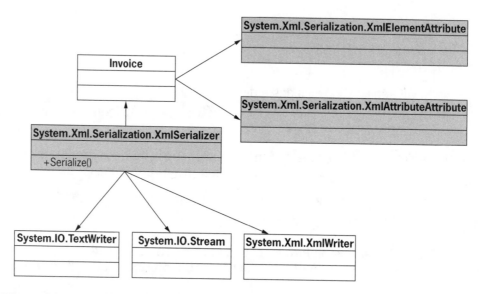

Figure 2.4 Some of the classes used in XML serialization. The shaded classes are part of the XML serialization framework.

and serialize them as XML to the supplied stream or writer. The XmlSerializer automatically determines the structure of the generated XML document unless you use attributes to influence that structure.

Figure 2.4 shows two of the commonly used attributes: XmlElementAttribute and XmlAttributeAttribute. These are .NET CLR attributes not XML attributes. .NET attributes are classes that inherit from System.Attribute and their names typically end with Attribute (by convention). These classes are used to add metadata to the assemblies, which can be used at runtime to add functionality. For example, by adding the XmlElementAttribute to a public property or field of your class, you are telling the XmlSerializer that you want this property or field to be serialized as an XML element with the specified name. For example, to specify that the invoiceNumber must be serialized to an <invNo> element:

```
<System.Xml.Serialization.XmlElement("invNo")> _
Public invoiceNumber As String
```

Note that the VB compiler lets you take off the Attribute suffix on the attribute's name so that it appears in your code as XmlElement instead of

`XmlElementAttribute`. This is advantageous for two reasons: It shortens the code so you type fewer characters, and it reduces the chance of confusion between .NET attributes and XML attributes by eliminating the word "Attribute." For the remainder of this chapter, I will omit the `Attribute` suffix on .NET attribute names.

Return to the example in Listing 2.10. I start the example by calling `CreateInvoice` to create a new invoice object and set its properties. In a real application, these property values may come from a database as part of processing shipped orders. I then create a new `XmlSerializer` using the constructor overload that accepts a type. This is the type of the object that you want to serialize, which in this case, I get by calling `inv.GetType`. Then I create a new `StreamWriter` passing it the file name, and call `XmlSerializer.Serialize` passing it the writer and the invoice object. The resulting XML is shown in Listing 2.8.

This simple example is sufficient if you just want to save the object to XML and reload it later. However, when building Web services, most likely you want your XML document to be schema-valid based on some existing schema. For example, if you represent a vendor who is sending out electronic invoices to buyers, you might sit down with the buyers and establish a schema for the invoice document. Assuming you have an `Invoice` class in your application, you'll want to serialize objects from that class according to the invoice schema. Similarly, the buyer will want to process the invoice you send him, possibly by deserializing the invoice document into another invoice object. It is very important to understand the following: The class the vendor uses to represent an invoice is different from the class the buyer uses to represent an invoice. The only common aspect between the two classes is that they both serialize/deserialize according to the same schema.

2.10.2 Schemas and XML Serialization

To show you how XSD and XML serialization are used in Web services, I put together an example vendor application that sends electronic invoices to a buyer application. The scenario is as follows: The buyer and seller establish a schema for the invoice document (shown in Listing 2.11). This schema will serve as the basis for the electronic document exchange that will take place between the two parties.

Listing 2.11 Invoice XML schema. This schema is used to validate invoice documents received by the buyer (VBWSClientCode\chapter2 \XmlDocuments\nwindInvoice.xsd).

```
<schema
targetNamespace=
"http://www.devxpert.com/nwind.net/schemas/invoice"
xmlns="http://www.w3.org/2001/XMLSchema"
xmlns:dx="http://www.devxpert.com/nwind.net/schemas/invoice"
elementFormDefault="qualified">
<element name="invoice">
   <complexType>
  <all>
   <element name="invoiceNumber" type="string" />
   <element name="supplierID" type="int" />
   <element name="invoiceDate" type="date" />
   <element name="poNumber" type="string" />
   <element name="subTotal" type="dx:USD" />
   <element name="salesTax" type="dx:USD" />
   <element name="paymentReceived" type="dx:USD" />
   <element name="amtDue" type="dx:USD" />
   <element name="terms" type="string" minOccurs="0" />
   <element name="contactName" type="string" minOccurs="0" />
   <element name="contactNumber" type="string" minOccurs="0" />
   <element name="promotion" type="string" minOccurs="0" />
   <element name="invoiceItems" type="dx:invoiceItemsType" />
  </all>
   </complexType>
</element>
<simpleType name="USD">
   <restriction base="decimal">
  <fractionDigits value="2" />
   </restriction>
</simpleType>
<complexType name="invoiceItemsType">
   <sequence>
      <element name="item" maxOccurs="unbounded">
        <complexType>
                <sequence>
```

REAL WORLD XML WEB SERVICES

```
      <element name="partNum" type="string" />
      <element name="quant" type="int" />
      <element name="unitPrice" type="dx:USD" />
      <element name="total" type="dx:USD" />
       </sequence>
       </complexType>
     </element>
  </sequence>
</complexType>
</schema>
```

This schema defines an element named `invoice` that has an anonymous complex type. This complex type is made up of elements that can appear in any order (hence the use of `<xsd:all>`). The schema also defines a new type called USD, which inherits from the built-in type `decimal` and restricts the number of digits after the decimal point to two. The type USD is used for elements such as `<subtotal>` and `<salesTax>`. There's also the `invoiceItemsType`, which contains any number of the `<item>` elements. The `item` element itself represents an invoice item with a part number, quantity, unit price, and total. Note that the schema specifies that `elementFormDefault` is `qualified`, so we expect all elements in the invoice document to belong to the target namespace: `http://www.devxpert.com/nwind.net/schemas/invoice`.

The seller will send an invoice as an XML document to the buyer. The buyer will then validate it using the invoice schema in Listing 2.6, process it, and return True or False to the seller indicating success or failure, respectively (see Figure 2.5).

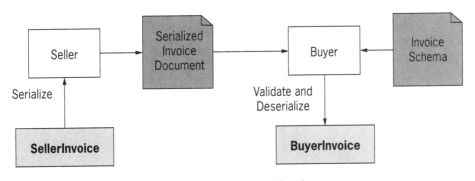

Figure 2.5 A scenario utilizing XSD and serialization

The buyer needs to create a new class to represent the invoice. The buyer will call this class `BuyerInvoice`. Given the invoice schema, the buyer uses a tool called `xsd.exe` to create the `BuyerInvoice` class. This tool is part of the .NET Framework SDK and can generate classes from schemas and vice versa. It can also infer a schema from an XML document, which would be a good starting point if you have a document and want to create the corresponding schema. To create the `BuyerInvoice` class, the buyer issues the following command:

```
xsd.exe invoice.xsd /classes /language:VB
```

The `/classes` option tells `xsd.exe` to generate classes from the specified schema, while the `/language` tells it to generate those classes in VB. Listing 2.12 shows the generated VB class after it has been renamed from invoice (based on the schema) to `BuyerInvoice`.

Listing 2.12   BuyerInvoice class created by xsd.exe from invoice schema (VBWSClientCode\chapter2 \NWIND\BuyerInvoice.vb)

```
'modified class name from invoice to BuyerInvoice
<System.Xml.Serialization.XmlRootAttribute( _
 [Namespace]:=
 "http://www.devxpert.com/nwind.net/schemas/invoice", _
 ElementName:="invoice", _
IsNullable:=False)> _
Public Class BuyerInvoice
    <System.Xml.Serialization.XmlElementAttribute( _
      IsNullable:=False)> _
    Public invoiceNumber As String
    Public supplierID As Integer
    <System.Xml.Serialization.XmlElementAttribute( _
      DataType:="date", IsNullable:=False)> _
    Public invoiceDate As Date
    <System.Xml.Serialization.XmlElementAttribute( _
      IsNullable:=False)> _
    Public poNumber As String
    Public subTotal As Decimal
    Public salesTax As Decimal
    Public paymentReceived As Decimal
    Public amtDue As Decimal
    <System.Xml.Serialization.XmlElementAttribute( _
      IsNullable:=False)> _
```

```
    Public terms As String
    <System.Xml.Serialization.XmlElementAttribute( _
      IsNullable:=False)> _
    Public contactName As String
    <System.Xml.Serialization.XmlElementAttribute( _
      IsNullable:=False)> _
    Public contactNumber As String
    <System.Xml.Serialization.XmlElementAttribute( _
      IsNullable:=False)> _
    Public promotion As String
    <System.Xml.Serialization.XmlArrayAttribute( _
      IsNullable:=False), _
     System.Xml.Serialization.XmlArrayItemAttribute( _
      "item", IsNullable:=False)> _
    Public invoiceItems() As invoiceItemsTypeItem
    'Added this method
    Public Function ProcessInvoice() As Boolean
        'always returns true for now
        Return True
    End Function
End Class

Public Class invoiceItemsTypeItem
    <System.Xml.Serialization.XmlElementAttribute( _
      IsNullable:=False)> _
    Public partNum As String
    Public quant As Integer
    Public unitPrice As Decimal
    Public total As Decimal
End Class
```

In addition to renaming the class, I also added the method `ProcessInvoice` that will be used later to process incoming invoices. Note that `xsd.exe` actually creates two classes: `invoice` and `invoiceItemsTypeItem`. The latter corresponds to the type of the `item` element that is itself part of the complex type `invoiceItemsType`, hence the name `invoiceItemsTypeItem`.

`Xsd.exe` places several serialization attributes within the generated class to ensure the class can be deserialized from schema instance documents (invoice documents). Working our way from the top, the `BuyerInvoice` class itself has an attribute called `XmlRoot`, which indicates that an object from the class corresponds to the document element in an invoice document. The

`Namespace` and `ElementName` properties of `XmlRoot` indicate the namespace URI and local name of the document element, respectively. So here it's saying that the document element is called invoice and belongs to the namespace `http://www.devxpert.com/nwind.net/schemas/invoice`. `IsNullable` indicates whether null (Nothing) values should be serialized with the `xsi:nil="true"` attribute. If you set this to `True`, then when you serialize an invoice object that is set to Nothing, the serializer will generate this XML element (namespace declarations removed):

```
<invoice xsi:nil="true"/>
```

However, since `IsNullable` is set to `False`, serializing a null object reference will generate the following XML (namespace declarations removed):

```
<invoice/>
```

Next, the `invoiceNumber` field has the `XmlElement` attribute, which indicates it gets serialized to an XML element, as we know from the schema, and that it is not nullable. Serializing to an XML element (with the same name as the field or property) is the default, so you actually don't need the `XmlElement` attribute unless you are specifying additional information such as `IsNullable` or `ElementName`. That's why `supplierID` does not have any attributes: It gets serialized to an XML element named `supplierID` and, because it is an `int`, it will never be null. Next is `invoiceDate` that has the `XmlElement` attribute, this time with an interesting property: `DataType="date"`.

Visual Basic's `Date` type maps to `System.DateTime` structure, which contains the date and the time. XSD's `date` type contains the date only (with an optional time zone). So the serializer must know to discard the time portion of the `invoiceDate` when serializing to XML. The value of `DataType` can be any of the built-in XSD types. Going down the class, you'll notice that all elements that were declared of type `dx:USD` in the schema correspond to fields of type `Decimal`. That's because there's no equivalent to XSD's ability to create new types that inherit existing types and declaratively restrict facets of the base type such as the number of digits after the decimal point. If you want to map this restriction to your VB class, you'll have to convert the fields to properties and add logic in the property Set procedures to enforce this restriction. The next interesting bit is the `invoiceItems` field, which is an array of type `invoiceItems-TypeItem`. This array has two attributes: `XmlArray` indicates that it is an array and that its contents should be serialized as a series of elements; `XmlArray-Item` indicates the name of the XML element used to represent each item in the array, in this case `<item>`.

So now the buyer will write some code to deserialize the XML invoices that he or she receives into this `BuyerInvoice` class. Listing 2.13 shows the example `SubmitInvoice` method, which validates and deserializes the received document in one step.

Listing 2.13 The buyer receives, validates, and deserializes the invoice document (VBWSClientCode\NWIND\InvoiceProcessor.vb)

```
Imports System.Xml
Imports System.Xml.Schema
Imports System.Xml.Serialization
Public Class InvoiceProcessor
    Public Const INVOICE_NS As String = _
        "http://www.devxpert.com/nwind.net/schemas/invoice"
    'modify this constant to point to your schema location
    Public Const SCHEMA_LOCATION As String = _

"D:\VBWSClientCode\chapter2\XmlDocuments\nwindInvoice.xsd"

    Public Function SubmitInvoice(ByVal InvoiceDoc As XmlNode) _
                As Boolean
        'This method validates the input invoice
        'and deserializes it into an object
        'the validating reader and the schema collection
        Dim vr As New XmlValidatingReader(InvoiceDoc.OuterXml, _
            XmlNodeType.Document, Nothing)
        Dim xsc As New XmlSchemaCollection()
        xsc.Add(INVOICE_NS, SCHEMA_LOCATION)
        vr.Schemas.Add(xsc)
        Dim Invoice As BuyerInvoice
        'the serializer
        Dim serializer As _
            NewXmlSerializer(GetType(BuyerInvoice))
```

```
              'deserializing will read from the validatingReader
              'this causes the document to be validated
              Invoice = CType(serializer.Deserialize(vr), BuyerInvoice)
              Return Invoice.ProcessInvoice()
         End Function
    End Class
```

To validate the document, the code uses an `XmlValidatingReader` and an `XmlSchemaCollection`. But instead of reading directly from the reader, the code creates an `XmlSerializer` and calls its `Deserialize` method passing it the validating reader. The `XmlSerializer` will read the document from the validating reader, causing it to be validated while deserialized. Finally, the code invokes `BuyerInvoice.ProcessInvoice` to process this new invoice. This particular example lacks the exception handling you saw in the validation example earlier in this chapter, and which should be present in real applications.

Assuming the seller *already has* an application that generates invoices using the `SellerInvoice` class, the seller must now determine a way to serialize objects from that class into XML documents according to the invoice schema. The seller can do this by simply adding the appropriate attributes to the `SellerInvoice` class. Listing 2.14 shows the `SellerInvoice` class after the seller added the necessary attributes. Note that these attributes have been added manually; not by using `xsd.exe` (xsd.exe cannot add attributes to an existing class).

Listing 2.14   SellerInvoice class with the necessary attributes to serialize it according to the schema (VBWSClientCode\SubmitInvoice\SellerInvoice.vb)

```
<XmlRoot([Namespace]:= _
"http://www.devxpert.com/nwind.net/schemas/invoice", _
 ElementName:="invoice", _
 IsNullable:=False)> _
Public Class SellerInvoice
    Private mInvoiceSubTotal As Decimal
    Private mSalesTax As Decimal
    Private mAmountDue As Decimal
    Private mInvoiceItems As ArrayList
    'public fields and properties
    <XmlIgnore()> _
    Public OrderNumber As String
```

```vb
<XmlElement(ElementName:="invoiceNumber", _
IsNullable:=False)> _
Public InvoiceNum As String

<XmlElement(ElementName:="supplierID", _
IsNullable:=False)> _
Public SupplierId As Integer

<XmlElement(ElementName:="invoiceDate", _
DataType:="date", _
IsNullable:=False)> _
Public InvoiceDate As Date

<XmlElement(ElementName:="poNumber", _
IsNullable:=False)> _
Public PONumber As String

<XmlElement(ElementName:="subTotal", _
IsNullable:=False)> _
Property SubTotal() As Decimal
    Get
        SubTotal = Me.mInvoiceSubTotal
    End Get
    Set(ByVal Value As Decimal)

    End Set
End Property

<XmlElement(ElementName:="salesTax", _
IsNullable:=False)> _
Property SalesTaxAmt() As Decimal
    Get
        SalesTaxAmt = Me.mSalesTax
    End Get
    Set(ByVal Value As Decimal)

    End Set
End Property

<XmlElement(ElementName:="paymentReceived", _
IsNullable:=False)> _
Public PreviousPayment As Decimal
```

```vb
<XmlElement(ElementName:="amtDue", _
IsNullable:=False)> _
Property AmountDue() As Decimal
    Get
        Return mAmountDue
    End Get
    Set(ByVal Value As Decimal)

    End Set
End Property

<XmlElement(ElementName:="terms", _
IsNullable:=False)> _
Public PayTerms As String

<XmlElement(ElementName:="contactName", _
IsNullable:=False)> _
Public ContactName As String

<XmlElement(ElementName:="contactNumber", _
IsNullable:=False)> _
Public ContactNumber As String

<XmlElement(ElementName:="promotion", _
IsNullable:=False)> _
Public CurrentPromotion As String

'Moved the InvoiceItems to the end of the class
<XmlArray(ElementName:="invoiceItems"), _
XmlArrayItem("item", GetType(InvoiceItem))> _
Property InvoiceItems() As ArrayList
    Get
        Return mInvoiceItems
    End Get
    Set(ByVal Value As ArrayList)

    End Set
End Property
'method to add a new invoice item
Public Sub AddItem(ByVal InvItem As InvoiceItem)
    InvItem.Total = Round(InvItem.UnitPrice * _
                InvItem.Quant, 2)
    mInvoiceItems.Add(InvItem)
End Sub
```

```
    'method to compute the invoice total
    Public Function ComputeTotal(ByVal SalesTaxPercent _
            As Decimal) As Decimal
        Dim ItemsTotal As Decimal
        Dim InvItem As InvoiceItem
        For Each InvItem In InvoiceItems
            ItemsTotal += InvItem.Quant * InvItem.UnitPrice
        Next
        Me.mInvoiceSubTotal = Round(ItemsTotal, 2)
        Me.mSalesTax = Round(Me.mInvoiceSubTotal * _
                    SalesTaxPercent, 2)
        Me.mAmountDue = Round(Me.mSalesTax + _
                    Me.mInvoiceSubTotal _
                    - Me.PreviousPayment, 2)
        Return Me.mAmountDue
    End Function

    Public Sub New()
        mInvoiceItems = New ArrayList()
    End Sub
End Class

Public Class InvoiceItem
    <XmlElement(ElementName:="partNum", _
    IsNullable:=False)> _
    Public PartNum As String
    <XmlElement(ElementName:="quant", _
    IsNullable:=False)> _
    Public Quant As Integer
    <XmlElement(ElementName:="unitPrice", _
    IsNullable:=False)> _
    Public UnitPrice As Decimal
    <XmlElement(ElementName:="total", _
    IsNullable:=False)> _
    Public Total As Decimal
End Class
```

This class is in a module that imports System.Xml.Serialization, therefore, class names such as XmlElement need not be fully qualified. The class
begins with the now familiar XmlRoot attribute. The next interesting thing is the
use of the XmlIgnore attribute to indicate that OrderNumber should not be
serialized. OrderNumber is only needed within the seller's application and is
not part of the invoice schema. Many of the names of properties and fields of

this class do not match those in the schema; for example, `InvoiceNum` and `invoiceNumber`. The solution for this mismatch is to use the `XmlElement` attribute and set its `ElementName` property to the name specified in the schema; for example, `invoiceNumber`. Although VB is not case sensitive, case does matter when you serialize an object to XML. The default name used for the XML element (or XML attribute), is the exact name that you use in your VB code. Because XML is case sensitive, if the schema declares an element named `SupplierID` and your serialized object contains an element called `SupplierId`, you have an invalid XML document. That's why the `SupplierId` field has the `XmlElement` attribute with its ElementName property set to SupplierID. Note that case does not matter when you deserialize an object from XML because the `XmlSerializer` ignores the case of members in your VB class when deserializing.

The `SellerInvoice` class contains the calculated properties: `SubTotal`, `SalesTaxAmt`, and `AmountDue`. These are exposed as properties (rather than fields) whose Set procedures do nothing. Ideally, you'd use read-only properties for a scenario like this; however, the serializer cannot serialize read-only properties. This is unfortunate because there are scenarios (like the one we are discussing) where you want to serialize an object to XML then use that XML to deserialize a different object. In these scenarios, having read-only properties on the first object makes sense.

Instead of using an array for the invoice items, the seller uses an `Array-List`. The serializer can handle `ArrayLists` provided you add the `XmlArray-Item` attribute to tell the serializer the data type of items in this `ArrayList`. `XmlArrayItem` also indicates the element name, in this case "item," to use for each item in the `ArrayList`. The `XmlArray` attribute is used to tell the serializer the name to use for the XML element name that represents the entire array.

Finally, the `SellerInvoice` class has two methods. `AddItem` adds a new invoice item to the `InvoiceItems ArrayList` and calculates the total cost for that item rounding it off to two digits after the decimal point. `ComputeTotal` calculates the sum of all item totals and stores it as the invoice subtotal. It also calculates the sales tax and the invoice total, rounding all these numbers to two digits after the decimal point.

Now the seller must add code to his or her application to serialize the invoice to a string and call the buyer's `SubmitInvoice` method, passing it that string. In a real application, `SubmitInvoice` would be exposed as part of a Web service that the seller can call. But we are not ready to invoke a Web service yet, so we will just call the method directly. This makes no difference in terms of how XSD and serialization are used. Listing 2.15 shows the seller's code.

Listing 2.15   Seller's code for serializing and submitting the invoice (VBWSClientCode\chapter2\SubmitInvoice\SubmitInvoice.vb)

```
Private Sub SubmitInvoice_Click( _
    ByVal sender As System.Object, _
    ByVal e As System.EventArgs) Handles SubmitInvoice.Click
        'string writer
        Dim strWriter As New StringWriter()
        Try
            'create a new invoice object
            'and set its properties
            Dim inv As SellerInvoice = CreateInvoice()
            Dim serializer As New XmlSerializer(inv.GetType)
            'serialize invoice to string writer
            serializer.Serialize(strWriter, inv)
            Dim InvoiceDoc As New XmlDocument()
            InvoiceDoc.LoadXml(strWriter.ToString())
            Dim BuyerInvProc As New Buyer.InvoiceProcessor()
            'send invoice to buyer
            If BuyerInvProc.SubmitInvoice(InvoiceDoc) Then
                MessageBox.Show("Invoice successfully submitted")
            End If
            strWriter.Close()
        Catch ex As Exception
            MessageBox.Show("Error submitting invoice: " _
                            & ex.Message)
        Finally
            strWriter.Close()
        End Try
    End Sub
```

The above code is very similar to what you have seen before except for the use of `StringWriter` instead of `StreamWriter` to serialize the invoice object to a string rather than a stream. The seller then creates an instance of the buyer's `InvoiceProcessor` and calls `SubmitInvoice`, passing it the serialized invoice string. If the invoice is schema-valid, this method returns `True`, indicating that the invoice has been successfully processed.

2.10.3 Overriding Serialization Attributes

Assume the seller now wants to send electronic invoices to another buyer. This buyer agrees to the invoice schema except for `invoiceNumber`: They insist that invoiceNumber must be an attribute of the `<invoice>` element. To satisfy this requirement, the seller continues to use the `SellerInvoice` class but applies a serialization override while serializing invoices. Serialization overrides let you specify at runtime how an object is to be serialized. They are applied to an object externally so you do not need the object's source code to control how it is serialized. Listing 2.16 shows the code that serializes an instance of `Seller-Invoice` with `invoiceNumber` as an attribute.

Listing 2.16   Using attribute overrides to control XML serialization (VBWSClientCode\chapter2\Serializer\Form1.vb)

```vb
Private Sub btnOverrides_Click( _
        ByVal sender As System.Object, _
        ByVal e As System.EventArgs) Handles btnOverrides.Click
        Dim inv As SellerInvoice = CreateSellerInvoice()

    'the following is the equivalent of
    'adding this attribute to InvoiceNum
    '<XmlAttribute(AttributeName:= "invoiceNumber", _
    'Form:=Schema.XmlSchemaForm.Unqualified)>
    Dim NewAttr As New XmlAttributeAttribute()
    NewAttr.AttributeName = "invoiceNumber"
    'the attribute name is unqualified attribute
    NewAttr.Form = Schema.XmlSchemaForm.Unqualified

    'Create an attributes collection
    'and add to it the NewAttr
    Dim Attribs As New XmlAttributes()
    Attribs.XmlAttribute = NewAttr
    'Create an attribute overrides object
    Dim AttribOverrides As New XmlAttributeOverrides()
    'add to it the object type, the member name,
```

```
            'and the overrides
            AttribOverrides.Add(GetType(Invoice), _
                "InvoiceNum", Attribs)
            'create a serializer with the overrides
            Dim serializer As New XmlSerializer( _
                GetType(Invoice), AttribOverrides)
            Dim file As String = _
                Environment.CurrentDirectory & "\InvoiceAttrs.xml"
            Dim writer As New StreamWriter(file)
            serializer.Serialize(writer, inv)
            writer.Close()
            MessageBox.Show("Serialized invoice to: " & file)
    End Sub
```

Looking closely at Listing 2.16, you'll see the full name of the serialization attribute XmlAttributeAttribute. When you use serialization overrides, you actually instantiate an object from the serialization attribute that you want to use, (for example, XmlAttributeAttribute). Therefore, you must use the full name of the serialization attribute, (for example, `XmlElementAttribute` and `Xml-AttributeAttribute`).

The example in Listing 2.16 creates an object of `XmlAttributeAttribute` and sets its `AttributeName` and `Form` properties. It then puts this object into the `XmlAttribute` property of an `XmlAttributes` object. The `XmlAttributes` object represents all XML serialization attributes that we want to apply to an object or a member of an object at runtime while serializing it. To associate the `XmlAttributeAttribute` with the `InvoiceNum` member of the `SellerInvoice`, I create a new `XmlAttributeOverrides` object and call its `Add` method passing it the `SellerInvoice` type, the `InvoiceNum` member name, and the `XmlAttributes` object that contains the `XmlAttributeAttribute`. The effect of doing this is exactly the same as if I had added `XmlAttributeAttribute` to the `InvoiceNum` field of the `SellerInvoice` class itself:

```
Public Class SellerInvoice
  'code omitted ...
  <XmlAttributeAttribute(AttributeName:="invoiceNumber")> _
  Public InvoiceNum As String
  'code omitted ...
End Class
```

Next, I create an `XmlSerializer`, this time passing it the `XmlAttribu-teOverrides` as the constructor's second parameter. When I call `XmlSeri-alizer.Serialize`, it takes into account the attribute overrides I passed and puts the value of `InvoiceNum` into an attribute called `invoiceNum`.

By using XML serialization attribute overrides, you can serialize a given object multiple ways, depending on your target schema. You can also control how objects are serialized without having access to their source code.

2.10.4 Inheritance, Interfaces and Serialization

Consider again the dessert example: how would you serialize the `Dessert-Menu`? The problem here is that the menu contains three `Dessert` items (`Item1`, `Item2`, and `Item3`) that actually contain objects of the derived types `IceCream` and `Cake`. The serializer cannot serialize the menu unless you tell it about the derived types `IceCream` and `Cake`. To do this, you add an `XmlIn-clude` attribute on the base class `Dessert` for each of the derived types `IceCream` and `Cake` as shown in Listing 2.17. The serializer reads this meta-data and understands that whenever it is asked to serialize a `Dessert` object, it should examine it to see if it's really an `IceCream` or a `Cake`. Now when you se-rialize the `DessertMenu` shown in Listing 2.17, you get the XML shown in List-ing 2.18. Note that each menu item has an `xsi:type` attribute indicating the type of that item.

Listing 2.17   The Dessert classes with XML serialization attributes added

```
'Dessert is the base class
'Use XmlInclude to indicate other types
'that inherit from Dessert
<XmlInclude(GetType(IceCream)), XmlInclude(GetType(Cake))> _
Public Class Dessert
    Public Calories As Long
End Class
'IceCream inherits from Dessert
Public Class IceCream
    Inherits Dessert
    Public Flavor As String
End Class
'Cake inherits from Dessert
```

```vbnet
Public Class Cake
    Inherits Dessert
    Public IsChocolate As Boolean
End Class

'This is the class we will serialize
Public Class DessertMenu
    Public Item1 As Dessert
    Public Item2 As Dessert
    Public Item3 As Dessert
    Public Sub New()
      'Code omitted that
      'puts IceCream in items 1 and 2
      'puts Cake in item 3
    End Sub
End Class
```

Listing 2.18   The serialized DessertMenu object

```xml
<DessertMenu
    xmlns:xsi="http://www.w3.org/2001/XMLSchema-instance"
    xmlns:xsd="http://www.w3.org/2001/XMLSchema">
  <Item1 xsi:type="IceCream">
    <Calories>3000</Calories>
    <Flavor>Oreo cookie</Flavor>
  </Item1>
  <Item2 xsi:type="IceCream">
    <Calories>3000</Calories>
    <Flavor>Oreo cookie</Flavor>
  </Item2>
  <Item3 xsi:type="Cake">
    <Calories>4000</Calories>
    <IsChocolate>true</IsChocolate>
  </Item3>
</DessertMenu>
```

While you can easily serialize polymorphic types, XML serialization does not support interface serialization primarily because of how XSD works. XSD has the concept of base types and derived types, but it doesn't have a concept of interfaces. So there's no direct equivalent to an interface in XSD. Although an interface can be thought of as an abstract base class, trying to map interfaces to XSD abstract base types would not work because XSD supports only single inheritance whereas a VB .NET class could implement multiple interfaces. This results in the following limitation: A serializer must know the real object's type to serialize it; it cannot serialize a property or field that returns an interface. For example, you might try to define an `IDessert` interface instead of the `Dessert` abstract class, and rewrite the `DessertMenu` to use that interface like this:

```
Public Class DessertMenu
    Public Item1 As IDessert
    Public Item2 As IDessert
    Public Item3 As IDessert
    'Code omitted
End Class
```

The serializer would not be able to serialize `DessertMenu` objects—it would throw an exception because it does not know the real type of the objects contained in each of `Item1`, `Item2`, and `Item3`.

2.10.5   XML Serialization and Remoting

The XML serialization classes you've seen so far all live in the `System.Xml.Serialization` namespace. There are other classes that live in `System.Runtime.Remoting.Serialization` and are also responsible for serialization. The two sets of classes satisfy different serialization needs. `System.Xml.Serialization` focuses on the needs of XML-based messaging. Therefore, it provides an easy way to serialize and deserialize an object's public data thereby saving you the hassle of generating and parsing XML yourself. But `System.Xml.Serialization` does not try to create faithful reproduction of the object through serialization then deserialization. In fact, you've seen an example where the seller serialized an object and the buyer used that XML to deserialize an object of a different type—it's all about the XML data.

On the other hand, `System.Runtime.Remoting.Serialization` satisfies the need of serializing entire object graphs and deserializing them on the other end thereby creating a faithful reproduction of the object graph including the object identities. With remoting, objects can be serialized to XML or to a binary format. `System.Runtime.Remoting.Serialization` makes the most sense when a .NET client and server (remote object) want to communicate over a Local Area Network (LAN) or an intranet, whereas `System.Xml.Serialization` is very useful for serializing public object state into XML for messaging.

2.11 Summary

The W3C's XSD Schema is the type system used formally to describe Web services messages. Schemas offer many built-in types and let you define your own types as well as the structure of XML messages and documents. You can also use XSD schemas with `MSXML4` or with the `XmlValidatingReader` to validate incoming messages thereby enforcing the agreed-upon messaging contract. In addition, if you are programming in .NET, you can take advantage of the XML serialization framework to easily generate XML documents according to a predefined schema and/or to process incoming XML messages without having to write abundant parsing code.

2.12 Resources

DevelopMentor's .NET Web discussion list:
>   http://discuss.develop.com/ dotnet-web.html

T. Bray, "XML Namespaces by Example": http://www.xml.com/pub/a/1999/01/namespaces.html, ©2002 O'Reilly & Associates, Inc., O'Reilly/XML.com, January 19, 1999.

2.12.1 Specifications

C.M. Sperberg-McQueen, H. Thompsen, W3C XML Schema specifications and resources: http://www.w3.org/XML/Schema, © 2000 W3C (MIT, INRIA, KEIO), April 2000.

T. Bray, D. Hollander, A. Layman, W3C Namespaces in XML Recommendation: http://www.w3.org/TR/1999/REC-xml-names-19990114/, © 1999 W3C (MIT, INRIA, KEIO), January 14, 1999.

R. Moats, IETF RFC 2141 URN Syntax: http://www.ietf.org/rfc/rfc2141.txt, May 1999.

T. Berners-Lee, R. Fielding, L. Masinter, IETF RFC 2396 Uniform Resource Identifiers (URI): Generic Syntax: http://www.ietf.org/rfc/rfc2396.txt, August 1998.

Chapter 3

SOAP: Invoking Web Services

I think there's a world market for about five computers.
—Thomas Watson

In Chapter 1, you learned how to invoke a Web service using the SOAP Toolkit and .NET. In this chapter, you will learn how these tools and others use SOAP messages to invoke Web services. I will explain the goals and architecture of SOAP and the ways it can be used, including messaging and RPC. Chapter 3 will teach you SOAP's capabilities and functionalities, so that you get a better understanding of the tools you'll be using, such as .NET and the SOAP Toolkit. Such understanding will come in handy when you need to invoke a Web service and you find the tools have limitations that prevent you from using them. This chapter and the next are tightly integrated and together complete the picture of how Web services work.

3.1   What Is SOAP?

Since 1994, the Web has grown tremendously and has become the Internet's "killer" application. The Internet itself provides basic network connectivity among millions of computers using TCP and IP as shown in Figure 3.1. This connectivity is valueless unless applications running on different machines can communicate with each other leveraging the underlying network. Traditionally, each type of application has invented and used its own application-level protocol that sits on top of TCP. For example, HTTP is an application-level protocol designed for use between the Web browser and Web server as shown in Figure 3.1. The arrows in Figure 3.1 show the logical communication that passes between peer layers on

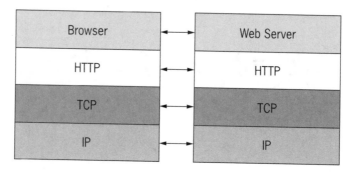

Figure 3.1 The Internet protocol stack used for browser/server communication

different hosts. The actual information flow goes down the stack on one host then up the stack on the other.

Despite HTTP's huge success as the Internet's killer application protocol, it is limited to fairly simple commands that center on requesting and sending resources (for example, GET, POST and PUT). This results in millions of interconnected computers that leverage the Internet primarily for browsing the Web but cannot, despite the connectivity, freely exchange data between applications. SOAP[1] proposes to solve this problem by defining a standard protocol that any application can use to communicate and exchange data with any other application. Figure 3.2 shows how SOAP can be used over TCP/IP leveraging of the current Internet infrastructure.

SOAP is an application-level protocol so it can work directly over a transport protocol such as TCP. However, today's Internet infrastructure is riddled with proxies and firewalls that typically allow HTTP traffic only. In order for all Internet-connected applications to communicate, SOAP must be able to flow over the current Internet infrastructure including firewalls and proxies. To achieve this, SOAP can be layered over HTTP as shown in Figure 3.3.

Layering SOAP over HTTP means that a SOAP message is sent as part of an HTTP request or response, which makes it easy to communicate over any net-

---

[1]SOAP was originally an acronym for Simple Object Access Protocol. However, the W3C's XML Protocol Working Group decided to use the name "SOAP" for the W3C standard XML protocol. In this case, "SOAP" will be the protocol name and not an acronym.

REAL WORLD XML WEB SERVICES

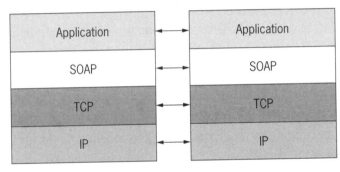

Figure 3.2   SOAP enables application-to-application communication over any transport protocol including TCP.

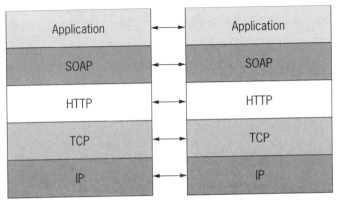

Figure 3.3   SOAP can be used over HTTP to enable application-to-application communications over existing Internet infrastructure with its firewalls and proxies.

work that permits HTTP traffic. HTTP is also a good choice because, just like Web browsers, it is pervasive on all computing platforms and devices.

To achieve platform independence and maximum interoperability, SOAP uses XML to represent messages exchanged between the client and the Web service. Like HTTP, XML is also pervasive and you can find an XML parser for nearly any computing platform (or you can write your own if necessary). By leveraging HTTP and XML, SOAP provides application-to-application communications between applications running on any platform and connected over the existing Internet infrastructure.

3.2 SOAP Architecture

The key architectural aspect of SOAP is its simple design, which is intended to encourage vendors to adopt and implement the protocol. SOAP doesn't try to solve all the problems of distributed applications communication; it focuses instead on the minimum standards required to send messages from one application to another. For example, SOAP does not include specifications for security or distributed transactions, both of which are commonly needed for distributed applications. The SOAP architecture, however, is flexible and extensible through the use of SOAP headers, which I'll discuss later in this chapter.

SOAP's architecture is centered on sending a SOAP message from the sender (the client) to the ultimate destination (the Web service) with optional intermediate nodes between the two as shown in Figure 3.4. Note that there's nothing in this architecture that talks about accessing objects and invoking methods remotely, as in a Remote Procedure Call. Instead, SOAP focuses on sending a message from a sender to a recipient. To understand SOAP fully, you need to think in terms of messages exchanged between client and Web service. Using SOAP for RPC is just a special application of messaging that combines two messages in opposite directions.

3.2.1 The SOAP Message

The SOAP message architecture consists of an Envelope which contains an optional Header and a mandatory Body as shown in Figure 3.5. The Body itself contains the payload (the data being sent) or optional error information.

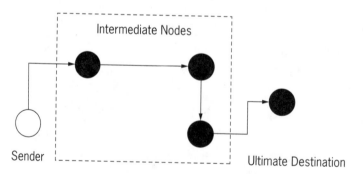

Figure 3.4 A SOAP message travels from the sender to the ultimate destination with optional intermediate nodes between the two.

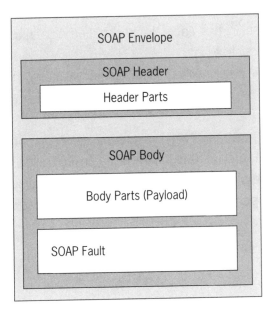

Figure 3.5 SOAP message architecture

A basic SOAP message is a well-formed XML document consisting of `<En-velope>` and `<Body>` elements that belong to the SOAP envelope namespace defined as `http://schemas.xmlsoap.org/soap/envelope/`. Listing 3.1 shows an example SOAP message with the `soapenv` prefix declared for the SOAP namespace. For the rest of this chapter, I'll refer to SOAP elements using `soapenv` as the namespace prefix, (for example, `<soapenv:Envelope>` and `<soapenv:Body>`).

Listing 3.1 An example SOAP message

```
<soapenv:Envelope
xmlns:soapenv="http://schemas.xmlsoap.org/soap/envelope/">
  <soapenv:Body>
    <SubmitInvoice
      xmlns="http://learnxmlws.com/nwind.net">
      <invoiceDoc>...</invoiceDoc>
    </SubmitInvoice>
  </soapenv:Body>
</soapenv:Envelope>
```

The `<soapenv:Envelope>` is the document element (top level element) of the SOAP message and usually has several namespace declarations, including the SOAP envelope namespace. Within the `<soapenv:Envelope>`, there's always one `<soapenv:Body>` element that contains the payload of data being sent. Looking at Listing 3.1, you see that the payload is `<SubmitInvoice>` and its contents.

In addition to `<soapenv:Body>`, `<soapenv:Envelope>` may also contain an optional `<soapenv:Header>` element which is used to send additional information to what's already in the `<soapenv:Body>` payload. Listing 3.2 shows the same SOAP message as in Listing 3.1 with a `<soapenv:Header>` added.

Listing 3.2   A SOAP message with headers

```
<soapenv:Envelope
xmlns:soapenv="http://schemas.xmlsoap.org/soap/envelope/">
  <soapenv:Header>
 <authHeader
   xmlns="http://learnxmlws.com/nwind.net">
    <authToken>
      4fthlE3GpY2cnrSvylSzYtV3HjL8ovFHm91P
    </authToken>
 </authHeader>
 </soapenv:Header>
 <soapenv:Body>
   <SubmitInvoice
     xmlns="http://learnxmlws.com/nwind.net">
     <invoiceDoc></invoiceDoc>
   </SubmitInvoice>
 </soapenv:Body>
</soapenv:Envelope>
```

In this example, the `<soapenv:Header>` is used to send an application-specific authentication header represented by the element `<authHeader>`. I'll discuss SOAP headers in more detail later in this chapter.

The last SOAP element is `<soapenv:Fault>`, which is used to communicate error information. If used, the `<soapenv:Fault>` appears as a child of the `<soapenv:Body>` and contains several child elements such as `<faultcode>` and `<faultstring>`. I'll explain the contents of `<soapenv:Fault>` and how to use it to communicate error information later in this chapter.

3.3 SOAP Message Formats

SOAP messages can have several different formats that differ in how the data inside `<soapenv:Body>` and potentially inside `<soapenv:Header>` is formatted.

To send data in a SOAP message, you must first serialize this data in a format that can be understood by the message recipient. For example, in Chapter 2 you learned how to use the `System.Xml.Serialization` namespace to easily serialize objects to an XML document. To send this XML document in a SOAP message, you can simply create the SOAP message and include this document within the `<soapenv:Body>`.[2] In this case, the message you end up with is said to follow document-style SOAP, has a literal payload, and is usually referred to as a document/literal message. Document and RPC are two styles of SOAP messages both defined in the SOAP specification. In a nutshell, here's what each term means:

- **Document:** `<soapenv:Body>` contains one or more child elements called parts. There are no SOAP formatting rules for what the `<soapenv:Body>` contains; it contains whatever the sender and the receiver agree upon.

- **RPC:** Here the `<soapenv:Body>` contains the name of the method or remote procedure you are invoking and an element for each parameter of that procedure. Section 7 of the SOAP specification defines exactly what the `<soapenv:Body>` contains when using RPC-style SOAP.

In addition to the two SOAP message styles, there are two formats for serializing data into XML. The format you choose determines how your data is serialized into the `<soapenv:Body>` and `<soapenv:Header>` elements. Here's a definition of each serialization format:

- **Encoded:** Data is serialized according to some encoding rules. The most common are the encoding rules specified in Section 5 of the SOAP specification, which define how objects, structures, arrays, and object graphs

---

[2]According to SOAP rules, an XML document contained within `<soapenv:Body>` cannot have an XML declaration, processing instructions, or a Document Type Declaration.

should be serialized. With Section 5 encoding, the client and the service deal with data in terms of objects and structures.

- **Literal:** Data is serialized according to an XML Schema, usually XSD. There are no special encoding rules that dictate how to serialize the data and the serialization format needed to convey the fact that the data came from an array, an object, and so forth. With literal format, the client and service deal with the data in terms of XML documents rather than objects and structures.

Figure 3.6 shows the `<soapenv:Body>` element and its contents with the labels indicating the effect of document or RPC, literal and encoded.

Theoretically, your choice of using document or RPC is independent of your choice of encoded or literal, giving you a total of four different combinations: document/literal, document/encoded, RPC/literal, and RPC/encoded.

Practically, most implementations tend to combine RPC with encoded and document with literal. This makes sense when you group SOAP applications into two categories. Those exchanging business documents, such as business-to-

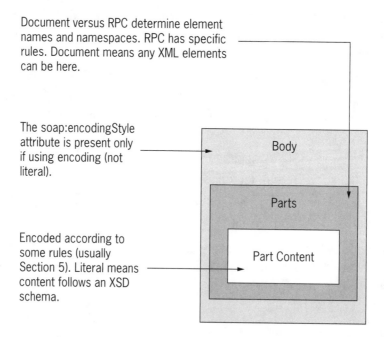

Figure 3.6   How RPC/document and literal/encoded affect the SOAP <Body> element and its content

REAL WORLD XML WEB SERVICES

business applications, tend to use document/literal SOAP messages. Applications using SOAP as an RPC protocol to invoke remote objects (instead of DCOM, for example) tend to use RPC/encoded SOAP messages.

When SOAP 1.1 came out, most people saw SOAP as a simple RPC protocol that can easily work over the Internet with its firewalls and proxies. As a result, there was a rush of SOAP implementations mostly focused on RPC and using Section 5 encoded messages. For example, the Microsoft SOAP Toolkit, which is designed to let you expose COM components as Web services, uses RPC/encoded SOAP messages by default. This makes sense because the objective is to remotely invoke a method on your COM component, which means you are thinking in terms of RPC. When using .NET you can expose Web services in two ways: Remoting and .NET Web services. Remoting uses RPC/encoded SOAP while .NET Web services, designed for document exchange via messaging, use document/literal SOAP by default (but can also be configured to use RPC/encoded). This stresses the appropriate usage of RPC/encoded versus document/literal SOAP messages.

Document/literal is the better fit for SOAP messaging because you have full control over the format of the message payload. If you are building a business-to-business application, you might be exchanging documents, such as invoices and purchase orders, whose schemas are predefined by a standards body. By using document/literal, you can control the exact message format and make it conform to this standard schema. Going forward, the only good reason to use RPC/encoded SOAP is when you are exposing server-side objects to be invoked by remote clients that are designed to use RPC. In the next two sections, I will show you how to use SOAP for messaging and RPC and practical applications of each.

3.4 Messaging with SOAP

SOAP messaging is actually very easy to implement. All you need to do is format your request as an XML document and insert it within the `<soapenv:Body>` of a document/literal message. How you create your request as XML depends on the nature of the request and where the data is coming from. If your application uses .NET objects internally to represent the request data, you can easily create the XML by using .NET Serialization as explained in Chapter 2. Alternatively, if the request data is coming from SQL Server, you can get the data out as XML using SQL Server's FOR XML clause or one of the many other XML features of SQL Server.

As an example of messaging, I built a simple Web service (explained later in this chapter) to receive invoice documents, validate them, save them in a SQL Server database, and return a receipt id. Listing 3.3 shows an example SOAP request and the corresponding response document for this particular Web service.

Listing 3.3 Document/literal request and response messages

```
<!-- Request document -->
<soapenv:Envelope
xmlns:xsi="http://www.w3.org/2001/XMLSchema-instance"
xmlns:xsd="http://www.w3.org/2001/XMLSchema"
xmlns:soapenv="http://schemas.xmlsoap.org/soap/envelope/">
<soapenv:Body>
  <invoice xmlns="http://schemas.learnxmlws.com/invoice">
  <invoiceNumber>123-YJK-9087</invoiceNumber>
  <supplierID>5</supplierID>
  <invoiceDate>2001-08-11</invoiceDate>
  <poNumber>PO-0983</poNumber>
  <subTotal>21.90</subTotal>
  <salesTax>9.86</salesTax>
  <paymentReceived>0</paymentReceived>
  <amtDue>31.76</amtDue>
  <terms>net 30</terms>
  <contactName>Yasser Shohoud</contactName>
  <contactNumber>(703) 626-6822</contactNumber>
  <promotion></promotion>
  <invoiceItems>
    <item>
      <partNum>1234-KUY</partNum>
      <quant>2</quant>
      <unitPrice>10.95</unitPrice>
      <total>21.90</total>
    </item>
  </invoiceItems>
  </invoice>
</soapenv:Body>
</soapenv:Envelope>
```

```
<!-- Response document -->
<soapenv:Envelope
xmlns:xsi='http://www.w3.org/2001/XMLSchema-instance'
xmlns:xsd='http://www.w3.org/2001/XMLSchema'
xmlns:soapenv='http://schemas.xmlsoap.org/soap/envelope/'>
  <soapenv:Body>
    <Receipt
    xmlns='http://schemas.learnxmlws.com/invoice'>9</Receipt>
  </soapenv:Body>
</soapenv:Envelope>
```

Both request and response documents are examples of document/literal SOAP messages. The request document begins with the `<soapenv:Envelope>` element that contains `<soapenv:Body>`, which in turn contains the invoice document. In this example, the invoice document is the request message's payload. The entire invoice document, beginning with `<invoice>` belongs to the namespace `http://schemas.learnxmlws.com/invoice`, which is the `targetNamespace` defined in the invoice's schema document invoice.xsd.

Following the same structure, the response message's payload contains a simple document with one element: `<Receipt>`, which contains the receipt number confirming that the invoice has been processed successfully.

3.4.1 SOAP over HTTP

While SOAP can be used over a variety of transports, HTTP is the most commonly used because of its ubiquity. HTTP requests are very easy to form; they consist simply of an HTTP command such as POST or GET followed by the URL you're requesting and the protocol version (for example, HTTP 1.0). An HTTP request or response usually contains HTTP headers, which are simple information organized in name-value pairs. For example, this is an HTTP GET request for the resource `/images/pp_header_02.jpg` with the two HTTP headers `Accept` and `Referer` (yes `Referer` has a typo; it's that way in the HTTP standard):

```
GET /images/pp_header_02.jpg HTTP/1.1
Accept: */*
Referer: http://localhost/Logon.asp?url=/Default.asp
```

When using SOAP over HTTP, there are two rules to remember. First, you must set the `Content-Type` header to `text/xml` telling the recipient that the HTTP request or response contains an XML document, that is, a SOAP message. Second, when sending a SOAP request, you must set the HTTP `SOAPAction` header. This special header always contains a quoted value and is designed to convey extra information about the SOAP message at the HTTP level. This can be useful, for example, for firewalls that filter SOAP/HTTP traffic based on certain values of the HTTP `SOAPAction` header. There are no rules for the value of `SOAPAction`; you have to set it to whatever the Web service expects it to be. This lack of clearly defined rules has caused much controversy over the use of `SOAPAction` and whether it's needed at all. Practically, you should not design your Web services to rely on `SOAPAction` unless you absolutely need to. Listing 3.4 shows an example HTTP request with the above SOAP request message and the `SOAPAction` and `Content-Type` headers.

Listing 3.4   A SOAP message sent over HTTP

```
POST /vbwsbook/chapter3/MessagingWS/invoiceMessaging.asp HTTP/1.0
SOAPAction: "urn:InvoiceAction"
Content-Type: text/xml
Accept-Language: en-us
Content-Length: 929
Accept: */*
User-Agent: Mozilla/4.0 (compatible; Win32;
WinHttp.WinHttpRequest.5)
Host: vbwsserver
Connection: Keep-Alive

<soapenv:Envelope
xmlns:xsi="http://www.w3.org/2001/XMLSchema-instance"
xmlns:xsd="http://www.w3.org/2001/XMLSchema"
xmlns:soapenv="http://schemas.xmlsoap.org/soap/envelope/">
...
</soapenv:Envelope>
```

3.4.2   Capturing SOAP Messages

For learning and troubleshooting purposes, throughout this chapter and the rest of the book, you'll need a way to capture SOAP messages exchanged between client and service. There are a few free tools that allow you to do this easily. One of the tools, Trace Utility, comes with the Microsoft SOAP Toolkit and can be used to intercept and record SOAP messages between the client and server. The tool works by inserting itself between the client and the Web server where your Web service is running. Basically, it listens on a specified port, and forwards all traffic it receives to a Web server and port that you also specify. Figure 3.7 shows an example of configuring it to listen on port 8080 and forwarding all traffic to the local server on port 80.

Once you configure the Trace Utility to listen to a port such as 8080, you must make your client send all requests to this port on the localhost. Therefore, instead of sending a SOAP request to http://hostname/myservice.asp, you'd send it to http://localhost:8080/myservice.asp. If you want to capture SOAP messages while running code in this chapter, simply run the Trace Utility and make it listen on port 8080 and replace the service URL in the code to point to port 8080 on the localhost. The Trace Utility will intercept and capture the request and response messages and display them in the trace window.

3.4.3 The Web Service
To show you how easy it is to create and process the messages in Listing 3.3, I created the example Web service in classic ASP using only the Microsoft XML parser MSXML version 4.0 as shown in Listing 3.5.

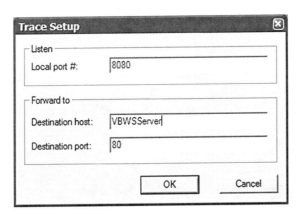

Figure 3.7   Configuring the Trace Utility

Listing 3.5 A classic ASP page that acts as a SOAP endpoint (VBWSServer\VBWSBook\Chapter3\MessagingWS\invoiceMessaging.asp)

```
<%@Language="VBScript" %>
<%
Const adVarChar=200
Const adInteger=3
Const adParamInput=1
Const adParamOutput=2
Const adCmdStoredProc=4
Dim CONNSTR
Dim NS
Dim XSD_LOC
Dim requestDoc
Dim doc
Dim schemaCache
Dim MY_ACTION

CONNSTR= _
"provider=SQLOLEDB;server=(local);database=WSBook;uid=sa;pwd=;"
NS="http://schemas.learnxmlws.com/invoice"
'Check the SOAPAction
Set requestDoc=Server.CreateObject("MSXML2.DOMDocument")
'Load the SOAP message
requestDoc.async=false
If Not requestDoc.Load(Request) Then
  Call SendFault("soap:Client", _
    "Error loading request doc", _
    "Message processor", _
    requestDoc.parseError.reason & _
    " at line " & _
    requestDoc.parseError.line, _
    requestDoc.parseError.errorCode)
  Response.End
Else
  Call requestDoc.setProperty("SelectionNamespaces", _
       "xmlns:vbws='" & NS & "'")
End If

XSD_LOC=Server.MapPath("./invoice.xsd")
Set doc=Server.CreateObject("MSXML2.DOMDocument")
Set schemaCache = Server.CreateObject("MSXML2.XMLSchemaCache")
On Error Resume Next
'Add the schema location and target namespace
```

```
Call schemaCache.Add(NS,XSD_LOC)
If Err.Number <> 0 Then
    Call SendFault("vbws:Application", _
        "Failed to add schema",Err.Source, _
        Err.Description,Err.number)Response.End
End If
'get the invoice document out of the
'SOAP message
Set doc.schemas = schemaCache
If Not doc.loadxml( _
  requestDoc.selectSingleNode("//vbws:invoice").xml) Then

  Call SendFault("soap:Client","Error validating invoice doc", _
    "Document validation", _
    doc.parseError.reason & " at line " & doc.parseError.line, _
    doc.parseError.errorCode)
        Response.End
Else


    Dim invNum
    Dim RegId
    Dim supplier
    Call doc.setProperty("SelectionNamespaces", _
 "xmlns:vbws='" & NS & "'")
    'get invoice number and supplier id
    invNum=doc.selectSingleNode("//vbws:invoiceNumber").text
    supplier=doc.selectSingleNode("//vbws:supplierID").text

    Dim cmd
    Set cmd=Server.CreateObject("ADODB.Command")
    cmd.ActiveConnection=ConnStr
    If Err.Number <> 0 Then
  Call SendFault("soap:Server","Error connecting to database", _
                "Importing invoice", _
                Err.Description,Err.Number)
        Response.End
    End If
    Dim param
    'call the stored procedure
    'to register the invoice
    Set param=cmd.CreateParameter( _
      "invoiceNumber",adVarChar, _
      adParamInput,50,invNum)
```

```
         cmd.Parameters.Append(param)
      Set param=cmd.CreateParameter("supplierId",adInteger, _
         adParamInput,0,supplier)
       cmd.Parameters.Append(param)
      Set param=cmd.CreateParameter("RegId",adInteger, _
         adParamOutput)
       cmd.Parameters.Append(param)
       cmd.CommandText="AddIncomingInvoice"
       cmd.CommandType=adCmdStoredProc
    cmd.Execute
       If Err.number <> 0 Then
       Response.Write Err.Description
       Response.End
       End If
       RegId=cmd.Parameters("RegId").Value
       cmd.ActiveConnection.Close
       Set cmd=Nothing
       'save the invoice document to disk
       Call doc.Save( _
       Server.MapPath("./" & supplier & "-" & invNum & ".xml"))
       Set doc=Nothing
       'write the response
    WriteSOAPResponse("<Receipt xmlns='" & NS & _
                "'>" & RegId & "</Receipt>")
End If


Sub SendFault(faultCode,faultString,source,descr,num)
   Dim faultMsg
   faultMsg = "<soap:Fault xmlns:vbws='" & NS & _
          "'><faultCode>" & faultCode & "</faultCode>" & _
         "<faultString>" & faultString & "</faultString>" & _
         "<detail><vbws:ErrNumber>" & num & _
         "</vbws:ErrNumber>" & _
         "<vbws:ErrDescr>" & descr & "</vbws:ErrDescr>" & _
         "<vbws:ErrSource>" & source & "</vbws:ErrSource>" & _
         "</detail></soap:Fault>"
   Call WriteSOAPResponse(faultMsg)
End Sub


Sub WriteSOAPResponse(msg)
    Response.ContentType="text/xml"
   Response.Write "<soap:Envelope xmlns:xsi=" & _
       "'http://www.w3.org/2001/XMLSchema-instance'" & _
       " xmlns:xsd='http://www.w3.org/2001/XMLSchema'" & _
```

```
"  xmlns:soap='http://schemas.xmlsoap.org/soap/envelope/'>" & _
        "<soap:Body>"
    Response.Write msg
    Response.Write "</soap:Body></soap:Envelope>"
End Sub

%>
```

I chose an ASP page instead of a COM component because it can easily receive an HTTP request and it's very easily deployed: just copy it to the server where you want to deploy it. Of course you will need to modify the database connection string to point to the book's database (see the CD readme file for more information on setting up the database).

First, I create an XML DOM Document and load the request message into it. Then I set the document's `SelectionNamespaces` property mapping the `vbws` prefix to the invoice namespace. This step is necessary because I will use XPath to retrieve elements from the document and I must use the fully qualified element names. Then I create an `XMLSchemaCache` object and add to it the invoice XSD schema and the invoice namespace to validate the incoming invoice document as shown in Chapter 2. Next, I pull out the incoming invoice document using `requestDoc.selectSingleNode("//vbws:invoice").xml` and load this in a new `DOMDocument`. At this point, the invoice is validated against the XSD schema so I catch any errors and send them back using `Response.Write`. Later in this chapter, I will add code to send error information back to the client using `<soapenv:Fault>`.

After the invoice is validated, I invoke a stored procedure called `AddIncomingInvoice`, passing it the supplier id and the invoice number from the incoming invoice document. The stored procedure registers the invoice and returns a receipt number. I save the invoice document to disk in the same folder where this ASP page exists. Finally, I send back a SOAP response with one element, `<Receipt>`, which contains the receipt number returned by the stored procedure.

3.4.4 The Client

On the client side, I wrote a utility called SOAPSender which easily lets you create and send SOAP messages. The utility is available in two versions: one written in VB 6 as a COM component using only MSXML 4.0, the other written in VB .NET using classes from the .NET Framework including `System.Xml` and `System.Net`. Then I wrote a Windows client using VB 6 and SOAPSender as shown in Listing 3.6.

Listing 3.6 A client submitting an invoice to the Web service (VBWSClientCode\Chapter3\SOAPSender\Form1.frm)

```
Private Const SERVICE_URL = _
"http://VBWSServer/vbwsbook/chapter3/MessagingWS/
➥InvoiceMessaging.asp"

Private Sub cmdSendInvoice_Click()
Dim doc As MSXML2.DOMDocument40
Set doc = New MSXML2.DOMDocument40
If Not doc.Load(txtInvoice.Text) Then
    MsgBox "Error loading XML document " & vbCrLf & _
        doc.parseError.reason, vbCritical
    Exit Sub
End If
Dim vbws As VBWSSoap.SOAPSender
Set vbws = New VBWSSoap.SOAPSender
On Error GoTo eh
vbws.ServiceUrl = SERVICE_URL
vbws.SoapAction = """"""
vbws.WriteBodyXml doc.documentElement.xml
vbws.send
If Not doc.loadXML(vbws.GetResponseString) Then
    MsgBox "Error loading response document " & vbCrLf & _
        doc.parseError.reason & vbCrLf & _
        "Response document is" & vbCrLf & _
        vbws.GetResponseString(), vbCritical
    Exit Sub
Else
    MsgBox "Response is " & vbws.GetResponseString
End If

Exit Sub
eh:
```

```
        MsgBox "Error sending invoice document" & _
   vbCrLf & ➡Err.Description
   End Sub
```

To send the invoice document, I first load it into a DOMDocument called doc using doc.Load. Then I create a SOAPSender object and set its ServiceUrl property to point to the URL of my ASP page. I also set its SoapAction property to a pair of double quotes (the equivalent of an empty SOAPAction) since this Web service does not rely on SOAPAction.

I call its WriteBodyXml method passing it the invoice document's XML. WriteBodyXml simply takes the XML you give it and stuffs it as the content of the `<soapenv:Body>` element. To send the invoice document, I simply call Send, and then retrieve the response using SOAPSender's GetResponseString method, which returns the entire response as a string. Because this example uses messaging, the client is not designed as if invoking a method on a remote object. Instead, it sends a document to a remote recipient. This is the key distinction between messaging and RPC.

As you can see, once you learn some SOAP fundamentals, the client and service code are straightforward and do not require a special SOAP tool. This is especially true for document/literal SOAP messages as their message payload can be any XML document. If you're building data exchange or business-to-business integration Web services, you should design them using document/literal. You can then implement them using any technology or toolset you prefer including rolling your own as I showed you here.

3.5   RPC with SOAP

When you have an existing distributed application with client and server pieces using DCOM to communicate between them, it's usually impractical to rearchitect and rewrite the application using XML messaging. Minimally, replacing DCOM with messaging requires major changes and additions to the server to receive and process incoming XML documents and to send responses as outgoing XML documents. Additionally, the client must be rewritten to format and send requests as XML documents and to receive and parse responses. These changes are small compared to the major change in programming model that developers must learn and adopt. Developers writing the client no longer instantiate a server object and call its methods passing them parameters and getting back a return value. Instead they must serialize all data to XML to send the request, and then deserialize data from XML upon receiving the response. Finally, if the existing application architecture does not lend itself to messaging, by using stateful server objects, for example, then a major rearchitecture and/or some custom SOAP extensions are needed to replace DCOM with SOAP messaging.

To ease converting existing applications from DCOM to SOAP, you can write a layer on the client side that acts as the Web service proxy. As a proxy, this layer would give the client the impression that it's calling methods on a server object. The proxy would be responsible for serializing the parameters to XML, sending them as parts of a SOAP message, then parsing and deserializing the response message and returning data to the client in native data types such as strings, integers, and arrays.

On the server side, you can write another layer that is responsible for receiving SOAP messages, deserializing their content to native data types, instantiating the server COM component and invoking the appropriate method, then serializing the return value and sending back a SOAP response. The proxy layer needs to communicate specific information about the RPC call to the server, such as the intended object, a method name, and the name, value, and content of each parameter. Similarly, the server needs to communicate back the return value and the output value of all in/out (ByRef) parameters. If you write both of these layers, you can communicate this information in any format you like as long as both layers agree to the format. However, if you are exposing the server side as a public Web service that many clients will have to communicate with, then all clients and the service must use a common format for communicating this information.

Section 7 of the SOAP specification defines a standard format for communicating this information when using SOAP for RPC. The SOAP specification also defines a standard way of serializing/deserializing native application types such as strings, arrays, and structures. This is especially important to enable interoperation among clients and servers. This standard serialization format is commonly called Section 5 encoding after the SOAP specification section where it is defined (I'll explain SOAP Section 5 encoding later in this chapter). According to the SOAP specification, you can use SOAP for RPC (also known as Section 7) without necessarily using the standard Section 5 encoding. (You can serialize your data in any format while still using SOAP for RPC.) However, it makes sense to use Section 5 encoding format when using RPC, especially when you care about interoperability, because most SOAP stacks and tools, such as the Microsoft SOAP Toolkit, combine RPC with Section 5 encoding.

In this section, I will show you an example of using SOAP for RPC with a VB 6 client that uses data binding to show a list of orders in a data grid for the selected employee (see Figure 3.8). The grid is bound to a Recordset returned from invoking a remote COM component using DCOM. I've replaced DCOM with SOAP and implemented a simple proxy as a VB 6 class with its `DataSource-Behavior` set to `vbDataSource` so that the data grid can bind to an instance of this proxy class.

On the server side, I added a stub layer written as a simple ASP page that receives the SOAP message, invokes the COM component, then serializes and returns the Recordset. The server COM component did not have to change at all. The client had to change in order to bind to the proxy class instead of directly to a Recordset. This change required exactly three lines of code. The

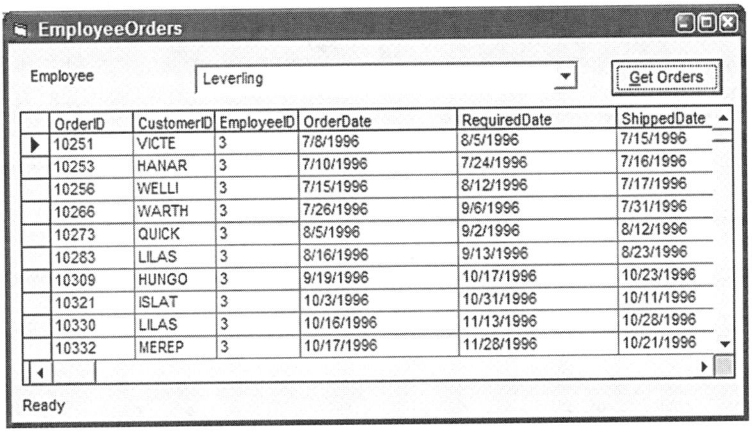

Figure 3.8 An example Visual Basic client using data binding to display employee orders

existing server-side COM component is called RecordsetExample and exposes a method called GetEmpOrders, which takes in an employee id and queries the Northwind Orders table for all orders with the given employee id and returns the result in an ADO Recordset:

```
Public Function GetEmpOrders(ByVal EmpId As Long) As Recordset
```

To expose the COM component as a Web service, I wrote the ASP page shown in Listing 3.7 which uses only MSXML 4.0 and ADO 2.6.

Listing 3.7 An ASP page to expose an existing COM component as a Web service (VBWSBook\Chapter3\EmployeeOrders\EmpOrders.asp)

```
<%@Language="VBScript" %>
<%
CONST adPersistXML=1

Dim NS
Dim requestDoc
Dim EmpId
Dim RpcEx
Dim rs


On Error Resume Next



NS="http://schemas.learnxmlws.com/employeeOrders"
Set requestDoc=Server.CreateObject("MSXML2.DOMDocument")
'Load the SOAP message
requestDoc.async=false
If Not requestDoc.Load(Request) Then
  Response.Write "Error loading request doc " & Err.Description
  Response.End
Else
  Call requestDoc.setProperty("SelectionNamespaces", _
      "xmlns:vbws='" & NS & "'")
End If

'get the employee id
EmpId=requestDoc.selectSingleNode( _
"//vbws:GetEmpOrders/EmpId").text
If Err.number <> 0 Then
  Response.Write "Error retrieving employee id: " & _
```

```
              Err.Description
     End If

     Set RpcEx =Server.CreateObject("RPCExamples.RecordsetExample")
     Set rs=RpcEx.GetEmpOrders(EmpId)
     If Err.number <> 0 Then
       Response.Write "Error retrieving data: " & Err.Description
     End If
     'write the response
      WriteSOAPResponse("<vbws:GetEmpOrdersResponse xmlns:vbws='" & _
          NS & "'" _
     "soapenv:encodingStyle=
  ➥'http://schemas.xmlsoap.org/soap/encoding/'>" & _
       "<theReturn>" & Rs2Xml(rs) & _
       "</theReturn></vbws:GetEmpOrdersResponse>")
     If Err.number <> 0 Then
       Response.Write "Error serializing data: " & Err.Description
     End If
     Function Rs2Xml(rs)
         Dim doc
         Set doc = Server.CreateObject("MSXML2.DOMDocument")
         rs.Save doc, adPersistXML
         Rs2Xml = "<![CDATA[" & doc.xml & "]]>"
     End Function
     Sub WriteSOAPResponse(msg)
         Response.ContentType="text/xml"
         Response.CharSet="iso-8859-1"
      Response.Write "<soapenv:Envelope " & _
      "xmlns:xsi='http://www.w3.org/2001/XMLSchema-instance'" & _
      "xmlns:xsd='http://www.w3.org/2001/XMLSchema'" & _
      "xmlns:soapenv='http://schemas.xmlsoap.org/soap/envelope/'>" & _
           "<soapenv:Body>"
       Response.Write msg
       Response.Write "</soapenv:Body></soapenv:Envelope>"
     End Sub
     %>
```

I start by loading the request message in a DOMDocument named requestDoc.
Then I retrieve the employee id using XPath to select the element called EmpId. I
instantiate an object from the example component RPCExamples.Recordset-
Example and call GetEmpOrders, passing it the employee id to get back an

ADO Recordset. Then I call `WriteSOAPResponse`, passing it the contents of `<soapenv:Body>` as in the example response message in Listing 3.6. To serialize the Recordset, I wrote a function called `Rs2Xml`, which creates a `DOMDocument` and passes it to `rs.Save`, then wraps the output XML in a CDATA section. Obviously, all the serialization heavy lifting is done by the Recordset itself. My legacy COM component is now exposed as a Web service and is ready to be invoked via SOAP RPC/encoded messages. Listing 3.8 shows the corresponding request and response SOAP RPC/Section 5 encoded messages.

Listing 3.8   Example request message passing an employee id and the response message containing an ADO Recordset with employee orders

```
POST /vbwsbook/chapter3/EmployeeOrders/EmpOrders.asp HTTP/1.0
SOAPAction: ""
Content-Type: text/xml
Accept-Language: en-us
Content-Length: 351
Accept: */*
User-Agent: Mozilla/4.0 (compatible; Win32;
➥WinHttp.WinHttpRequest.5)
Host: VBWSServer
Connection: Keep-Alive


<soapenv:Envelope
xmlns:xsi="http://www.w3.org/2001/XMLSchema-instance"
xmlns:xsd="http://www.w3.org/2001/XMLSchema"
xmlns:soapenv="http://schemas.xmlsoap.org/soap/envelope/">
<soapenv:Body>
  <vbws:GetEmpOrders
    xmlns:vbws="http://schemas.learnxmlws.com/employeeOrders"
    soapenv:encodingStyle=
    "http://schemas.xmlsoap.org/soap/encoding/">
  <EmpId xsi:type="xsd:int">3</EmpId>
  </vbws:GetEmpOrders>
</soapenv:Body>
</soapenv:Envelope>


HTTP/1.1 200 OK
Server: Microsoft-IIS/5.1
Date: Mon, 03 Sep 2001 13:52:26 GMT
Connection: keep-alive
```

```
Connection: Keep-Alive
Content-Length: 49198
Content-Type: text/xml; Charset=iso-8859-1
Cache-control: private
<soapenv:Envelope
xmlns:xsi='http://www.w3.org/2001/XMLSchema-instance'
xmlns:xsd='http://www.w3.org/2001/XMLSchema'
xmlns:soapenv='http://schemas.xmlsoap.org/soap/envelope/'>
<soapenv:Body>
<vbws:GetEmpOrdersResponse
xmlns:vbws='http://schemas.learnxmlws.com/employeeOrders'
soapenv:encodingStyle=
'http://schemas.xmlsoap.org/soap/encoding/'>
<theReturn xsi:type='xsd:string'>
<![CDATA[
<xml
xmlns:s="uuid:BDC6E3F0-6DA3-11d1-A2A3-00AA00C14882"
xmlns:dt="uuid:C2F41010-65B3-11d1-A29F-00AA00C14882"
xmlns:rs="urn:schemas-microsoft-com:rowset"
xmlns:z="#RowsetSchema">
...
</xml>
]]>
</theReturn>
</vbws:GetEmpOrdersResponse>
</soapenv:Body>
</soapenv:Envelope>
```

Looking at Listing 3.8, you'll see that the request message uses HTTP POST with `SOAPAction ""` because the Web service does not rely on SOAPAction. Within the request message's `<soapBody>`, there's a single element that must have the same name as the method, that is, `GetEmpOrders`. This element's namespace is called the operation namespace and is determined by the creator of the Web service, which in this example, I decided to make `http://schemas.learnxmlws.com/employeeOrders`. The `soapenv:encoding-Style` attribute indicates the type of encoding used for the method parameters, with the value `http://schemas.xmlsoap.org/soap/encoding/` indicating SOAP Section 5 encoding.

`<GetEmpOrders>` must contain an element for each parameter of the method being invoked with the same name as the parameter: `EmpId` in this case. Note that according to SOAP Section 5 rules, these elements must not belong to any namespace, so `<EmpId>` has no namespace prefix or default namespace declaration. `EmpId` is a VB `Long which maps to` an XSD `int` and, when serialized according to Section 5 encoding rules, comes out as the string "3". Although this is simple and quite intuitive, it is important to standardize to enable interoperability among different SOAP implementations. Otherwise, someone might decide to serialize the integer value 3 as 0x03, which would be incompatible with my Web service. Note that `xsi:type="xsd:int"` is used to indicate the type of `<EmpId>`, which might be helpful for the server when it tries to deserialize this parameter. xsi:type is not the only way to specify parameter types nor is it required. In Chapter 4 you will learn how an XSD schema as part of a WSDL document serves the same purpose and can be used instead of inline type information.

Still looking at Listing 3.8, the response begins with HTTP status code 200, which indicates that the RPC call completed successfully. Within `<soap-env:Body>` there's one element that, only by convention, is named after the method name with "Response" appended to it, that is, `<GetEmpOrdersResponse>`. The method's return value is represented by an element that must be the first child of `<GetEmpOrdersResponse>`. The name of the return value element, for example, `<theReturn>` is insignificant. In this example, the method call returns an ADO Recordset so I use its `Save` method to serialize it to XML. I cannot, however, just stuff the serialized Recordset into `<theReturn>` because the result would be invalid according to Section 5 encoding rules. Instead, I enclose it in a CDATA section and make it appear as if it were just a string with no XML markup, hence as far as SOAP is concerned, the return value's type is simply a string, that is, `xsi:type="xsd:string"`.

On the client side, the proxy will extract this string, load it in a `DOMDocument`, then deserialize or rehydrate an ADO Recordset from it and return it to the client application, which doesn't know how this Recordset was created or where it came from.

Listing 3.9 shows the proxy class used by the client to invoke this Web service. This class relies on SOAPSender to form and send the SOAP request message. Then it parses the response document, extracts the XML that represents the serialized Recordset, and loads it into a new Recordset.

Listing 3.9 The Web service proxy class that acts as a data source (VBWSClientCode\chapter3\EmployeeOrdersClient\CEmployeeOrders.cls)

```
Private Sub Class_GetDataMember(DataMember As String, _
Data As Object)
On Error GoTo eh
    Dim soapMsg As MSXML2.DOMDocument
    Dim doc As MSXML2.DOMDocument
    Dim vbws As SOAPSender
    Set vbws = New SOAPSender
    'write the element representing
    'the method call
    vbws.BeginBodyPart "vbws:GetEmpOrders", NS
    'write the EmpId parameter
    vbws.BeginElement "EmpId", ""
    vbws.AddAttribute "xsi:type", XSI_NS, "xsd:int"
    'write the employee id
    vbws.WriteText CStr(mEmpId)
    vbws.EndElement
    vbws.EndBodyPart
    vbws.ServiceUrl = _
    "http://vbwsserver/vbwsbook/chapter3/EmployeeOrders/
➥EmpOrders.asp"
    vbws.SoapAction = """urn:EmployeeOrders"""
    vbws.Send
    Set soapMsg = New MSXML2.DOMDocument
    If Not soapMsg.loadXML(vbws.GetResponseString) Then
        MsgBox "Error loading response document " & vbCrLf & _
            soapMsg.parseError.reason & vbCrLf & _
          "Response document is" & vbCrLf & _
            vbws.GetResponseString(), vbCritical
        Exit Sub
    Else
        Call soapMsg.setProperty("SelectionNamespaces", _
         "xmlns:vbws='" & NS & "'")
        Set doc = New MSXML2.DOMDocument
        doc.loadXML soapMsg.selectSingleNode( _
          "//vbws:GetEmpOrdersResponse").firstChild.Text
        Set Data = New ADODB.Recordset
        Data.Open doc
        Set doc = Nothing
    End If
```

```
Exit Sub
eh:
    MsgBox "Error sending request" & vbCrLf & Err.Description
End Sub
```

Listing 3.10 shows the three lines of code that the client application uses to bind a data grid to the returned Recordset. The client (outside of the proxy class shown in Listing 3.9) doesn't really know where the Recordset is coming from.

Listing 3.10 Three lines of code is all it takes to invoke the Web service proxy and bind the data grid (VBWSClientCode\chapter3\EmployeeOrdersClient\ frmMain.frm).

```
Private Sub cmdGetOrders_Click()

    Set empOrdersData = New CEmployeeOrders
    empOrdersData.EmpId = cboEmp.ItemData(cboEmp.ListIndex)
    Set DataGrid1.DataSource = empOrdersData

End Sub
```

As a data source, the proxy class implements GetDataMember, which the grid calls to get the ADO Recordset. To create and send the request message, I create a SOAPSender object and call its BeginBodyPart method, which writes an element as a direct child of <soapenv:Body>. As in the example request message in Listing 3.8, the body part is called GetEmpOrders and belongs to the operation namespace. Then I call BeginElement followed by AddAttribute to write <EmpId xsi:type="xsd:int"> with no namespace for the EmpId element itself. The call to WriteText writes the employee id, which is a property of the proxy class that must be set by the client application. Then I set the ServiceUrl and SoapAction properties and call Send to send the request message. Next I load the response SOAP message into a DOMDocument called soapMsg and use XPath to get the text of the first child of <GetEmpOrdersResponse>.

The SOAP RPC rules (SOAP Section 7) specify that the first child of <GetEmpOrdersResponse> must be the method's return value. Recall that the returned string is an XML representation of an ADO Recordset, so I load it into a

`DOMDocument` called `doc`. Then I create a new Recordset and call its `Open` method, passing it this `DOMDocument`. The Recordset handles deserializing itself from XML and the client application can use it to bind the data grid. Using SOAP RPC, I was easily able to transform this existing application to one that can be easily deployed over an intranet or the Internet even in the presence of firewalls and proxies. This is a classic example of using SOAP to facilitate application deployment and smooth operation over existing network infrastructure. However, as I explained in Chapter 1, you should replace DCOM communication with SOAP only in cases where doing so makes business sense and adds value by enabling application deployment or usage patterns not possible or practical with DCOM.

3.5.1 Section 5 Encoding

The majority of the SOAP specification is in Section 5 and represents about 40 percent of the specification in terms of number of pages. It includes detailed rules on serializing application data including arrays and objects that are implemented by most SOAP stacks available today. Although Section 5 is a major part of the SOAP specification, I won't go into details because the tools you use, such as the SOAP Toolkit and .NET, will support Section 5 encoding so that you do not need to learn its details. Additionally, document/literal messaging, where you define your own messages using XSD schemas, is a better long-term strategy because each industry is likely to have a set of standard XSD schemas that define industry-specific messages. I will, however, give an overview of Section 5 encoding to enable you to read and troubleshoot SOAP requests and responses as necessary. I don't expect that you'll need to know more about Section 5 than what I explain in this section.

Section 5 encoding supports all the XSD built-in types defined in the "XML Schema Part 2: Datatypes" specification. The following examples represent a string, date, and float, respectively. Note that I've included the `xsi:type` attribute on each element to illustrate the element's type; however, this is optional and some SOAP implementations, such as the SOAP Toolkit, do not include this attribute on serialized data.

```
<!-- this is a string -->
<empName xsi:type="xsd:string">Eddie Willers</empName>
<!-- this is a date -->
<bdate xsi:type="xsd:date">1969-01-17</bdate>
<!-- this is a float -->
<temperature xsi:type="xsd:float">250.0938</temperature>
```

A class (or a struct) is serialized as an element with a child element for each member of the class (or struct) that SOAP calls accessors. Listing 3.11 shows an example VB .NET structure and the corresponding Section 5 encoded format.

Listing 3.11   An example VB .NET Structure and a Section 5 encoded instance of it. The root element, `<theOrder>`, represents the structure instance while each of the other elements represents a structure member.

```
Structure OrderInfo
    Public OrderNum As String
    Public OrderDate As Date
    Public CustomerId As Integer
End Structure

<theOrder>
  <OrderNum xsi:type="xsd:string">XYZ-98-023</OrderNum>
  <OrderDate xsi:type="xsd:date">2002-03-01</OrderDate>
  <CustomerId xsi:type="xsd:int">423</CustomerId>
</theOrder>
```

Section 5 also defines specific rules for encoding arrays including multi-dimensional, sparse, and partially-transmitted arrays. SOAP defines an element called Array that belongs to the SOAP encoding namespace, that is, `http://schemas.xmlsoap.org/soap/encoding/`.[3] I'll use the `soapenc` prefix to refer to this namespace throughout this chapter; hence the SOAP Array element's fully qualified name is `soapenc:Array`. To serialize an array according to Section 5 rules, you write a `soap-enc:Array` element inside which you write a child

---

[3]Note that this string, `http://schemas.xmlsoap.org/soap/encoding`, serves two purposes in SOAP. It is the namespace for the Array type and other elements defined in Section 5 and it is also the value of the soapenv:encodingStyle attribute that indicates the use of Section 5 encoding.

element for each item in the array in the same sequence as the array items. For example the VB .NET array

```
Dim MyInts() As Integer = {9, 2, 17}
```

would be serialized as an element with three child elements:

```
<soapenc:Array
    soapenc:arrayType="xsd:int[3]">
  <e1>9</e1>
  <e2>2</e2>
  <e3>17</e3>
</soapenc:Array>
```

Here `soapenc:arrayType` indicates the type and number of array items. Note that the number between square brackets is the number of elements, *not* the upper bound. Therefore, `int[3]` means an array of three integers unlike VB where `Public AnArray(3) As Integer` means an array of four integers. Array items are identified by their position: the first element, `<e1>` represents the first array item and so on. The element names, `e1`, `e2`, and `e3` are not significant—only the element positions matter.

Besides the `soap-enc:Array` element, SOAP also defines a `soap-enc:Array` *type*. This allows you to declare new elements of `type` `soap-enc:Array` or a type derived from it, and then use these elements as arrays in a SOAP message. For example, if you use XSD to declare a new element called `MyInts` like this:

```
<element name="MyInts" type="soapenc:Array"/>
```

you can then serialize the `MyInts` VB array shown above like this:

```
<MyInts
    soapenc:arrayType="xsd:int[3]">
  <e1>9</e1>
  <e1>2</e1>
  <e1>17</e1>
</MyInts>
```

Using `Variant` in VB 6 and `System.Object` in VB .NET, you can create arrays that have items of different types. Here's a VB .NET array that contains a string, an integer, an instance of the `OrderInfo` structure, and a double:

```
Dim theOrder As OrderInfo
Dim AssortedArray() = {"a string", 12, theOrder, 98.5}
```

To serialize this array according to Section 5 rules, you'll need to indicate each array item's type using `xsi:type` as shown in Listing 3.12.

Listing 3.12 Serializing an array with elements of different types

```
<soapenc:Array
soapenc:arrayType="xsd:anyType[3]">
  <e1 xsi:type="xsd:string">a string</e1>
  <e2 xsi:type="xsd:int">12</e2>
  <e3 xsi:type="vbws:OrderInfo">
    <OrderNum xsi:type="xsd:string">XYZ-98-023</OrderNum>
    <OrderDate xsi:type="xsd:date">2002-03-01</OrderDate>
    <CustomerId xsi:type="xsd:int">423</CustomerId>
  </e3>
  <e4 xsi:type="xsd:double">98.5</e4>
</soapenc:Array>
```

The array itself is of type `xsd:anyType`, which is XSD's equivalent of the .NET `System.Object` type, while each element has an `xsi:type` attribute identifying its XSD type. The third element, `<e3>`, is of type `vbws:OrderInfo`, assuming the `OrderInfo` type is defined in a schema with a target namespace identified by the `vbws` prefix.

In this section I've covered the basic Section 5 encoding rules related to types you are most likely to encounter and use. Armed with this information, you can now read and understand SOAP requests and responses and troubleshoot serialization-related interoperability issues that might arise when communicating between different SOAP stacks.

3.6 When Things Go Wrong

As part of invoking Web services, SOAP specifies a standard method of communicating error information to the client using the `<soapenv:Fault>` element and its subelements. The three pre-defined subelements are `<faultCode>`, `<faultString>`, and `<detail>`. You can also define your own subelements that belong to an application-specific namespace.

3.6.1 <faultCode>

The contents of `<faultCode>` can be any fully-qualified name that you define for your application optionally with multiple parts of this name separated by a dot. For example, I might define the following string to indicate a database error in my application: `vbws:Application.Database`, where `vbws` is a namespace prefix declared as `http://schemas.learnxmlws.com/myApp/`. There are a few standard fault codes defined in the SOAP spec including `soapenv:Client` and `soapenv:Server`, which define message processing errors at the SOAP level rather than the application level. `soapenv:Client` indicates an error in the message content (for example, message content might not be properly encoded). `soapenv:Server` indicates errors in message processing that are not due to bad message content. For example, the server might fail to instantiate the COM component or .NET class that represents the requested Web service. `soapenv:Client` and `soapenv:Server` fault codes are generally used for errors raised by the SOAP stack you use, while application-specific errors can be communicated back as custom fault codes such as `vbws:Application.Database`.

3.6.2 <faultString>

This is where you convey text information about the error that occurred. On the client side, you should parse out the contents of `<faultString>` and present it to the user in a message box, status panel, or log file. There is no limit on the string length, but since it is only text (no markup), it cannot easily convey structured information.

3.6.3 <detail>

This is an optional subelement of `<soapenv:Fault>` where you can put any other error information as one or more child elements of `<detail>`. These child elements are application-defined and must belong to some application-defined namespace. You might use this facility to communicate runtime error or exception information such as `Err.Number`, `Err.Description` and `Err.Source` for VB 6 and VB Script.

3.6.4 Communicating Error Information

Going back to the invoice messaging application, I added a simple procedure called `SendFault` to invoiceMessaging.asp. I also changed the error handling code in invoiceMessaging.asp to invoke this new procedure with the right parameters and end the response. Listing 3.13 shows this procedure along with two examples of calling it.

Listing 3.13 Communicating error information using `<soapenv:Fault>` **and custom** `<detail>` **child elements (VBWSBook\Chapter3\MessagingWS\ invoiceMessaging.asp)**

```
'An example of calling SendFault
'To indicate the schema document could not be loaded
Call schemaCache.Add(NS,XSD_LOC)
If Err.Number <> 0 Then
    Call SendFault("vbws:Application","Failed to add
schema",Err.Source,Err.Description,Err.number)
    Response.End
End If
'...


'SendFault procedure
Sub SendFault(faultCode,faultString,source,descr,num)
  Dim faultMsg
  faultMsg = "<soapenv:Fault xmlns:vbws='" & NS & _
"'><faultCode>" & _
    faultCode & "</faultCode>" & _
    "<faultString>" & faultString & "</faultString>" & _
    "<detail><vbws:ErrNumber>" & num & "</vbws:ErrNumber>" & _
    "<vbws:ErrDescr>" & descr & "</vbws:ErrDescr>" & _
    "<vbws:ErrSource>" & source & "</vbws:ErrSource>" & _
    "</detail></soapenv:Fault>"
  Call WriteSOAPResponse(faultMsg)
End Sub
```

The parameters to `SendFault` are `faultCode`, `faultString`, which are re-ported in `<faultCode>` and `<faultString>`, respectively; and `source`, `descr`, and `num`, which are reported in the custom detail child elements `<vbws:ErrSource>`, `<vbws:ErrDescr>`, and `<vbws:ErrNumber>`, respectively. Listing 3.14 shows an example response message with fault information in response to a failure to load the XSD schema, respectively.

Listing 3.14   Example SOAP responses with error information in `<soapenv:Fault>`

```
<!-- response to schema not found error -->
<soapenv:Envelope
xmlns:xsi='http://www.w3.org/2001/XMLSchema-instance'
xmlns:xsd='http://www.w3.org/2001/XMLSchema'
xmlns:soapenv='http://schemas.xmlsoap.org/soap/envelope/'>
<soapenv:Body>
  <soapenv:Fault
  xmlns:vbws='http://schemas.learnxmlws.com/invoice'>
  <faultCode>vbws:Application</faultCode>
  <faultString>Failed to add schema</faultString>
  <detail>
  <vbws:ErrNumber>-2146697210</vbws:ErrNumber>
  <vbws:ErrDescr>System error: -2146697210.</vbws:ErrDescr>
  <vbws:ErrSource>msxml4.dll</vbws:ErrSource>
  </detail>
  </soapenv:Fault>
</soapenv:Body>
</soapenv:Envelope>
```

Note that I used the custom fault code `vbws:Application` for communicating the application-specific error of failing to load the schema.

3.7   Extending SOAP

SOAP provides only the bare minimum functionality required to invoke Web services and leaves it up to implementors to extend it in ways to meet client and service needs. SOAP header elements are a means of extending SOAP functionality by communicating information that is not necessarily part of the message data but is needed to process the message, such as user credentials, session id, or transaction id. `<soapenv:Header>` is an optional child element of

`<soapenv:Envelope>` that can be used to convey such information in the form of application-defined child elements. Headers can be sent with the request and response messages to communicate information to the service or the client, respectively. A Web service might define an `<authInfo>` header element that contains two subelements for the user id and password as shown in Listing 3.15. Clients invoking this Web service would then insert user credentials into this header with each request to the Web service.

Listing 3.15 Providing user credentials in SOAP headers

```
<soapenv:Envelope
xmlns:xsi='http://www.w3.org/2001/XMLSchema-instance'
xmlns:xsd='http://www.w3.org/2001/XMLSchema'
xmlns:soapenv='http://schemas.xmlsoap.org/soap/envelope/'>
<soapenv:Header>
 <authInfo
  xmlns="http://schemas.learnxmlws.com/appHeader">
   <uid>jgalt</uid>
   <pwd>motor</pwd>
 </authInfo>
</soapenv:Header>
...
</soapenv:Envelope>
```

Since custom header elements are application-defined, a client might send a header element to a service that does not understand this header. In many cases, the sender (whether client or service) of a SOAP message with a particular, application-defined header might require that the recipient understand this header. To satisfy this requirement, SOAP defines a `soapenv:mustUnderstand` attribute that can be placed on a header element and set to "1", which means that the recipient must understand this header or send back a `<soapenv:Fault>` indicating that it does not understand the header. For example, a client invokes a Web service and specifies a quality of service (QoS) header indicating that it needs the response within 200 milliseconds or less. If the Web service does not understand the `<QoS>` header, it might process the message anyway taking longer than the requested 200 milliseconds and not meet the client's needs. To ensure the service understands the header or returns a

`<soapenv:Fault>`, the client adds `soapenv:mustUnderstand="1"` to the `<QoS>` header as shown in Listing 3.16.

Listing 3.16   Using soapenv:mustUnderstand

```
<soapenv:Envelope
xmlns:xsi='http://www.w3.org/2001/XMLSchema-instance'
xmlns:xsd='http://www.w3.org/2001/XMLSchema'
xmlns:soapenv='http://schemas.xmlsoap.org/soap/envelope/'>
<soapenv:Header>
<QoS
  xmlns="http://schemas.learnxmlws.com/appHeader"
  soapenv:mustUnderstand="1">
   <resp>200</resp>
 </QoS >
</soapenv:Header>
...
</soapenv:Envelope>
```

3.8   Handling Binary Data

A SOAP message is an XML document which, according to the XML specification, must contain only legal characters in the document's character encoding. This means you can't just insert binary data into a SOAP message and ship it over the network. Therefore, sending images, files, and other binary data with SOAP requires special handling.

You can choose between several different methods for handling binary data based on the size of the data and the nature of the application. In this section, I will briefly explain three such methods and when you'd want to use each.

3.8.1   Base64 Encoding

For binary content of relatively small size, you can encode the bits into a legal character representation using any encoding/decoding scheme that is most convenient for your service and its clients. Base64 is one such encoding scheme that's fairly widespread and available in many implementations. Both the .NET Framework and the SOAP Toolkit support Base64 encoding/decoding of data. You can also use third-party components to apply Base64 encoding/decoding yourself if your SOAP stack does not support it. To show you Base64 encoding, I created a

.NET Web service (VBWSBook\Chapter3\BinExample\theService.asmx.vb) that exposes one method called `GetArray` that returns a `Byte` array with ten items. Listing 3.17 shows the SOAP response from this method with the `Byte` array encoded using Base64 and the `xsi:type` attribute that indicates its XSD type as `base64Binary`.

Listing 3.17   A 10-item Byte array encoded using Base64 and transmitted in a SOAP message

```
<?xml version="1.0" encoding="utf-8"?>
<soapenv:Envelope
xmlns:soapenv="http://schemas.xmlsoap.org/soap/envelope/"
xmlns:tns="http://tempuri.org/"
xmlns:xsi="http://www.w3.org/2001/XMLSchema-instance"
xmlns:xsd="http://www.w3.org/2001/XMLSchema">
  <soapenv:Body
   soapenv:encodingStyle=
   "http://schemas.xmlsoap.org/soap/encoding/">
    <tns:GetArrayResponse>
      <GetArrayResult
          xsi:type="xsd:base64Binary">
          9U69nNJ+iH73wA==
      </GetArrayResult>
    </tns:GetArrayResponse>
  </soapenv:Body>
</soapenv:Envelope>
```

This encoding was done for me by the .NET Framework. I just declared the return value as a `Byte` array and returned the array. Similarly, a .NET client proxy would automatically extract the encoded characters and decode them into a `Byte` array, then return it to the client application. While Base64 encoding works well for small content size, it becomes impractical for large content such as images and files because of the processing required to encode/decode the content and the significant increase in size of the encoded content compared with the original content size.

3.8.2   SOAP with Attachments

The SOAP with Attachments specification defines how a SOAP message can be transmitted along with arbitrary binary content such as images and files in their original format, all combined into one document. This document is called a MIME multipart/related message (MIME) and contains several parts, one containing the SOAP message and one for each individual binary content, each part with a unique content id. Listing 3.18 shows an example message from the SOAP with Attachments specification.

Listing 3.18 An example SOAP message with attachments. This example is from the SOAP with Attachments specification.

```
MIME-Version: 1.0
Content-Type: Multipart/Related; boundary=MIME_boundary;
➥type=text/xml;
         start="<claim061400a.xml@claiming-it.com>"
Content-Description: This is the optional message description.

--MIME_boundary
Content-Type: text/xml; charset=UTF-8
Content-Transfer-Encoding: 8bit
Content-ID: <claim061400a.xml@claiming-it.com>

<?xml version='1.0' ?>
<SOAP-ENV:Envelope
xmlns:SOAP-ENV="http://schemas.xmlsoap.org/soap/envelope/">
<SOAP-ENV:Body>
..
<theSignedForm href="cid:claim061400a.tiff@claiming-it.com"/>
..
</SOAP-ENV:Body>
</SOAP-ENV:Envelope>

--MIME_boundary
Content-Type: image/tiff
Content-Transfer-Encoding: binary
Content-ID: <claim061400a.tiff@claiming-it.com>

...binary TIFF image...
--MIME_boundary--
```

The message in Listing 3.18 contains a SOAP message and a TIFF image. The SOAP message contains an element called `<theSignedForm>` that references the TIFF image part with its content id, `claim061400a.tiff@claiming-it.com`. This reference tells the message recipient that the content of the `<the-`

SignedForm> is the TIFF image found further down in the message with id claim061400a.tiff@claiming-it.com. Note that the TIFF image is in its native binary format so that no encoding/decoding is required.

Today, the .NET Framework does not support SOAP with attachments, which means you'll need a third party SOAP stack or your own implementation if you want to write and support it. The SOAP Toolkit provides an extensibility mechanism that allows you to implement features such as SOAP with Attachments. In fact, the SOAP Toolkit comes with a sample SOAP with Attachments implementation using this extensibility mechanism.

3.8.3 A Simple Solution

There's a simple solution to the binary content problem that can be used in many situations. Instead of sending the binary content with the SOAP message, you can send a URL to the binary content and let the client retrieve the content from this URL. I wrote a test Web service using .NET that returns current weather conditions for a given zip code.[4] The Web service returns current temperature and humidity, barometric pressure, and general conditions such as "partly cloudy" or "sunny." It also returns a URL to a GIF image that depicts these current conditions. If the client wants to display the GIF image, it extracts the URL out of the SOAP response and uses HTTP GET to fetch the image from that URL. Listing 3.19 shows an example SOAP response from my weather Web service where <IconUrl> contains the GIF image's URL.

Listing 3.19 An example SOAP message. Instead of a GIF image, this message contains a URL to that image.

```
<?xml version="1.0" encoding="utf-8"?>
<soapenv:Envelope
xmlns:soapenv="http://schemas.xmlsoap.org/soap/envelope/"
xmlns:soapenc="http://schemas.xmlsoap.org/soap/encoding/"
xmlns:tns="http://tempuri.org/"
xmlns:types="http://tempuri.org/encodedTypes"
xmlns:xsi="http://www.w3.org/2001/XMLSchema-instance"
```

---

[4]This Web service is intended for educational purposes only. It extracts weather information from the National Weather Service's Web site. Chapter 13 shows you how to build a similar weather service.

```
xmlns:xsd="http://www.w3.org/2001/XMLSchema">
  <soapenv:Body
      soapenv:encodingStyle="http://schemas.xmlsoap.org/soap/
encoding/">
    <tns:GetWeatherResponse>
      <GetWeatherResult xsi:type="types:CurrentWeather">
        <LastUpdated
          xsi:type="xsd:string">
          Wednesday, September 5, at 2:51 PM
        </LastUpdated>
        <IconUrl
          xsi:type="xsd:string">
        http://image.weather.com/web/common/wxicons/52/30.gif
        </IconUrl>
        <Conditions
        xsi:type="xsd:string">Partly Cloudy</Conditions>
        <CurrentTemp xsi:type="xsd:float">79</CurrentTemp>
        <Humidity xsi:type="xsd:float">0.45</Humidity>
        <Barometer xsi:type="xsd:float">30.12</Barometer>
        <BarometerDirection
        xsi:type="xsd:string">falling</BarometerDirection>
      </GetWeatherResult>
    </tns:GetWeatherResponse>
  </soapenv:Body>
</soapenv:Envelope>
```

This approach works even when the binary content is not in a static file such as a GIF or JPG image. You can return a URL to a dynamic resource such as an ASP or ASPX page that generates the binary content and sends back. For example, if the Weather icon were dynamically generated, the icon URL in Listing 3.19 could've been:

```
http://www.learnxmlws.com/wicon.aspx?id=8920
```

Alternatively, the service could save the dynamically-generated binary content to a disk file and send the URL to that file. An example of this is the Xara 3D Web service[5], which dynamically generates a 3D text graphic based on input parameters, saves it to a GIF file, and returns the file's URL so that the client can retrieve it.

---

[5]The Xara 3D Web service is located at http://ws.xara.com/graphicrender/render3d.asp with several example clients at http://ws.xara.com/graphicrender/soap/render3d/examples.asp.

This simple solution revolves around sending the binary content's location instead of the binary content itself, which assumes that the message recipient can then make an HTTP request to retrieve the binary content. This assumption is usually valid when the recipient is a client that needs to retrieve a binary resource from a Web service, but it's usually *invalid* if the recipient is the Web service that needs to receive a binary resource from the client. That's because most clients are not running Web servers and therefore they can send outgoing HTTP requests but cannot handle incoming ones. Therefore, if you design a Web service where clients must send binary content as part of the SOAP request messages, chances are clients will have to Base64 encode this binary content or, if the content is too large, you'll have to implement SOAP with Attachments on both client and service sides.

3.9 Summary

The Simple Object Access Protocol is a de facto standard for cross-platform messaging and RPC that can be used over a variety of transport protocols of which HTTP is the most common. You can think of SOAP as the Internet's application-to-application protocol enabling applications to communicate over the existing Internet infrastructure. XML-based messaging is the essence of SOAP with RPC being built on top of that, mostly to enable existing applications to invoke remote services and objects over the Web. When using SOAP, there are always client-side and server-side pieces that handle serializing/deserializing application data into the appropriate XML format to send and receive SOAP messages. You can write your own client and server pieces especially if you want a highly-specialized custom solution or you can use off-the-shelf SOAP stacks such as the SOAP Toolkit and the .NET Framework.

3.10 Resources

DevelopMentor's SOAP discussion list: http://discuss.develop.com/soap.html.

3.10.1 Specifications

R. Fielding, J. Getts, J. Mogul, H. Frystyk Nielsen, T. Berners-Lee. Hypertext Transfer Protocol—HTTP/1.1: http://www.ietf.org/rfc/rfc2068.txt, IETF, January 1997.

D. Box, D. Ehnebuske, G. Kakivaya, A. Layman, N. Mendelshon, H. Frystyk Nielsen, S. Thatte, D. Winer. SOAP 1.1 W3C Note: http://www.w3.org/TR/SOAP/, © 2000 DevelopMentor, International Business Machines Corporation, Lotus Development Corporation, Microsoft, UserLand Software, May 8, 2000.

Editors: M. Gudgin, M. Hadley, J. Moreau, H. Frystyk Nielson, SOAP 1.2 W3C Working Draft: http://www.w3.org/TR/2001/WD-soap12-20010709/, W3C (MIT, INRIA, KEIO), July 9, 2001.

J. Berton, S. Thatte, H. Frystyk Nielsen, SOAP Message with Attachments: http://www.w3.org/TR/SOAP-attachments, December 11, 2000.

G. Levinson, The MIME Multipart/Related Content-type: http://www.ietf.org/rfc/rfc2387.txt, IETF, August 1998.

Chapter 4

Describing Web Services

> It would be possible to describe everything scientifically, but it would
> make no sense; it would be without meaning, as if you described a
> Beethoven symphony as a variation of wave pressure. —Albert Einstein

Just as XML Schemas are used to describe data types exposed by Web services, there is a need for a language that can be used to describe the complete interfaces exposed by them. In this chapter, I explain the concepts and terminology behind the most commonly used language for describing Web service interfaces—the Web Services Description Language (WSDL). I will show you how to write WSDL documents that describe your Web service's interface and how to read WSDL documents for services that you want to invoke. The goal of this chapter is to teach you to create the SOAP request messages, and parse response messages based on reading a WSDL document. Tools, such as the SOAP Toolkit, can do this most of the time, but sometimes they fail, especially if there are errors in the WSDL file. By knowing how to read and understand WSDL you can solve these problems yourself and go on to invoke the Web service or enable clients to invoke your Web service.

4.1 Why Describe Web Services?

If I create a service called `WeatherRetriever` that exposes one method called `GetTemperature` like this:

```
Public GetTemperature(ByVal ZipCode As String) As Single
```

I want developers to invoke my Web service so I put together an HTML page that gives people the information they need to invoke it, which is

- The name of the operation (the method) that it exposes, which in this case is GetTemperature. Clients would also need to know that the method takes in the zip code as an xsd:string and returns the current temperature as an xsd:float.
- The protocol they can use to invoke this Web service. In this case, the service is accessible using SOAP over HTTP.
- Whether the service is expecting RPC or document style SOAP messages.
- Whether the service is expecting literal, SOAP encoded, or other type of messages.
- The Web service's location, for example http://www.learnXmlws.com/services/WeatherRetriever.asmx.

Developers can read this information and start writing clients that will invoke my Web services. But there are some problems associated with providing this information in an informal way such as an HTML page.

First, the HTML page I come up with to publish this information is not a standard. So every Web service creator will have his or her own way of describing the service. As a developer, you will have to figure out how a particular Web service is described, read the description, and try to understand it.

Second, using HTML or the back of a napkin to describe a Web service hardly provides a formal description that can be read and processed by your development tools. For example, if you make a mistake when reading my service description and you write a client that expects the temperature back as an xsd:int instead of an xsd:float, the error will manifest itself at runtime only, when your client actually invokes the Web service. Without a formal, machine-readable description of a Web service, there's nothing your compiler can do to help you catch such errors at compile time.

Given a machine-readable Web service description, a development tool can be smart enough to check the names of operations you're calling and the types of parameters you're passing at compile time, which can save you hours of debugging. A better development tool would read the Web service description and generate the client code needed to invoke the Web service, thereby eliminating manual work by you. In fact, there are many tools that do exactly that; including wsdl.exe (part of the .NET Framework SDK) and Visual Studio .NET.

WSDL is an XML grammar for describing Web service interfaces, the protocols supported by the Web service, and the Web service location. Version 1.1 of the WSDL specification was authored by IBM Research and Microsoft and can be found at http://www.w3c.org/TR/wsdl. Although WSDL is not a W3C standard, or a required part of building and invoking Web services, it is supported by many SOAP stacks. Some tools, like wsdl.exe, use it to facilitate clients to invoke Web services.

On the server side, when you expose a Web service with VB 6 and the SOAP Toolkit or with VB .NET, you automatically get a WSDL document describing your service. Other developers can read this WSDL document to learn your service's interface and how to invoke it. On the client side, there are two ways to use a WSDL document. A development tool, like wsdl.exe, can read the WSDL document at design time and generate the client code necessary to invoke it as shown in Figure 4.1. This is analogous to using a type library (the WSDL equivalent in the COM world) and early binding to invoke a COM component. Alternatively, a development tool can read the WSDL document at runtime to generate the necessary requests and process the responses as shown in Figure 4.2. This is analogous to using late binding to invoke a COM component. By default, .NET clients use early binding while clients using the SOAP Toolkit use late binding. This is just the default way of doing things using these two tools, but, with some extra work on your part, each tool can be used for both early and late binding.

4.2 WSDL Overview

Figure 4.3 shows one client invoking a Web service using SOAP and another invoking the same service using HTTP GET. Figure 4.4 shows the same process with the various pieces labeled with WSDL terminology.

In WSDL, a **service** exposes groups of **operations** (methods). Each group of operations is called a **portType**, which is roughly analogous to an interface in the COM world. To invoke an operation, the client sends an input message and gets back an output message. The input message contains the data going to the

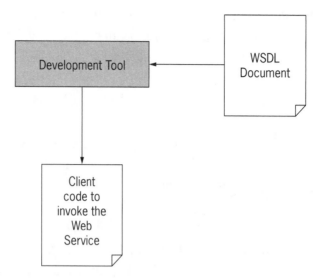

Figure 4.1   A development tool (for example, wsdl.exe) can use a WSDL document at design time to generate client code that invokes the Web service.

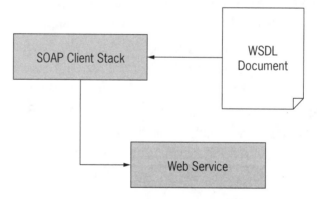

Figure 4.2   A client-side SOAP stack can use a WSDL document at runtime to formulate the Web service request message and understand the response message.

service and the output message contains the data coming back from the service. Each item of data in a message is called a message part or simply **part**. The actual protocol used to invoke an operation and the actual format of the input and output messages are specified in a **binding**. The service itself is ex-

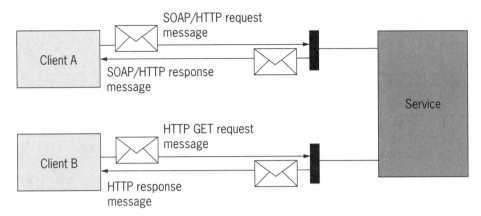

Figure 4.3 Two clients invoking a Web service. Client A is using SOAP over HTTP while client B is using HTTP GET.

posed to the world via one or more ports. Each **port** specifies two things: A network address where it's located (for example, http://www.learnXm-lws.com/services/WeatherRetriever.asmx) and the binding used with this port. A service may expose multiple ports each with different bindings. For example, the service in Figure 4.4 exposes two ports: one with a binding for SOAP and the other with a binding for HTTP GET.

Figure 4.5 shows the components of a WSDL document and how they relate to each other. The boxes show the containment relations and the arrows show the reference relations.

A service contains one or more ports and each port references a binding. Each binding references a portType, the operations within that portType, and the messages that make up each operation. Each portType contains zero or more operations. Each operation has an input and output message (I'll discuss other message combinations later in this chapter). Each message has zero or more parts and each part is of some data type. The part's type can be an XSD built-in type such as `xsd:int` or it can be a custom simple or complex type that's defined using XSD.

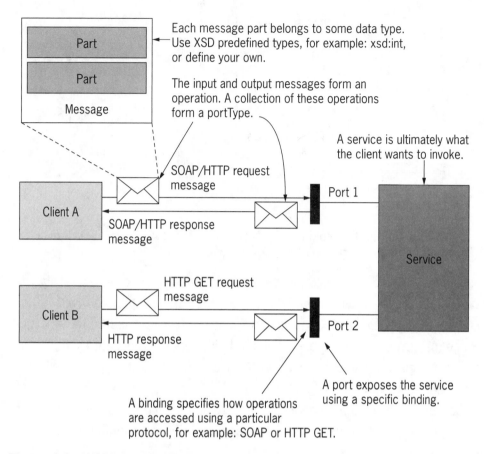

Each message part belongs to some data type. Use XSD predefined types, for example: xsd:int, or define your own.

The input and output messages form an operation. A collection of these operations form a portType.

A service is ultimately what the client wants to invoke.

A port exposes the service using a specific binding.

A binding specifies how operations are accessed using a particular protocol, for example: SOAP or HTTP GET.

Figure 4.4   WSDL terminology labeling the various parts of a client-service interaction

4.3   A WSDL Example

Let's take a look at a simple example Web service and the corresponding WSDL document. I created a VB 6 COM component called VB6Weather with one method:

```
Public Function GetTemperature(ByVal zipcode As String, _
                      ByVal celsius As Boolean) As Single

'code omitted

End Function
```

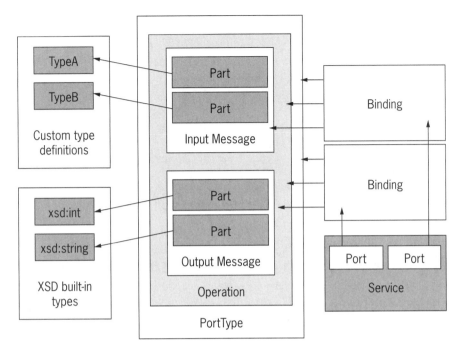

Figure 4.5 **The components of a WSDL document and how they relate to each other**

Then I ran the SOAP Toolkit's WSDL Generator to create the corresponding WSDL which is shown in Listing 4.1.

Listing 4.1 A WSDL document created by the SOAP Toolkit's WSDL Generator (VBWSBook\Chapter4\ExampleWSDLs\VB6Weather.wsdl)

```
<?xml version='1.0' encoding='UTF-8' ?>
 <!-- Generated 08/16/01 by Microsoft SOAP Toolkit
 WSDL File Generator, Version 1.02.813.0 -->
<definitions  name ='VB6Weather'
   targetNamespace = 'http://tempuri.org/wsdl/'
   xmlns:wsdlns='http://tempuri.org/wsdl/'
   xmlns:typens='http://tempuri.org/type'
   xmlns:soap='http://schemas.xmlsoap.org/wsdl/soap/'
   xmlns:xsd='http://www.w3.org/2001/XMLSchema'
   xmlns:stk=
   'http://schemas.microsoft.com/soap-toolkit/wsdl-extension'
   xmlns='http://schemas.xmlsoap.org/wsdl/'>
 <types>
```

```
          <schema targetNamespace='http://tempuri.org/type'
            xmlns='http://www.w3.org/2001/XMLSchema'
            xmlns:SOAP-ENC='http://schemas.xmlsoap.org/soap/encoding/'
            xmlns:wsdl='http://schemas.xmlsoap.org/wsdl/'
            elementFormDefault='qualified'>
          </schema>
        </types>
        <message name='VB6Weather.GetTemperature'>
          <part name='zipcode' type='xsd:string'/>
          <part name='celsius' type='xsd:boolean'/>
        </message>
        <message name='VB6Weather.GetTemperatureResponse'>
          <part name='Result' type='xsd:float'/>
        </message>
        <portType name='VB6WeatherSoapPort'>
          <operation name='GetTemperature'
          parameterOrder='zipcode celsius'>
            <input message='wsdlns:VB6Weather.GetTemperature' />
            <output
            message='wsdlns:VB6Weather.GetTemperatureResponse' />
          </operation>
        </portType>
        <binding name='VB6WeatherSoapBinding'
                 type='wsdlns:VB6WeatherSoapPort' >
          <stk:binding preferredEncoding='UTF-8'/>
          <soap:binding
             style='rpc'
             transport='http://schemas.xmlsoap.org/soap/http' />
          <operation name='GetTemperature' >
            <soap:operation
            soapAction=
               'http://tempuri.org/action/VB6Weather.GetTemperature' />
            <input>
              <soap:body use='encoded'
                namespace='http://tempuri.org/message/'
                encodingStyle=
                  'http://schemas.xmlsoap.org/soap/encoding/' />
            </input>
            <output>
              <soap:body use='encoded'
                namespace='http://tempuri.org/message/'
                encodingStyle=
                  'http://schemas.xmlsoap.org/soap/encoding/' />
            </output>
```

```
      </operation>
    </binding>
    <service name='VB6Weather' >
      <port
        name='VB6WeatherSoapPort'
        binding='wsdlns:VB6WeatherSoapBinding' >
        <soap:address
        location=
          'http://vbwsserver/webtest/vb6weather/VB6Weather.ASP' />
      </port>
    </service>
  </definitions>
```

In Chapter 3, you learned that there are four styles of SOAP messages: RPC/encoded, RPC/literal, document/encoded, and document/literal. RPC/encoded is the default for exposing Web services using the Microsoft SOAP Toolkit, therefore the corresponding WSDL in Listing 4.1 is for RPC/encoded messages. In the next section, I'll explain how the WSDL differs for the other three styles.

Looking at the document in Listing 4.1, you see that the default namespace is declared as `http://schemas.xmlsoap.org/wsdl/`, which is the WSDL namespace. The document starts with the `<definitions>` element, which is the document element (the topmost element) of a WSDL document and usually contains a few namespace declarations such as you see here. The `<definitions>` element has an optional attribute called `targetNamespace`, which defines the containing namespace for all WSDL items defined in this document such as messages, operations, and portTypes. The WSDL `targetNamespace` attribute is functionally similar to the XSD `targetNamespace` attribute discussed in Chapter 2.

The next element down is the `<types>` element, which contains an XSD schema. This schema is where you'd define custom types to use with message parts such as `TypeA` and `TypeB` in Figure 4.5. In this particular example, there are no custom types because all the parameters and return value of the `GetTemperature` method can be represented using XSD built-in types.

Next comes the definition of messages using the `<message>` element. Each message has a unique name indicated by its `name` attribute. There are two messages: One represents the request and one represents the response. In this case, the SOAP Toolkit uses the names `VB6Weather.GetTemperature` and `VB6Weather.GetTemperatureResponse` following its `Component.Method` and `Component.MethodResponse` naming convention. Note that this is just the naming convention that the SOAP Toolkit follows, there is no standard way to name the messages; you can name them anything you like. The request message contains two parts corresponding to the two parameters, `zipcode` and `celsius`, of the `GetTemperature` method.

When using SOAP RPC, these part names must match the method parameter names because that's a rule of SOAP RPC as discussed in Chapter 3. Each part type is the XSD-equivalent of the VB parameter type. For example, A VB `Boolean` becomes an `xsd:boolean` and a VB `Single` becomes an `xsd:float`. The response message contains one part that corresponds to the method return value. If there were any `ByRef` parameters (in/out parameters), you would see the corresponding parts in both the request and response messages. If a Web service method has out parameters, they would be represented here as parts inside the response message. Although you cannot create methods with `out` parameters in Visual Basic, other languages such as C# allow you to, so you might encounter Web services that have `out` parameters.[1]

The `<portType>` element defines the collection of methods exposed by the Web service so you can think of it as an interface implemented by the Web service. Each `portType` must have a unique name, which in this example is `VB6WeatherSoapPort`, but that name can be anything you like. Inside the `<portType>`, an `<operation>` element represents each method and contains a reference to the input (request) and output (response) messages using `<input>` and `<output>` element. An important thing to note is that when referring to a message, you must use its fully qualified name. This is because a message belongs to the `targetNamespace` as defined in the `<definitions>` element. Looking back at the `<definitions>` element in Listing 4.1, you'll notice that the `targetNamespace` is defined as `http://tempuri.org/wsdl/` and that

---

[1] Of course if you are using C# you would not use the SOAP Toolkit to create your Web services. You'd use the .NET Framework for that. Regardless of what tools you use, your knowledge of WSDL still will be applicable.

the prefix `wsdlns` also maps to the same namespace. Therefore, when you want to refer to the message called `VB6Weather.GetTemperature`, you have to prefix the message name with the `targetNamespace` prefix, which in this example is `wsdlns`. This is exactly the same mechanism that XSD uses for specifying the `targetNamespace` of custom types and then for referring to those types later within your schema (see Chapter 2).

The `<operation>` element itself has the optional attribute `parameter-Order`, which lists all method parameters in the order in which they appear in the method declaration. This attribute is optional, but you'll usually see it in WSDL documents for Web services that use RPC-style SOAP (rather than document-style). At this point, you might be wondering how a development tool (for example, wsdl.exe) figures out whether each `<part>` is in, `in/out`, `out`, or the return value. The rules for determining this depend on the `parameter-Order` attribute as follows: For each parameter that appears in the `parameterOrder` list, if there's a `<part>` with the same name in the input and output messages, then the parameter is in/out (`ByRef`). If there's a `<part>` with the same name in the input message only, then the parameter is an in parameter (`ByVal`). If there's a `<part>` with the same name in the output message only, then the parameter is an out parameter. Finally, if there's a `<part>` in the output message that is not listed in the `parameterOrder` attribute that `<part>` is considered the method's return value. Keep in mind that `parameterOrder` is *optional*, so if you encounter a WSDL document that does not specify `parameterOrder`, don't be surprised. In fact, most tools will not write a `parameterOrder` attribute when they generate a WSDL for a Web service that uses document style SOAP. This makes sense because with document style there are no parameters, just XML documents being exchanged within the SOAP envelope.

You might ask: Why is `parameterOrder` needed at all? Couldn't we infer the order of parameters from the order of the `<part>` elements? (That is, the first `<part>` element is the first parameter, and so forth.) This would actually work well if all Web services were created with languages that do not support `out` parameters. The problem lies with methods that have a mix of `in` and `out` parameters. For example, here are two messages describing a method with `in`, `in/out`, and `out` parameters as well as a return value.

```
<message name="ExampleIn">
  <part name="inParam" type="s:int" />
  <part name="inoutParam" type="s:float" />
</message>
<message name="ExampleOut">
  <part name="RetVal" type="s:string" />
  <part name="outParam" type="s:string" />
  <part name="inoutParam" type="s:float" />
</message>
```

Just by looking at these messages, you can tell that the `inoutParam` is the last parameter of the method because it comes last in both the input and output messages. But is `inParam` or `outParam` the first method parameter? You cannot make that determination without the `paramterOrder` attribute.

The next element is `<binding>`, which also has a unique name and provides information on how to invoke operations of a particular portType using a particular protocol. In this example, the binding provides information on how to access the `VB6WeatherSoapPort` portType. The first element within the binding (`<stk:binding>`) is not part of WSDL at all. It is an element used by the SOAP Toolkit to indicate the preferred encoding to use when invoking operations. You can tell that `<stk:binding>` is not part of WSDL because its namespace is `http://schemas.microsoft.com/soap-toolkit/wsdl-extension`, which is not the WSDL namespace. However, WSDL does allow you to extend it using your own elements, which are referred to as extensibility elements. You normally would not need to do this, but if you decide to extend a WSDL document by adding your own extensibility elements, keep in mind that the clients that read this WSDL may not understand what's meant by those elements (unless of course you are also writing the clients). The next element is `<soap:binding>`, which belongs to the namespace `http://schemas.xml-soap.org/wsdl/soap/` and provides information on whether to use RPC or document-style SOAP and what transport protocol to use with SOAP.[2] The

---

[2]Recall from Chapter 3 that SOAP may be used over any transport protocol including, but not limited to, HTTP.

`<soap:binding>` element is defined in the WSDL specification along with six other elements as part of the SOAP WSDL binding. Table 4.1 lists all seven elements, where each element may appear in a WSDL document, and a brief description of each.

Table 4.1   The SOAP WSDL Extension Elements

Element	Location	Description
`<soap:address>`	As a child of a `<port>` element	Provides the URL of the SOAP end point
`<soap:binding>`	As a child of a `<binding>` element	Specifies whether to use document or RPC style soap and the transport protocol to use
`<soap:body>`	As a child of an `<input>` or `<output>` element that's a child of a `<binding>` element	Specifies the namespace of the SOAP `<Body>` contents and whether they are to be literal or encoded and which encoding style to use
`<soap:fault>`	As a child of a `<fault>` element	Defines the name of a SOAP fault, its namespace, encoded/literal, and the encoding style
`<soap:header>`	As a child of an `<input>` or `<output>` element that is a child of a `<binding>` element	Specifies the message that this header is used with, the header namespace, encoded/literal, and the encoding style
`<soap:header-fault>`	As a child of an `<input>` or `<output>` element that is a child of a `<binding>` element	Specifies the message that this header fault corresponds to, the header fault namespace, encoded/literal, and the encoding style
`<soap:operation>`	As a child of an `<operation>` element that is the child of a `<binding>` element	Specifies the SOAPAction value to use when invoking this operation and whether to use RPC or document style SOAP

The `<soap:binding>` element in Listing 4.1 specifies that clients must use RPC-style SOAP over HTTP. The URI `http://schemas.xmlsoap.org/soap/http` indicates the HTTP protocol. This is neither a namespace nor a URL, it's just a unique name that is defined within the context of SOAP WSDL binding to mean HTTP.

Each operation of the portType `VB6WeatherSoapPort` has a corresponding `<operation>` element inside the `<binding>` element. This `<operation>` element provides the information actually needed to invoke the operation using the specified protocol. The example in Listing 4.1 has an `<operation>` element called `GetTemperature` with a `<soap:operation>` that specifies a `soapAction` of `http://tempuri.org/action/VB6Weather.GetTemperature`. It also contains an `<input>` and an `<output>` element that corresponds to the operation's input and output messages, respectively. Within the `<input>` and `<output>` elements, `<soap:body>` elements specify that the contents of the `<Body>` element in the SOAP message must be part of the namespace `http://tempuri.org/message/` and must be encoded according to the encoding style `http://schemas.xmlsoap.org/soap/encoding/`, which is the SOAP Section 5 encoding style. To summarize, here's the information that the client gets from reading the `<binding>` in Listing 4.1:

- This binding is for the portType `VB6WeatherSoapPort`.
- To invoke operations in this binding, the client must use RPC style SOAP over HTTP.
- The `SOAPAction` HTTP header for the `GetTemperature` operation is `http://tempuri.org/action/VB6Weather.GetTemperature`.
- The contents of the `<Body>` element in the SOAP request should be encoded according to SOAP Section 5 and should belong to the namespace `http://tempuri.org/message/`.
- The contents of the `<Body>` element in the SOAP response will be encoded according to SOAP Section 5 and will belong to the namespace `http://tempuri.org/message/`.

Reading down in Listing 4.1, you see the `<service>` element that is called `VB6Weather`. The SOAP Toolkit's WSDL Generator asks you for the service name and uses it as the value of the `<service>` name attribute here. The

`<service>` contains zero or more `<port>` elements that specify how this service can be accessed. In this example, the port refers to the binding called `VB6WeatherSoapBinding` and contains a `<soap:address>` element that tells the client where the SOAP end point is located. The client reads the value of the `location` attribute from the `<soap:address>` and sends the SOAP request to this location. Therefore, if this location is incorrect, the client will not be able to reach the Web service.

4.4 WSDL SOAP Binding

In this section, I will take a look at the details of how WSDL describes SOAP-based Web services. Document/literal SOAP messages are commonly used and their WSDL is the simplest to understand, so we'll start with them. Next I'll discuss the WSDL for RPC/encoded SOAP messages because this format is also commonly used; especially when you are exposing existing applications as Web services. The other two formats: document/encoded and RPC/literal are rarely used and exist mostly because the SOAP and WSDL standards allow them. To spare you unnecessary details, I won't discuss them here.

You already know the definitions of the terms RPC, document, literal, and encoded within the context of SOAP messages. Let's define these terms within the context of WSDL and using WSDL terminology:

- **Document:** When you are using document, you are thinking of sending an XML document with the request message and getting back an XML document with the response message. Therefore, each `<message>` contains one or more `<part>`s that make up the XML document you are sending or receiving. The primary difference between document and RPC is that with document, `<part>`s do not correspond to method parameters; they just represent the XML document being transmitted.

- **RPC:** When you are using RPC, you are thinking in terms of invoking methods, passing parameters, and getting return values. Therefore, input and output `<message>`s contain `<part>`s that correspond to the method parameters and return value.

- **Encoding** within the context of WSDL: Encoding means the contents of each part will adhere to some agreed upon encoding rules such as SOAP Section 5 encoding. Each `<part>` has some type, but that type alone does not provide all the information you need to serialize the data into the message. That's why sometimes it's called an abstract part type: You need more information to make it concrete. To serialize the data, you must know the encoding rules used, which are usually the SOAP Section 5 rules. The `<part>` type and `name` attributes, the `namespace` attribute of `<soap:body>`, and the SOAP Section 5 encoding rules work together to tell you how to serialize the data into the message.

- **Literal** within the context of WSDL: Using literal means you create a schema that describes the exact contents of each message part. Each `<part>` is of a type that is specified using an XSD schema. This is also called a concrete type because by looking at the schema you can determine how to serialize the data into the message.

To explain the WSDL for document/literal and RPC/encoded, I will use the .NET Web service in Listing 4.2, which exposes a document/literal operation called ExampleDocLit and an RPC/encoded operation called ExampleRpcEnc.

Listing 4.2   The Example VB .NET Web service with an RPC/encoded and a document/literal method. Note that the methods return types are Object to demonstrate how various types are mapped from VB (VBWSBook\Chapter4\ Combos\Example.asmx.vb).

```
Public Structure theStruct
    Public theName As String
    Public theNumber As Double
    Public theDate As Date
End Structure

Public Class Example
    <WebMethod(), SoapRpcMethod()> _
    Public Function ExampleRpcEnc(ByVal a As Integer, _
                    ByVal b As Single(), _
                    ByVal c As theStruct) As Object
        Dim ret As Double = 9.99
        Return ret
    End Function

    <WebMethod(), SoapDocumentMethod()> _
    Public Function ExampleDocLit(ByVal a As Integer, _
                    ByVal b As Single(), _
                    ByVal c As theStruct) As Object
        Dim ret As Double = 9.99
```

```
        Return ret
    End Function
End Class
```

As you learned in Chapter 1, you can obtain the WSDL for a .NET Web service by navigating to the service's .asmx file and adding WSDL as a query string. The next two sections show and explain the contents of this auto-generated WSDL beginning with the document/literal method.

4.4.1 Document/Literal

Listing 4.3 shows a modified version of the auto-generated WSDL for the `ExampleDocLit` method in Listing 4.2. The original auto-generated WSDL contains definitions for both methods: `ExampleDocLit` and `ExampleRpcEnc`. To make the WSDL easier to read, I separated the two definitions so that you can focus on each one individually. In addition (also to make the core WSDL easier to read), I removed the `<types>` section and put it in a separate listing (Listing 4.4).

Listing 4.3 WSDL document for the document/literal combination. Note that the `<types>` section has been removed to make the document easier to read (VBWSBook\Chapter4\ExampleWSDLs\DocLitExample.wsdl).

```
<definitions
xmlns:s="http://www.w3.org/2001/XMLSchema"
xmlns:soap="http://schemas.xmlsoap.org/wsdl/soap/"
xmlns:s1="http://tempuri.org/"
targetNamespace="http://tempuri.org/"
xmlns="http://schemas.xmlsoap.org/wsdl/">

<!-- <types> section removed from here -->

  <message name="ExampleDocLitSoapIn">
    <part name="parameters" element="s1:ExampleDocLit" />
  </message>
  <message name="ExampleDocLitSoapOut">
    <part name="parameters" element="s1:ExampleDocLitResponse" />
  </message>
  <portType name="ExampleSoap">
    <operation name="ExampleDocLit">
      <input message="s1:ExampleDocLitSoapIn" />
      <output message="s1:ExampleDocLitSoapOut" />
    </operation>
```

```
    </portType>
    <binding name="ExampleSoap" type="s1:ExampleSoap">
      <soap:binding
          transport="http://schemas.xmlsoap.org/soap/http"
          style="document" />
      <operation name="ExampleDocLit">
        <soap:operation
          soapAction="http://tempuri.org/ExampleDocLit"
          style="document" />
        <input>
          <soap:body use="literal" />
        </input>
        <output>
          <soap:body use="literal" />
        </output>
      </operation>
    </binding>
    <service name="Example">
      <port name="ExampleSoap" binding="s1:ExampleSoap">
        <soap:address
          location=
          "http://VBWSServer/vbwsbook/Chapter4/Combos/Example.asmx"
        />
      </port>
    </service>
  </definitions>
```

The first thing you'll notice about Listing 4.3 is that each of the input and output messages contains only one `<part>`. When you are using document style messages, the message content can be anything that you define. This is because document style means you are sending and receiving documents with no implication of methods and method parameters. In this example, .NET defines two elements in the `<types>` section as shown by: `ExampleDocLit` and `ExampleDocLitResponse`, both of which belong to the schema `targetNamespace`, which is `http://tempuri.org/`. The first element, `ExampleDocLit`, represents the input to the method and contains three elements named a, b, and c. Element b is of type `ArrayOfFloat`, which is defined further down in the schema as having a sequence of elements called `<float>` with type `xsd:float`. Similarly, the element c is of type `theStruct`, which is also defined in the schema as having a sequence of three elements: `theName`, `theNumber`, and `theDate`.

Essentially, when you use document/literal, .NET defines an element with the same name as the method. This element contains an element for each parameter of your method with the same name as the parameter. .NET also defines an element that acts as a wrapper around parameters, for example, Example-DocList. This element contains an element for each parameter and .NET defines an XSD complex type for each parameter that has a non-primitive type such as arrays, structs, and classes.

These are the rules that .NET uses for defining the schema used with document/literal operations. But there isn't *one* correct way of defining this schema; you can define any schema you like as long as it meets your needs. For example, I can eliminate the `ExampleDocLit` element from the type definitions and rewrite the input message directly to contain the three elements `a`, `b`, and `c`:

```
<message name="ExampleDocLitSoapIn">
    <part name="one" element="s1:a" />
    <part name="two" element="s1:b" />
    <part name="three" element="s1:c" />
</message>
```

Note that I also used the names `one`, `two`, and `three` for the message parts. When using document (as opposed to RPC), there are no restrictions on the part names because we aren't thinking in terms of method parameters; we are just passing XML documents.

Going back to Listing 4.3, you'll see `ExampleDocLitResponse` element declared with a complex type that contains one element called `Example-DocLitResult`. The interesting thing about this `ExampleDocLitResult` element is that it has no `type` attribute. According to the XML Schema Part 1 recommendation, an element with a missing type attribute has the default type `anyType`. You might remember from Chapter 2 that `anyType` is at the root of the XSD type system: All XSD types derive (directly or indirectly) from `anyType`. This makes `anyType` the equivalent of the `System.Object` type in the .NET type system, which is why the return value's type is `anyType`.

Also in Listing 4.3, you'll see that the `style` attribute of the `<soap:bind-ing>` element indicates that the default SOAP message style is document. The `<soap:operation>` also has a `style` attribute, which in this case is set to document. If the `style` attributes of `<soap:binding>` and `<soap:opera-tion>` have conflicting values, the `<soap:operation>`'s `style` is the one you should pay attention to because the `<soap:binding>`'s style is meaningful only if the `<soap:operation>` does not have a `style` attribute. The `soapAction` attribute of `<soap:operation>` tells you the value of the `SOA-PAction` HTTP header to use when invoking this particular operation.

Next, the `use` attribute of `<soap:body>` is set to `literal` for both `<in-put>` and `<output>` messages. This tells you that the contents of the SOAP `<Body>` in the request and response messages are fully described using the schema declaration for the elements `ExampleDocLit` and `ExampleDocLit-Response`. That is, there are no additional rules that you have to be aware of to format the request and response messages; all the information you need is in the schema that's in the `<types>` section. Contrast this to encoded messages, which require that you know the rules of encoding used, (for example, SOAP Section 5 encoding rules).

The `<service>` element contains one port that points to the binding I just discussed. The `<port>` also contains a `<soap:address>` with the location attribute telling you where the service is located, (that is, where to send your SOAP request message to invoke this service).

When you use document/literal style all you really need is a schema describing the input and output message content, the value of the `SOAPAction`, and the end point (service) URL. Therefore the WSDL for document/literal style is very simple with the `<types>` section containing most of the information.

Listing 4.4   The `<types>` section for the document/literal combination. This section was extracted from the WSDL document in Listing 4.3.

```
<types>
  <s:schema attributeFormDefault="qualified"
            elementFormDefault="qualified"
            targetNamespace="http://tempuri.org/">
    <s:element name="ExampleDocLit">
      <s:complexType>
```

```
        <s:sequence>
          <s:element minOccurs="1" maxOccurs="1" name="a"
                type="s:int" />
          <s:element minOccurs="1" maxOccurs="1" name="b"
                nillable="true"
                type="s1:ArrayOfFloat" />
          <s:element minOccurs="1" maxOccurs="1" name="c"
                type="s1:theStruct" />
        </s:sequence>
      </s:complexType>
    </s:element>
    <s:complexType name="ArrayOfFloat">
      <s:sequence>
        <s:element minOccurs="0" maxOccurs="unbounded"
                  name="float"
              type="s:float" />
      </s:sequence>
    </s:complexType>
    <s:complexType name="theStruct">
      <s:sequence>
        <s:element minOccurs="1" maxOccurs="1" name="theName"
                nillable="true"
                type="s:string" />
        <s:element minOccurs="1" maxOccurs="1" name="theNumber"
                type="s:double" />
        <s:element minOccurs="1" maxOccurs="1" name="theDate"
                type="s:dateTime" />
      </s:sequence>
    </s:complexType>
    <s:element name="ExampleDocLitResponse">
      <s:complexType>
        <s:sequence>
          <s:element minOccurs="1" maxOccurs="1"
                name="ExampleDocLitResult"
                nillable="true" />
        </s:sequence>
      </s:complexType>
    </s:element>
  </s:schema>
</types>
```

4.4.2 RPC/Encoded

Looking at the `ExampleRpcEnc` method in Listing 4.2, you'll notice the `SoapRpcMethod()` attribute that tells .NET that this method is accessible using RPC/Section 5 encoded SOAP messages.

Listing 4.5 shows the interesting parts of the generated WSDL. Again, I have removed the `<types>` section and put it in Listing 4.6 to keep you focused on the big picture.

Listing 4.5 WSDL document for the RPC/encoded combination. Note that the `<types>` section has been removed to make the document easier to read (VBWSBook\Chapter4\ExampleWSDLs\RpcEncExample.wsdl).

```
<definitions xmlns:s="http://www.w3.org/2001/XMLSchema"
xmlns:soap="http://schemas.xmlsoap.org/wsdl/soap/"
xmlns:soapenc="http://schemas.xmlsoap.org/soap/encoding/"
xmlns:s0="http://tempuri.org/encodedTypes"
targetNamespace="http://tempuri.org/"
xmlns="http://schemas.xmlsoap.org/wsdl/">
  <!-- <types> section removed from here -->
  <message name="ExampleRpcEncSoapIn">
    <part name="a" type="s:int"/>
    <part name="b" type="s0:ArrayOfFloat"/>
    <part name="c" type="s0:theStruct"/>
  </message>
  <message name="ExampleRpcEncSoapOut">
    <part name="ExampleRpcEncResult" type="s:anyType"/>
  </message>
  <portType name="ExampleSoap">
    <operation name="ExampleRpcEnc">
      <input message="s1:ExampleRpcEncSoapIn"/>
      <output message="s1:ExampleRpcEncSoapOut"/>
    </operation>
  </portType>
  <binding name="ExampleSoap" type="s1:ExampleSoap">
    <soap:binding
       transport="http://schemas.xmlsoap.org/soap/http"
        style="document"/>
    <operation name="ExampleRpcEnc">
      <soap:operation
             soapAction="http://tempuri.org/ExampleRpcEnc"
              style="rpc"/>
```

```
    <input>
      <soap:body use="encoded" namespace="http://tempuri.org/"
            encodingStyle=
                "http://schemas.xmlsoap.org/soap/encoding/"/>
    </input>
    <output>
      <soap:body use="encoded" namespace="http://tempuri.org/"
            encodingStyle=
                "http://schemas.xmlsoap.org/soap/encoding/"/>
    </output>
  </operation>
  </binding>
  <service name="Example">
    <port name="ExampleSoap" binding="s1:ExampleSoap">
      <soap:address
        location=
        "http://vbwsserver/vbwsbook/Chapter4/Combos/Example.asmx"
        />
    </port>
  </service>
</definitions>
```

The first difference you'll notice between RPC/encoded and document/literal is that the input message, `ExampleRpcEncSoapIn`, has three parts corresponding to the three in parameters `a`, `b`, and `c`.[3] Each `<part>` has a `type` attribute that identifies the parameter type. This is another difference compared to document/literal where each `<part>` has an `element` attribute instead of `type`.

Looking at the part types, you'll notice that the array of `Singles` is represented as an XSD complex type called `ArrayOfFloat` and `theStruct` structure is represented by another complex type called `theStruct`. Both types are defined in the `<types>` section shown in Listing 4.6.

The complex type `ArrayOfFloat` is defined as derived from the base type `soapenc:Array`. This is inline with the SOAP Section 5 rule discussed in Chapter 3: An array must derive from the base type `soapenc:Array`. In addition to being derived from `soapenc:Array`, `ArrayOfFloat` also adds the `soap-`

---

[3]To be specific, this is a difference between RPC and document; that is, encoded and literal have nothing to do with how many `<part>`s there are within the `<message>`.

enc:arrayType attribute which, as discussed in Chapter 3, is used within the SOAP message to indicate the type and number of items in the array.

theStruct complex type consists of a sequence of three elements each corresponding to the three members of theStruct structure as defined in Listing 4.2.

The output message, Example1SoapOut, has one part that corresponds to the method's return value and has the XSD type anyType which, as explained above, corresponds to the .NET System.Object type.

The <soap:binding> element has its style attribute set to document indicating that document is the default style for the service's operations. The <soap:operation> element, however, overrides this default because it has its style attribute set to rpc.

When reading WSDL documents, first look at the style attribute of the <soap:operation> to determine an operation's style. If that attribute is missing, then look at the style attribute of the <soap:binding>, which acts as the default style.

For both the <input> and <output> messages, the <soap:body> element has its use attribute set to encoded and the encodingStyle attribute set to http://schemas.xmlsoap.org/soap/encoding/, which together indicate the use of Section 5 encoding for the contents of the SOAP <Body> element.

The <service> element and its contents are exactly the same as in the document/literal case.

Listing 4.6 The `<types>` section for the RPC/encoded combination. This section was extracted from the WSDL document in Listing 4.5.

```
<types>
    <s:schema targetNamespace="http://tempuri.org/encodedTypes">
        <s:complexType name="ArrayOfFloat">
            <s:complexContent mixed="false">
                <s:restriction base="soapenc:Array">
                    <s:attribute n1:arrayType="s:float[]"
                     ref="soapenc:arrayType"
                    xmlns:n1="http://schemas.xmlsoap.org/wsdl/"/>
```

```
      </s:restriction>
    </s:complexContent>
  </s:complexType>
  <s:complexType name="theStruct">
    <s:sequence>
      <s:element minOccurs="1" maxOccurs="1"
            name="theName" type="s:string"/>
      <s:element minOccurs="1" maxOccurs="1"
            name="theNumber" type="s:double"/>
      <s:element minOccurs="1" maxOccurs="1"
            name="theDate" type="s:dateTime"/>
    </s:sequence>
  </s:complexType>
  </s:schema>
</types>
```

4.4.3 SOAP Header

SOAP headers provide an easy way to extend SOAP and are an important part of
the architecture of any Web service. Therefore, WSDL provides facilities for describing SOAP headers so that clients can understand what headers each operation expects or sends back. Listing 4.7 shows an example SOAP message with
a header called `MyHeader` that contains two elements: `<Item1>` and
`<Item2>`.

Listing 4.7 An example SOAP message with a header

```
<soap:Envelope ...>
  <soap:Header>
    <MyHeader xmlns="http://tempuri.org/">
      <Item1>A value</Item1>
      <Item2>2090.201</Item2>
    </MyHeader>
  </soap:Header>
  <soap:Body>
      ...
  </soap:Body>
</soap:Envelope>
```

Headers are defined using the `<soap:header>` element that is part of the
WSDL SOAP binding as shown in Listing 4.8. Again, to make things easier to
read, I pulled out the `<types>` section and put it in Listing 4.9.

Listing 4.8 WSDL document showing an example header definition (VBWSBook\Chapter4\ExampleWSDLs\Headers.wsdl)

```
<definitions ...>
<!-- types section has been omitted -->

  <!-- The input and output messages have been omitted -->
  <message name="ExampleHeaderDocMyHeader">
    <part name="MyHeader" element="s1:MyHeader" />
  </message>
  <portType name="ExampleSoap">
    <operation name="ExampleHeaderDoc">
      <input message="s1:ExampleHeaderDocSoapIn" />
      <output message="s1:ExampleHeaderDocSoapOut" />
    </operation>
  </portType>
  <binding name="ExampleSoap" type="s1:ExampleSoap">
    <soap:binding
            transport="http://schemas.xmlsoap.org/soap/http"
            style="document" />
    <operation name="ExampleHeaderDoc">
      <soap:operation
          soapAction="http://tempuri.org/ExampleHeaderDoc"
          style="document" />
      <input>
        <soap:body use="literal" />
        <soap:header n1:required="true"
            message="s1:ExampleHeaderDocMyHeader"
            part="MyHeader"
            use="literal"
            xmlns:n1="http://schemas.xmlsoap.org/wsdl/" />
      </input>
      <output>
        <soap:body use="literal" />
      </output>
    </operation>
  </binding>
  ...
</definitions>
```

In this particular example, the `<soap:header>` element indicates that the header is required and that the header contents are defined by the part called

`MyHeader` (defined in the message called `ExampleHeaderDocMyHeader`). Also, the use attribute of `<soap:header>` is set to `literal` to indicate that the header should be serialized according to the schema provided. The message called `ExampleHeaderDocMyHeader` is defined in Listing 4.8 as having one part called `MyHeader`, which points to the element called `MyHeader`. The `MyHeader` element is declared in the `<types>` section in Listing 4.9.

Listing 4.9   The `<types>` section extracted from the WSDL for the operations using headers (VBWSBook\Chapter4\ExampleWSDLs\Headers.wsdl)

```
<types>
   <s:schema targetNamespace="http://tempuri.org/encodedTypes">

   </s:schema>
   <s:schema attributeFormDefault="qualified"
             elementFormDefault="qualified"
             targetNamespace="http://tempuri.org/">

<!-- element declarations for input
and output message parts have been omitted -->

      <s:element name="MyHeader" type="s1:MyHeader" />
      <s:complexType name="MyHeader">
        <s:sequence>
          <s:element minOccurs="1" maxOccurs="1"
                     name="Item1" nillable="true"
                     type="s:string" />
          <s:element minOccurs="1" maxOccurs="1"
                     name="Item2" type="s:double" />
        </s:sequence>
      </s:complexType>
   </s:schema>
</types>
```

`MyHeader` element declaration has a complex type that contains two elements: `Item1` and `Item2`, exactly as the header example in Listing 4.7 shows. Therefore by looking at this WSDL document, a client can understand that the operation called `ExampleHeaderDoc` expects to receive a required header that looks like the one in Listing 4.7.

4.4.4 SOAP Fault

SOAP lets you communicate error information using the SOAP `<Fault>` element. Within the `<Fault>` element, the `<detail>` element may contain application-specific information about the error. So you could have a `<Fault>` like the one in Listing 4.10.

Listing 4.10 An example `<Fault>` element with application-specific information in the `<detail>` element

```
<soap:Fault>
  <faultcode>soap:Server</faultcode>
  <faultstring>Errors occurred while processing the message
                  </faultstring>
  <detail>
    <validationErrors xmlns="http://tempuri.org/">
    <field>
      <name>CompanyName</name>
      <error>Is not unique</error>
    </field>
    <field>
      <name>CurrencyCode</name>
      <error>Must be USD</error>
    </field>
    </validationErrors>
  </detail>
</soap:Fault>
```

Since your Web service clients rely on WSDL to understand the format of the request and response messages, your WSDL document should describe the fault details returned by your Web service. Listing 4.11 shows the WSDL for the document/literal example from earlier in this chapter with fault information added.

Listing 4.11 The document/literal example with fault information added (VBWSBook\Chapter4\ExampleWSDLs\DocLitExamplewithFault.wsdl)

```
<definitions ...>
  <types>
    <s:schema
    attributeFormDefault="qualified"
    elementFormDefault="qualified"
    targetNamespace="http://tempuri.org/">
      <s:element name="validationErrors">
```

```
        <s:complexType>
          <s:sequence>
            <s:element minOccurs="1"
                   maxOccurs="unbounded"
                   name="field" type="s1:FieldType"/>
          </s:sequence>
        </s:complexType>
      </s:element>
      <s:complexType name="FieldType">
        <s:sequence>
          <s:element minOccurs="1"
                   maxOccurs="1"
                   name="name" type="s:string"/>
          <s:element minOccurs="1"
                   maxOccurs="1"
                   name="error" type="s:string"/>
        </s:sequence>
      </s:complexType>
    </s:schema>
</types>
...
<message name="FaultMsg">
  <part name="validationErrors"
         element="s1:ValidationErrors"/>
</message>
<portType name="ExampleSoap">
  <operation name="ExampleDocLit">
    <input message="s1:ExampleDocLitSoapIn"/>
    <output message="s1:ExampleDocLitSoapOut"/>
    <fault name="ExampleFault" message="s1:FaultMsg"/>
  </operation>
</portType>

<binding name="ExampleSoap" type="s1:ExampleSoap">
  ...
  <operation name="ExampleDocLit">
    <soap:operation
         soapAction="http://tempuri.org/ExampleDocLit"
         style="document"/>
    <input>
      <soap:body use="literal"/>
    </input>
    <output>
      <soap:body use="literal"/>
```

```
      </output>
      <fault>
        <soap:fault name="s1:ExampleFault" use="literal"/>
      </fault>
    </operation>
  </binding>
  ...
</definitions>
```

You'll notice a message called `FaultMsg` in Listing 4.11 that has one `<part>` called `validationErrors`, which points to the `validationErrors` element declared in the schema within the `<types>` section. If you examine the element declaration for `validationErrors`, you'll see it describes the `<validationErrors>` element in Listing 4.10. Now that you have the `FaultMsg` defined, you need to define a `<fault>` for the particular operation that returns this error information. The `ExampleDocLit` operation contains `<input>` and `<output>` elements and a `<fault>` element called `ExampleFault`. This `<fault>` element's `message` attribute points back to the `FaultMsg` message.

Now for the binding part: The corresponding `<operation>` element inside the `<binding>` also has a `<fault>` element. Within this `<fault>` element, you'll see a `<soap:fault>` element that defines how the error information should be serialized. In this example, the error information is serialized using `literal` style.

4.5 Using WSDL Documents

In this section I will show you how to read a Web service's WSDL document and create the SOAP request message to invoke the Web service. I will do this using three different Web services, two of which are live on the Web.

To simplify things, we will make the SOAP request messages using simple string concatenation and use MSXML.XMLHTTP to send the message using HTTP POST. You should never use string concatenation to form a SOAP request in a real production application. There are many problems with this approach, including how easy it is to end up with XML that's neither valid nor well-formed. This approach, however, works well for learning examples as it keeps the code very simple and lets you focus on the SOAP message you're creating—not on how you're creating it.

4.5.1 Product Checker

The first Web service I'll discuss takes in a product id and returns the product information from the Northwind database. The Web service itself is included with the book's code (VBWSBook\Chapter4\ProductChecker) so you can run it on your own machine. I won't tell you what language the Web service is written in because, from a client perspective, it doesn't matter. As someone who wants to invoke the Web service, all you need is a WSDL document for the service. Listing 4.12 shows the WSDL for the `ProductChecker` Web service with its one operation: `CheckProducts`.

Listing 4.12   WSDL for ProductChecker

```
<definitions xmlns:s="http://www.w3.org/2001/XMLSchema"
xmlns:soap="http://schemas.xmlsoap.org/wsdl/soap/"
xmlns:s0="http://tempuri.org/"
targetNamespace="http://tempuri.org/"
xmlns="http://schemas.xmlsoap.org/wsdl/">
  <types>
    <s:schema
        attributeFormDefault="qualified"
        elementFormDefault="qualified"
        targetNamespace="http://tempuri.org/">
    <s:element name="CheckProducts">
      <s:complexType>
        <s:sequence>
          <s:element minOccurs="1"  maxOccurs="1"
                    name="productId" type="s:int" />
        </s:sequence>
      </s:complexType>
    </s:element>
    <s:element name="CheckProductsResponse">
      <s:complexType>
        <s:sequence>
          <s:element minOccurs="1" maxOccurs="1"
                    name="CheckProductsResult"
                    type="s0:ProductInfo" />
        </s:sequence>
```

```xml
          </s:complexType>
        </s:element>
        <s:complexType name="ProductInfo">
          <s:sequence>
            <s:element minOccurs="1" maxOccurs="1"
                       name="ProductID" type="s:int" />
            <s:element minOccurs="1"
                       maxOccurs="1"
                       name="ProductName"
                  nillable="true" type="s:string" />
            <s:element minOccurs="1" maxOccurs="1"
                       name="UnitPrice" type="s:decimal" />
            <s:element minOccurs="1" maxOccurs="1"
                       name="UnitsInStock" type="s:short" />
            <s:element minOccurs="1" maxOccurs="1"
                       name="UnitsOnOrder" type="s:short" />
          </s:sequence>
        </s:complexType>
      </s:schema>
    </types>
    <message name="CheckProductsSoapIn">
      <part name="parameters" element="s0:CheckProducts" />
    </message>
    <message name="CheckProductsSoapOut">
      <part name="parameters"
            element="s0:CheckProductsResponse" />
    </message>
    <portType name="ProductCheckerSoap">
      <operation name="CheckProducts">
        <input message="s0:CheckProductsSoapIn" />
        <output message="s0:CheckProductsSoapOut" />
      </operation>
    </portType>
    <binding name="ProductCheckerSoap"
            type="s0:ProductCheckerSoap">
      <soap:binding
        transport="http://schemas.xmlsoap.org/soap/http"
        style="document" />
      <operation name="CheckProducts">
        <soap:operation
          soapAction="http://tempuri.org/CheckProducts"
          style="document" />
        <input>
          <soap:body use="literal" />
```

```
      </input>
      <output>
        <soap:body use="literal" />
      </output>
    </operation>
  </binding>
  <service name="ProductChecker">
    <port name="ProductCheckerSoap"
          binding="s0:ProductCheckerSoap">
      <soap:address
       location=
"http://vbwsserver/vbwsbook/Chapter4/ProductChecker/
➥ProductChecker.asmx" />
    </port>
  </service>
</definitions>
```

Listing 4.13 shows the client code that invokes the `CheckProducts` operation. This code is written in VB 6 and requires MSXML 4.0.

Listing 4.13 Creating the SOAP message to invoke the ProductChecker service (VBWSClientCode\Chapter4\ReadingWSDL\Form1.frm)

```
Private Sub cmdProductInfo_Click()
Dim msg As String
msg = "<soap:Envelope "
msg = msg & _
   "xmlns:xsi='http://www.w3.org/2001/XMLSchema-instance' "
msg = msg & _
   "xmlns:xsd='http://www.w3.org/2001/XMLSchema' "
msg = msg & _
   "xmlns:soap='http://schemas.xmlsoap.org/soap/envelope/'>"
msg = msg & "<soap:Body>"
msg = msg & "<CheckProducts xmlns='http://tempuri.org/'>"
msg = msg & "<productId>20</productId>"
msg = msg & "</CheckProducts>"
msg = msg & "</soap:Body>"
msg = msg & "</soap:Envelope>"

Dim http As New MSXML2.XMLHTTP40
Dim ServiceURL As String
ServiceURL = _
"http://vbwsserver/vbwsbook/Chapter4/ProductChecker/
➥ProductChecker.asmx"
```

```
http.open "POST", ServiceURL, False
http.setRequestHeader "SOAPAction", _
   """http://tempuri.org/CheckProducts"""
http.setRequestHeader "Content-Type", "text/xml"
http.send msg
MsgBox (http.responseText)
End Sub
```

Looking at the top of Listing 4.12, you'll see that the `<definitions>` element contains namespace declarations for the 2001 XML Schema recommendation. This tells you that the Web service supports this latest version of XSD. So you begin to build your SOAP request message by writing the SOAP `<Envelope>` element with the appropriate namespace declarations for the xsd, xsi, and soap prefixes. Inside the `<Envelope>` element, you write the SOAP `<Body>` element that will contain the message payload. Going back to Listing 4.12, you'll see that the `CheckProducts` operation has an input message called `CheckProductsSoapIn`. This message is defined in the WSDL as having one part that is the element `CheckProducts`. In the `<types>` section in Listing 4.12, the `<CheckProducts>` element is declared as containing one element called `<productId>` that is of type `xsd:int`. You also notice that the `targetName-space` for the schema is `http://tempuri.org/`. You ask yourself the question: Do I need to use SOAP Section 5 encoding for this message? To answer the question you look for the `<binding>` section in Listing 4.12. You find that the `<input>` and `<output>` messages for the `CheckProducts` operation contain a `<soap:body>` element with its use attribute set to literal, meaning that you do not need to use any special encoding for the contents of the SOAP `<Body>`. You just need to follow the schema. You also find that the `CheckProducts` operation uses document style SOAP as defined by the `<soap:operation>` element.

Armed with this information, you continue to construct the SOAP message by adding the `<CheckProducts>` element directly inside the `<Body>` element (because of document style). Then you add a default namespace declaration using the schema's `targetNamespace`. Inside `<CheckProducts>` you add one element called `<productId>` that contains an `xsd:int`, for example, 20.

Now you have the SOAP message and you're ready to send it using HTTP POST. You get the service URL from the `<port>` element's location attribute and you use that with the `Open` method of an MSXML2.XMLHTTP40 object. You also get the `SOAPAction` value from the `<soap:operation>` element and use `setRequestHeader` with that value within double quotes. Finally, you set the `Content-Type` header to `text/xml` to describe the HTTP payload type. Now you're ready to send the message by calling the `Send` method and passing it the SOAP message string. To get the response, you use the `responseText` property that returns whatever the service sent back.

To understand what the `CheckProducts` operation will return, you go back to Listing 4.12 and look for the operation's `<output>` message that is called `CheckProductsSoapOut`. This message has one part that references the element `CheckProductsResponse`. This element is declared as containing one child element called `CheckProductsResult`, which is of type `ProductInfo`. The `ProductInfo` type contains a `ProductID`, `ProductName`, `UnitPrice`, `UnitsInStock`, and `UnitsOnOrder`.

Figure 4.6 shows the actual SOAP message we get back from the service. The `<Body>` element contains a `CheckProductsResponse` element with all the right content exactly as declared in the schema.

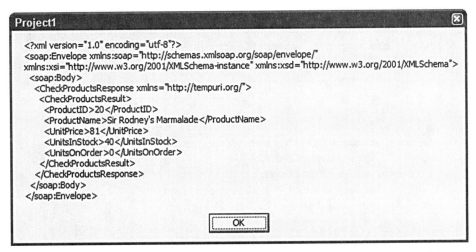

Figure 4.6 The result of invoking CheckProducts with a product id of 20

4.5.2 The Weather Service

The weather service is a live Web service running on www.LearnXmlws.com for educational purposes only. It has two methods: `GetTemperature` and `GetWeather`. Both methods take in a string parameter containing a zip code. `GetTemperature` returns the current temperature at this zip code and `GetWeather` returns more detailed information including humidity and barometric pressure. I'm only going to show you how to invoke `GetWeather`, so I simplified the WSDL by deleting everything that has to do with `GetTemperature`. The service's modified WSDL document is in Listing 4.14.

Listing 4.14   WSDL for the weather retriever service (VBWSClientCode\Chapter4\ProductCheckerClient\ LearnXmlwsWeather.wsdl)

```
<?xml version="1.0" encoding="utf-8"?>
<definitions xmlns:s="http://www.w3.org/2001/XMLSchema"
xmlns:soap="http://schemas.xmlsoap.org/wsdl/soap/"
xmlns:soapenc="http://schemas.xmlsoap.org/soap/encoding/"
xmlns:s0="http://tempuri.org/encodedTypes"
xmlns:s1="http://tempuri.org/"
targetNamespace="http://tempuri.org/"
xmlns="http://schemas.xmlsoap.org/wsdl/">
  <types>
    <s:schema targetNamespace="http://tempuri.org/encodedTypes">
      <s:complexType name="CurrentWeather">
        <s:sequence>
          <s:element minOccurs="1"
          maxOccurs="1" name="LastUpdated"
           type="s:string" />
          <s:element minOccurs="1"
            maxOccurs="1" name="IconUrl"
            type="s:string" />
          <s:element minOccurs="1"
            maxOccurs="1" name="Conditions"
            type="s:string" />
          <s:element minOccurs="1"
            maxOccurs="1" name="CurrentTemp"
            type="s:float" />
          <s:element minOccurs="1"
            maxOccurs="1" name="Humidity"
            type="s:float" />
          <s:element minOccurs="1"
```

```
            maxOccurs="1" name="Barometer"
            type="s:float" />
          <s:element minOccurs="1"
            maxOccurs="1" name="BarometerDirection"
            type="s:string" />
        </s:sequence>
      </s:complexType>
    </s:schema>
  </types>
<message name="GetWeatherSoapIn">
  <part name="zipCode" type="s:string" />
</message>
<message name="GetWeatherSoapOut">
  <part name="GetWeatherResult" type="s0:CurrentWeather" />
</message>
<portType name="WeatherRetrieverSoap">
  <operation name="GetWeather">
    <input message="s1:GetWeatherSoapIn" />
    <output message="s1:GetWeatherSoapOut" />
  </operation>
</portType>
<binding name="WeatherRetrieverSoap"
      type="s1:WeatherRetrieverSoap">
  <soap:binding
    transport="http://schemas.xmlsoap.org/soap/http"
    style="rpc" />
  <operation name="GetWeather">
    <soap:operation
    soapAction="http://tempuri.org/GetWeather"
    style="rpc" />
    <input>
      <soap:body use="encoded"
      namespace="http://tempuri.org/"
     encodingStyle="http://schemas.xmlsoap.org/soap/encoding/"
        />
    </input>
    <output>
      <soap:body use="encoded" namespace="http://tempuri.org/"
     encodingStyle="http://schemas.xmlsoap.org/soap/encoding/"
        />
    </output>
  </operation>
</binding>
<service name="WeatherRetriever">
```

```
        <port name="WeatherRetrieverSoap"
            binding="s1:WeatherRetrieverSoap">
          <soap:address
          location=
"http://www.learnxmlws.com/services/WeatherRetriever.asmx"
            />
        </port>
      </service>
    </definitions>
```

In the `<binding>` section, the `<soap:operation>` element indicates that the `GetWeather` operation is using RPC style SOAP messages. Also, the `use` and `encodingStyle` attributes of the `<soap:body>` element indicate that the parameter and return value data are to be encoded according to SOAP Section 5 encoding rules. This service uses RPC/encoded SOAP messages while the `ProductChecker` service uses document/literal messages. Listing 4.15 shows the client code for invoking `GetWeather`.

Listing 4.15   Client code to invoke the weather retriever service (VBWSClientCode\Chapter4\ReadingWSDL\Form1.frm)

```
Private Sub cmdWeather_Click()
    Dim http As New MSXML2.XMLHTTP40
    Dim msg As String

    msg = "<soap:Envelope " & _
    "xmlns:xsi='http://www.w3.org/2001/XMLSchema-instance' " & _
    "xmlns:xsd='http://www.w3.org/2001/XMLSchema' " & _
    "xmlns:soap='http://schemas.xmlsoap.org/soap/envelope/'>"
    msg = msg & "<soap:Body>"
    msg = msg & _
        "<mns:GetWeather xmlns:mns='http://tempuri.org/'>"
    msg = msg & "<zipCode " & _
    " soap:encodingStyle=" & _
    "'http://schemas.xmlsoap.org/soap/encoding/'>" & _
    "20171</zipCode>"
    msg = msg & "</mns:GetWeather>"
    msg = msg & "</soap:Body>"
    msg = msg & "</soap:Envelope>"

    http.open "POST", _
    "http://www.learnXmlws.com/services/ _
    WeatherRetriever.asmx", False
```

```
        http.setRequestHeader "SOAPAction", _
        """http://tempuri.org/GetWeather"""
        http.setRequestHeader "Content-Type", "text/xml"
        http.send msg
        MsgBox (http.responseText)
    End Sub
```

The `<Envelope>` element has the usual namespace declarations for xsd, xsi, and soap. Within the `<Body>` element, there's one element named after the operation's name as it appears in the WSDL document (`GetWeather`). This element belongs to the namespace indicated by the namespace attribute of the `<soap:body>` element, that is, `http://tempuri.org/`. The operation uses RPC; therefore, each message part represents a method parameter with the same name as the parameter. These message parts appear as child elements of `<GetWeather>`. In this case, there's one `<part>` called `zipCode` which corresponds to the `zipCode` parameter. Note that when using RPC, the message part elements, for example, `<zipCode>`, do not belong to any namespace. The `soap:encodingStyle` attribute on `<zipCode>` indicates that this parameter is encoded according to SOAP Section 5 encoding, which is what the service expects as indicated by the `encodingStyle` attribute of `<soap:body>` in Listing 4.14.

The `SOAPAction` is set to `"http://tempuri.org/GetWeather"` as indicated by the `soapAction` attribute of `<soap:operation>`. Finally, the entire message is sent via HTTP POST to the service location as given by the `location` attribute of `<soap:address>`. Looking at the `GetWeather-SoapOut` message in Listing 4.14, you'll see that the response message contains one part of type `CurrentWeather`, which is a complex type that contains the elements `LastUpdated`, `IconUrl`, `Conditions`, `CurrentTemp`, `Humidity`, `Barometer` and `BarometerDirection`. Listing 4.16 shows the response message you get. The element `<GetWeatherResult>` represents the method's return value. The actual returned data is encoded, according to SOAP Section 5 encoding, in a structure of type `CurrentWeather` with `id="id1"`. `<GetWeatherResult>` references this structure using `href="#id1"`.

Listing 4.16   Response message from GetWeather

```
<soap:Envelope
xmlns:soap="http://schemas.xmlsoap.org/soap/envelope/"
xmlns:soapenc="http://schemas.xmlsoap.org/soap/encoding/"
xmlns:tns="http://tempuri.org/"
xmlns:types="http://tempuri.org/encodedTypes"
xmlns:xsi="http://www.w3.org/2001/XMLSchema-instance"
xmlns:xsd="http://www.w3.org/2001/XMLSchema">
  <soap:Body
   soap:encodingStyle=
   "http://schemas.xmlsoap.org/soap/encoding/">
   <tns:GetWeatherResponse>
     <GetWeatherResult href="#id1" />
   </tns:GetWeatherResponse>
   <types:CurrentWeather id="id1"
      xsi:type="types:CurrentWeather">
    <LastUpdated xsi:type="xsd:string">
    Jan 10, 2002 at 04:51 PM EST
   </LastUpdated>
    <IconUrl xsi:type="xsd:string">
    http://www.learnxmlws.com/services/images/weather.gif
   </IconUrl>
    <Conditions xsi:type="xsd:string">Cloudy</Conditions>
    <CurrentTemp xsi:type="xsd:float">53</CurrentTemp>
    <Humidity xsi:type="xsd:float">0.63</Humidity>
    <Barometer xsi:type="xsd:float">29.84</Barometer>
    <BarometerDirection
       xsi:type="xsd:string">rising</BarometerDirection>
   </types:CurrentWeather>
  </soap:Body>
</soap:Envelope>
```

4.5.3   Quote of the Day

The Quote of the Day Web service is also live on the Web at `http://www.lemurlabs.com:80/rpcrouter`. It's called the "Fortune" service but it really doesn't return fortunes, just quotes and word definitions. Although this Web service is written in Java and uses the Apache SOAP implementation, you'll be able to call it just like the first two Web services without any problems. Listing 4.17 shows the WSDL for this Web service.

Listing 4.17 WSDL for Quote of the Day service

```
<definitions name = "FortuneService"
targetNamespace =
"http://www.lemurlabs.com/projects/soap/fortune/
➥FortuneService.wsdl"
xmlns:tns=
"http://www.lemurlabs.com/projects/soap/fortune/
➥FortuneService.wsdl"
xmlns:xsd = "http://www.w3.org/1999/XMLSchema"
xmlns:soap = "http://schemas.xmlsoap.org/wsdl/soap/"
xmlns = "http://schemas.xmlsoap.org/wsdl/">
  <types>
    <schema
     targetNamespace =
       "http://www.lemurlabs.com/projects/soap¬
        /fortune/FortuneService.xsd"
       xmlns= "http://www.w3.org/1999/XMLSchema">
    </schema>
  </types>
  <message name = "getFortuneByDictionaryRequest">
    <part name = "dictionaryName" type="xsd:string"/>
  </message>
  <message name = "getFortuneByDictionaryResponse">
    <part name = "return" type="xsd:string"/>
  </message>
  <portType name = "FortunePortType">
    <operation name = "getFortuneByDictionary">
      <input message = "tns:getFortuneByDictionaryRequest"
             name="getFortuneByDictionary"/>
      <output message = "tns:getFortuneByDictionaryResponse"
             name="getFortuneByDictionaryResponse" />
    </operation>
  </portType>
  <binding name = "FortuneBinding" type = "tns:FortunePortType">
    <soap:binding style = "rpc"
                  transport =
                  "http://schemas.xmlsoap.org/soap/http"/>
    <operation name = "getFortuneByDictionary">
      <soap:operation/>
      <input>
        <soap:body use = "encoded"
                   namespace = "urn:lemurlabs-Fortune"
                   encodingStyle =
              "http://schemas.xmlsoap.org/soap/encoding/"/>
```

```
        </input>
        <output>
          <soap:body use = "encoded"
                     namespace = "urn:lemurlabs-Fortune"
                     encodingStyle =
              "http://schemas.xmlsoap.org/soap/encoding/"/>
        </output>
      </operation>
    </binding>
    <service name = "FortuneService">
      <port name = "FortunePort"
        binding = "tns:FortuneBinding">
        <soap:address
            location = "http://www.lemurlabs.com:80/rpcrouter"/>
      </port>
    </service>
  </definitions>
```

The first thing you'll notice is that the XML Schema namespace refers to the 1999 version of XSD, which is not the final version. This Web service is using an older version of XSD so we must be mindful of this when formatting the request message and parsing the response message. To invoke the operation called `getFortuneByDictionary`, you must look at the `<input>` message called `getFortuneByDictionaryRequest`. This message has one part called `dictionaryName` of type `xsd:string`. Looking at the `<binding>` section, you'll see that RPC is the default style for all operations as indicated by the `style` attribute of `<soap:binding>`. You can also see from `<soap:body>` that the operation's input and output messages are encoded according to Section 5 encoding rules. Therefore, this operation uses RPC/encoded style messages. Listing 4.18 shows the client code to invoke the getFortuneByDictionary operation.

Listing 4.18   Client code to invoke Quote of the Day service (VBWSClientCode\Chapter4\ReadingWSDL\Form1.frm)

```
Private Sub cmdFortune_Click()
    Dim http As New MSXML2.XMLHTTP
    'this example uses an older schema style
    Dim msg As String
    msg = "<soap:Envelope "
```

```
    msg = msg & _
        "xmlns:xsi='http://www.w3.org/1999/XMLSchema-instance' "
    msg = msg & _
        "xmlns:xsd='http://www.w3.org/1999/XMLSchema' "
    msg = msg & _
        "xmlns:soap='http://schemas.xmlsoap.org/soap/envelope/'>"
    msg = msg & "<soap:Body>"
    msg = msg & _
      "<mns:getFortuneByDictionary " & _
      "xmlns:mns='urn:lemurlabs-Fortune'>"
    msg = msg & "<dictionaryName "
    msg = msg & _
        "soap:encodingStyle=" & _
        "'http://schemas.xmlsoap.org/soap/encoding/' "
    msg = msg & _
        "xsi:type='xsd:string'>definitions</dictionaryName>"
    msg = msg & "</mns:getFortuneByDictionary>"
    msg = msg & "</soap:Body>"
    msg = msg & "</soap:Envelope>"

    http.open "POST", _
  "http://www.lemurlabs.com:80/rpcrouter", False
    http.setRequestHeader "SOAPAction", """"""
    http.setRequestHeader "Content-Type", "text/xml"
    http.send msg
    MsgBox (http.responseText)
  End Sub
```

The <soap:Envelope> contains the usual namespace declarations, but this time using the 1999 XML Schema namespaces. The <soap:Body> contains one element that is named after the operation's name, that is, <getFortuneByDictionary>. This element's namespace is urn:lemurlabs-Fortune, which is the value of the namespace attribute of the <soap:body> element in the WSDL in Listing 4.17. This element contains one element that corresponds to the method's only input parameter, that is, <dictionaryName>. Note that <dictionaryName> does not belong to any namespace as dictated by SOAP RPC style rules. In this example, I'm passing definitions as the value of the dictionaryName parameter. There are two important attributes on the <dictionaryName> element: encodingStyle and xsi:type. encodingStyle simply says that the contents of dictionaryName are encoded according to the SOAP Section 5 rules. The `xsi:type` attribute indicates the type of the element as explained in Chapter 2. While the SOAP specification does not require this to be present, some implementations do require it. For example, earlier versions of Apache SOAP needed this `xsi:type` information on the server side to know how to handle the data that's coming in. Other implementations, such as the Microsoft SOAP Toolkit rely on the WSDL document on the server side to determine the type of a particular parameter. If the server requires the `xsi:type` and you do not pass it, the call will fail and you will get back a message with a `<Fault>` indicating the error. I'll discuss these types of issues and many others in Chapter 12.

Looking at the `<soap:operation>` in Listing 4.17, you'll notice it has no `soapAction` attribute. This means you should use an empty value for the `SOAPAction` HTTP header, which according to the SOAP specification, is indicated by two double quotes ("").

Running the code in Listing 4.8 will invoke the Web service and display the response message in a message box that will contain a random word definition enclosed within a CDATA section. You'll get a different definition each time you invoke the operation. The particular response I got is shown in Figure 4.7 and offers an interesting view of quality control.

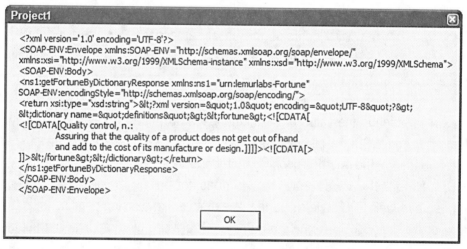

Figure 4.7   An example response from invoking the definitions Web service. This particular example offers an interesting definition for "quality control."

4.6 Other WSDL Features

4.6.1 Documenting Your WSDL

The WSDL documents you've seen so far contain lots of information on the operations, messages, and parameters exposed by a Web service. They do not, however, contain any information on what each operation actually does. For example, the quote of the day service had an operation called `getFortuneBy-Dictionary`, which had one input parameter called `dictionaryName`. How would a client know what values to pass in as the `dictionaryName`? And how would it know exactly what the method does, that is, how would it know that the method returns quotes and definitions?

To provide such information, you can add documentation to your WSDL using `<document>`, which may appear inside any WSDL element such as `<operation>` or `<message>`. The `<document>` element has mixed content, that is, it can contain any combination of elements and text. This is very useful because not only can you have documentation in the form of simple text, but you can also have HTML tags around parts of the documentation. You might even want to structure your documentation using XML, then apply an XSLT transformation to transform this XML documentation to HTML for the clients to read.

4.6.2 WSDL Imports

In many of the previous examples, I separated the `<types>` section into a separate listing to make the document easier to read. For readability and reusability of WSDL documents, you may want to do the same in a production environment. For example, if a team of developers is building several Web services, there might be a need to reuse some of the type definitions or other parts of the WSDL across those Web services. You can do this by separating out the various pieces that you want to reuse then using the WSDL `<import>` element to import those pieces back into the WSDL document. For example, you might create a document for type definitions that contains only the schema section. Or you might create another document for interface definitions that contains messages, portTypes, and bindings. Finally, a third document would contain the service and port elements as shown in Listings 4.19, 4.20, and 4.21.

**Listing 4.19   Separating type definitions
(VBWSBook\Chapter4\ExampleWSDLs\RPCEncTypes.xsd)**

```
<!-- This schema is in a file located at
http://VBWSServer/VBWSBook/Chapter4/ExampleWSDLs/RPCEncTypes.xsd
-->
<s:schema
xmlns:s="http://www.w3.org/2001/XMLSchema"
xmlns:soapenc="http://schemas.xmlsoap.org/soap/encoding/"
xmlns:s0="http://tempuri.org/encodedTypes"
xmlns:s1="http://tempuri.org/"
targetNamespace="http://tempuri.org/encodedTypes"
targetNamespace="http://tempuri.org/encodedTypes">
<s:complexType name="ArrayOfFloat">
  <s:complexContent mixed="false">
    <s:restriction base="soapenc:Array">
      <s:attribute n1:arrayType="s:float[]"
          ref="soapenc:arrayType"
          xmlns:n1="http://schemas.xmlsoap.org/wsdl/" />
    </s:restriction>
  </s:complexContent>
</s:complexType>
<s:complexType name="theStruct">
  <s:sequence>
    <s:element minOccurs="1" maxOccurs="1" name="theName"
            type="s:string" />
    <s:element minOccurs="1" maxOccurs="1" name="theNumber"
            type="s:double" />
    <s:element minOccurs="1" maxOccurs="1" name="theDate"
            type="s:dateTime" />
  </s:sequence>
</s:complexType>
</s:schema>
```

**Listing 4.20   Separating out interface elements (messages, portTypes and
bindings) using `<import>` to import `<types>`
(VBWSBook\Chapter4\ExampleWSDLs\RPCEncInterface.wsdl)**

```
<definitions xmlns:s="http://www.w3.org/2001/XMLSchema"
xmlns:soap="http://schemas.xmlsoap.org/wsdl/soap/"
xmlns:soapenc="http://schemas.xmlsoap.org/soap/encoding/"
xmlns:s0="http://tempuri.org/encodedTypes"
targetNamespace="http://tempuri.org/"
xmlns:s1="http://tempuri.org/"
xmlns="http://schemas.xmlsoap.org/wsdl/">
```

```
<import
    namespace="http://tempuri.org/encodedTypes" location=
    "http://vbwsserver/VBWSBook/Chapter4/ExampleWSDLs/
➡RpcEncTypes.xsd"/>
<types/>

<message name="ExampleRpcEncSoapIn">
  <part name="a" type="s:int"/>
  <part name="b" type="s0:ArrayOfFloat"/>
  <part name="c" type="s0:theStruct"/>
</message>
<message name="ExampleRpcEncSoapOut">
  <part name="ExampleRpcEncResult" type="s:anyType"/>
</message>
<portType name="ExampleSoap">
  <operation name="ExampleRpcEnc">
    <input message="s1:ExampleRpcEncSoapIn"/>
    <output message="s1:ExampleRpcEncSoapOut"/>
  </operation>
</portType>
<binding name="ExampleSoap" type="s1:ExampleSoap">
  <soap:binding
    transport="http://schemas.xmlsoap.org/soap/http"
     style="document"/>
  <operation name="ExampleRpcEnc">
    <soap:operation
        soapAction="http://tempuri.org/ExampleRpcEnc"
         style="rpc"/>
    <input>
      <soap:body use="encoded" namespace="http://tempuri.org/"
        encodingStyle=
            "http://schemas.xmlsoap.org/soap/encoding/"/>
    </input>
    <output>
      <soap:body use="encoded" namespace="http://tempuri.org/"
        encodingStyle=
            "http://schemas.xmlsoap.org/soap/encoding/"/>
    </output>
  </operation>
</binding>
</definitions>
```

Listing 4.21 Separate document for `<service>`. **The documents containing types and interface definitions are imported using** `<import>` **(VBWSBook\Chapter4\ExampleWSDLs\RPCEncService.wsdl).**

```
<?xml version="1.0" encoding="utf-8"?>
<definitions xmlns:s="http://www.w3.org/2001/XMLSchema"
xmlns:soap="http://schemas.xmlsoap.org/wsdl/soap/"
xmlns:soapenc="http://schemas.xmlsoap.org/soap/encoding/"
xmlns:s0="http://tempuri.org/encodedTypes"
targetNamespace="http://services.learnxmlws.com/"
xmlns:s1="http://tempuri.org/"
xmlns="http://schemas.xmlsoap.org/wsdl/">
<import
    namespace="http://tempuri.org/encodedTypes"
    location="http://vbwsserver/VBWSBook/Chapter4/¬
            ExampleWSDLs/RpcEncTypes.xsd"/>
  <import namespace="http://tempuri.org/" location=
      "http://vbwsserver/VBWSBook/Chapter4/¬
      ExampleWSDLs/RpcEncInterface.wsdl"/>
  <types/>
<service name="Example">
  <port name="ExampleSoap" binding="s1:ExampleSoap">
    <soap:address
        location=
    "http://VBWSServer/vbwsbook/Chapter4/Combos/Example.asmx"/>
    </port>
  </service>
</definitions>
```

In this example, the schema part lives in the document at http://vbwsserver/ VBWSBook/Chapter4/ExampleWSDLs/RpcEncTypes.xsd and has the target namespace http://tempuri.org/encodedTypes. The messages, (portTypesm, operations, and bindings), all live in the document at http://vbwsserver/VBWSBook/ Chapter4/ExampleWSDLs/RpcEncInterface.wsdl. The message parts refer to types defined in the schema document, for example, `ArrayOfFloat` and `theStruct`. Therefore, the RPCEncInterface.wsdl document imports the schema document using the WSDL `<import>` element. The namespace attribute of the `<import>` element indicates the target namespace of the imported document. In this case, the imported schema document has the target namespace `http://tempuri.org/encodedTypes`. The `<import>` location attribute simply points to the physical location of the document to be imported.

Similarly, Listing 4.21 shows the concrete aspects of the WSDL, that is, the `<service>` and `<port>` elements, with an `<import>` element pointing to the RPCEncInterface.wsdl document and its target namespace.

4.6.3 Extending WSDL

The WSDL specification defines only a handful of elements that can be used to describe a Web service. In many cases, you'll want to provide additional information to your clients or to client development tools. All the SOAP binding elements you've seen, such as `<soap:operation>` and `<soap:body>` are called WSDL extensibility elements—elements designed to extend parts of WSDL by providing more information specific to SOAP.

You can add your own extensibility elements to a WSDL document describing, for example, the guaranteed availability of the Web service or an average response time from a specific operation. To do this, you define some elements that belong to a namespace that you own (for example, `http://www.vbws.com/wsdl/extension/`) then include those elements within relevant parts of the WSDL document. Appendix A 3 of the WSDL 1.1 specification lists the places within a WSDL document where you can add your own extensibility elements.

Listing 4.22 shows an example of using an extensibility element called `ResponseTime` that I defined. This element tells the client the average and maximum response time in milliseconds of the `ExampleRpcEnc` operation.

Listing 4.22 Adding your own WSDL extensibility elements

```
<definitions xmlns:vbws="http://www.vbws.com/wsdl/extension/"
...>
<binding ...>
  <operation name="ExampleRpcEnc">
      <vbws:ResponseTime average="130" maximum="500"/>
      <soap:operation
            soapAction="http://tempuri.org/ExampleRpcEnc"
              style="rpc"/>
      <input>
```

```
            <soap:body use="encoded" namespace="http://tempuri.org/"
                encodingStyle=
                    "http://schemas.xmlsoap.org/soap/encoding/"/>
        </input>
        <output>
            <soap:body use="encoded" namespace="http://tempuri.org/"
                encodingStyle=
                    "http://schemas.xmlsoap.org/soap/encoding/"/>
        </output>
      </operation>
    </binding>
  </definitions>
```

Clients may use this response time to determine whether or not the service is fast enough for their needs. If it's not fast enough, the client might look for another service that can provide the same functionality with a faster, guaranteed response time.

4.6.4 WSDL Operations

The examples you've seen in this chapter have shown operations with input and output messages. The WSDL specification calls these request-response operations because the client sends a request and then the service sends back a response. WSDL defines four types of operations: one-way, request-response, solicit-response, and notification. These are abstract operations that say nothing about how they are physically implemented. For example, a request-response operation might be implemented as an HTTP request followed by an HTTP response or it might be implemented as an outgoing MSMQ message on Queue A followed by an incoming MSMQ message on Queue B. Here's a definition of each of these abstract operations and when each may be useful:

- **Request-response operation:** All examples in this chapter show request-response operations. A request-response operation contains two messages: An input message and an output message. A request-response operation may also contain any number of optional `<fault>` elements that describe error information returned by the operation. Today's Web services mostly use request-response operations, especially when using HTTP, because they correspond nicely to the HTTP request-response model.

- **One-way operation:** One-way operations contain only input messages. They represent operations that receive input but do not produce any response when invoked. This type of operation is most useful when using one-directional transports such as MSMQ or SMTP where the client just sends the message and does not expect a response.

- **Solicit-response operation:** A solicit-response operation looks like a reversed request-response operation. It contains an output and input message, in that order. It also contains any number of optional fault elements similar to the request-response operation. Solicit-response operations represent callbacks from the service to the client. This is equivalent to the notion of events that the service raises and the client handles. Using solicit-response operations, events can be defined as part of a Web service's interface. There's one important issue to be aware of here: When using HTTP, solicit-response messages require that the client be able to receive HTTP requests that come from the Web service. This is the reverse of typical HTTP traffic between a client and a service. Practically speaking, implementing solicit-response over HTTP requires some form of Web server running on the client machine. It also requires that the client machine be accessible from the Web service, which usually means the client needs to have a real IP address as opposed to a network translated address (using NAT).

- **Notification operation:** This is similar to a one-way operation, but going from the service to the client. A notification operation contains only an output message. You can think of notification operations as callbacks from the service to the client that do not produce a response message. Since the service is sending a message to the client, the client will need to be running an HTTP (Web) server to receive HTTP messages.

4.6.5 HTTP Binding

All the examples you've seen in this chapter used WSDL SOAP binding to describe how operations can be invoked using SOAP. The WSDL specification also defines a binding for invoking operations using HTTP GET or POST requests. While this is not something you'd want to do for new Web services, it is a good feature for exposing parts of an existing Web application as a Web service. For example, I created an ASP page called prodCheck.asp for retrieving product information similar to the Product Checker Web service. This page supports both

GET and POST so you could invoke it by simply navigating to it and including the product id in the query string like this:

```
http://vbwsserver/VBWSBook/Chapter4/HTTPService/Prod
➥Check.asp?pid=20
```

Alternatively, you can invoke it using an HTML form with `method="POST"`. I provided an example form for you called prodInfo.htm. Either way, the response is an XML document that contains product information:

```
<ProductInfo xmlns='http://tempuri.org/'>
  <ProductID>20</ProductID>
  <ProductName>Sir Rodney's Marmalade</ProductName>
  <UnitPrice>81</UnitPrice>
  <UnitsInStock>40</UnitsInStock>
  <UnitsOnOrder>0</UnitsOnOrder>
</ProductInfo>
```

You can easily turn this ASP page into a Web service by creating the appropriate WSDL document. Listing 4.23 shows the WSDL document I created for this Web service with HTTP GET and POST bindings.

Listing 4.23   A WSDL document for a Web service using HTTP GET

```
<definitions xmlns:xsd="http://www.w3.org/2001/XMLSchema"
xmlns:http="http://schemas.xmlsoap.org/wsdl/http/"
xmlns:tns="http://tempuri.org/"
targetNamespace="http://tempuri.org/"
xmlns="http://schemas.xmlsoap.org/wsdl/"
xmlns:mime="http://schemas.xmlsoap.org/wsdl/mime/">
  <types>
    <xsd:schema attributeFormDefault="qualified"
      elementFormDefault="qualified"
      targetNamespace="http://tempuri.org/">
    <xsd:element name="ProductInfo"
            type="tns:ProductInfoType"/>
    <xsd:complexType name="ProductInfoType">
      <xsd:sequence>
        <xsd:element minOccurs="1"
            maxOccurs="1" name="ProductID"
            type="xsd:int"/>
        <xsd:element minOccurs="1"
            maxOccurs="1" name="ProductName"
```

```
                 nillable="true" type="xsd:string"/>
        <xsd:element minOccurs="1"
               maxOccurs="1" name="UnitPrice"
               type="xsd:decimal"/>
        <xsd:element minOccurs="1"
               maxOccurs="1" name="UnitsInStock"
               type="xsd:short"/>
        <xsd:element minOccurs="1"
               maxOccurs="1" name="UnitsOnOrder"
               type="xsd:short"/>
      </xsd:sequence>
    </xsd:complexType>
  </xsd:schema>
</types>
<message name="ProdCheckIn">
  <part name="pid" type="xsd:string"/>
</message>
<message name="ProdCheckOut">
  <part name="ProdInfo" element="tns:ProductInfo"/>
</message>
<portType name="ProdCheckPortType">
  <operation name="ProdCheck">
    <input message="tns:ProdCheckIn"/>
    <output message="tns:ProdCheckOut"/>
  </operation>
</portType>
<binding name="ProdCheckGET"
         type="tns:ProdCheckPortType">
  <http:binding verb="GET"/>
  <operation name="ProdCheck">
    <http:operation location="/ProdCheck.asp"/>
    <input>
      <http:urlEncoded/>
    </input>
    <output>
      <mime:mimeXml part="ProdInfo"/>
    </output>
  </operation>
</binding>
<binding name="ProdCheckPOST" type="tns:ProdCheckPortType">
  <http:binding verb="POST"/>
  <operation name="ProdCheck">
    <http:operation location="/ProdCheck.asp"/>
    <input>
```

```
        <mime:content
            type="application/x-www-form-urlencoded"/>
      </input>
      <output>
        <mime:mimeXml part="ProdInfo"/>
      </output>
    </operation>
  </binding>
  <service name="ProductChecker">
    <port name="ProdCheckGETPort" binding="tns:ProdCheckGET">
      <http:address
      location="http://vbwsserver/vbwsbook/Chapter4/HTTPService"
      />
    </port>
    <port name="ProdCheckPOSTPort" binding="tns:ProdCheckPOST">
      <http:address
      location="http://vbwsserver/vbwsbook/Chapter4/HTTPService"/
      ➡>
    </port>
  </service>
</definitions>
```

This WSDL document is very similar to other examples you've seen throughout this chapter. The first interesting thing you might notice is the presence of two `<binding>` elements: one for HTTP GET and one for HTTP POST as indicated by the verb attribute of `<http:binding>`. The `ProdCheck` operation appears in each binding with the location attribute of `<http:operation>` set to `/ProdCheck.asp`. When using HTTP to invoke an operation, the client must append this location to the URL that's in the `<port>` element's location. In this case, the complete location becomes:

```
http://vbwsserver/vbwsbook/Chapter4/HTTPService/ProdCheck.asp.
```

For the HTTP GET binding, the `<http:urlEncoded>` element indicates that the input parameters are to be passed in the query string using name value pairs. In this example there's only one input parameter called pid; therefore, the operation's URL with the value 20 for `pid` would be:

```
http://vbwsserver/vbwsbook/Chapter4/HTTPService/
➡ProdCheck.asp?pid=20
```

which is exactly the URL you'd use to invoke the ASP page from a browser. Similarly, the HTTP POST binding indicates that the input is of MIME type `application/x-www-form-urlencoded`, which is the MIME type for data in an HTML FORM submitted via POST.

In both cases, GET and POST, the output is defined using `<mime:mimeXml>`, which indicates that the response contains an XML document that is not SOAP (that is, there's no SOAP Envelope). Looking at the output message called `Prod-CheckOut`, you'll see that it has one part that is the element `<ProductInfo>`. This element is declared in the schema near the top of Listing 4.23.

With this WSDL document, the ASP page becomes a legitimate Web service that can be invoked by a client that supports HTTP GET or POST. In fact, you could run wsdl.exe against this WSDL document, as you learned in Chapter 1, to produce a VB or C# proxy that invokes this Web service using HTTP GET or POST. The client never needs to know that this is an ASP page!

4.6.6 MIME Binding

The WSDL document in Listing 4.23 uses a `<mime:mimeXml>` element to indicate that the response message contains an XML document. `<mimeXml>` is part of the WSDL MIME binding namespace: `http://schemas.xmlsoap.org/wsdl/mime/`. Elements in this namespace are used to indicate the exact type of one or more message parts. For example, if your Web service returned a GIF image, you could use `<mime:content>` to indicate that:

```
<mime:content part="myPicture" type="image/gif"/>
```

Here, `myPicture` refers to the name of a message part declared earlier in the document. The value of the `type` attribute can be any MIME type. In addition to `<mime:content>` and `<mime:Xml>`, WSDL also defines the `<mime:multipartRelated>` element that lets you group together several related message parts into one message. This is useful if the individual message parts make sense only when processed together as one aggregate entity. For example, if your Web service operation returns a separate SOAP response and JPEG image that must be processed together by the client, then you could use `<mime:multipartRelated>` to group the two parts. Assuming the SOAP response part is called contract and the JPEG part is called signature, you would write:

```
<mime:multipartRelated>
    <mime:part>
        <soap:body parts="contract" use="literal"/>
    </mime:part>
    <mime:part>
        <mime:content part="signature" type="image/jpeg"/>
    </mime:part>
</mime:multipartRelated>
```

4.7 Summary

The Web Services Description Language is an XML grammar used formally to describe Web service interfaces and protocol bindings. Many tools today can generate WSDL documents for you based on your Web service methods. In this chapter, you learned how to read a WSDL document and form the SOAP request to invoke the Web service. This skill will prove useful as you build and invoke Web services, especially when you are interoperating with other platforms.

4.8 Resources

DevelopMentor's SOAP discussion list: http://discuss.develop.com/soap.html
WSDL discussion list: http://groups.yahoo.com/group/wsdl/.

E. Christensen, F. Curlbera, G. Meredith, S. Weerawarana, Web Services Description Language (WSDL) 1.1: http://www.w3.org/TR/wsdl, © 2001 Ariba, International Business Machines Corporation, Microsoft, W3C, March 15, 2001.

D. Box, D. Ehnebuske, G. Kakivaya, A. Layman, N. Mendelshon, H. Frystyk Nielson, S. Thatte, D. Winer, SOAP 1.1 W3C Note: http://www.w3.org/TR/SOAP/, © 2000 DevelopMentor, International Business Machines Corporation, Lotus Development Corporation, Microsoft, UserLand Software, W3C, May 8, 2000.

Editors: M. Gudgin, M. Hadley, J. Moreau, H. Frystyk Nielson, SOAP 1.2 W3C Working Draft: http://www.w3.org/TR/2001/WD-soap12-20010709/, W3C (MIT, INRIA, KEIO), July 9, 2001.

Chapter 5

The Microsoft SOAP Toolkit

He who controls the past commands the future. He who commands the
future conquers the past. —George Orwell

Most of the time you'll use development tools to help you expose and invoke
Web services. Chapter 5 focuses on the Microsoft SOAP Toolkit as one of these
tools. The toolkit is COM-based and can be used with any COM-capable programming language, including Visual Basic 6.0, VBScript, and Visual C++. This chapter explains the toolkit's components and architecture and shows you how to use
it to expose and invoke Web services.

5.1 Toolkit API Architecture

The SOAP toolkit is made up of two main parts that can be used together or in-
dependently. The first part is the client, which is made up of several COM components that allow you to invoke SOAP-based Web services. The second part is
the server components used to expose Web services, usually implemented as
COM components. A client application calls a Web service using the SOAP Toolkit's client API as shown in Figure 5.1. The toolkit's client reads the WSDL describing the Web service, creates the SOAP message, and sends an HTTP
request to the Web server. On the server, you can choose an ASP page or an
ISAPI extension, as the listener for incoming requests. The listener captures the
request and invokes the toolkit's SoapServer30 component that instantiates the
appropriate COM component and invokes the requested method. SoapServer30
relies on information in a .wsml file to determine the ProgID of the component to
instantiate and the DispID of the method to call. WSML is a toolkit-specific XML

file format used to provide additional information needed to invoke the Web service. After invoking the COM component's method, SoapServer30 takes the return value and any ByRef parameters and creates the response SOAP message. The Web server then sends the response message back to the client as the HTTP response.

The toolkit provides a high level API that encapsulates all the SOAP messaging and makes it almost trivial to expose and invoke Web services. For cases where you need more control, the toolkit exposes a low level API that allows you to control every aspect of SOAP messaging, (requiring extra coding). This high level of control sometimes comes in handy when trying to interoperate with Java-based and other Web services.

5.2 Exposing Web Services

From a business standpoint, there are great benefits to be gained by exposing existing COM-based server components as Web services. The most obvious benefit is easier integration with other platforms. As explained in Chapter 1, most business functions today span multiple supporting applications running on several

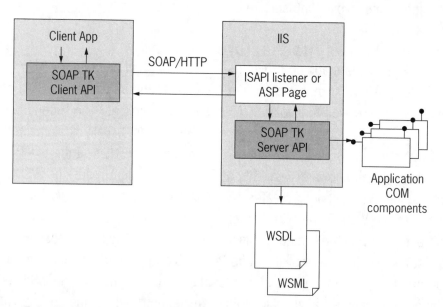

Figure 5.1   Data flow through the SOAP Toolkit

platforms. Integrating these applications can improve the overall business process by removing or reducing some of the seams and gaps in existing solutions.

Businesses can also benefit from exposing existing data to other applications rather than people. In the past six to seven years, there's been an explosion of intranet applications designed to make business information readily available to more workers. A typical Web application's architecture is based on a COM-based middle tier with an ASP-based front end. If this describes your applications, you've already done the hard part: You've created business logic and data access code in the form of COM components. To extend the reach of your application, you can expose these existing components (or some of them) as Web services for consumption by other applications. Doing this increases the usefulness of existing multi-tier applications and allows other systems to integrate nicely with yours (back to integration again).

Finally, a huge business benefit is the ease of deployment of client applications. Again, if you've built the server COM components, you've already taken care of the server side of things. Exposing these components as Web services makes it easier to deploy clients that require only HTTP access to the server. Simplifying deployment and network configuration translates into saved time, money, and frustration. So how do you expose existing COM components as Web services?

It's generally a bad idea to try to expose each COM component as a Web service and each interface method as a Web service operation. Instead, you should design a new layer on top of existing server-side (for example, MTS or COM+) components as in Figure 5.2. This Web Services Layer (WSL) is a new set of stateless COM components designed to expose the services that clients need in order to perform their business functions.

When designing the WSL, think in terms of business services and documents, not in terms of object models. For example, don't design an Order object with properties such as order number and amount, and methods such as Save, Update, and Delete. Instead, design an OrderMgmt Web service with PlaceOrder and DeleteOrder operations[1] that take in an Order XML document and return an

---

[1]If you are exposing transactional COM+ or MTS components, they are probably designed around stateless, service-oriented calls that make them easier to expose as Web services.

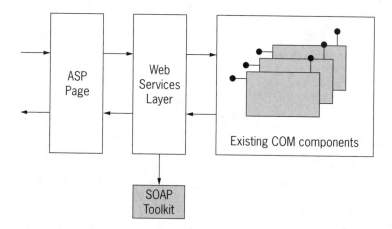

Figure 5.2 Creating a Web Services Layer to expose existing COM components

OrderReceipt document. Use XML Schemas to define each of your service documents. Each of the service operations, (for example, PlaceOrder), would aggregate several existing COM components to perform a specific and complete business function.

The WSL uses the SOAP Toolkit to handle incoming SOAP requests and to send outgoing responses. You use either the high level API or the low level API to do this. I usually recommend using the low level API because it is a consistent API that gives you lots of control over the transmitted messages. However, there are many cases where the high level API might be sufficient, especially if you are building quick prototypes. First, I will explain the use of the high level API for exposing and invoking Web services, then I'll show you how the low level API works.

5.3 Using the High Level API

5.3.1 Exposing Web Services
Now that you understand when and why to expose COM components and Web services, let's examine how it's done. This section covers the mechanics used to expose COM components with the SOAP Toolkit's high level API.

To expose a COM component, you need a WSDL document that describes the Web service operations as explained in Chapter 4. When using the high level API, you also need a WSML document that maps services to COM components and service operations to interface methods. Instead of creating these documents manually, you use the WSDL Generator that comes with the toolkit.[2] This wizard reads a COM component's type library and lets you choose which methods you want to expose. Then it generates the necessary documents based on information in the type library.

Consider the simple component in Listing 5.1, with one method called GetStore-Sales that returns a sales figure given a store id. Let's walk through the steps of exposing it as a Web service.

Listing 5.1   A GetStoreSales method to be exposed as a Web service operation (VBWSBook\Chapter5\HLServer\Stores.cls)

```
Option Explicit
Private Const UID As String = "admin"
Private Const PWD As String = "admin"
Public Function GetStoreSales(ByVal user As String, _
          ByVal password As String, _
          ByVal StoreId As String) As Double
    If user = UID And password = PWD Then
        Select Case StoreId
            Case "6380"
                GetStoreSales = 120490.87
            Case "7066"
                GetStoreSales = 190100.04
            Case "7896"
                GetStoreSales = 115900.56
        End Select
    Else
        GetStoreSales = 0
    End If
End Function
```

When you launch the wizard, it asks you if you want to use an existing configuration file. When you use the wizard you can save your selections and input to a configuration file and then use this file as a starting point the next time. Since

---

[2]The WSDL Generator works on Windows NT 4, Windows 2000, and Windows XP.

this is the first time you have run the wizard, you won't use an existing configuration file. On the next screen you enter a Web service name and the COM component's path as in Figure 5.3. On the next screen, you pick from a list of components and methods available in the selected .dll.

When you click next, the screen asks you to specify SOAP listener information. You decide on the type of listener: ASP or ISAPI. Generally, an ISAPI listener is slightly faster than an ASP listener. However, you can learn more from examining the code within an ASP listener, so go ahead and select ASP listener for this example. Later in this chapter, I will explain how the ISAPI listener works and how to use it.

You must also specify the listener's URL. Here's a tip to ensure that you enter the right URL: First, create a folder on your hard drive where you want the listener and other service files to reside, (for example, D:\VBWSBook\HLServer\).

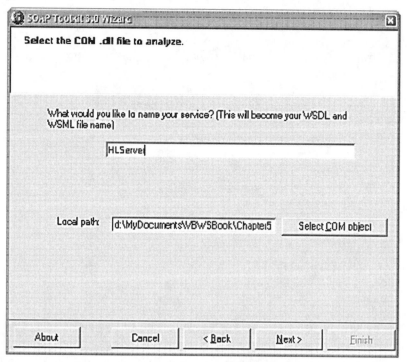

Figure 5.3 Specifying service name and selecting a .dll

Then open the IIS administration console and create a new virtual directory called HLServer that maps to the folder you created (be sure to enable directory browsing). To ensure you configured things correctly, open Internet Explorer and enter the URL to this new virtual directory, (for example, http://VBWSServer/HLServer). If everything is right, you will see a directory listing of the folder you created, which at this point is empty.

Now copy the URL from IE's address bar and paste it in the wizard's URI field as shown in Figure 5.4. When you click next, you see the screen in Figure 5.5 asking you to specify four URIs. The first URI is the WSDL target namespace (see Chapter 4). The second one is the schema target namespace (see Chapter 2). The third one is the SOAP operation namespace (see Chapter 3). Finally, the last URI is the value of the SOAPAction HTTP header (see Chapter 3).

If you're building a new Web service (as opposed to implementing a pre-defined Web service interface), the URI values are defined by you. Just be

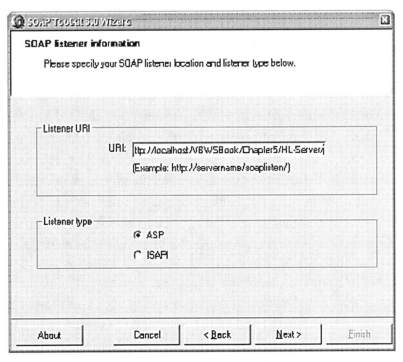

Figure 5.4   Specifying the listener type and URL

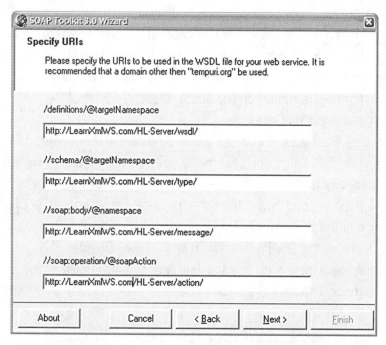

Figure 5.5 Specifying URIs used in the service's WSDL

consistent in what you choose and try to use your organization's Internet domain name if possible.

The next screen (Figure 5.6) asks you to pick the character set to be used for SOAP messages. For maximum interoperability, you should pick UTF-8 unless you know you'll need to use characters from the UTF-16 character set. You also must enter two paths. The first is where the generated WSDL, WSML, and ASP files will be saved. This must be the same folder you created and configured as a virtual directory (for example D:\VBWSBook\HLServer\). The second path is where the WSDL Generator's configuration file will be saved. You can choose any folder to store the configuration file. It doesn't have to be Web-accessible.

When you click next, the wizard generates the three files and saves them to the specified folder. Listing 5.2 shows an example of a generated WSDL document.

REAL WORLD XML WEB SERVICES

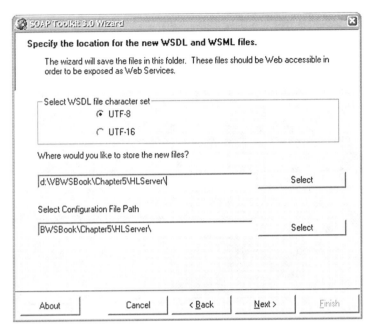

Figure 5.6 Specifying location to store configuration and output files. Output file location must correspond to the service URL specified earlier.

Listing 5.2 A WSDL document generated by the wizard (VBWSBook\Chapter5\HLServer\HLServer.WSDL)

```xml
<?xml version="1.0" encoding="UTF-8"?>
<definitions
 name="HLServer"
 targetNamespace="http://LearnXmlWS.com/HLServer/wsdl/"
 xmlns:wsdlns="http://LearnXmlWS.com/HLServer/wsdl/"
 xmlns:typens="http://LearnXmlWS.com/HLServer/type/"
 xmlns:soap="http://schemas.xmlsoap.org/wsdl/soap/"
 xmlns:xsd="http://www.w3.org/2001/XMLSchema"
 xmlns:stk=
"http://schemas.microsoft.com/soap-toolkit/wsdl-extension"
 xmlns="http://schemas.xmlsoap.org/wsdl/">
  <types>
    <schema
      targetNamespace="http://LearnXmlWS.com/HLServer/type/"
      xmlns="http://www.w3.org/2001/XMLSchema"
      xmlns:SOAP-ENC="http://schemas.xmlsoap.org/soap/encoding/"
      xmlns:wsdl="http://schemas.xmlsoap.org/wsdl/"
```

```
                elementFormDefault="qualified"/>
    </types>
    <message name="Stores.GetStoreSales">
      <part name="user" type="xsd:string"/>
      <part name="password" type="xsd:string"/>
      <part name="StoreId" type="xsd:string"/>
    </message>
    <message name="Stores.GetStoreSalesResponse">
      <part name="Result" type="xsd:double"/>
    </message>
    <portType name="StoresSoapPort">
      <operation
                name="GetStoreSales"
                parameterOrder="user password StoreId">
        <input message="wsdlns:Stores.GetStoreSales"/>
        <output message="wsdlns:Stores.GetStoreSalesResponse"/>
      </operation>
    </portType>
    <binding name="StoresSoapBinding" type="wsdlns:StoresSoapPort">
      <stk:binding preferredEncoding="UTF-8"/>
      <soap:binding
            style="rpc"
            transport="http://schemas.xmlsoap.org/soap/http"/>
      <operation name="GetStoreSales">
        <soap:operation
        soapAction=
        "http://LearnXmlWS.com/HLServer/action/
➥Stores.GetStoreSales"/>
        <input>
          <soap:body use="encoded"
        namespace="http://LearnXmlWS.com/HLServer/message/"
        encodingStyle="http://schemas.xmlsoap.org/soap/encoding/"
        parts="user password StoreId"/>
        </input>
        <output>
          <soap:body use="encoded"
        namespace="http://LearnXmlWS.com/HLServer/message/"
        encodingStyle="http://schemas.xmlsoap.org/soap/encoding/"
        parts="Result"/>
        </output>
      </operation>
    </binding>
    <service name="HLServer">
      <port name="StoresSoapPort"
```

```
        binding="wsdlns:StoresSoapBinding">
      <soap:address
        location=
"http://VBWSServer/VBWSBook/Chapter5/HLServer/HLServer.ASP"/>
    </port>
  </service>
</definitions>
```

The generated WSDL contains no type definitions because the only method we exposed uses simple types (for example, strings and double). There are two messages in this WSDL: Stores.GetStoreSales and Stores.GetStoreSalesResponse. There's also one operation named GetStoreSales and one SOAP binding named StoresSoapBinding. This SOAP binding uses RPC/encoded messages as indicated by the style and use attributes in Listing 5.2. The service end point URL is specified in the `<soap:address>` location attribute. This URL points to the generated ASP page because you chose to use an ASP listener.

Listing 5.3 shows the WSML document generated for the example HLServer.

Listing 5.3   A WSML document generated by the wizard (VBWSBook\Chapter5\HLServer.WSML)

```
<?xml version="1.0" encoding="UTF-8"?>
<servicemapping name="HLServer">
  <service name="HLServer">
    <using PROGID="HLServer.Stores" cachable="0"
    ID="StoresObject"/>
    <port name="StoresSoapPort">
      <operation name="GetStoreSales">
        <execute uses="StoresObject"
                method="GetStoreSales" dispID="1610809344">
          <parameter callIndex="-1"
                  name="retval" elementName="Result"/>
          <parameter callIndex="1"
                  name="user" elementName="user"/>
          <parameter callIndex="2"
                  name="password" elementName="password"/>
          <parameter callIndex="3"
                  name="StoreId" elementName="StoreId"/>
        </execute>
      </operation>
```

```
      </port>
    </service>
  </servicemapping>
```

A WSDML document provides the necessary information to map a SOAP request message to the corresponding component and method. The one in Listing 5.3 provides a mapping for the HLServer service as indicated by the `<service>` name attribute. The specific COM component exposing this service is identified by the `<using>` element's PROGID attribute. Each Web service operation defined in the WSDL document has a corresponding `<operation>` element in the WSML document that specifies the method name, dispID, and parameters. Note that you must regenerate the WSML document if you change the dispID of one or more methods, (for example, by reordering methods on your VB classes).

Listing 5.4 shows the generated ASP page that acts as the Web service listener.

Listing 5.4   An ASP listener generated by the wizard (VBWSBook\Chapter5\HLServer\HLServer.asp)

```
<%@ LANGUAGE=VBScript %>
<%
Option Explicit
On Error Resume Next
Response.ContentType = "text/xml"
Dim SoapServer
If Not Application("HLServerInitialized") Then
  Application.Lock
  If Not Application("HLServerInitialized") Then
    Dim WSDLFilePath
    Dim WSMLFilePath
    WSDLFilePath = Server.MapPath("HLServer.wsdl")
    WSMLFilePath = Server.MapPath("HLServer.wsml")
    Set SoapServer = Server.CreateObject("MSSOAP.SoapServer30")
    If Err Then SendFault "Cannot create SoapServer object. " & _
        Err.Description
    SoapServer.Init WSDLFilePath, WSMLFilePath
    If Err Then SendFault "SoapServer.Init failed. " & _
           Err.Description
    Set Application("HLServerServer") = SoapServer
    Application("HLServerInitialized") = True
  End If
```

```
      Application.UnLock
End If
Set SoapServer = Application("HLServerServer")
SoapServer.SoapInvoke Request, Response, ""
If Err Then SendFault "SoapServer.SoapInvoke failed. " & _
        Err.Description


Sub SendFault(ByVal LogMessage)
  Dim Serializer
  On Error Resume Next
  ' "URI Query" logging must be enabled for AppendToLog to work
  Response.AppendToLog " SOAP ERROR: " & LogMessage
  Set Serializer = Server.CreateObject("MSSOAP.SoapSerializer30")
  If Err Then
    Response.AppendToLog _
                "Could not create SoapSerializer30 object. " & _
                Err.Description
    Response.Status = "500 Internal Server Error"
  Else
    Serializer.Init Response
    If Err Then
      Response.AppendToLog "SoapSerializer.Init failed. " & _
              Err.Description
      Response.Status = "500 Internal Server Error"
    Else
      Response.Status = "500 Internal Server Error"
      Serializer.startEnvelope
      Serializer.startBody
      Serializer.startFault "Server", _
          "The request could not be processed due to a " & _
          "problem in the server. Please contact the " & _
          "system admistrator. " & LogMessage
      Serializer.endFault
      Serializer.endBody
      Serializer.endEnvelope
      If Err Then
        Response.AppendToLog "SoapSerializer failed. " & _
            Err.Description
        Response.Status = "500 Internal Server Error"
      End If
    End If
  End If
  Response.End
End Sub
%>
```

Most of the code in Listing 5.4 handles initialization and errors; the code that does the real work is a few lines only. The page sets the response type to text/xml as required by SOAP messages. Then it reads a flag called HLServerInitialized out of the ASP Application object. This flag is used to determine if there's a cached version of the SoapServer30 object that can be used to process this request. The first time you call the service this flag will be false, so the code will lock the Application and then obtain the WSDL and WSML file paths by using Server.MapPath. Note that the assumption is that both files reside in the same folder as this ASP page. If that's not the case you must change the parameter to Server.MapPath or set WSDLFilePath and WSMLFilePath to the right file paths directly.

The next line creates a SoapServer30 object that will process this and future incoming requests. If an error occurs, a SOAP Fault is returned to the client. The procedure called SendFault in Listing 5.4 handles the details of constructing the SOAP Fault using a SoapSerializer30 object (more on this later), then calls Response.End to end execution. If the SoapServer object was created successfully, the page calls Init, passing it the WSDL and WSML file paths. It adds the initialized SoapServer to the ASP Application object as an item called HLServerServer (name of your service with the word Server appended) and sets the HLServerInitialized flag to true and unlocks the Application. Subsequent calls to this service will be processed by the same instance of SoapServer30.

If you make changes to the service and regenerate the WSDL and WSML files, you need to stop and restart the IIS application. Otherwise, clients will continue to use the cached instance of SoapServer30 that was initialized with the older WSDL and WSML documents.

Now the real work happens: The page calls SoapServer30.SoapInvoke, passing it the ASP Request and Response objects. The third parameter to SoapInvoke is an optional default value for the SOAPAction header. Since the incoming request should have a SOAPAction header, SoapServer30 can read it directly from the ASP Request object so no default value is needed.

Calling SoapServer.SoapInvoke does all the real work. It reads the incoming SOAP message, finds out which COM component and method are requested, deserializes incoming data into the right types, invokes the desired method, serializes the return value, and sends the response SOAP message. Figure 5.7 shows a *pseudo* sequence diagram of the interaction between the client, ASP listener, SoapServer30, and your server COM component.

You can modify the ASP listener page to suit your needs. For example, you can ask it to send an email if a certain type of error occurs while processing a request. If you modify this page, be careful not to replace it if you rerun the WSDL generator.

5.3.2 Invoking Web Services

When you use the high level API to invoke a Web service, your client application primarily uses a `SoapClient30` object as shown in Figure 5.8. You might also create a class that implements `IHeaderHandler` to send and/or receive SOAP headers from the Web service.

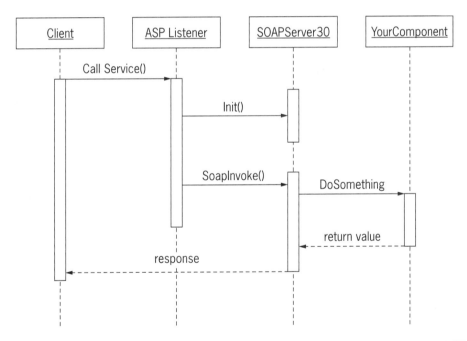

Figure 5.7 A pseudo sequence diagram showing interaction between an ASP listener, an instance of SoapServer30, and the service's COM component

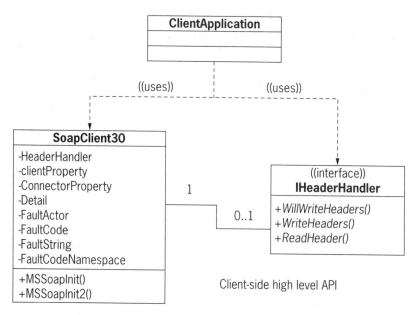

Figure 5.8 The client-side high level API

To invoke a Web service, first you instantiate a `SoapClient30` object and call its `MSSoapinit` method, passing it the URL to the service's WSDL document as shown in Listing 5.1.

Listing 5.5   Using the high level API to invoke a Web service (VBWSClientCode\HLClient\frmClient.frm)

```
Private Sub cmdSales_Click()
    On Error GoTo eh
    Dim soap As MSSOAPLib30.SoapClient30
    Set soap = New MSSOAPLib30.SoapClient30
    'For completeness, we specify the
    'service name (HLServer) and
    'the port name (StoresSoapPort)
    'but they are optional when
    'the WSDL doc contains
    'one service with one SOAP port
    soap.MSSoapInit WSDL_URL, "HLServer", "StoresSoapPort"

    'the following 3 lines use a proxy
    'For example you can use ProxyTrace
    'for troubleshooting
```

```
    If chkProxy.Value Then
        soap.ConnectorProperty("ProxyServer") = "localhost"
        soap.ConnectorProperty("ProxyPort") = "8080"
        soap.ConnectorProperty("UseProxy") = True
    End If

    Dim Sales As Double
    'this is the Web service call
    Sales = soap.GetStoreSales(UID, PWD, cboStoreId.Text)
    lblSales.Caption = "Sales for this store are: $" & CStr(Sales)
    Exit Sub
eh:
    Dim msg As String
    msg = Err.Description & "Fault Code: " & soap.FaultCode
    msg = msg & vbCrLf & "Fault String: " & soap.FaultString
    msg = msg & vbCrLf & "Fault Detail: " & soap.Detail
    MsgBox msg, vbCritical, "Error calling service"

End Sub
```

After calling `MSSoapinit`, you call the Web service operation as if it were a method on `SoapClient30` object. The example in Listing 5.1 calls an operation named `GetStoreSales` that takes in a user id, a password, and the store id and then returns the monthly sales for that store. Note that `SoapClient30` doesn't actually have a `GetStoreSales` method, so you will not get this method in intellisense, nor will the compiler catch errors such as passing the wrong number of arguments or arguments of the wrong type.

SoapClient30 exposes a ConnectorProperty that lets you set various HTTP-related properties. For example, Listing 5.5 shows an example of using ConnectorProperty to configure a proxy server. The SOAP Toolkit will automatically use the same HTTP proxy settings that you have configured in Internet Explorer's connection settings. Therefore, you don't need to set ProxyServer and Proxy-Port explicitly, unless you don't want to use the same settings as IE. You do need to set UseProxy to True.

5.3.3 Error Handling

When an error occurs you can use SoapClient30 properties to get information from the SOAP Fault element. SoapClient30 exposes Fault information in five properties: FaultActor, FaultCode, FaultCodeNamespace, FaultString, and Detail. Listing 5.5 shows how you can read some of this information in an error handler and present it to the user.

5.3.4 Troubleshooting with the Trace Utility

When things go wrong and you want to troubleshoot your client and/or service, I recommend that you begin by viewing request/response messages to determine if everything is being sent as you expected. The SOAP Toolkit comes with a handy Trace Utility that can capture and display HTTP requests as shown in Figure 5.9.

The Trace Utility runs on the same machine as the client and listens on the port that you configure, (for example, port 8080). Instead of sending requests directly to the service, the client sends all requests to the Trace Utility on the local host. Upon receiving a request, the Trace Utility forwards it to the service, which can be on any host (not necessarily the localhost). The service sends back an HTTP response and the Trace Utility forwards the response to the client.

To display captured messages, you can choose a formatted trace that displays formatted XML using Internet Explorer's default stylesheet as in Figure 5.10; or you can choose an unformatted trace that displays message content in hex as shown in Figure 5.11.

The trick is to get the client to send messages to the Trace Utility rather than to the service. By default, the client sends requests to the URL specified in the

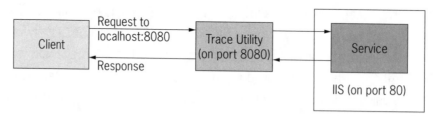

Figure 5.9 Using the Trace Utility to capture and display SOAP messages

REAL WORLD XML WEB SERVICES

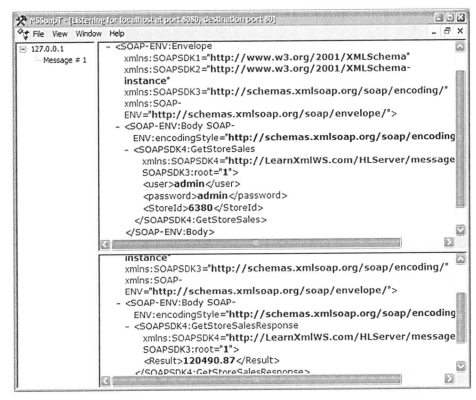

Figure 5.10 A formatted trace captured with the toolkit's Trace Utility

WSDL port element. To override this URL, you can use the EndPointURL connector property to specify the Trace Utility's URL. For example:

```
soap.ConnectorProperty("EndPointURL") = _
  "http://localhost:8080/VBWSBook/Chapter5/HLServer/HLServer.asp"
```

You want to do this after you call MSSoapInit but before you begin calling Web service operations.

5.3.5 Using High Level API from Classic ASP

To invoke Web services from a classic ASP page, you use the SoapClient30 object much like a VB client would. There's only one extra step you need to be

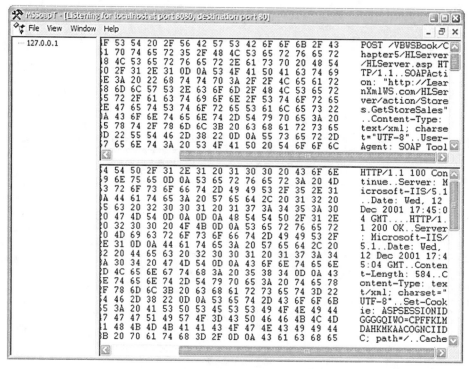

Figure 5.11 **An unformatted trace displayed request and response messages in hex**

aware of: If you use HTTP to load the WSDL file, you must set the Server-HTTPRequest client property to True. Listing 5.6 shows an example ASP page that calls a Web service using the high level API.

Listing 5.6 **An example ASP page invoking a Web service with the SOAP toolkit (VBWSBook\Chapter5\weather.asp)**

```
<%

    Dim zipCode
    zipCode=Request.QueryString("zip")
    Dim soap
    Set soap = Server.CreateObject("MSSOAP.SoapClient30")
    soap.ClientProperty("ServerHTTPRequest")=True
    soap.MSSoapInit _
        "http://www.learnxmlws.com/services/
➥weatherRetriever.asmx?wsdl"
```

```
      Dim temperature
      temperature=soap.GetTemperature(zipCode)
%>
<html>
<body>
<p>The temperature at <% =zipCode %> is <b><% =temperature %></b>
degrees</p>
</body>
</html>
```

There are two interesting things in Listing 5.6. First, notice that you create the client using Server.CreateObject with the ProgID MSSOAP.SoapClient30. Also, notice the line:

```
soap.ClientProperty("ServerHTTPRequest")=True
```

This line is required because the WSDL document is loaded using HTTP as indicated by the URL used with MSSoapInit. Note that when you set ServerHTTPRequest to True, you must use ProxyCfg, the WinHTTP Proxy Configuration tool, to configure proxy settings even if you are *not* using a proxy. You can download this tool from http://msdn.microsoft.com/msdn-files/027/001/468/Proxycfg.exe.

5.4 Serialization in the High Level API

The high level API abstracts your application from the underlying SOAP messages. It can also abstract your application from dealing with XML by automatically serializing application data to XML and deserializing XML into application data on the other end. The example in Listing 5.5 uses simple types only (for example, strings and doubles), which are easier to serialize than complex types. The SOAP toolkit also supports complex type serialization with built-in type mappers and the ability to create your own custom type mappers.

You can skip complex type serialization altogether by passing/returning XML nodes instead of objects to/from Web service operations. Even with the high level API, the SOAP toolkit lets you do this by passing or returning an IXML-DOMNodeList, which is a list of DOM nodes. This approach has many benefits and I recommend using it whenever you can. I'll explain the details and benefits of using this approach later in this section. First, I'll give you a quick overview of other options for serializing complex types.

5.4.1 Generic Type Mapper

The generic type mapper handles serialization to/from application objects. It serializes object properties to XML elements and deserializes XML elements back into object properties. Consider a server COM component with the GetStore-Sales method shown in Listing 5.7.

Listing 5.7   A GetSoreSales method that returns a Store object (VBWSBook\Chapter5\ComplexTypeServer\Stores.cls)

```
Public Function GetStoreSales(ByVal user As String, _
        ByVal password As String, _
        ByVal StoreId As String) As Store
    If user = UID And password = PWD Then
        Dim objStore As Store
        Set objStore = New Store
        Select Case StoreId
            Case "6380"
                objStore.Sales = 120490.87
            Case "7066"
                objStore.Sales = 190100.04
            Case "7896"
                objStore.Sales = 115900.56
        End Select
    Else
        objStore.Sales = 0
    End If
    Set GetStoreSales = objStore
End Function
```

This simple method instantiates a new Store object using the Store class shown in Listing 5.8. It then sets properties of this object and returns it to the caller.

Listing 5.8   The Store class
(VBWSBook\Chapter5\ComplexTypeServer\Store.cls)

```
'store class
Private mvarStoreId As String 'local copy
Private mvarSales As Double 'local copy
Private mvarIncome As Double 'local copy
Public Property Let Income(ByVal vData As Double)
    mvarIncome = vData
End Property
Public Property Get Income() As Double
    Income = mvarIncome
End Property
Public Property Let Sales(ByVal vData As Double)
    mvarSales = vData
    Me.Income = vData * 0.7
End Property
Public Property Get Sales() As Double
    Sales = mvarSales
End Property
Public Property Let StoreId(ByVal vData As String)
    mvarStoreId = vData
End Property
Public Property Get StoreId() As String
    StoreId = mvarStoreId
End Property
```

There's nothing earth-shattering about the Store class; it's a simple class with a few properties. The Sales property Let procedure also sets the income property to 70 percent of sales (pretty healthy income). When you run the WSDL Generator Wizard to expose this server component, the generated WSDL will include a complex type definition corresponding to the Stores class. The complex type is named after the COM interface name, (that is, `store` as shown in Listing 5.9).

There are two limitations to be aware of when using the generic type mapper. First, it always maps object properties to XML elements and vice versa. Therefore, there must be a one-to-one correspondence between elements in the SOAP message and properties on your application objects—XML attributes are not supported. Second, the generic type mapper does not support object structures with loops. For example, if you have an object graph where object A references object B, object B references object C, which in turn references object A, the generic mapper wouldn't know how to handle this. By tracing the object references, the generic mapper would get into an infinite loop while trying to serialize such a structure.

Listing 5.9   The WSDL types section defining a `_Store` **type (VBWSBook\Chapter5\ComplexTypeServer\ComplexTypeServer.wsdl)**

```
<types>
  <schema
   targetNamespace=
   "http://LearnXmlWS.com/ComplexTypeServer/type/"
   xmlns="http://www.w3.org/2001/XMLSchema"
   xmlns:SOAP-ENC="http://schemas.xmlsoap.org/soap/encoding/"
   xmlns:wsdl="http://schemas.xmlsoap.org/wsdl/"
   elementFormDefault="qualified">
    <complexType name="_Store">
      <sequence>
        <element name="Income" type="double"/>
        <element name="Sales" type="double"/>
        <element name="StoreId" type="string"/>
      </sequence>
    </complexType>
  </schema>
</types>
```

The wizard does a good job of mapping object properties to their corresponding XSD types as shown in Listing 5.9. It also creates two WSML files: one for server use and one for client use. Both files contain identical `<types>` sections that define how to handle the `_Store` complexType as shown in Listing 5.10.

Listing 5.10   Both server and client WSML files contain identical `<types>` **sections (VBWSBook\Chapter5\ComplexTypeServer\ ComplexTypeServer.wsml)**

```
<types>
  <type
    name='_Store'
    targetNamespace=
    'http://LearnXmlWS.com/ComplexTypeServer/type/'
    uses='GCTM'
    targetClassId='{CB1C1344-96A8-4C67-8AEF-383941143E0F}'
    iid='{D92E1F9B-7AEA-4ECD-AED2-5A2E2245ECAC}'/>
</types>
```

The type information in Listing 5.10 specifies the COM CLSID and IID for the COM class that should be used to handle the `complexType _Store`. These ids are the same in the client and server WSML, which means you must have the same COM class (Store) registered on the server and client machines. If the Store class you use on the client is different from the one you use on the server, you can edit the client's WSML file and manually enter the appropriate CLSID and IID. Make sure, however, that the Store class you use on the client has the same properties names and data types as those on the server.

This is one of the reasons why I recommend that you skip built-in serialization/deserialization and simply use XML: You don't need to deploy the Store class to the client. In my experience, deployment is usually a source of headaches in COM-based client applications. Anything you can do to minimize the number of components deployed will ultimately save you time and money.

Assuming you use the generic type mapper, a client can invoke GetStore-Sales and get the output as an instance of Store. As mentioned previously, the Store component must be deployed and registered on client machines (put it in a separate DLL, not the same DLL as the server component). The client project will have to add a reference to the Store component in order to compile. Listing 5.11 shows an example client calling GetStoreSales and retrieving the output as an instance of Store.

Listing 5.11   A client calling GetStoreSales to retrieve a Store object (VBWSClientCode\Chapter5\ComplexTypeClient\frmClient.frm)

```
Private Sub cmdSales_Click()
    On Error GoTo eh
    Dim soap As MSSOAPLib30.SoapClient30
    Set soap = New MSSOAPLib30.SoapClient30

    soap.MSSoapInit WSDL_URL, , , WSML_URL

    'the following 3 lines use a proxy
    'For example you can use ProxyTrace
    'for troubleshooting
    'replace VBWSServer with the name of your proxy server
    If chkProxy.Value Then
        soap.ConnectorProperty("ProxyServer") = "localhost"
        soap.ConnectorProperty("ProxyPort") = "8080"
```

```
        soap.ConnectorProperty("UseProxy") = True
    End If

    Dim objStore As Store
    'this is the Web service call
    Set objStore = soap.GetStoreSales(UID, PWD, cboStoreId.Text)
    lblSales.Caption = "Sales for this store are: $" & _
                    CStr(objStore.Sales)
    lblSales.Caption = lblSales.Caption & vbCrLf & _
                    "Income is: $" & CStr(objStore.Income)

    Exit Sub
eh:
    Dim msg As String
    msg = Err.Description & "Fault Code: " & soap.FaultCode
    msg = msg & vbCrLf & "Fault String: " & soap.FaultString
    msg = msg & vbCrLf & "Fault Detail: " & soap.Detail
    MsgBox msg, vbCritical, "Error calling service"
End Sub
```

This client is similar to the one in Listing 5.5 that was using only simple types, but it must pass the WSML document URL to the SoapClient30 MSSoapInit method. It also uses Store as the return value from GetStoreSales instead of a double. The returned object contains both store sales and income, which can be accessed by the client by invoking the object's properties.

5.4.2   User-Defined Data Type Mapper

The SOAP Toolkit has a built-in User-Defined Type (UDT) mapper. As the name implies, this mapper knows how to serialize and deserialize UDTs. Listing 5.12 shows an example server that uses a Store UDT instead of a class. Listing 5.13 shows the corresponding client code. These listings are very similar to those using a Store class (Listings 5.7 and 5.11). The primary difference is the use of the Set keyword when you set an object reference.

**Listing 5.12   A server method returning a User Defined Type
(VBWSBook\Chapter5\UDTServer\Stores.cls)**

```
Public Type Store
    Sales As Double
    Income As Double
    StoreId As String
```

```
      End Type
      Public Function GetStoreSales(ByVal user As String, _
                ByVal password As String, _
                ByVal StoreId As String) As Store

          If user = UID And password = PWD Then
              Dim theStore As Store
              Select Case StoreId
                  Case "6380"
                      theStore.Sales = 120490.87
                  Case "7066"
                      theStore.Sales = 190100.04
                  Case "7896"
                      theStore.Sales = 115900.56
              End Select
          Else
              theStore.Sales = 0
          End If
          theStore.Income = theStore.Sales * 0.7
          GetStoreSales = theStore
      End Function
```

Listing 5.13 A client calling the UDTServer (VBWSClientCode\Chapter5\UDTClient\frmClient.frm)

```
      Private Sub cmdSales_Click()
          On Error GoTo eh
          Dim soap As MSSOAPLib30.SoapClient30
          Set soap = New MSSOAPLib30.SoapClient30

          soap.MSSoapInit WSDL_URL, , , WSML_URL

          'other code removed ...

          Dim theStore As Store
          'this is the Web service call
          theStore = soap.GetStoreSales(UID, PWD, cboStoreId.Text)
          lblSales.Caption = "Sales for this store are: $" & _
                          CStr(theStore.Sales)
          lblSales.Caption = lblSales.Caption & vbCrLf & _
                      "Income is: $" & CStr(theStore.Income)

          'other code removed ...

      End Sub
```

5.4.3 Custom Type Mappers

If the built-in generic and UDT mappers don't work for you, you can build your own custom mapper. For example, if there isn't a one-to-one correspondence between your application class's properties and elements, you might want to implement a custom type mapper.

To use a custom type mapper, you must create a COM class that implements the ISoapMapper interface. At runtime, the SOAP toolkit components call methods of this interface asking your implementation to serialize or deserialize the custom types. To tell the SOAP toolkit about this type mapper, you must define a complexType in the service's WSDL document and then define your custom type mapper as the mapper for this complexType in the service's WSML document.

I will not go into the details of how to implement custom type mappers. I recommend instead that you use XML directly via the IXMLDOMNodeList.

5.4.4 Complex Types As IXMLDOMNodeList

Instead of playing the serialization/deserialization game, you can use XML as the native data format within your applications. This lets you easily deposit XML in outgoing SOAP messages and pull out XML from incoming messages without the need for complicated serialization/deserialization logic. Using XML as your application's internal data format has many benefits over using classes as data containers. Here's a list of these benefits:

- **Less code:** Although it might seem that a client using the XML DOM to manipulate data is using a lot of code, it is usually less than a client using classes as data containers (remember you must factor in the data container code itself). For example, Listing 5.14 shows a client that calls the same complexTypeServer from Listing 5.7.

Listing 5.14   A client invoking complexTypeServer and getting the result in an IXMLDOMNodeList (VBWSClientCode\Chapter5\XmlClient\frmClient.frm)

```
Private Sub cmdSales_Click()
    On Error GoTo eh
    Dim soap As MSSOAPLib30.SoapClient30
    Set soap = New MSSOAPLib30.SoapClient30

    soap.MSSoapInit WSDL_URL
```

```
        'other code omitted

    Dim nl As IXMLDOMNodeList
    'this is the Web service call
    Set nl = soap.GetStoreSales(UID, PWD, cboStoreId.Text)
    Dim doc As MSXML2.DOMDocument40
    'put the returned node list in the document
    Set doc = MakeDoc(nl, "Store")
    lblSales.Caption = "Sales for this store are: $" & _
            doc.selectSingleNode("/Store/Sales").Text
    lblSales.Caption = lblSales.Caption & vbCrLf & _
              "Income is: $" & _
            doc.selectSingleNode("/Store/Income").Text


        'other code omitted
End Sub


'MakeDoc function
Private Function MakeDoc( _
            nl As IXMLDOMNodeList, _
            elemName As String) _
              As DOMDocument40
    Dim doc As New MSXML2.DOMDocument40
    doc.LoadXml "<" & elemName & "/>"
    Dim n As IXMLDOMNode
    For Each n In nl
        Select Case n.nodeType
            Case NODE_ATTRIBUTE
                doc.documentElement.setAttribute _
                            n.nodeName, n.nodeValue
            Case NODE_ELEMENT, NODE_TEXT
                doc.documentElement.appendChild n
        End Select

    Next
    Set MakeDoc = doc
End Function
```

The interesting part about this client is that it captures the return value from GetStoreSales in an IXMLDOMNodeList. Then it calls the general purpose, reusable function (MakeDoc), which takes in the node list and puts the nodes from the list into a DOM document. The client then uses SelectSingle-Node with XPath to extract the specific nodes that it needs.

When you compare this code with the ComplexTypeClient in Listing 5.11 you'll find it has a few extra lines of code; but this assessment is incorrect. First, note that the MakeDoc function is reusable, so it can be encapsulated in a .bas module (or even COM component) that can be reused by many clients. Second, the ComplexTypeClient in Listing 5.11 relies on the Store class from Listing 5.8 so you should include the number of lines of code in the Store class when comparing the two techniques.

- **Easier deployment:** Beyond the number of code lines, consider ease of deployment. Using type mappers implies custom application classes or UDTs that must be deployed to client machines. If you have thousands of clients, this becomes an issue because of the all-too-familiar hassle of deploying components and maintaining and versioning them. When using XML on the client, there's nothing to deploy but the client itself (the client machine needs MSXML anyway in order to use the SOAP Toolkit).

- **Easier maintenance:** When you eliminate classes that act as data containers, you eliminate unnecessary code that must be maintained and versioned as the data schema changes. It's a lot of work to version your data and your logic; why add another layer of data containers that you must version and maintain with each change to your data? Many organizations built elaborate systems for mapping relational data stores to application classes. But now that XML has a mature API (the DOM) and a rich type system (XML Schemas), there's no reason to do this. Instead, use the DOM as your data container. Move DOM documents and nodes between your logic components and within the client. Ultimately, this will result in a more maintainable architecture.

- **Data is readily available as XML:** This one applies to the server side. Whatever relational database you use on the back end, chances are you can get your data out of it as XML. By leveraging built-in support such as SQL Server 2000, or by using features of the data access technology such as ADO 2.5+, you can easily get your data as an XML document. Compare this to reading data out of a relational database then copying values out of an ADO recordset into properties of an application object. It's preferable to get your data as an XML document and pass that document to your business logic components. When it's time to send data out of a SOAP-exposed method, simply return an IXMLDOMNodeList that contains all the nodes inside this document (or the nodes inside the document's element). By eliminating data holders you simplify the application's architecture and improve maintainability.

- **XML provides a rich programming model:** Once you have your data in XML, a world of possibilities opens up. Suddenly, you can use XPath to navigate and select from complex document structures instead of creating classes upon classes and collections of those classes. You can also transform your data with XSLT to generate simple HTML, elaborate SVG, or SQL INSERT statements to insert the data into a database! Want to validate your data? Use an XML Schema instead of writing code to validate a number as a valid zip code or a string as a valid telephone number. XML Schemas are extremely powerful (see Chapter 2) and should be used for these purposes. When applying these technologies, you'll find yourself writing less code and pulling out application elements in separate, portable, and maintainable modules (XSLT transformations, XSD schemas, and so forth).

For these reasons, I recommend that you skip automatic serialization/ deserialization of application types (except in simple cases where there's just one class with a couple of properties and few clients to deploy). A custom type mapper might be useful on the server side if you are exposing methods on existing COM components that return application objects. In most cases you can use the generic type mapper. If not, you can always wrap the existing COM components with new ones that return an IXMLDOMNodeList. Inside these new components, call the existing ones and generate the XML yourself. This is preferable to using a custom type mapper because you now have an application façade that returns XML and is not tied to the SOAP toolkit. This opens up the possibility of reusing the facade in other ways in the future.

5.5 Implementing Header Handlers

In Chapter 3, you saw how SOAP headers can extend SOAP by sending information outside the message body. The SOAP toolkit lets you send and receive SOAP headers by implementing an interface called IHeaderHandler. In this section I'll show you how to expose services that use headers and how to invoke a service that requires them.

5.5.1 Exposing Services with Headers

Consider the simple server class called Stores in Listing 5.15. This server exposes two properties named UserId and Password. At runtime, it assumes these properties have been populated before GetStoreSales is called.

Listing 5.15   A GetStoreSales implementation that relies on SOAP headers for getting user id and password (VBWSBook\HLHeaderServer\Stores.cls)

```
Option Explicit
Private Const UID As String = "admin"
Private Const PWD As String = "admin"
Private m_UID As String
Private m_PWD As String
Public Function GetStoreSales(ByVal StoreId As String) As Double
    If m_UID = UID And m_PWD = PWD Then
        'code omitted
    End If
End Function
Public Property Let UserId(ByVal newVal As String)
    m_UID = newVal
End Property
Public Property Let Password(ByVal newVal As String)
    m_PWD = newVal
End Property
```

To set the properties, a class called AuthHeader implemented IHeaderHandler to read user id and password out of the incoming message and used them to set the server's UserId and Password properties. Listing 5.16 shows the AuthHeader class.

Listing 5.16   A class implementing IHeaderHandler to read user id and password (VBWSBook\Chapter5\HLHeaderServer\AuthHeader)

```
Option Explicit
Implements IHeaderHandler
Private Function IHeaderHandler_readHeader( _
        ByVal par_Reader As MSSOAPLib30.ISoapReader, _
        ByVal par_HeaderNode As MSXML2.IXMLDOMNode, _
        ByVal par_Object As Object) As Boolean

    On Error GoTo eh
    'For complex headers, you can optionally
    'load the par_HeaderNode xml
```

```
'into a DOM document and
'validate it using an XSD schema

par_Object.UserId = _
      par_HeaderNode.selectSingleNode("UserId").Text
par_Object.Password = _
      par_HeaderNode.selectSingleNode("Password").Text
IHeaderHandler_readHeader = True
Exit Function
eh:
App.LogEvent "Error " & Err.Description
IHeaderHandler_readHeader = False
End Function

Private Function IHeaderHandler_willWriteHeaders() As Boolean
IHeaderHandler_willWriteHeaders = False
End Function
Private Sub IHeaderHandler_WriteHeaders( _
    ByVal par_Serializer As MSSOAPLib30.ISoapSerializer, _
    ByVal par_Object As Object)

End Sub
```

IHeaderHandler has three methods. ReadHeader is used to read data out of the SOAP headers. To write headers out to the SOAP message, you first return True from WillWriteHeaders, then you implement WriteHeaders where you do the actual writing.

The first parameter to ReadHeader is an object that implements ISoapReader that can be used to read the contents of the SOAP message. When used on the server side, the second parameter to ReadHeaders is a reference to the request handler on the server, that is, an instance of the Stores class shown in Listing 5.15. The third parameter to ReadHeader is an IXMLDOMNode that represents the incoming SOAP header node. IHeaderHandler_readHeader should return True if it read and understood the SOAP header passed in.

To read incoming headers, the code in Listing 5.16 uses selectSingleNode to extract the UserId and Password elements and to get their text content. It uses the extracted values to set the UserId and Password properties of the Store object, then returns True to indicate the header was understood.

Because you get access to the header as an IXMLDOMNode, you can easily validate the header XML using the MSXML4 parser and an XML Schema as explained in Chapter 2.

5.5.2 Invoking Services with Headers

In addition to exposing services that require SOAP headers, the toolkit also lets clients send and receive headers when invoking services. Listing 5.17 shows an example class called AuthHeader that implements IHeaderHandler to send a user id and password as a SOAP header.

Note that this AuthHeader class is not the same AuthHeader class used by the server. The server's implementation is concerned with reading a SOAP header while the client implementation writes the SOAP header.

Listing 5.17   An implementation of IHeaderHandler to write user id and password in SOAP header (VBWSClientCode\Chapter5\HLHeaderClient\ AuthHeader.cls)

```
Private Function IHeaderHandler_ReadHeader( _
  ByVal par_Reader As MSSOAPLib30.ISoapReader, _
  ByVal par_HeaderNode As MSXML2.IXMLDOMNode, _
  ByVal par_Object As Object) As Boolean
 IHeaderHandler_ReadHeader = False
End Function


Private Function IHeaderHandler_WillWriteHeaders() As Boolean
 IHeaderHandler_WillWriteHeaders = True
End Function


Private Sub IHeaderHandler_WriteHeaders( _
 ByVal par_Serializer As MSSOAPLib30.ISoapSerializer, _
 ByVal par_Object As Object)

    par_Serializer.startHeaderElement _
            "AuthInfo", _
            "http://LearnXmlWS.com/type"
    par_Serializer.startElement "UserId"
    par_Serializer.SoapAttribute "type", _
        "http://www.w3.org/2001/XMLSchema-instance", "xsd:string"
    par_Serializer.writeString m_UID
    par_Serializer.endElement
```

```
        par_Serializer.startElement "Password"
        par_Serializer.SoapAttribute "type", _
            "http://www.w3.org/2001/XMLSchema-instance", "xsd:string"
        par_Serializer.writeString m_PWD
        par_Serializer.endElement
        par_Serializer.endHeaderElement
    End Sub


    Property Let ClientUserId(ByVal newVal As String)
        m_UID = newVal
    End Property
    Property Let ClientPassword(ByVal newVal As String)
        m_PWD = newVal
    End Property
```

The example in Listing 5.17 does not read any headers; therefore, it returns False from ReadHeader. WillWriteHeaders returns True, indicating the class wants to write SOAP headers to outgoing SOAP messages. All the action is in WriteHeaders implementation where it actually writes the user id and password information. The first parameter to WriteHeaders is an object that implements ISoapSerializer. You use this object to write out the SOAP header XML. First, to write the header element itself, you call ISoapSerializer.startHeaderElement passing it the element's name and namespace. To write child elements inside the header, you call ISoapSerializer.startElement with the element's name and an optional namespace. For example, the code in Listing 5.17 uses startElement to write the UserId and Password elements. To write attributes on an element, you call ISoapSerializer.SoapAttribute passing it the attribute's name, namespace, and value.

To ensure the XML is well-formed, each startElement call must be paired with an endElement and the startHeaderElement call must be paired with an end-HeaderElement call.

Listing 5.17 uses ISoapSerializer.WriteString to write out the values in m_UID and m_PWD. Before invoking the service, the client application sets these values by calling the class's ClientUserId and ClientPassword properties. Listing 5.18 shows an example client application that uses the AuthHeader class.

Listing 5.18 A client using AuthHeader to send the password and user id in a SOAP header (VBWSClientCode\Chapter5\HLHeaderClient\frmClient.frm)

```
Private Sub cmdSales_Click()
On Error GoTo eh
    Dim soap As MSSOAPLib30.SoapClient30
    Set soap = New MSSOAPLib30.SoapClient30

    soap.MSSoapInit WSDL_URL

    If chkProxy.Value Then
        soap.ConnectorProperty("ProxyServer") = "localhost"
        soap.ConnectorProperty("ProxyPort") = "8080"
        soap.ConnectorProperty("UseProxy") = True
    End If

    'set the header handler
    Dim theHeader As AuthHeader
    Set theHeader = New AuthHeader
    theHeader.ClientUserId = UID
    theHeader.ClientPassword = PWD
    Set soap.HeaderHandler = theHeader

    lblSales.Caption = "Sales for this store are: $" & CStr( _
            soap.GetStoreSales(cboStoreId.Text))
    Exit Sub
eh:
    MsgBox Err.Description, vbCritical, "Error calling service"

End Sub
```

The client first instantiates a SoapClient object. Then it instantiates an Auth-Header object called theHeader and sets its ClientUserId and ClientPassword properties. Before calling the Web service, the client sets the SoapClient's HeaderHandler property to theHeader, allowing it to write headers when the service is called. The client then invokes GetStoreSales, which causes the SoapClient to call theHeader's implementation of IHeaderHandler.WillWriteHeaders then IHeaderHandler.WriteHeaders. Figure 5.12 shows the SOAP message with the AuthInfo header as it was sent to the service. Notice that the namespace prefixes SOAPSDK4 and SOAPSDK2 are automatically assigned by the toolkit; I only specified the namespace URIs.

```
<?xml version="1.0" encoding="UTF-8" standalone="no" ?>
- <SOAP-ENV:Envelope xmlns:SOAPSDK1="http://www.w3.org/2001/XMLSchema"
    xmlns:SOAPSDK2="http://www.w3.org/2001/XMLSchema-instance"
    xmlns:SOAPSDK3="http://schemas.xmlsoap.org/soap/encoding/" xmlns:SOAP-
    ENV="http://schemas.xmlsoap.org/soap/envelope/">
  - <SOAP-ENV:Header>
    - <SOAPSDK4:AuthInfo xmlns:SOAPSDK4="http://LearnXmlWS.com/type">
        <UserId SOAPSDK2:type="xsd:string">admin</UserId>
        <Password SOAPSDK2:type="xsd:string">admin</Password>
      </SOAPSDK4:AuthInfo>
    </SOAP-ENV:Header>
  - <SOAP-ENV:Body SOAP-
      ENV:encodingStyle="http://schemas.xmlsoap.org/soap/encoding/">
    - <SOAPSDK5:GetStoreSales
        xmlns:SOAPSDK5="http://LearnXmlWS.com/HLHeaderServer/message/"
        SOAPSDK3:root="1">
        <StoreId>6380</StoreId>
      </SOAPSDK5:GetStoreSales>
    </SOAP-ENV:Body>
  </SOAP-ENV:Envelope>
```

Figure 5.12   A request message with a SOAP header that contains user id and password

5.6   Using the Low Level API

In addition to the high level API, the SOAP Toolkit provides another way of exposing and invoking Web services, called the low level API. When I hear "low level
API" I think of opening a TCP socket and sending/receiving network packets,
something that most VB developers would like to avoid. But the toolkit's low level
API is nothing like that. Instead, it's a nice, clean COM-based object model that
lets you form and parse SOAP messages directly. Since you already know XSD,
SOAP, and WSDL (you've read Chapters 2 through 4 haven't you?), you have
nothing to fear. You should embrace this low level API as the quickest way to get
the results you need even with the most complex SOAP message requirements.
I'll explain how to expose existing COM components using the low level API, then
I'll show you how to invoke services with it.

5.6.1   Exposing Services with Low Level API

Because of the simplicity, control, and consistency, I recommend that you
use the low level API to invoke existing COM components. When using the low
level API to expose Web services, there are two primary objects you interact

with: SoapReader30 and SoapSerializer30 as shown in Figure 5.13. You use SoapReader30 to read from incoming SOAP messages and SoapSerializer30 to write to outgoing SOAP messages. I will not go into the details of every method and property of these two objects; it's in the documentation. Instead I'll show you working examples of these objects in action.

Listing 5.19 shows an example service using the low level API. The service project exposes one method called ProcessRequest. This method is called by the ASP page that receives the request. The page is only two lines of code to instantiate the server and call ProcessRequest:

```
<%@ LANGUAGE=VBScript %>
<%
    Set LLServer = Server.CreateObject("LLServer.Stores")
    Call LLServer.ProcessRequest (Request, Response)
%>
```

For the server to access the ASP Request and Response objects, it must add a reference to the Microsoft Active Server Pages Object Library. The server starts by creating a new SoapReader30 object and calling its Load method, passing it the ASP Request object. The Load method is one of the ways to load a SOAP message into the SoapReader30; you can also use loadXML or LoadWithParser. The Load method can read a SOAP message from a file, a URL, or a Stream. The ASP Request object is a stream—that's why you can pass it directly to the Load method.

The server then uses the BodyEntry method to extract the request element by specifying the element's name and namespace. If no request element is found, the server throws an error. If a request element is found, the server uses getElementsByTagName to read the user id, password, and store id from the request. Then it makes a call to the GetStoreSales function, also in Listing 5.19. (Or this could be a call to an existing COM component or an aggregation of such calls.)

Now it's time to form the response SOAP message. First, the server sets the HTTP response content type to text/xml, which is the format clients expect. Then it instantiates a SoapSerializer30 object and calls its Init method, passing it

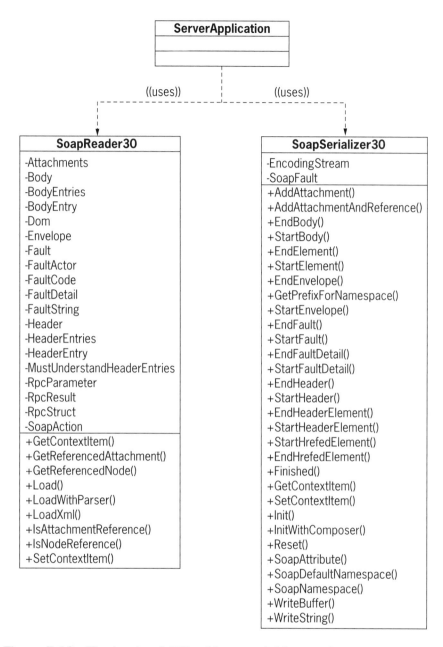

Figure 5.13   The low level API's object model for services

the ASP Response object. The serializer now knows that the response SOAP message should be written to the Response object.

As you've learned in the section on implementing header handlers, SoapSerializer30 exposes intuitive methods to create the response SOAP message. For example, StartEnvelope and StartBody write out the SOAP Envelope and Body, respectively. The server code in Listing 5.19 starts the SOAP Envelope, then Body, then uses StartElement to write out a return element. Within this return element, the server writes out the sales figure returned from Get-StoreSales. Note that each call to StartElement must be paired with a call to EndElement. When serialization is finished, the server exits and the SOAP response message is returned to the client.

Take a close look at the server code in Listing 5.19. It may seem like a lot of code, but it is actually simple XML reading and writing. Best of all, it is consistent: Whether you are sending a simple sales figure as in this example, or a complex XML document according to some standard schema, you can do it all using the same API. It also gives you total control over the message content, which can help you solve interoperability problems if they arise.

Listing 5.19   An example service using the low level API (VBWSBook\Chapter5\LLServer\Stores.cls)

```
Public Sub ProcessRequest(ByVal Request _
                          As ASPTypeLibrary.Request, _
                          ByVal Response _
                          As ASPTypeLibrary.Response)


    'This method acts as a SOAP
    'request processor and
    'dispatches the call to the
    'appropriate component and method
    Dim UserId As String
    Dim password As String
    Dim StoreId As String
    Dim Sales As Double
    Dim Serializer As MSSOAPLib30.SoapSerializer30
    Dim Rdr As MSSOAPLib30.SoapReader30
    Dim MethodName As String
```

```vb
    On Error GoTo eh
    Set Rdr = New MSSOAPLib30.SoapReader30
    'Load the SOAP request
    Rdr.Load Request
    'get the request element
    Dim reqElem As IXMLDOMElement
    Set reqElem = Rdr.BodyEntry(REQ_NAME, REQ_NS)

    If reqElem Is Nothing Then
        Err.Raise 1234 + vbObjectError, _
            "LLServer", _
            "Unknown request element name or namespace"
    End If

    'pull data out of the request
    UserId = reqElem.getElementsByTagName("user").Item(0).Text
    password = _
        reqElem.getElementsByTagName("password").Item(0).Text
    StoreId = _
        reqElem.getElementsByTagName("StoreId").Item(0).Text
    'make the call
    'this could invoke an
    'existing COM component
    Sales = GetStoreSales(UserId, password, StoreId)

    'now write the response
    Response.ContentType = "text/xml"
    Set Serializer = New MSSOAPLib30.SoapSerializer30
    Serializer.Init Response
    Serializer.StartEnvelope
    Serializer.StartBody
    Serializer.StartElement RETURN_NAME, RETURN_NS, _
                            "NONE", "vbws"
    Serializer.WriteString CStr(Sales)
    Serializer.EndElement
    Serializer.EndBody
    Serializer.EndEnvelope
    Serializer.Finished
Exit Sub
eh:
'should return a SOAP Fault here
App.LogEvent Err.Description
End Sub
Private Function GetStoreSales(ByVal user As String, _
```

```
            ByVal password As String, _
            ByVal StoreId As String) As Double
    If user = UID And password = PWD Then
        Select Case StoreId
            Case "6380"
                GetStoreSales = 120490.87
            Case "7066"
                GetStoreSales = 190100.04
            Case "7896"
                GetStoreSales = 115900.56
        End Select
    Else
        GetStoreSales = 0
    End If
End Function
```

5.6.2 Invoking Services with the Low Level API

In addition to SoapReader30 and SoapSerializer30, clients using the low level API use an HttpConnector30 to send the HTTP request and receive the response. Figure 5.14 shows the toolkit's low level API classes that a client application uses. To see how these classes are used, let's examine a client that uses the low level API to invoke the server in Listing 5.19. Listing 5.20 shows a simple client that does this.

Note: You do not have to use the low level API to invoke a service that uses the low level API. The client and service can each use the low or high level API, independent of the other.

**Listing 5.20   A client using the low level API
(VBWSClientCode\Chapter5\LLClient\frmClient.frm)**

```
Option Explicit
Private Const UID As String = "admin"
Private Const PWD As String = "admin"
Private Const SERVICE_URL As String = _
    "http://VBWSServer/VBWSBook/Chapter5/LLServer/LLServer.ASP"
Private Const SOAP_ACTION As String = "irrelevant"
Private Const OPERATION_NAME As String = "GetStoreSales"
Private Const OPERATION_NS = "http://LearnXMLWS.com/message/"
Private Const XSD_NS As String = _
        "http://www.w3.org/2001/XMLSchema"
Private Const XSI_NS As String = _
        "http://www.w3.org/2001/XMLSchema-instance"
```

```
Private Sub cmdLLAPI_Click()
On Error GoTo eh

    Dim Serializer As SoapSerializer30
    Dim Connector As SoapConnector30
    Dim Rdr As SoapReader30
    Dim SalesElem As IXMLDOMElement


    Set Connector = New HttpConnector30
    Connector.Property("EndPointURL") = SERVICE_URL
    Connector.Property("SoapAction") = SOAP_ACTION
    If chkPrxy.Value Then
        Connector.Property("ProxyServer") = "VBWSServer"
        Connector.Property("ProxyPort") = "8080"
        Connector.Property("UseProxy") = True
    End If

    'establish connection
    Connector.Connect
    Connector.BeginMessage
    'SoapSerializer uses the Connector
    Set Serializer = New SoapSerializer30
    Serializer.Init Connector.InputStream
    'write the SOAP message
    Serializer.startEnvelope
    Serializer.startBody
    Serializer.startElement OPERATION_NAME, OPERATION_NS
    'declare the xsi and xsd namespaces
    Serializer.SoapNamespace "xsi", XSI_NS
    Serializer.SoapNamespace "xsd", XSD_NS
    'write user id
    Serializer.startElement "user"
    'add the xsi:type attribute
    Serializer.SoapAttribute "type", XSI_NS, "xsd:string", "xsi"
    Serializer.writeString UID
    Serializer.endElement
    'write password
    Serializer.startElement "password"
    'add the xsi:type attribute
     Serializer.SoapAttribute "type", XSI_NS, "xsd:string", "xsi"
    Serializer.writeString PWD
    Serializer.endElement
    'can also use writeXML
```

```
Serializer.writeXML "<StoreId xsi:type='xsd:string'>" & _
                cboStoreId.Text & "</StoreId>"

Serializer.endElement
Serializer.endBody
Serializer.endEnvelope
Serializer.Finished
'send the message
Connector.EndMessage

'get the response
Set Rdr = New SoapReader30
Rdr.Load Connector.OutputStream

'need to add error checking and handling here

lblSales.Caption = "Sales for this store are: $" & _
    Rdr.BodyEntry(RETURN_NAME, RETURN_NS).Text

Exit Sub
eh:
MsgBox Err.Description, vbCritical, _
        "Error calling service"
End Sub
```

The client begins by instantiating an HttpConnector30 object that is responsible for handling the HTTP aspects of the SOAP request. It sets the connector's End-PointURL to the service's URL. It also sets the SoapAction property to a constant defined as "irrelevant." I did this intentionally to show you that the value of SOAP-Action is irrelevant in this case because the server ignores it.

After the usual five lines that set the proxy server, the client calls Connector.Connect then Connector.BeginMessage to establish the HTTP connection and signal the beginning of serialization. Then it instantiates a SoapSerializer30 and calls its Init method, passing it the connector's InputStream. The serializer writes out the SOAP message to this stream. The client uses the now familiar serializer methods to start the message SOAP Envelope, Body, and to write out the request element. Inside the request element, the client writes out the user id, password, and store id. Note that the client writes out the xsi:type attribute on each element. While this is not required by this particular server, some non-

Microsoft SOAP implementations are easier to use if the SOAP message contains this attribute on each element (more on this in Chapter 12). For demonstration purposes, I used the serializer's writeXML method, which lets you write an XML string directly to the message stream. After finishing the message, the client calls EndMessage, which sends the SOAP message to the service.

To read the response, the client instantiates a SoapReader30 and calls its Load method, passing it the connector's output stream. The soap reader reads the response message out of this stream and gives the client easy access to the message's contents. The client then uses SoapReader30.BodyEntry to read out the return element's text content (the sales figures that the client is after).

5.7 The ISAPI Listener

All examples in this chapter have used an ASP listener to receive and process SOAP requests. The toolkit's documentation recommends that for maximum performance you use an ISAPI listener. I haven't run benchmarks comparing the performance of ISAPI versus ASP listeners but intuitively, I agree with the documentation's recommendation. You should use an ASP listener only if you want to preprocess incoming SOAP messages before passing them on to SoapServer30; otherwise you should use an ISAPI listener.

The ISAPI listener is based on the ISAPI extension architecture where a file type (a file extension) is mapped to a DLL that knows how to handle requests for files of that type.

The toolkit's ISAPI listener is an ISAPI extension that handles requests for .wsdl files. To configure the listener, you need to tell IIS to forward requests with a URL ending in .wsdl to the ISAPI listener. You can do this using the IIS administration console by opening the properties of the virtual directory where your service resides, clicking on "configuration" then clicking on "Add" to add a new mapping. Then you enter the path to SOAPIS30.dll (usually C:\Program Files\Common Files\MSSoap\Binaries\SOAPIS30.dll) and .wsdl as the extension as in Figure 5.15. You also want to limit the HTTP verbs to those that can be handled by the listener, namely GET, POST, and HEAD.

When a client sends an HTTP GET, POST, or HEAD request for a .wsdl file within this virtual directory, IIS passes this request along to the ISAPI listener.

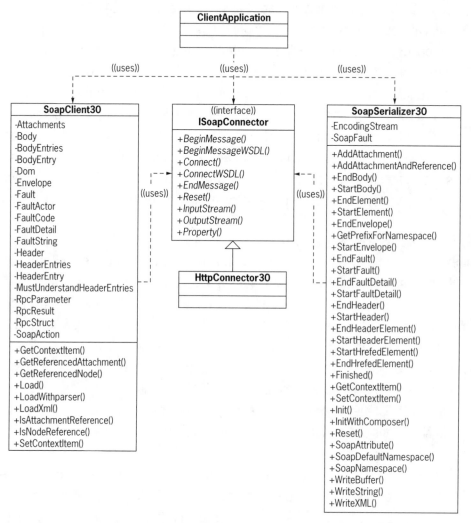

Figure 5.14   The low level API object model for clients

The listener processes the request using a SoapServer30 object much like the ASP listener does.

You can also configure the ISAPI listener by using a command line utility called soapvdir.cmd. This utility can be used to create a new virtual directory and configure the ISAPI filter on it at the same time. For example,

```
Soapvdir.cmd CREATE VBWSBOOK D:\VBWSBOOK
```

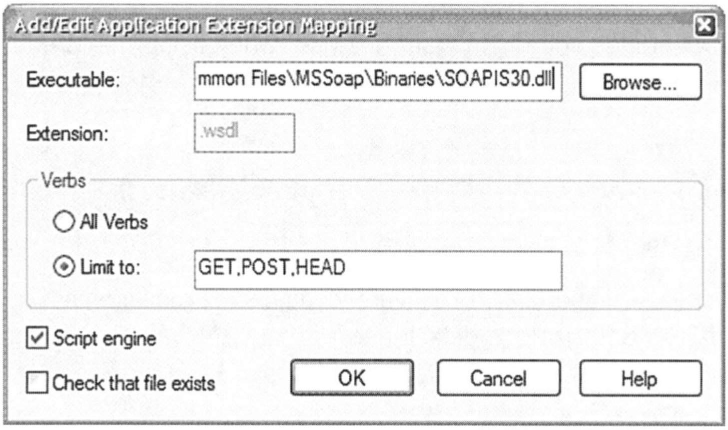

Figure 5.15   Configuring the ISAPI listener on a virtual directory

creates a new virtual directory called VBWSBOOK, which maps to the folder
D:\VBWSBOOK and configures the ISAPI listener on this new virtual directory. If
you are using Windows NT 4 or 2000 server with multiple Web sites configured,
this utility will use the first site by default unless you specify another site number
with the –s switch.

If you already have a virtual directory and simply want to configure the ISAPI
listener on it, use the UPDATE command instead of CREATE:

```
Soapvdir.cmd UPDATE VBWSBOOK D:\VBWSBOOK
```

This will look for an existing VBWSBOOK virtual directory and configure it to use
the ISAPI listener.

When you run the WSDL generator wizard and select ISAPI listener, the service's location in the generated WSDL points to the WSDL document itself rather
than an ASP page (there is no ASP page because you are using an ISAPI listener). For example, the HLServer's WSDL would be:

```
<service name="HLServer">
  <port name="StoresSoapPort"
     binding="wsdlns:StoresSoapBinding">
   <soap:address
   location=
   "http://VBWSServer/VBWSBook/Chapter5/HLServer/HLServer.WSDL"/>
  </port>
</service>
```

5.7.1 Tweaking the ISAPI Listener

There are a few settings you might want to tweak when using the ISAPI listener in a production application. These settings are registry values located in the registry key

```
HKEY_LOCAL_MACHINE\SOFTWARE\Microsoft\MSSOAP\SOAPISAP
```

Here is a list of settings:

- *MaxPostSize* is important to configure if you expect request messages that exceed 100KB in size (the default permissible size). When you change this setting, be sure to switch to Decimal base and keep in mind that 1KB = 1024 Bytes.

- *NoNagling* turns off the nagling delay. By default, when a service responds with a small message, this response might be buffered before being sent to the client. This is a TCP optimization that tries to maximize the payload sent with each TCP packet by waiting to see if there's more data to send before sending a packet. Normally, having nagling delay on is a good thing but if your service's response messages are small and the performance you're getting is much worse than expected, you can try to turn it off by setting the NoNaggling value to 1.

- *NumThreads* is the number of threads handling incoming requests. Normally the default (two threads per CPU plus an extra thread) is close to optimum. You should try to increase this number only if the request queue gets too long (as indicated by the queue length perf counter). You should know, however, that too many threads is not a good thing: It causes CPUs to spend too many processing cycles switching among thread contexts rather than performing useful work.

- *ObjCachedPerThread* is the number of objects cached per thread. The ISAPI listener will cache a SoapServer30 object for each Web service you have exposed (just like the ASP listener does). So this number should be at least the number of Web services exposed via the ISAPI listener.

5.8 Summary

Today's reality is that we all have COM-based server applications that can benefit from integrating with other applications via Web services. In addition, most desktops already have the Visual Basic runtime installed but do not or cannot have the .NET runtime installed. Both of these realities make the SOAP Toolkit a valuable tool in your Web Services toolbox. The SOAP Toolkit lets you easily expose and invoke Web services with the high level API. For complete control, you can use the toolkit's low level API and take matters into your own hands.

The SOAP toolkit is also relatively mature since it's been out the longest compared to most other SOAP stacks (if you include its v1.0 predecessor which had a different architecture). Having a mature COM-based SOAP stack with two different programming models means you can feel confident about architecting Web service solutions around the SOAP toolkit.

5.9 Resources

Microsoft's SOAP home page: http://msdn.microsoft.com/library/en-us/dnsoapspec/html/soapspecindex.asp.

Microsoft's SOAP Toolkit's newsgroup: news://msnews.microsoft.com/microsoft.public.xml.soapsdk.

Chapter 6

.NET Web Services

It is new fancy rathert than taste which produces so many new
fashions. —Voltaire

In Chapter 1 you learned how easy it is to create and invoke a simple Web service using .NET. This was a good start and was intended to get you hooked on
creating Web services. Practically however, the Web services you create will
need to do much more than just add two numbers. This chapter will build on
what you've learned in Chapters 1 through 4 and dive deeper into the details of
creating and invoking Web services using .NET. You will learn how to build .NET
Web services, customize their WSDL, and invoke them using .NET clients. Even
if you have not read Chapters 2 through 4, you can still learn a lot from this
chapter. If you skipped the earlier chapters, you might want to go back and read
them after you've read this chapter and worked through the code.

6.1   Creating Web Services with VS .NET

Web services are part of the ASP.NET framework, which means you do not need
a special IDE to write a .NET Web service; you can build one using Notepad. A
.NET Web service consists of a file with the .asmx extension and an optional assembly (for example .dll or .exe). This .asmx file is considered the Web service's
end point; therefore, it must be placed in a Web accessible folder such as a Web
application's vroot. The .asmx file contains a WebService processing directive
such as:

```
<%@ WebService Language="vb" Class="MathService" %>
```

The Language attribute specifies the language in which the Web service code is written. The Class attribute specifies the name of the class that represents the Web service. This includes the class's namespace if there is one. The rest of the .asmx file can contain the Web service implementation and any supporting code, such as private classes. For example, a Web service that exposes one method called Add can be implemented in an .asmx file like this:

```
<%@ WebService Language="vb" Class="MathService" %>
Imports System.Web.Services

Public Class MathService
  <WebMethod()> _
  Public Function Add(ByVal a As Double, _
                      ByVal b As Double) As Double
    return a + b
  End Function
End Class
```

Putting all implementation code in a single file is usually a bad idea because it's easy to accidentally change the code on a production server. It is also easier to maintain code that is logically divided into different files. To do this, you should compile the Web service implementation in an assembly, (for example, a .dll) and place this assembly in the application's bin folder. For example, if your Web server has an application vroot called /services, you would place the .asmx files directly in /services and place the Web service implementation assemblies in /services/bin. The resulting .asmx file contains only the WebService directive:

```
<%@ WebService Language="vb" Class="MathService" %>
```

The actual Web service implementation is in an assembly inside the application's bin folder. If you use Visual Studio .NET to create a Web service, it will automatically create the *servicename*.asmx file and another file called *servicename*.asmx.vb (or .cs if you are using C#). For example, Listing 6.1 shows the equivalent math service built with Visual Studio .NET.

Listing 6.1   Contents of the .asmx and .asmx.vb files that VS .NET auto-matically generates. Note that the code in this listing is from two different files.

```
'Contents of MathService.asmx
<%@ WebService Language="vb"
  Codebehind="MathService.asmx.vb"
  Class="ClassWS.MathService" %>


'Contents of MathService.asmx.vb
Imports System.Web.Services

Public Class MathService
    Inherits System.Web.Services.WebService
    <WebMethod()> _
    Public Function Add(ByVal a As Double, _
                        ByVal b As Double) As Double
        Return a + b
    End Function
End Class
```

Figure 6.1 shows how the .asmx and .asmx.vb file relate to each another. The .asmx file contains a WebService directive that has an additional attribute called Codebehind, which names the file that contains the Web service implementation. This attribute is not needed by the ASP.NET framework, but VS .NET needs it to correlate the .asmx file with the corresponding .asmx.vb file.

The .asmx.vb file is a regular source file that contains the Web service class and the implementation code. Note that by default, the MathService class belongs to the project's namespace which in this example is ClassWS. The WebService directive's Class attribute uses the fully qualified class name, which in this example, is ClassWS.MathService.

6.1.1   Creating a Web Service

Although you can create a Web service by creating an .asmx file with any text editor, using Visual Studio .NET makes it easy to code and debug Web services. Simply start Visual Studio .NET and choose File, New, and Project. Then choose the ASP.NET Web Service project template. In the location field, enter the URL

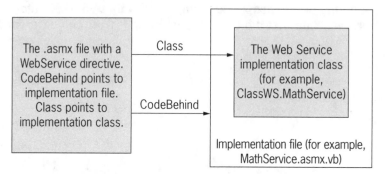

Figure 6.1   Relation between .asmx and .asmx.vb files

where you want the new project to be located. The project name is automatically derived from the last segment of this URL (the word after the last forward slash). The project name is displayed in the Name field but you cannot edit it there. Figure 6.2 shows a project being created. This new project is called Chapter6 and project files are located at the URL `http://VBWSServer/VBWSBook/Chapter6/`. Visual Studio creates a new IIS virtual directory called VBWSBook/Chapter6 (if it doesn't exist) and configures it to allow scripting and program execution.

If you have an existing IIS application in which you want to place a new project, select the project template called "New Project In Existing Folder" and enter the new project name. On the next screen you'll be asked to enter a folder name; instead enter the URL where you want the new project to be located, for example, `http://VBWSServer/VBWSBook/chapter6`, as shown in Figure 6.3. When you click OK, Visual Studio puts the new project in this virtual directory, instead of creating a new virtual directory.

When you create an ASP.NET Web Service project, you can add multiple Web services to it. You can also add new Web services to other project types such as ASP.NET Web Applications. (I've even added Web services to Windows applications, not that you'd want to do that!) Don't assume that you need to create a new project for every new Web service that you want to add.

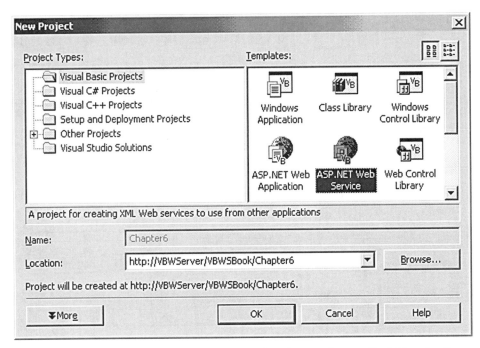

Figure 6.2   Creating a new ASP.NET Web Service project called Chapter6

If you've created a new ASP.NET Web Service project, you will see several files in Solution Explorer. One of these files, service1.asmx, is a Web service. There are actually two files, service1.asmx and service1.asmx.vb, but by default VS .NET shows you only the .asmx file.

To see the file service1.asmx.vb, go to the Project menu and select Show All Files. You will see a plus (+) next to service1.asmx. Clicking on this expands the tree and you see service1.asmx.vb.

The file name, service1, appears in five different places. First you have the two filenames, service1.asmx and service1.asmx.vb. Then, if you open the code view for service1.asmx (by right clicking on service1.asmx and choosing View Code, or selecting it and pressing F7), it opens service1.asmx.vb and you see the class that implements the Web service:

```
Public Class Service1
```

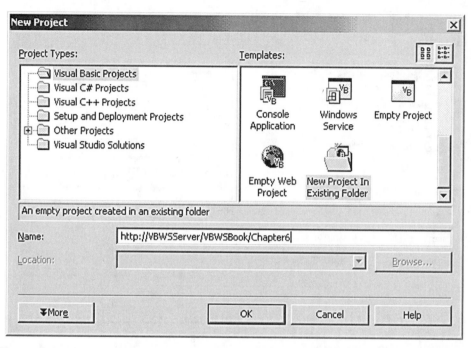

Figure 6.3 Creating a new project in an existing folder. When asked to enter a folder location, enter the URL where you want the new project to be created.

Finally, if you right-click on service1.asmx, choose Open With, and choose Source Code (Text) Editor, you get the real .asmx file that contains the WebService directive as explained above:

```
<%@ WebService
    Language="vb" Codebehind="Service1.asmx.vb"
    Class="Chapter6.Service1" %>
```

This directive contains the name Service1 twice: In the codebehind file name and in the class name. Renaming a Web service requires changing all five occurrences of Service1. Unfortunately, when you rename an .asmx file in VS .NET, it will not rename the Web service class nor will it update the class name in the WebService directive. Therefore, the easiest thing to do when you create a new Web service project is to delete Service1.asmx and add a new Web service from the Project menu and specify the service name, (for example, DataService).

Then open the code view for DataService.asmx and you will see a class called `DataService` and an example `HelloWorld` method that's commented out.

To add methods to your Web service, simply add a Function or Sub, like you normally would, making sure it is Public and prefixing it with the `WebMethod` attribute. The `WebMethod` attribute makes your methods accessible as operations on the Web service. Listing 6.2 shows an example method that returns the server time.

Listing 6.2   Adding a WebMethod to your Web service (VBWSBook\Chapter6\DataService.asmx.vb)

```
<WebMethod()> _
Public Function GetServerTime() As DateTime
     Return System.DateTime.Now()
End Function
```

Note that you can put the `WebMethod` attribute on the same line as the method definition. For example, the following works just as well:

```
<WebMethod()> Public Function GetServerTime() As DateTime
```

To test your project, right-click on DataService.asmx, choose Set As Start Page, and choose Start from the Debug menu or press F5 to build and run the project. This will launch Internet Explorer with the service documentation page which should look like the one in Figure 6.4.

If you click on the GetServerTime link, it will take you to a test page as shown in Figure 6.5, where you can click on Invoke to test the operation. You will get a new Internet Explorer window with a `<dateTime>` element that contains the current date and time on the machine where the service is running. If you close Internet Explorer, debugging will automatically stop; you can go back and edit the code, rebuild, and so on.

6.2   Invoking Web Services with Visual Studio .NET

The next logical step after creating and testing a Web service is to create a client for that service. You can call a Web service from practically any kind of application. The rule is: If you can send an HTTP POST request to the Web server, you can

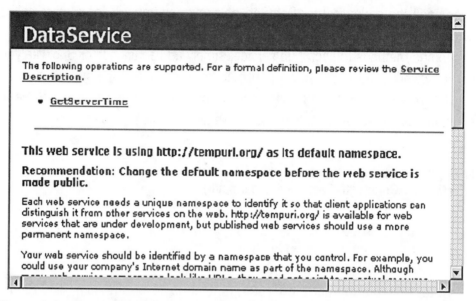

Figure 6.4 The default documentation page that is automatically generated when you navigate to an .asmx file with a browser

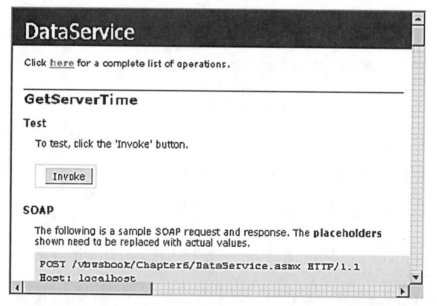

Figure 6.5 You can test your Web service methods from this HTML page by clicking Invoke

invoke the Web service. To create a Windows Forms client, start Visual Studio
.NET and create a new project using the Windows Application template. This creates the project file and adds a form called Form1. As you learned in Chapter 1,
you can use wsdl.exe to create a proxy class that makes it easy to invoke the Web
service. VS .NET can generate this proxy class for you by choosing Add Web Reference from the project menu, which will bring up the dialog shown in Figure 6.6.
Here you type the Web service URL (for example, `http://VBWSServer/vbws-
book/Chapter6/DataService.asmx`) and hit Enter, which will bring up the
service documentation page and enable the Add Reference button on the bottom
right. Clicking on Add Reference will generate the proxy class and add it to your
project. By default, this new class belongs to a .NET namespace that's taken from
the host name where the Web service is located. For example, if the Web service
is on the VBWSServer, the namespace is simply VBWSServer. Similarly, if the Web
service is at www.LearnXmlws.com, the namespace is com.learnxmlws.www.

Examining the project files in Solution Explorer reveals a new folder called
Web References that contains within it another folder called VBWSServer (Figure
6.7 top). Switching to Class View (Figure 6.7 bottom), you'll see a namespace
called `VBWSServer` that contains the generated proxy class called `DataSer-
vice` (same name as the service).

You might want to change the VBWSServer namespace to something more
meaningful such as `LocalServices`. You do this by selecting the VBWSServer
folder in Solution Explorer and renaming it to `LocalServices`. Then you can instantiate an object from the proxy class and call its `GetServerTime` method,
which in turn will invoke the Web service and return the server time. Listing 6.3
shows a button click event handler that invokes the Web service and displays the
returned server time in a message box.

**Listing 6.3 Invoking a Web service in .NET
(VBWSClientCode\Chapter6\WSClient\Form1.vb)**

```
Private Sub Button1_Click( _
    ByVal sender As System.Object, _
    ByVal e As System.EventArgs) Handles Button1.Click
    Dim ws As New LocalServices.DataService()
    MessageBox.Show(ws.GetServerTime().ToString())
End Sub
```

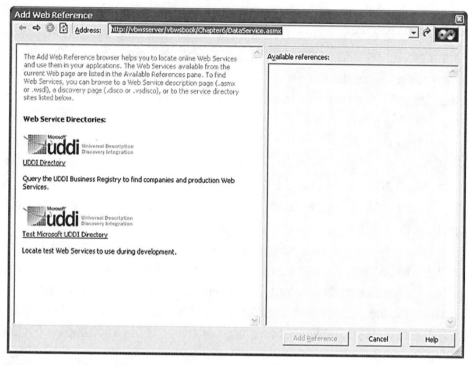

Figure 6.6   Using the Add Web Reference dialog

6.2.1   Using an HTTP Proxy

Some local area networks have HTTP proxies installed to help secure machines on the LAN. An HTTP proxy works by receiving requests from clients and forwarding those requests to their ultimate destination. The proxy receives the response from the Web server and forwards it back to the client.

Note that the term proxy is overloaded: An HTTP proxy or proxy server is a network device that receives and forwards HTTP requests. A Web service proxy is a class that acts as a wrapper to the Web service calls like the one VS .NET generates when you add a Web reference. Throughout this discussion, I'll use the terms proxy server and Web service proxy to avoid confusion.

If you have a proxy server on your network, you might already have Internet Explorer configured to use that server. If that's the case, .NET will use the same proxy server settings by default. You can also programmatically specify a proxy server when invoking a Web service. To do this you instantiate a

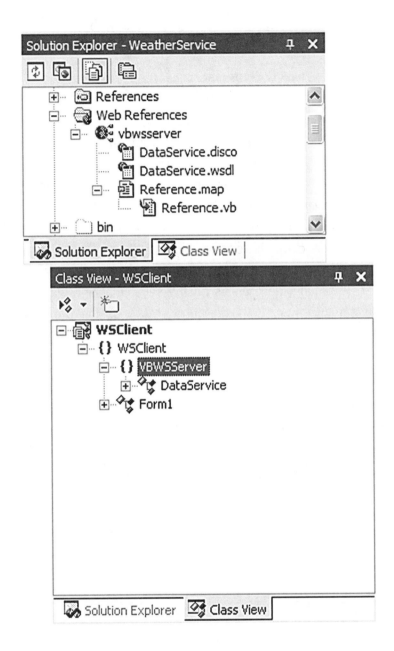

Figure 6.7 Solution Explorer (top) and Class View (bottom) showing the files and classes created when you add a Web reference. This view has "show all files" turned on.

`System.Net.WebProxy` object and use it to set the Web service's `Proxy` property, for example:

```
Dim ws As New LocalServices.DataService()
ws.Proxy = New System.Net.WebProxy("http://proxyserveraddress")
```

Using an HTTP proxy can also be extremely useful for debugging. There's an excellent utility called ProxyTrace that you can download from http://www.pocketsoap. com/tcptrace/pt.asp (for your convenience, ProxyTrace is also on the CD included with this book).[1] This tool acts as a proxy server, receiving and forwarding requests while showing you the content of those requests. When you run ProxyTrace.exe, you get a dialog where you can configure the port on which it will listen (shown in Figure 6.8). This can be any available port on your machine; for example, 8080. Then you can update the client code to make it go through this proxy server. Assuming the client is on the same machine that's running ProxyTrace, you can use `http://localhost:8080` as the proxy server's address:

```
Dim ws As New LocalServices.DataService()
ws.Proxy = New System.Net.WebProxy("http://localhost:8080")
```

When you run the client and invoke the Web service, you'll see the request and response messages in ProxyTrace as shown in Figure 6.9. This is an extremely

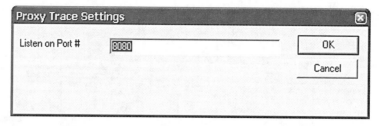

Figure 6.8   Configuring ProxyTrace to use port 8080

---

[1]Double thanks to Simon Fell for making this possible. First, thanks for creating ProxyTrace and providing it free of charge. Second, thanks for letting me include it on the book's CD. Please be sure to visit Simon's site at www.pocketsoap.com where he also publishes a free implementation of SOAP for the PocketPC.

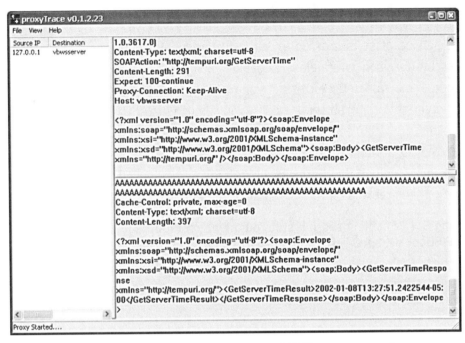

Figure 6.9 ProxyTrace captures and displays HTTP requests and responses

valuable tool when troubleshooting Web service problems, especially those concerned with interoperability.

Note: If the client is using a localhost address to access the Web service, .NET will not use an HTTP proxy even if you tell it to. Therefore, you should use the machine name instead of localhost to invoke the Web service if you want to capture request/response messages using ProxyTrace.

6.3 Leveraging the ASP.NET Framework

.NET Web services execute within the ASP.NET runtime and can leverage many of ASP.NET's useful features. This section explains how you can take advantage of features such as ASP.NET sessions, output caching, and distributed transactions (a feature of .NET Enterprise services). There are many other features of ASP.NET that don't make much sense in the context of Web services. For example, cookie-less sessions are very cool and useful for Web applications but they rely on URL munging, which doesn't work for Web services.

6.3.1 Using ASP.NET Sessions

When a client invokes a Web method on your service, a new instance of your Web service class is created to serve that request. Therefore, a Web service class by definition is stateless because each request is served by a new instance of the Web service class. If you want to retain some state information on the server between Web service calls, you can use the ASP.NET session object.[2] Sessions are disabled by default; to enable session state, you must set the `WebMethod` attribute's `EnableSession` property to `True`. Listing 6.3 shows an example method that retrieves and returns a value called `TheData` out of the session, then replaces it with the input parameter.

Listing 6.4   Enabling session state on a Web method (VBWSBook\Chapter6\DataService.asmx.vb)

```
<WebMethod(EnableSession:=True)> _
Public Function SessionData(ByVal newVal As String) As String
    Dim oldVal As String
    If Session("TheData") Is Nothing Then
        Session("TheData") = newVal
        oldVal = "Session was empty"
    Else
        oldVal = Session("TheData")
        Session("TheData") = newVal
    End If
    Return oldVal
End Function
```

To invoke the Web service and retain session state, the client must receive the session cookie, then send it back with each subsequent request. The Web service proxy doesn't support cookies by default (and that's a good thing); you have to set its `CookieContainer` property to a new instance of `System.Net.CookieContainer` to enable cookie support. Listing 6.5 shows how a client can invoke `SessionData` while maintaining session state.

---

[2]By default, session state is stored in-process. While this gives you great performance, it prevents you from creating a Web server farm to scale out with increased application load. ASP.NET solves this problem by letting you store session information optionally on a dedicated server using either a Windows service or a back-end SQL Server database. This is useful when your Web services are running on a Web server farm.

When you change a Web service, (for example, by adding a new Web method like the DataService example), clients must also regenerate the Web service proxy. First, compile the Web service itself, then open the client project, right click on the Web service proxy (for example, `LocalService` folder) in Solution Explorer and choose Update Web Reference. Visual Studio will read the new WSDL document and regenerate the proxy class with the new `Session-Data` method.

Listing 6.5 Invoking a Web service that uses sessions. Note that the client must keep the Web service proxy object alive between requests (VBWSClientCode\Chapter6\WSClient\Form1.vb).

```
Dim m_ws As LocalServices.DataService
Private Sub Form1_Load( _
    ByVal sender As System.Object, _
    ByVal e As System.EventArgs) Handles MyBase.Load
    m_ws = New LocalServices.DataService()
    'use ProxyTrace to show request/response messages
    m_ws.Proxy = New System.Net.WebProxy("http://localhost:8080")
    m_ws.CookieContainer = New System.Net.CookieContainer()
End Sub
Private Sub btnSession_Click( _
    ByVal sender As System.Object, _
    ByVal e As System.EventArgs) Handles btnSession.Click
    MessageBox.Show(m_ws.SessionData(txtSessionVal.Text))
End Sub
```

Note that the Web service proxy is declared as a form member variable and instantiated in the form load event. Also in the form load event, the Web service proxy is configured to use a proxy server (to capture the request/response messages) and its `CookieContainer` property is set to a new `System.Net.CookieContainer` object. Then in the `btnSession` click event, the `SessionData` method is called passing it the contents of the text box called `txtSessionVal`. Figure 6.10 shows an example request/response message pair. Note the Set-Cookie: ASP.NET_SessionId in the HTTP header of the response message. This is the value of the session cookie being sent to the client. The client stores this cookie in the cookie container and resends it to the server with each subsequent request.

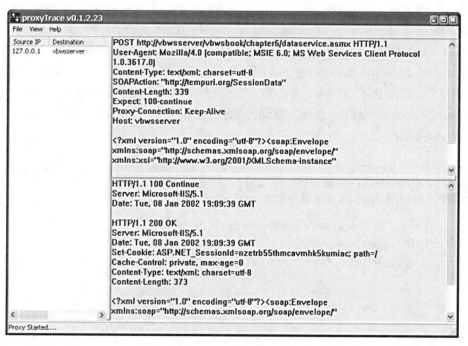

```
proxyTrace v0.1.2.23
File   View   Help

Source IP    Destination    POST http://vbwsserver/vbwsbook/chapter6/dataservice.asmx HTTP/1.1
127.0.0.1    vbwsserver     User-Agent: Mozilla/4.0 (compatible; MSIE 6.0; MS Web Services Client Protocol
                            1.0.3617.0)
                            Content-Type: text/xml; charset=utf-8
                            SOAPAction: "http://tempuri.org/SessionData"
                            Content-Length: 339
                            Expect: 100-continue
                            Proxy-Connection: Keep-Alive
                            Host: vbwsserver

                            <?xml version="1.0" encoding="utf-8"?><soap:Envelope
                            xmlns:soap="http://schemas.xmlsoap.org/soap/envelope/"
                            xmlns:xsi="http://www.w3.org/2001/XMLSchema-instance"

                            HTTP/1.1 100 Continue
                            Server: Microsoft-IIS/5.1
                            Date: Tue, 08 Jan 2002 19:09:39 GMT

                            HTTP/1.1 200 OK
                            Server: Microsoft-IIS/5.1
                            Date: Tue, 08 Jan 2002 19:09:39 GMT
                            Set-Cookie: ASP.NET_SessionId=nzetrb55thmcavmhk5kumiac; path=/
                            Cache-Control: private, max-age=0
                            Content-Type: text/xml; charset=utf-8
                            Content-Length: 373

                            <?xml version="1.0" encoding="utf-8"?><soap:Envelope
                            xmlns:soap="http://schemas.xmlsoap.org/soap/envelope/"

Proxy Started....
```

Figure 6.10   An example request/response to a service using sessions. Notice the Set-Cookie header in the HTTP response. This cookie is sent back with each subsequent request.

6.3.2   Enabling Output Caching

ASP.NET output caching lets you retain in memory the output from a Web method for a specified period of time. During this time, requests to the same method with the same parameter values will get the output directly from cache without really invoking the Web method. This works well for Web methods designed to return data without having any side effects on the server. For example, a Web method that returns the current temperature for a given zip code benefits from output caching. To enable output caching, you set the `WebMethod`'s `CacheDuration` property to the number of seconds that the output should be retained in memory:

```
<WebMethod(CacheDuration:=10)> _
Public Function CachedGetServerTime() As DateTime
```

Output caching is not an option if this Web method also inserts a record into a database to keep a log of all requests. This is because the Web method would not be called for some requests and therefore the database log would not reflect the actual number of requests. To fully leverage output caching, be mindful of it while designing your Web service. Whenever possible, methods that you expect to be highly accessed should be designed to take advantage of output caching by not having any side effects, such as writing to the event log or to a database.

6.3.3 Using Data Caching

If your Web service design requires such side effects (for example, you must log every single request because you will be billing your customers at the end of the month), you can still benefit from another type of caching called data or programmatic caching.

Instead of caching the entire response, your Web method uses the cache object to cache specific pieces of data in the first request. With subsequent requests, your Web method retrieves the data from the cache and returns it. Listing 6.6 shows two examples of using data caching in a Web service: DataCatchingFileDependency and DataCachingTimeout.

Listing 6.6   Using data caching with a file dependency and with a timeout value (VBWSBook\Chapter6\DataService.asmx.vb)

```
<WebMethod()> _
Public Function DataCachingFileDependency() As String
    Dim data As String
    data = Context.Cache.Get("MyDataDep")
    If data Is Nothing Then
        Dim cd As New System.Web.Caching.CacheDependency( _
            Context.Server.MapPath("DataFile.txt"))
        Context.Cache.Insert("MyDataDep", "cached at " + _
        System.DateTime.Now.ToString(), cd)
        data = "Was not yet cached"
    End If
    Return data
End Function
<WebMethod()> _
Public Function DataCachingTimeOut() As String
    Dim data As String
```

```
    data = Context.Cache.Get("MyDataTimeOut")
    If data Is Nothing Then
        Context.Cache.Insert("MyDataTimeOut", "cached at " + _
                System.DateTime.Now.ToString(), Nothing,
                System.DateTime.Now.AddMinutes(20), _
                TimeSpan.Zero)
        data = "Was not yet cached"
    End If
    Return data
End Function
```

Data caching is exposed via the Context.Cache property, which returns an object of type System.Web.Caching.Cache. This object lets you add and remove items to and from the cache using simple methods. The caching model is quite flexible in letting you specify the criteria for when cached items should expire. For example, the DataCachingFileDependency method in Listing 6.6 gets an item from the cache using Context.Cache.Get and passes it the item's key (which in this example is MyDataDep). If the item is not in the cache (the Get method returned Nothing), it creates a CacheDependency object, passing it the path to a file named DataFile.txt. Then it calls Context.Cache.Insert to insert a new item called MyDataDep. The actual item's data is the string "cached at" followed by the current data and time. The last parameter to the Insert method is the CacheDependency object. This means any changes to DataFile.txt will automatically invalidate the item in the cache (remove it from the cache). This is an example of caching data with the expiration criteria, depending on changes to a file. When you create the CacheDependency object you can also specify an array of files so that changes to any of them would invalidate cached data.

The second method, DataCachingTimeout, shows an example of specifying a time when cached data should be invalidated. Instead of passing a CacheDependency object to the Insert method, it passes a specific time, namely the current time plus twenty minutes, meaning the data will be invalid in 20 minutes.

Notice that the last parameter is TimeSpan.Zero. You can use the last parameter to specify a duration of inactivitiy after which the cache becomes invalid. For example, if you want the cache to become invalid if not used in the last 60 minutes, you specify this parameter as TimeSpan.FromMinutes(60). This gives the cached item a sliding scale of 60 minutes from the last-used time. You can't combine absolute timeout and sliding scale timeout. If you specify an absolute timeout, you must specify TimeSpan.Zero (as in Listing 6.5). If you specify a sliding scale TimeSpan, you must specify System.DateTime.MaxValue for the absolute timeout.

One last note: Output and data caching use memory. Therefore, the caching mechanisms are implemented so that data may be removed from the cache if the system resources are low. Which data gets removed from the cache is based on heuristics that take into account cached data usage and cache misses. This means that although you specified that data should be cached, it may be removed from the cache prematurely due to low available memory.

6.3.4 Distributed Transactions

In certain scenarios, you might want a Web method to act as the root of a distributed transaction so that all transactional components that are invoked from that method participate in one transaction. There are two scenarios when distributed transactions make sense: First, if the Web method needs to do work against two or more transactional resources (for example updating two relational databases or inserting into a database and writing to a transactional message queue). Second, if the Web method utilizes several transactional components that need to participate in the same transaction. Practically, you shouldn't run into this second scenario unless you are building a sophisticated system where transactional components can be used together in different ways and can participate in different types of business transactions.

If you decide you need distributed transactions, you can set the `Web-Method`'s `TransactionOption` property to `TransactionOption.Required` or `TransactionOption.RequiresNew`. The `TransactionOption` enumeration is defined in `System.EnterpriseServices` and has five possible values: `Disabled`, `NotSupported`, `Supported`, `Required`, and `RequiresNew`. A Web method cannot participate in an existing distributed transaction; therefore, both `Required` and `RequiresNew` mean that the Web method will always start a new distributed transaction. The other three values `Disabled`, `NotSupported`, and `Supported` mean that the Web method will not run in a transaction.

When a transactional Web method completes successfully, the transaction is automatically committed to release resources such as database locks. To abort a transaction, the Web method must either throw an exception or call `System.EnterpriseServices.ContextUtil.SetAbort`.

At the risk of being repetitious: *Before using distributed transactions, consider using your database's built-in transactions (for example, T-SQL transactions) or ADO.NET transactions.* If neither of these satisfies your application's requirements, you can easily use distributed transactions by setting the `TransactionOption` property.

MSDN has an article titled "Performance Comparison: Transaction Control" that compares the performance of TSQL, ADO.NET, and COM+ (Enterprise Services) transactions. At the time of this writing, the article can be found at: http://msdn.microsoft.com/library/default.asp?url=/library/en-us/dnbda/html/bdadotnetarch13.asp.

6.4   Customizing the Service's WSDL

In Chapters 3 and 4, you learned about SOAP messages and WSDL documents. You saw examples of WSDL and learned how WSDL is used to specify a Web service's interface. This section explains how you can control the auto-generated WSDL document and the service's SOAP messages to accommodate your requirements.

6.4.1   Disabling Protocols

By default, .NET lets you invoke Web services using HTTP GET, HTTP POST, and SOAP over HTTP. In fact, the auto-generated test page relies on HTTP GET to test the Web service. While supporting various protocols is a good thing for testing purposes, you might want to remove some of these protocols before you go into production. To remove HTTP GET and POST support from your Web service, you need to edit the Web application's web.config file. You must add a `<webServices>` section to this config file. Within this new section add a `<protocols>` element and add a `<remove>` element for each protocol that you want to remove. For example, this web.config removes HTTP GET and HTTP POST:

```
<configuration>
  <system.web>
    <webServices>
      <protocols>
        <remove name="HttpGet"/>
        <remove name="HttpPost"/>
      </protocols>
    </webServices>
  </system.web>
</configuration>
```

Configuring your Web service this way has three effects: First, the removed protocols are excluded from the service's WSDL document. Second, clients receive an error if they attempt to use these protocols to invoke the web service. Finally, disabling HTTP GET will disable the auto-generated test page, which is a bit of an inconvenience especially if you rely on that page for quick testing.[3]

You can apply these settings to all Web services running on a given machine by editing the machine.config file, which contains a `<webServices>` section, that by default, enables all three protocols. You can remove the protocols you want to disable from that section, which will affect all Web services running on that machine.

6.4.2 Names and Namespaces

A Web service's auto-generated WSDL document contains many names and namespaces that are based on various identifiers you use in your code. For example, the service name is by default, the same as the name of the class that implements this service. You might want to use characters in the service name that are legal for XML element names but illegal for VB class names (for example, a period). To change the default service name and namespace, you apply the `WebService` attribute to the class that implements the Web service. Listing 6.7 shows an example of a class called `CustomWS`, which exposes a Web service called `MyWeb.Service`. In this example, the `Namespace` property is set to `urn:my-unique-namespace` (instead of the default `http://tempuri.org`)

---

[3]You can use Web Services Studio for testing Web services instead of the auto-generated test page. This free tool, available on GotDotNet, lets you easily send a SOAP request to a Web service and view the response. Download it from www.GotDotNet.com.

and the name property is set to `MyWeb.Service`. I also set the `Description` property to display some useful documentation. Note that you can include HTML tags in your `Description` and they will be rendered as HTML on the default documentation page.

Listing 6.7   Setting the Web service's name and namespace using WebService(). Also setting a method's message name using WebMethod() (VBWSBook\Chapter6\CustomWS.asmx.vb).

```
'Using the Namespace property to control the service namespace
'Using the Name property to set the web service name
'with a . which is illegal in a VB class name
'And the Description property to document the service
'with html tags in the documentation
<WebService([Namespace]:="urn:my-unique-namespace", _
Name:="MyWeb.Service", _
Description:="Example of customizing Web services. " + _
"Written by <a href='mailto:shohoudy@devxpert.com'>" + _
"Yasser Shohoud</a>")> _
Public Class CustomWS
    Inherits System.Web.Services.WebService
    'using Description to display a useful
    'method description
    'Also MessageName to control the name of
    'the SOAP message
    <WebMethod( _
      Description:="This method has a custom operation name", _
      MessageName:="My.Message")> _
    Public Function CustomMsgName() As Integer
        Return 0
    End Function

End Class
```

You can add a description to each method by setting the `WebMethod`'s `Description` property. The `WebMethod` attribute in Listing 6.7 has both its `Description` and `MessageName` properties set. The `MessageName` property of `WebMethod` lets you control the name of the SOAP message as defined in the WSDL binding. In this example, I set the `MessageName` to `My.Message`, which is revealed as the input and output message names in the WSDL (shown in Figure 6.11). You can also use MessageName with overloaded Web methods to

```
    - <operation name="CustomMsgName">
        <documentation>This method has a custom operation name</documentation>
        <input name="My.Message" message="tns:My.MessageSoapIn" />
        <output name="My.Message" message="tns:My.MessageSoapOut" />
      </operation>
    </portType>
  - <binding name="MyWeb.ServiceSoap" type="tns:MyWeb.ServiceSoap">
      <soap:binding transport="http://schemas.xmlsoap.org/soap/http" style="document" />
    - <operation name="CustomMsgName">
        <soap:operation soapAction="urn:my-unique-namespace/My.Message" style="rpc" />
      - <input name="My.Message">
          <soap:body use="encoded" namespace="urn:my-unique-namespace"
          encodingStyle="http://schemas.xmlsoap.org/soap/encoding/" />
        </input>
      - <output name="My.Message">
          <soap:body use="encoded" namespace="urn:my-unique-namespace"
          encodingStyle="http://schemas.xmlsoap.org/soap/encoding/" />
        </output>
      </operation>
    </binding>
  - <service name="MyWeb.Service">
      <documentation>Example of customizing Web services. Written by <a
      href="mailto:shohoudy@devxpert.com">Yasser Shohoud</a></documentation>
    - <port name="MyWeb.ServiceSoap" binding="tns:MyWeb.ServiceSoap">
        <soap:address location="http://localhost/vbwsbook/Chapter6/CustomWS.asmx" />
      </port>
    </service>
  </definitions>
```

Figure 6.11   WSDL for the CustomWS Web service. Notice the service name is MyWeb.Service and the input and output message names are My.Message.

give them different message names in the generated WSDL (because a Web service cannot have two messages with the same name).

Pulling up this service's documentation page, you'll see the name My-Web.Service and the custom description at the top as shown in Figure 6.12. You'll also note the absence of the long recommendation about changing the Web service's namespace to something other than http://tempuri.org because we've already done that.

6.4.3   Controlling SOAP Message Style

.NET Web services use document/literal SOAP messages by default. This is generally acceptable because messaging Web services are centered on XML documents and their schemas. In some cases, however, you'll need to use RPC/encoded SOAP messages (for example, if you want to expose your Web service to clients that understand only RPC/encoded SOAP).

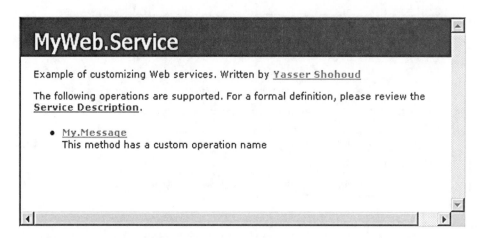

Figure 6.12   The documentation page for CustomWS

At the Web service level, you control the style of SOAP messages by applying `SoapRpcService` or `SoapDocumentService` (the default) attributes to the class that implements the Web service. For finer-grained control at the method level, you apply `SoapRpcMethod` or `SoapDocumentMethod` attributes on each individual method.

You can apply SoapRpcMethod and SoapDocumentMethod to different methods in the same Web service. Before you mix RPC/encoded and document/literal SOAP messages in the same Web service, be sure that your target clients' tools support such combinations. .NET clients have no problem with this but others might.

Both `SoapRpcMethod` and `SoapDocumentMethod` expose four properties that let you specify the request and response element names and namespaces. The property names are `RequestElementName`, `RequestElementNamespace`, `ResponseElementName`, and `ResponseElementNamespace`.

Listing 6.8 shows an example of applying `SoapDocumentMethod` and setting the `RequestNamespace` property to `http://xmlws.com/messages`. Listing 6.9 shows the resulting SOAP request message with the custom namespace.

Listing 6.8   Setting the request namespace for a specific method

```
'set the namespace to use
'for the body payload in the
'SOAP request message
<WebMethod(), _
SoapDocumentMethod(RequestNamespace:= _
"http://xmlws.com/messages")> _
Public Function CustomNS() As Integer
...
End Function
```

Listing 6.9   The resulting SOAP request message corresponding to CustomNS method

```
<soap:Envelope ...>
  <soap:Body>
    <CustomNS xmlns="http://xmlws.com/messages" />
  </soap:Body>
</soap:Envelope>
```

6.4.4   Parameter Encoding

When using document-style SOAP messages, .NET lets you specify whether you want to use encoded or literal parameters. The default is literal, which is by far the most common parameter format for document-style messages. However, if for some reason you need to use document/encoded messages, you can easily do this at the service or method levels by setting the `Use` property of `SoapDocumentService` or `SoapDocumentMethod`, respectively. The three possible values are `Literal`, `Encoded` and `Default`. If you use `Default` with `SoapDocumentMethod`, it'll default to whatever the containing service is using. Using `Default` with `SoapDocumentService` means you are accepting the default setting which is literal. Listing 6.10 shows an example method that uses document/encoded messages and Listing 6.11 shows the corresponding operation binding definition. Note that .NET supports three of the four message styles: Document/literal, document/encoded, and RPC/encoded. RPC/literal is not supported, but that's acceptable, because as mentioned in Chapters 3 and 4, practically only two message styles are used: Document/literal and RPC/encoded—and both are supported by .NET.

Listing 6.10   Using Document/encoded SOAP by setting the Use property of SoapDocumentMethod

```
<WebMethod(), _
SoapDocumentMethod(Use:=SoapBindingUse.Encoded, _
RequestNamespace:="http://xmlws.com/messages")> _
Public Function CustomNS() As Integer
   ...
End Function
```

Listing 6.11   The resulting WSDL binding information

```
<operation name="CustomNS">
  <soap:operation
      soapAction="urn:my-unique-namespace/CustomNS"
      style="document" />
  <input>
    <soap:body use="encoded"
       namespace="http://xmlws.com/messages"
       encodingStyle="http://schemas.xmlsoap.org/soap/encoding/"
   />
  </input>
  <output>
    <soap:body use="encoded"
        namespace="urn:my-unique-namespace/encodedTypes"
        encodingStyle="http://schemas.xmlsoap.org/soap/encoding/"
   />
  </output>
</operation>
```

`SoapDocumentMethod` and `SoapDocumentService` expose a property called `ParameterStyle`, which you can use to control whether method parameters and return value appear directly inside the `<soap:Body>` element (`ParameterStyle := SoapParameterStyle.Bare`) or are wrapped within another element (`ParameterStyle := SoapParameterStyle.Wrapped`). Listing 6.12 shows the effect of setting this property on request SOAP messages for an operation that takes two parameters like this:

```
Public Function ParamStyleTest( _
         ByVal a As Integer, _
         ByVal b As String) As  String
```

Listing 6.12   Two SOAP messages showing wrapped and bare parameter styles, respectively

```
<!-- this message corresponds to ParameterStyle := Wrapped -->
<soap:Envelope ...>
  <soap:Body>
    <ParamStyleTest xmlns="urn:my-unique-namespace">
      <a>int</a>
      <b>string</b>
    </ParamStyleTest>
  </soap:Body>
</soap:Envelope>
<!-- this message corresponds to ParameterStyle := Bare -->
<soap:Envelope ...>
  <soap:Body>
    <a xmlns="urn:my-unique-namespace">int</a>
    <b xmlns="urn:my-unique-namespace">string</b>
  </soap:Body>
</soap:Envelope>
```

`SoapParameterStyle.Bare` is especially useful when you want to have full control over what goes inside the `<Body>` element and you don't want .NET to add wrapper elements around your data. You'll see an example Web service implemented with `SoapParameterStyle.Bare` in Chapter 13.

6.4.5   One-Way Operations

As explained in Chapter 4, WSDL defines four types of operations. One of those operations is the **request-only operation**, where a client sends a request message and receives nothing back—not even error information. If you have such a method, you can apply a `SoapDocumentMethod` or a `SoapRpcMethod` attribute and set its `OneWay` property to `True`. This tells .NET that your method will not return an output message, which means incoming requests will return as soon as the method *begins* execution. For example, the method definition in Listing 6.13 results in the WSDL operation in Listing 6.14. Note that the WSDL operation has no output message.

Listing 6.13 A one-way Web method

```
<WebMethod(), SoapDocumentMethod(OneWay:=True)> _
Public Sub OneWayMethod(ByVal theData As String)
    ...
End Sub
```

Listing 6.14 The WSDL binding information for a one-way method

```
<operation name="OneWayMethod">
  <input message="s0:OneWayMethodSoapIn" />
</operation>
```

6.4.6 Ignoring/Specifying SOAP Action

By default, the SOAP Action HTTP header value is generated by combining the Web service namespace with the operation (method) name. Also by default, .NET reads the SOAP Action value for each Web service request and uses it to determine which operation is to be invoked. Although this works in most cases, it's better not to rely on SOAP Action because it is a highly controversial topic in the SOAP world today.

At the time of this writing, the SOAP 1.2 W3C *Working Draft* states that SOAP-Action is an optional feature and should not be required by a Web service unless there's a particular purpose for doing so.

Listing 6.15 shows an example of setting the SoapDocumentServiceAttribute.RoutingStyle property not to rely on SOAPAction.

Listing 6.15 Specifying that requests are to be routed based on element name, not SOAP Action

```
<SoapDocumentService( _
   RoutingStyle:=SoapServiceRoutingStyle.RequestElement)> _
Public Class CustomWS
   ...
End Class
```

Both `SoapDocumentService` and `SoapRpcService` have a `RoutingStyle` property that you can set to `SoapServiceRoutingStyle.RequestElement` in order to specify that the SOAPAction value should be ignored. Note that this property can only be set at the service level—not the method level.

If you use `SoapServiceRoutingStyle.RequestElement` with `Soap-ParameterStyle.Bare` parameter style, you must be careful about the number of parameters (must be exactly one) and parameter names for each Web method. That's because you are telling .NET to route incoming messages to the corresponding methods based on the name of the child of the `<soap:Body>` element. At the same time, you're telling it to include method parameters as direct children of `<soap:Body>` with no wrapper element. Although this can be tricky, .NET lets you get away with this combination provided that the method has exactly one parameter and that each method parameter is serialized to a different element name. .NET needs this restriction so it can tell which Web method to invoke based on the incoming element name. You'll see an example of this combination in Chapter 13.

It's also possible to set the required SOAP Action value for each method individually using the Action property of `SoapRpcMethod` or `SoapDocument-Method`. Whatever string you specify as this property value becomes the `soapAction` attribute value in the WSDL SOAP binding section.

Listing 6.16 shows the completed CustomWS Web service with the Web methods and attributes discussed in this section.

**Listing 6.16 The complete CustomWS Web service
(VBWSBook\Chapter6\CustomWS.asmx.vb)**

```
<SoapDocumentService( _
    RoutingStyle:=SoapServiceRoutingStyle.SoapAction), _
    WebService([Namespace]:="urn:my-unique-namespace", _
Name:="MyWeb.Service", _
Description:="Example of customizing Web services. " + _
"Written by <a href='mailto:shohoudy@devxpert.com'>" + _
"Yasser Shohoud</a>")> _
Public Class CustomWS
    Inherits System.Web.Services.WebService

    <WebMethod( _
      Description:="This method has a custom operation name", _
      MessageName:="My.Message")> _
    Public Function CustomMsgName() As Integer

    End Function
```

```
<WebMethod(), _
SoapDocumentMethod( _
  RequestNamespace:="http://xmlws.com/messages")> _
Public Function CustomNS() As Integer

End Function

<WebMethod(), _
SoapDocumentMethod(ParameterStyle:=SoapParameterStyle.Bare)> _
Public Function ParamStyleTest( _
        ByVal a As Integer, ByVal b As String)_
          As String

End Function
<WebMethod(), SoapDocumentMethod(OneWay:=True)> _
Public Sub OneWayMethod(ByVal theData As String)

End Sub
End Class
```

Now that you know how to create and customize Web services, the next section explains how .NET Web service clients work and how you can customize them to meet your needs.

6.5 Understanding Web Service Clients

A Web service proxy class inherits from either `HttpGetClientProtocol`, `HttpPostClientProtocol`, or `SoapHttpClientProtocol` depending on whether it uses HTTP GET, HTTP POST, or SOAP to invoke the Web service. As I mentioned earlier, HTTP GET and POST are somewhat interesting for quickly testing the service, but any real-world Web service will likely use SOAP, which means the Web service proxy will inherit from `SoapHttpClientProtocol`. Figure 6.13 shows the class hierarchy for a Web service proxy. Note that `SoapHttpClientProtocol` inherits from `HttpWebClientProtocol`, which in turn inherits from `WebClientProtocol`.

A Web service proxy class that uses SOAP inherits from `SoapHttpClientProxy`. Similarly, if the proxy uses HTTP GET or POST, it inherits from `HttpGetClientProtocol` or `HttpPostClientProtocol`, respectively.

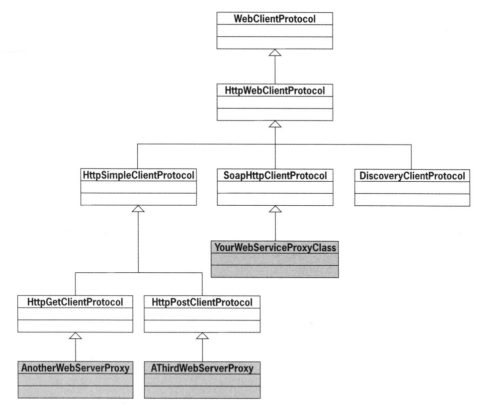

Figure 6.13 Inheritance hierarchy for a Web service proxy class. The classes at the bottom of the hierarchy are Web service proxies.

Each class in this inheritance hierarchy is responsible for a different portion of the task of sending a Web service request and receiving the response. For example, `HttpWebClientProtocol` implements functionality that is specific to HTTP such as the `Proxy` property explained above. On the other hand, `SoapHttpClientProtocol` exposes an interesting method called Invoke, which is responsible for invoking the Web service. This method does all the heavy lifting including serializing input parameters, sending the SOAP request, parsing the response, and deserializing all output parameters and return value. Invoke takes in the name of the method you want to invoke and an array of objects that contains the input parameters (that is, the parts of the input message) and returns an array of objects that contains the output parameters and return value (the parts of the output message):

```
Protected Function Invoke( _
    ByVal methodName As String, _
    ByVal parameters() As Object _
) As Object()
```

Note that `Invoke` is protected, which means you can't instantiate a `SoapHttp-ClientProtocol` object and call `Invoke` on it; you must inherit from `Soap-HttpClientProtocol`, then call `Me.Invoke`. Listing 6.17 shows an example custom proxy that calls the `GetServerTime` Web method from Listing 6.2.

Listing 6.17   A proxy class that inherits from SoapHttpClientProtocol and calls the GetServerTime method (VBWSClientCode\Chapter6\CustomClient\ CustomProxy.vb)

```
Imports System.Web.Services.Protocols
Imports System.Web.Services
<WebServiceBinding()> _
Public Class CustomProxy
    Inherits SoapHttpClientProtocol

    <SoapDocumentMethod("http://tempuri.org/GetServerTime", _
    RequestNamespace:="http://tempuri.org/", _
    ResponseNamespace:="http://tempuri.org/")> _
    Public Function GetServerTime() As DateTime
        Dim ret() As Object
        Me.Url = _
         "http://VBWSServer/vbwsbook/Chapter6/DataService.asmx"
        ret = Me.Invoke("GetServerTime", New Object(-1) {})
        Return CType(ret(0), DateTime)
    End Function

    End Class
```

In Listing 6.17, `CustomProxy` inherits from `SoapHttpClientProtocol` and adds the `GetServerTime` method. When `GetServerTime` is called, it sets the base class's `Url` property to the Web service end point URL, then calls `SoapHttpClientProtocol.Invoke` and passes it the Web method name

(GetServerTime) and an array of objects. This array normally contains an object for each input parameter that the Web method takes. In this case, it is empty because the Web method takes no parameters. The output from this call is an object array that is stored in the variable called `ret`. This array contains the Web method's return value and any returned `ByRef` parameters. In this case, the first (and only) item in this array is the method return value that represents the server's time. The next line takes this return value out of the array, converts it to a `DateTime,` and returns it.

You'll notice a `SoapDocumentMethod` attribute on the `GetServerTime` proxy method; this is needed so that `SoapHttpClientProtocol` will know how to form the SOAP request. Generally, the attributes you use on the service to control the SOAP message can also be used on the client to match the service definition. If, for example, the service defines a one-way method like this:

```
<WebMethod(), SoapDocumentMethod(OneWay := True)> _
Public Function OneWayMethod(ByVal a As Integer, _
        ByVal b As String) As String
```

the corresponding proxy method would look almost the same minus the `Web-Method` attribute:

```
<SoapDocumentMethod(OneWay := True)> _
Public Function OneWayMethod(ByVal a As Integer, _
        ByVal b As String) As String
```

Now that you know the fundamentals of how client proxies work, let's examine the proxy that Visual Studio .NET auto generates.

Listing 6.18 shows the proxy class that was generated by adding a Web reference to the `CustomWS` Web service shown in Listing 6.16.

Listing 6.18 A proxy class automatically generated for CustomWS. Some methods were removed to make it easier to read (VBWSClientCode\Chapter6\ CustomClient\Web References\VBWSServer\Reference.vb).

```
Namespace vbwsserver

<WebServiceBindingAttribute( _
Name:="MyWeb.ServiceSoap", _
```

```
[Namespace]:="urn:my-unique-namespace")> _
Public Class MyWebService
        Inherits SoapHttpClientProtocol

    <DebuggerStepThroughAttribute()> _
    Public Sub New()
        MyBase.New()
        Me.Url = "http://localhost/vbwsbook/Chapter6/CustomWS.asmx"
    End Sub


<DebuggerStepThroughAttribute(), _
SoapDocumentMethodAttribute( _
 "urn:my-unique-namespace/My.Message", _
RequestElementName:="My.Message", _
RequestNamespace:="urn:my-unique-namespace", _
ResponseElementName:="My.MessageResponse", _
ResponseNamespace:="urn:my-unique-namespace", _
Use:= SoapBindingUse.Literal, _
ParameterStyle:=SoapParameterStyle.Wrapped)> _
 Public Function CustomMsgName() As _
     <XmlElement("My.MessageResult", IsNullable:=False)> Integer
    Dim results() As Object = _
            Me.Invoke("CustomMsgName", New Object(-1) {})
    Return CType(results(0), Integer)
 End Function



<DebuggerStepThroughAttribute(), _
SoapDocumentMethodAttribute( _
 "urn:my-unique-namespace/ParamStyleTest", _
Use:= SoapBindingUse.Literal, _
ParameterStyle:=SoapParameterStyle.Bare)> _
Public Function ParamStyleTest( _
  <XmlElement ([Namespace]:="urn:my-unique-namespace", _
  IsNullable:=False)> ByVal a As Integer, _
  <XmlElement ([Namespace]:="urn:my-unique-namespace", _
  IsNullable:=True)> ByVal b As String) As _
<XmlElement ([Namespace]:="urn:my-unique-namespace", _
  IsNullable:=True)> String
   Dim results() As Object = Me.Invoke( _
            "ParamStyleTest", New Object() {a, b})
   Return CType(results(0), String)
End Function
```

```vb
<DebuggerStepThroughAttribute(), _
 SoapDocumentMethodAttribute( _
"urn:my-unique-namespace/OneWayMethod", _
RequestNamespace:="urn:my-unique-namespace", _
OneWay:=True, _
Use:= SoapBindingUse.Literal, _
ParameterStyle:=SoapParameterStyle.Wrapped)> _
Public Sub OneWayMethod(ByVal theData As String)
    Me.Invoke("OneWayMethod", New Object() {theData})
End Sub

End Class
End Namespace
```

I removed some of the methods in the auto-generated proxy and reformatted it to make it easier to read. The proxy begins with a namespace called `vb-wsserver` that is derived from the name of the host where the Web service is located. You can change this namespace to anything you like or remove it completely and the proxy class will continue to work. The proxy class is called `My-WebService`, which is based on the `Name` property of the `WebService` attribute in Listing 6.16 (that is, in the name of the `<service>` element in the service's WSDL document). This class has a `WebServiceBindingAttribute` with `Name` and `Namespace` properties. I'll discuss bindings in more detail in Chapter 8.

The proxy class's constructor (`Sub New()`) calls the base class's constructor, then sets the `Url` property to point to the Web service location. At runtime, `SoapHttpClientProtocol` sends HTTP requests to the URL in this property. The next method is `CustomMsgName`, which has two attributes on it. `Debugger-StepThroughAttribute` tells the debugger to skip the code in this method and go directly to the Web service method. This means when you debug the client and step into the call to the proxy's `CustomMsgName`, the debugger will try to take you to the Web service's `CustomMsgName` instead. This gives the illusion that you are calling directly into the Web service with no proxy class in between. The other attribute on `CustomMsgName` is `SoapDocumentMethod`, which specifies several aspects of the request and response SOAP message. The first parameter, `"urn:my-unique-namespace/My.Message"`, is the SOAP Action value re-

.NET WEB SERVICES   269

quired for this method. The next four properties indicate the request and response element names and namespaces. Normally these are optional, but in this example there's a custom message name as indicated by the `MessageName := "My.Message"` property on the Web method. The `Use` property indicates that message parts are literal (not encoded) and `ParameterStyle` indicates that message parts are to be wrapped into a single element. Both of these values are the default so removing them has no impact (remember this is auto-generated code).

The return value has an `XmlElement` attribute that specifies that the return element's name is `My.MessageResult`. The method implementation is very similar to what you saw above: It calls `Invoke` on the base class, passing it the method name and an array of input parameters (an empty array in this case) and gets back an array that contains the return value.

The next interesting method is `ParamStyleTest`. This Web method is defined to use the `Bare` parameter style, which means that each method parameter will be represented by a child element of `<soap:Body>`. The auto-generated proxy reflects this by setting the `ParameterStyle` property of `SoapDocumentMethod` to `Bare` and by adding `XmlElement` attribute on each of the parameters and the return value. Finally, `OneWayMethod` has the `SoapDocumentMethod`'s `OneWay` property set to `True` just as on the service side. At runtime, this property means that no response should be expected. Without this property on the client side, the client will look for a SOAP response message and throw an exception when it doesn't get one.

6.6 Summary

The .NET Framework provides a rich set of classes and tools for building and consuming Web services and Visual Studio .NET makes it even easier. In this chapter, you learned how to create .NET Web services and how to customize the Web service's WSDL to meet your needs. You also learned how .NET Web service clients are generated and how they work. The next two chapters build on this knowledge to show you how to perform advanced tasks such as utilizing SOAP headers and interface-based Web services development.

6.7 Resources

.NET Framework SDK documentation http://msdn.microsoft.com/library/en-us/
cpref/html/frlrfSystemWebServices.asp.

Developmentor's .NET Web discussion list:
discuss.develop.com/dotnet-web.html.

.NET Webservice Studio:
http://www.gotdotnet.com/team/tools/web_svc/default.aspx.

Chapter 7

SOAP Header and Fault

> There are two ways to write error-free programs. Only the third one
> works. —Anonymous

In Chapter 3, you learned how SOAP headers can be used to extend SOAP by including information in the SOAP message outside of the message payload. Applications of SOAP headers include custom session keys (when your application is managing its own sessions), security keys, and digital signatures. .NET makes it easy to send and receive SOAP headers by providing a framework of objects that you use to define your headers and to specify which Web methods will use them. In this chapter, you will learn how to implement SOAP headers with .NET to send additional information between client and service. You'll also learn to communicate error information in a rich, standard way using SOAP Fault elements.

7.1 Defining SOAP Headers

The first step in using SOAP headers is to define a class that represents the header you want to send or receive. This class must inherit from the base class `System.Web.Services.Protocols.SoapHeader` and add public members that represent the header information you need. Listing 7.1 shows two classes that represent two different SOAP headers, each with two public fields.

Listing 7.1 Two SOAP header classes (VBWSBook\Chapter7\ DataService.asmx.vb)

```
Public Class HeaderClass1
    Inherits SoapHeader
    Public field1 As Integer
    Public field2 As String
```

```
End Class
Public Class HeaderClass2
    Inherits SoapHeader
    Public fielda As Integer
    Public fieldb As String
End Class
```

Because your SOAP headers are simply classes, they can also contain proper-ties and methods. Also, you can use XML serialization attributes such as `Xml-Element` and `XmlArrayItem` to control how public members of your header classes get serialized into SOAP messages.

7.2   Using Headers on the Service

After defining your header classes, you need to specify which Web methods will use these headers. First, you declare public member variables of the types of headers you want to use. For example, Listing 7.2 shows a Web service with two member variables: one of type HeaderClass1 and one of type HeaderClass2. Note that the member variables must be public.

Listing 7.2   A Web service with two member variables representing two SOAP headers (VBWSBook\Chapter7\DataService.asmx.vb)

```
Public Class DataService
    Inherits System.Web.Services.WebService

    'header fields must be public
    Public inputHeader As HeaderClass1
    Public outputHeader As HeaderClass2
End Class
```

You add a `SoapHeaderAttribute` attribute to each Web method that needs to send or receive SOAP headers. This attribute lets you specify the name of the member variable that represents the SOAP header, the direction of the header (in, out, or in/out), and if the header is required. Listing 7.3 shows two Web methods that use the two headers defined in Listing 7.1.

Listing 7.3 Two Web methods that use the two SOAP headers defined in Listing 7.1 (VBWSBook\Chapter7\DataService.asmx.vb)

```
<WebMethod(), _
    SoapHeaderAttribute("inputHeader", _
            Direction:=SoapHeaderDirection.In, _
            Required:=True)> _
    Public Function ProcessHeader() As String

        Return "The information the service received " + _
            in the header is """ + _
            inputHeader.field1.ToString() + """ and """ + _
            inputHeader.field2 + """"
    End Function

    <WebMethod(), _
    SoapHeaderAttribute("outputHeader", _
            Direction:=SoapHeaderDirection.Out, _
            Required:=True)> _
    Public Sub ReturnHeader()
        outputHeader = New HeaderClass2()
        outputHeader.fielda = 122
        outputHeader.fieldb = "the data sent back in the header"
    End Sub
```

Looking at the first method, `ProcessHeader`, you'll note that `SoapHeaderAttribute`'s constructor takes in the name of the member variable that represents the SOAP header. For the first method, `ProcessHeader`, the member variable name is `inputHeader`, which we declared earlier. This means when a header is received in the SOAP request, it will automatically be deserialized into an instance of `HeaderClass1` and stored in the `inputHeader` variable. `SoapHeaderAttribute` also has a `Direction` property that is set to `SoapHeaderDirection.In` indicating that incoming SOAP messages will contain this header. Finally, the `Required` property is set to `True`, which means the header must be present in an incoming SOAP message; otherwise, an exception is returned to the client before your Web method is executed.

When the code inside `ProcessHeader` executes, you can assume that the input message contained a valid SOAP header that was deserialized into `inputHeader`. The example in Listing 7.3 reads `field1` and `field2` from `inputHeader` and returns them in a string to demonstrate that it received the SOAP header.

The second method, `ReturnHeader`, is different because it returns a SOAP header instead of receiving one. To indicate this, it has the `SoapHeaderAttribute`'s direction property set to `SoapHeaderDirection.Out`. It also has the `Required` property set to `True` which, for out headers, means that the service must return this header. Therefore, if *after* `ReturnHeader` executes it does not return the required header, the client gets an exception indicating this.

To return a header, the `ReturnHeader` code first instantiates a new `HeaderClass2` object and stores it in the member variable called `outputHeader`. Then it sets the members of this new object with the header information. `outputHeader` is automatically serialized to XML and included as a SOAP header in the response message.

You can use more than one SOAP header in a Web method by applying multiple `SoapHeader` attributes to it. For example, a Web method can have input and output headers defined using multiple `SoapHeader` attributes.

7.3   Using Headers on the Client

When you add a Web reference to a Web service that uses SOAP headers, the generated code contains a class for each SOAP header defined in the Web service. Listing 7.4 shows an example proxy class for the above service. To improve readability, I removed all attributes and other code not relevant to this discussion.

Listing 7.4   An example proxy class that calls a Web service with SOAP headers (VBWSClientCode\Chapter7\CustomClient\Web References\ VBWSServer1\Reference.vb)

```
Public Class DataService
    Inherits SoapHttpClientProtocol

    Public HeaderClass1Value As HeaderClass1
    Public HeaderClass2Value As HeaderClass2
```

```
    <SoapHeaderAttribute("HeaderClass2Value", _
    Direction:=SoapHeaderDirection.Out)> _
    Public Sub ReturnHeader()
        Me.Invoke("ReturnHeader", New Object(-1) {})
    End Sub

    <SoapHeaderAttribute("HeaderClass1Value")> _
    Public Function ProcessHeader() As String
        Dim results() As Object = _
          Me.Invoke("ProcessHeader", New Object(-1) {})
        Return CType(results(0), String)
    End Function
End Class

<XmlRootAttribute( _
[Namespace]:="http://tempuri.org/", IsNullable:=False)> _
Public Class HeaderClass1
    Inherits SoapHeader
    Public field1 As Integer
    Public field2 As String
End Class

<XmlRootAttribute( _
[Namespace]:="http://tempuri.org/", IsNullable:=False)> _
Public Class HeaderClass2
    Inherits SoapHeader
    Public fielda As Integer
    Public fieldb As String
End Class
```

The proxy class in Listing 7.4 has two member variables that represent the two headers used by the Web service. The classes `HeaderClass1` and `HeaderClass2` are both automatically generated and placed at the bottom of the file. Each Web method that uses headers, (for example, `ReturnHeader`), has a `SoapHeaderAttribute` that mimics the one on the service side except it uses the names of the member variables defined on the client, (`HeaderClass1Value` and `HeaderClass2Value`). Although the `Required` property is not set for each `SoapHeaderAttribute` in this example, the default is `True`. `SoapHttpClientProtocol` is smart enough to recognize when the client does not send a required input header, and it throws an exception without even attempting to send the SOAP request to the service.

Listing 7.5 shows how a client can use this proxy to send and receive SOAP headers.

Listing 7.5   A client that uses the proxy class in Listing 7.4 (VBWSClientCode\Chapter7\CustomClient\Form1.vb)

```
Private Sub Button6_Click( _
    ByVal sender As System.Object, _
    ByVal e As System.EventArgs) Handles Button6.Click
  Dim ws As New vbwsserver1.DataService()
  Dim theheader As New vbwsserver1.HeaderClass1()
  theheader.field1 = 77
  theheader.field2 = "some information the service needs"
  ws.HeaderClass1Value = theheader
  MessageBox.Show(ws.ProcessHeader())
End Sub

Private Sub Button7_Click( _
    ByVal sender As System.Object, _
    ByVal e As System.EventArgs) Handles Button7.Click
  Dim ws As New vbwsserver1.DataService()
  ws.ReturnHeader()
  Dim msg As String
  msg = "The header that came back contains """ + _
          ws.HeaderClass2Value.fielda.ToString() + _
          """ and """ + ws.HeaderClass2Value.fieldb + """"
  MessageBox.Show(msg)
End Sub
```

The first procedure, `Button6_Click`, calls `ProcessHeader`, which expects an input SOAP header. To send this header, the first step is to instantiate an object, in this case called `theheader`, from `vbwsserver1.HeaderClass1`. Note that `vbwsserver1` is the namespace in which Visual Studio put the proxy code. Next, you set the new header object's properties with the information you want to send in this header. Then you tell the proxy about this header object by setting the proxy's member variable `HeaderClass1Value` to `theheader`. When you call `ProcessHeader`, the header object will be automatically serialized and included in the request message.

`Button7_Click` calls `ReturnHeader`, which returns a SOAP header. The returned header is deserialized and stored in the proxy's `HeaderClass2Value` member variable so you can access the header information by simply reading the properties of this variable. The example code in Listing 7.5 calls `ReturnHeader`, then reads `HeaderClass2Value.fielda` and `HeaderClass2Value.fieldb` and displays them in a message box.

7.4 Mystery Headers

So far you've seen how a service can declare the headers it expects and how a client can send it those headers. It's possible for a client to send headers to the service that the service didn't know about at design time. If this happens, the service will most likely not care about those headers since it doesn't know what to do with them to begin with. However, you might have a scenario where you want to retrieve those headers and log or process them. You need a catch-all member variable that can be used to access all unknown headers. This member variable must be either a single instance or an array of `SoapUnknownHeader`. A single instance will capture the first unknown header while an array will capture all unknown headers. Then you add a `SoapHeaderAttribute` with this member variable's name to each method in which you want to access unknown headers. Listing 7.6 shows an example of this.

Listing 7.6   A Web method that reads all SOAP headers from the request message (VBWSBook\Chapter7\DataService.asmx.vb)

```
Public Class DataService
     Inherits System.Web.Services.WebService

     'the catch all header variable
     Public mysteryHeaders As SoapUnknownHeader()

     <WebMethod(), _
     SoapHeader("mysteryHeaders", _
           Direction:=SoapHeaderDirection.In, _
           Required:=False)> _
     Public Function WhatHeaders() As String
        Dim msg As String
        Dim unknownHeader As SoapUnknownHeader
        For Each unknownHeader In mysteryHeaders
```

```
                    msg = msg + "Header xml: " + _
                        unknownHeader.Element.OuterXml + vbCrLf
            Next
            Return msg
        End Function
    End Class
```

When WhatHeaders is called, all incoming SOAP headers will be deserialized into `SoapUnknownHeader` objects and added to the `mysteryHeaders` array. The code inside `WhatHeaders` loops through all headers in this array and gets each header's XML using `SoapUnknownHeader`'s Element property, which returns the header as an XML element. `WhatHeaders` then returns the headers XML back to the client as a demonstration that it received the header.

Listing 7.7 shows an example proxy for invoking `WhatHeaders` with a couple of undefined headers.

Listing 7.7 An example proxy that invokes WhatHeaders with two different SOAP headers (VBWSClientCode\Chapter7\CustomClient\Web References\VBWSServer1\Reference.vb)

```
'The following two classes were not
'auto-gen'd they were manually created
Public Class SessionInfo
    Inherits SoapHeader
    Public SessionId As String
    Public LastUsed As DateTime
End Class
Public Class TransactionInfo
    Inherits SoapHeader
    Public TransactionId As String
    Public MyVote As Boolean
End Class
<System.Web.Services.WebServiceBindingAttribute( _
 Name:="DataServiceSoap", [Namespace]:="http://tempuri.org/")> _
Public Class DataService
    Inherits System.Web.Services.Protocols.SoapHttpClientProtocol

    'The following two lines were not
    'auto-gen'd they were manually created
    Public theSession As SessionInfo
    Public tx As TransactionInfo
```

```
    <System.Diagnostics.DebuggerStepThroughAttribute()> _
    Public Sub New()
        MyBase.New()
        Me.Url = _
            "http://VBWSServer/vbwsbook/Chapter7/DataService.asmx"
    End Sub


    'The following 2 SoapHeaderAttributes
    'were added manually
    'and not auto gen'd
     <SoapHeaderAttribute("theSession"), _
      SoapHeaderAttribute("tx"), _
      SoapDocumentMethodAttribute( _
      "http://tempuri.org/WhatHeaders")> _
    Public Function WhatHeaders() As String
        Dim results() As Object = _
            Me.Invoke("WhatHeaders", New Object(-1) {})
        Return CType(results(0), String)
    End Function
End Class
```

The classes `SessionInfo` and `TransactionInfo` both inherit from `Soap-Header` and represent the two header types that we will send to the service. The proxy class, which is called `DataService`, has a member variable called `theSession` and another one called `tx`. These represent the instances of the headers that we will send to the service. I've manually added two `SoapHeader-Attributes` on the `WhatHeaders` method to indicate that I want to send `theSession` and `tx` as SOAP headers. Listing 7.8 shows client code using this proxy to invoke the service.

Listing 7.8   Example client code that uses the proxy in Listing 7.7 (VBWSClientCode\Chapter7\CustomClient\Form1.vb)

```
Private Sub Button8_Click( _
        ByVal sender As System.Object, _
        ByVal e As System.EventArgs) Handles Button8.Click
    Dim ws As New localhost1.DataService()
    ws.theSession = New localhost1.SessionInfo()
    ws.theSession.LastUsed = DateTime.Now
    ws.theSession.SessionId = "abcbdef1234e"
    ws.tx = New localhost1.TransactionInfo()
    ws.tx.MyVote = True
```

```
      ws.tx.TransactionId = "0fa9eb0374"
      MessageBox.Show(ws.WhatHeaders())
   End Sub
```

The client instantiates the proxy, then sets `theSession` member to a new instance of `SessionInfo` and populates its properties. Similarly, it sets the tx member to a new instance of `TransactionInfo` and populates its properties. Finally, it calls `WhatHeaders` and displays the returned string in a messagebox. Figure 7.1 shows the result, which is simply the XML representation of the SessionInfo and TransactionInfo headers as echoed back from the service.

7.5 You Must Understand This

If the client can send you arbitrary headers, there's a good chance your service will not understand what to do with them. This can cause problems if the client is counting on your service to process the headers. To solve this problem, the client can mark those headers with `soap:mustUnderstand="1"` to indicate that the service has to understand and process the header or return a `<soap:Fault>`.

You can do this using the SoapHeader's DidUnderstand property, which is a Boolean indicating if the service understood the specified header.

Listing 7.9 shows an example Web method that looks through all undefined attributes and sets each attribute's `DidUnderstand` property to False unless

Figure 7.1 WhatHeaders echoes the XML content of each header it receives

the attribute is called `TransactionInfo` and belongs to the `http://tempuri.org` namespace.

Listing 7.9 An example Web method that reads all headers but understands only a header called TransactionInfo (VBWSBook\Chapter7\ DataService.asmx.vb)

```
<WebMethod(), _
    SoapHeader("mysteryHeaders", _
            Direction:=SoapHeaderDirection.In, _
            Required:=False)> _
    Public Sub DoYouUnderstand()
        Dim unknownHeader As SoapUnknownHeader
        For Each unknownHeader In mysteryHeaders
            If unknownHeader.Element.Name = "TransactionInfo" _
                And unknownHeader.Element.NamespaceURI = _
                                    "http://tempuri.org/" Then
                unknownHeader.DidUnderstand = True
            Else
                unknownHeader.DidUnderstand = False
            End If
        Next
    End Sub
```

On the client side, the proxy looks like the one in Listing 7.10 and indicates that `theSession` header should be sent with calls to this Web method.

Listing 7.10 Proxy class for invoking DoYouUnderstand (VBWSClientCode\ Chapter7\CustomClient\Web References\VBWSServer1\Reference.vb)

```
'The following SoapHeaderAttribute
'was added manually
<SoapHeaderAttribute("theSession"), _
 SoapDocumentMethodAttribute( _
 "http://tempuri.org/DoYouUnderstand")> _
Public Sub DoYouUnderstand()
    Me.Invoke("DoYouUnderstand", New Object(-1) {})
End Sub
```

The client code is in Listing 7.11. The client first instantiates the Web service proxy and sets `theSession` member variable as explained. In addition, the client sets `theSession`'s `MustUnderstand` property to `True`. `MustUnderstand` is another property of `SoapHeader` that the client uses to tell the service it has to understand this header.

Listing 7.11   Client code using proxy class in Listing 7.10 (VBWSClientCode\Chapter7\CustomClient\Form1.vb

```
Private Sub Button9_Click( _
    ByVal sender As System.Object, _
    ByVal e As System.EventArgs) _
                Handles Button9.Click
    Dim ws As New localhost1.DataService()
    ws.theSession = New localhost1.SessionInfo()
    ws.theSession.LastUsed = DateTime.Now
    ws.theSession.SessionId = "abcbdef1234e"
    'the service must understand this header
    ws.theSession.MustUnderstand = True
    Try
        ws.DoYouUnderstand()
    Catch ex As Exception
        MessageBox.Show(ex.Message)
    End Try
End Sub
```

If the service doesn't understand a header that has `soap:mustUnderstand="1"`, a `<soap:Fault>` is automatically returned, which is translated to an exception on the client side. The Catch block in Listing 7.11 displays this exception in a message box as shown in Figure 7.2.

Figure 7.2   A SoapHeaderException is thrown indicating that the service did not understand a header marked with mustUnderstand = "1"

7.6 Communicating Errors

SOAP provides a standard mechanism for reporting error information using the `<soap:Fault>` element as discussed in Chapter 3. When using .NET, any exceptions not caught in the Web method get reported to the client as a `<soap:Fault>`. Similarly, .NET clients throw a `SoapException` whenever they receive a `<soap:Fault>`. In the simplest case, you can communicate errors from a service by throwing an exception, for example:

```
Throw New Exception("This is the error information")
```

For more sophisticated scenarios, you can send structured error information as XML elements inside `<soap:Fault>`. To do this, you create a new `SoapException` and pass it an array of XML elements that you want to send to the client. `SoapException` has six overloaded constructors, two of which take in an XML node that represents the returned `<detail>` element. For example:

```
Public Sub New( ByVal message As String, _
            ByVal code As System.Xml.XmlQualifiedName, _
            ByVal actor As String, _
            ByVal detail As System.Xml.XmlNode)
```

The first parameter, `message`, is the error message that you want to send. This string is sent as the text of the `<faultstring>` element. The second parameter is the value of `<faultcode>`; it can be any namespace-qualified name. The `code` value is usually the standard `soap:Client` and `soap:Server` codes, which you can send by passing in `SoapException.ClientFaultCode` or `SoapException.ServerFaultCode` as the value of the code parameter. `actor` is a string that indicates the SOAP node that is sending this fault information. You usually set `actor` to an empty string unless you have a chain of Web services and you want to indicate which service within that chain is sending the error. The detail parameter is an XML element that represents the `<detail>` child of `<soap:Fault>`.

According to the SOAP specification, you're allowed to send a `<detail>` element only if the error occurred while processing the contents of `<soap:Body>`. If, however, an error occurred while processing a SOAP header, it is illegal to send a `<detail>` element. In that case, you throw a `SoapHeaderException`, which works similarly to `SoapException` except that it doesn't have a detail property.

Listing 7.12 shows an example Web method that receives an invoice document (the one from Chapter 2), validates it using the invoice schema, and returns detailed error information by calling another method that throws a `SoapException`.

Listing 7.12   An example method that receives an invoice document (VBWSBook\Chapter7\CustomWS.asmx.vb)

```
<WebMethod()> _
Public Sub ReceiveInvoice(ByVal inv As XmlNode)
    'validate the invoice
    Dim proc As New InvoiceProcessor()
    Try
        proc.ValidateInvoice(inv)
    Catch ex As XmlSchemaException
        ThrowCustomEx("Validation", _
            ex.LineNumber, _
            ex.LinePosition, _
            "A validation error occurred " + _
            ex.Message)
    End Try
End Sub
```

`ReceiveInvoice` takes in an invoice document, then creates a new `InvoiceProcessor` object and calls its `ValidateInvoice` method to validate it. The code in `InvoiceProcessor.ValidateInvoice` is the same as the validation code using `XmlValidatingReader` that you saw in Chapter 2. Any validation errors result in an `XmlSchemaException`, which is caught by the `Catch` block. The code in the `Catch` block calls `ThrowCustomEx`, (shown in Listing 7.13), passing it the procedure that caused the error, the exact line and column position of the input invoice that caused the error, and a string that indicates the exception message, which provides more detailed information.

Listing 7.13 ThrowCustomEx throws a SoapException with detailed error information (VBWSBook\Chapter7\CustomWS.asmx.vb).

```vb
'this procedure throws the SoapException
Public Sub ThrowCustomEx(ByVal procName As String, _
        ByVal LineNumber As Integer, _
        ByVal LinePosition As Integer, _
        ByVal errInfo As String)
    Const MY_NS As String = "http://services.vbws.com/Supplier17/"
    Dim doc As New System.Xml.XmlDocument()
    Dim detail As System.Xml.XmlNode = _
            doc.CreateNode(XmlNodeType.Element, _
        SoapException.DetailElementName.Name, _
        SoapException.DetailElementName.Namespace)

    'the procedure name
    Dim procNode As System.Xml.XmlNode = _
        doc.CreateNode(XmlNodeType.Element, _
        "Procedure", MY_NS)
    procNode.InnerText = procName
    'the line number where the error occurred
    Dim lineNode As System.Xml.XmlNode = _
        doc.CreateNode(XmlNodeType.Element, _
        "Line", MY_NS)
    lineNode.InnerText = LineNumber.ToString()
    'the position within the line where the error occurred
    Dim posNode As System.Xml.XmlNode = _
        doc.CreateNode(XmlNodeType.Element, _
        "Position", MY_NS)
    posNode.InnerText = LinePosition.ToString()
    detail.AppendChild(procNode)
    detail.AppendChild(lineNode)
    detail.AppendChild(posNode)
    'Throw the exception
    Dim ex As New SoapException(errInfo, _
        SoapException.ClientFaultCode, _
        "", detail)
    Throw ex
    Return
End Sub
```

In `ThrowCustomEx`, I start by creating a new XML DOM document, called `doc`, used to create the XML elements that will contain the custom error information.

The next line uses `doc.CreateNode` to create a `<detail>` element. To specify the detail element's name and namespace, you use `SoapException.DetailElementName.Name` and `SoapException.DetailElementName.Namespace`. Then I create another element called `<Procedure>` and set its `InnerText` property to the name of the procedure that caused the error. Similarly, I create a `<Line>` element for the line number where the error occurred and a `<Position>` element for the column position. To send these custom elements, I append them as children of the detail element.

Now that the detail element is ready to be sent, I create a new `SoapException` and pass it the error message in `errInfo`, `SoapException.ClientFaultCode` as the faultcode, an empty string for the faultactor, and the detail element (along with its child nodes). Finally, I throw this new `SoapException`, which then gets serialized and sent to the client as a `<soap:Fault>` shown in Listing 7.14.

Listing 7.14   The serialized SoapException results in a `<soap:Fault>`

```
<soap:Envelope

    xmlns:soap="http://schemas.xmlsoap.org/soap/envelope/">
    <soap:Body>
     <soap:Fault>
       <faultcode>soap:Client</faultcode>
       <faultstring>System.Web.Services.Protocols.SoapException:
           A validation error occurred: The
           'http://www.vbws.com/nwind.net/schemas/invoice:subTotal'
           element has an invalid value according to its data type.
           An error occurred at (1, 530). at
           Chapter7.CustomWS.ThrowCustomEx(
           String procName, Int32 LineNumber, Int32 LinePosition,
           String errInfo)at Chapter7.CustomWS.ReceiveInvoice(
           XmlNode inv)</faultstring>
       <detail>
         <Procedure xmlns=
           "http://services.vbws.com/Supplier17/">
           Validation</Procedure>
         <Line
         xmlns="http://services.vbws.com/Supplier17/">1</Line>
         <Position xmlns="http://services.vbws.com/Supplier17/">
           530</Position>
```

```
        </detail>
      </soap:Fault>
    </soap:Body>
  </soap:Envelope>
```

Examining the SOAP message in Listing 7.14, you'll notice that it contains all the information sent by `ThrowCustomEx`. First, the faultcode is `soap:Client`, which indicates that the fault was caused by something the client did wrong (sent a bad invoice document). Faultstring contains the short error message, "A validation error occurred ..." along with the exception's message. `<detail>` contains the custom elements I created: `Procedure`, `Line`, and `Position`.

The client gets access to this rich error information through a `SoapException` object that can be used to prompt the user with a detailed, user-friendly error message. On the client side, you write code to catch and process this `SoapException` as shown in Listing 7.15.

Listing 7.15 Catching SoapExceptions on the client side (VBWSClientCode\Chapter7\CustomClient\frmMain.vb)

```vb
Private Sub btnInvoice_Click(ByVal sender As System.Object, _
        ByVal e As System.EventArgs) Handles btnInvoice.Click
    Dim doc As New Xml.XmlDocument()
    doc.Load("BadInvoice.xml")
    Dim ws As New vbwsserver.MyWebService()
    ws.Proxy = New System.Net.WebProxy("http://localhost:8080")
    Try
        ws.ReceiveInvoice(doc.DocumentElement)
    Catch ex As SoapException
        Dim sb As New System.Text.StringBuilder( _
                    "The <faultstring> is: ")
        sb.Append(vbCrLf)
        sb.Append(ex.Message)
        sb.Append(vbCrLf)
        Dim detail As Xml.XmlElement = ex.Detail
        Dim node As Xml.XmlNode
        For Each node In detail.ChildNodes
            If node.NodeType = Xml.XmlNodeType.Element Then
                sb.Append(node.LocalName)
                sb.Append(": ")
                sb.Append(node.InnerText)
                sb.Append(vbCrLf)
```

```
            End If
        Next
        MessageBox.Show(sb.ToString())
    Catch ex As Exception
        MessageBox.Show(ex.Message)
    End Try
End Sub
```

In the example in Listing 7.15, I create a new DOM document called doc and use it to load an invoice document from the file BadInvoice.xml. This document has an error in the `<subTotal>` element that contains a string instead of a number. Next, I instantiate the Web service proxy called ws, set it to use Proxy-Trace so I can capture the SOAP messages, and call `ReceiveInvoice`, passing it the document element of the invoice document (the topmost element with all its children). I pass the document element rather than the document itself because I don't want to pass the XML declaration. XML declarations, for example, `<?xml version="1.0" encoding="utf-8"?>`, are not allowed in the SOAP `<Body>` contents per the SOAP specification.

The interesting part is the first `Catch` block where I handle any `SoapExceptions`. I create a stringbuilder and append the exception's message to it. Then I loop through each child element of detail and append the element's name and text. When complete, I report the entire string in a MessageBox that looks like the one in Figure 7.3.

If the type of exception is anything other than `SoapException`, the second `Catch` block catches that and displays the exception's message. Other exception types may include `System.Net.WebException`, which indicates a Web-related error such as server down or file not found.

It's always a good idea to present rich error information to your clients to help them determine the cause of the problem. Using custom XML elements and SoapException, you can communicate rich, structured error information from the service in a standard, SOAP-compliant way.

7.7 Summary

In this chapter, you learned how to use SOAP headers to extend the SOAP protocol by sending extra information in request and response messages and indicat-

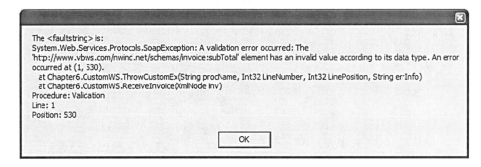

The <faultstring> is:
System.Web.Services.Protocols.SoapException: A validation error occurred: The
'http://www.vbws.com/nwinc.net/schemas/invoice:subTotal' element has an invalid value according to its data type. An error
occurred at (1, 530).
   at Chapter6.CustomWS.ThrowCustomEx(String procName, Int32 LineNumber, Int32 LinePosition, String errInfo)
   at Chapter6.CustomWS.ReceiveInvoice(XmlNode inv)
Procedure: Validation
Line: 1
Position: 530

OK

Figure 7.3   Displaying custom error information from SoapException

ing whether those headers are required. You also learned how to communicate
error information in a standard way using `<soap:Fault>` so that Web service
clients on any platform can access this error information.

The next chapters build on this knowledge and discuss common tasks such
as handling relational and structured data in Web services and more advanced
tasks such as extending .NET Web services Framework using SoapExtensions.

7.8   Resources

DevelopMentor's SOAP discussion list: http://discuss.develop.com/soap.html.

DevelopMentor's .NET Web discussion list: http://discuss.develop.com/dotnet-
  web.html.

SOAP 1.1 W3C Note: http://www.w3.org/TR/SOAP/.

SOAP 1.2 W3C Working Draft: http://www.w3.org/TR/2001/WD-soap12-
  20010709/.

Chapter 8

Interface-Based Web Service Development

> The goal of education is the advancement of knowledge and the dissemination of truth. —John F. Kennedy

Interface-based programming was popularized with component-based development in the 1990s. Using technologies like COM, you could define an interface and have several components implement it. Clients could utilize any of those components by programming against the interface. As your Web services evolve and mature, you will find it necessary to factor out Web service methods into interfaces, implement existing standard interfaces on your Web services, and program clients against an interface rather than a specific Web service. Interfaces can also be useful for versioning Web services by leaving the old interface intact and implementing a new interface on the same service.

WSDL bindings make this possible. In Chapter 4 you learned about WSDL bindings and how they define a concrete set of operations and provide the information needed to invoke those operations. A Web service implements one or more bindings and exposes them at a particular location defined by the port. Even if you haven't read Chapter 4, you can read this chapter and learn how to do interface-based programming. However, you will gain much more from this chapter if you read Chapter 4 first.

8.1 Defining Interfaces

The first step in interface-based programming is to define the interfaces you want to implement. When you build a Web service, you should always start with defining the interface. Today, tools like Visual Studio .NET do not provide direct support for this. I am hopeful that future versions will provide the needed support for defining Web service interfaces.

Although you can use Notepad to create a WSDL document from scratch, you'll probably want a more productive and less error-prone way to define your interfaces. An easy way to define a Web service interface is to create a Web service and define the Web methods you want the interface to have. If you have parameters with complex types, you define those types in schemas, then use xsd.exe to generate classes from the schemas (see Chapter 2 for more information on xsd.exe).

By default, all of a Web service's methods belong to the same binding. That binding (interface) has the same name as the Web service class with the word Soap appended. If you've created COM components in Visual Basic, you may know that each component you create has a default interface that is given the name _ClassName. Therefore, the concept of auto-generated interfaces shouldn't be new to you.

To control the binding's name and namespace, you use the `WebService-Binding` attribute on the Web service class to specify that binding's name and namespace. On each Web method that the service exposes, you add `SoapDocumentMethod` or `SoapRpcMethod` and set its `Binding` property to the binding name. Listing 8.1 shows an example class called `SupplierIface1` that exposes its methods in a binding called `ISupplier`.

Listing 8.1 A Web service example that exposes a binding called ISupplier (VBWSBook\Chapter8\Supplier1.asmx.vb)

```
Namespace Supplier1
    Public Structure Order
        Public CustomerEmail As String
        Public ShipVia As Shipper
        Public ShipName As String
        Public ShipAddress As String
```

```
        Public ShipCity As String
        Public ShipState As String
        Public ShipZipCode As String
        Public OrderItems() As OrderItem 'array of OrderItems
End Structure
Public Structure OrderItem
        Public ProductID As Integer
        Public Quantity As Integer
End Structure
Public Enum Shipper
        FedEx = 1
        UPS
        USPS
End Enum
Public Enum OrderStatus
        Pending
        Shipped
        Delivered
End Enum
Public Structure OrderInfo
        Public Status As OrderStatus
        Public ShippingType As String
        Public DeliveredDate As Date
        Public DeliveredTo As String
End Structure
Public Structure QuoteInfo
        Public ProductCost As Double
        Public Tax As Double
        Public Shipping As Double
        Public TotalCost As Double
End Structure
<WebServiceBinding( _
Name:="ISupplier", _
[Namespace]:="http://LearnXmlWS.com/Supplier"), _
WebService([Namespace]:="http://LearnXmlWS.com/Supplier", _
 Description:="The supplier's Web service")> _
Public Class SupplierIface1
        Inherits System.Web.Services.WebService
        <WebMethod( _
            Description:= _
            "Places the order then returns the new order id"), _
        SoapDocumentMethod(Binding:="ISupplier")> _
        Public Function PlaceOrder(ByVal newOrder As Order) _
                                    As String
```

```
                    'returns a new order id
        End Function
        <WebMethod(), _
        SoapDocumentMethod(Binding:="ISupplier")> _
        Public Function CheckStatus(ByVal OrderId As String) _
                                As OrderInfo
             'returns an orderinfo structure
        End Function
        <WebMethod(), _
        SoapDocumentMethod(Binding:="ISupplier")> _
        Public Function GetPriceQuote(ByVal newOrder As Order)
                                As QuoteInfo
             'returns an orderinfo structure
        End Function

    End Class
End Namespace
```

The first part of Listing 8.1 defines the data types that will be used by the service methods (for example, `Order`, `OrderItem`, `Shipper`, `OrderStatus`, `Order-Info`, and `QuoteInfo`). The `SupplierIface1` class has two attributes applied to it. `WebServiceBinding` has its name property set to `ISupplier` and its namespace property set to `http://LearnXmlWS.com/Supplier`. Each of the Web service methods has a `SoapDocumentMethod` applied to it with the `Binding` property set to `ISupplier`, making the methods part of the interface called `ISupplier`. The resulting WSDL document contains the binding definition and the service definition.

To get a pure interface definition, you can save this WSDL document to disk and remove the `<service>` element, which specifies a particular implementation for the interface. The edited WSDL document, shown in Listing 8.2 now contains your interface definition, which you can give to other developers who can use it to implement the same binding (interface) on their services.

Listing 8.2   The interface WSDL after removing the `<service>` element (VBWSBook\Chapter8\SingleInterface.wsdl)

```
<?xml version="1.0" encoding="utf-8"?>
<definitions xmlns:http="http://schemas.xmlsoap.org/wsdl/http/"
xmlns:soap="http://schemas.xmlsoap.org/wsdl/soap/"
```

```
xmlns:s="http://www.w3.org/2001/XMLSchema"
xmlns:s0="http://LearnXmlWS.com/Supplier"
xmlns:soapenc="http://schemas.xmlsoap.org/soap/encoding/"
xmlns:tm="http://microsoft.com/wsdl/mime/textMatching/"
xmlns:mime="http://schemas.xmlsoap.org/wsdl/mime/"
targetNamespace="http://LearnXmlWS.com/Supplier"
xmlns="http://schemas.xmlsoap.org/wsdl/">
  <types>
    <s:schema elementFormDefault="qualified"
        targetNamespace="http://LearnXmlWS.com/Supplier">
      <s:element name="PlaceOrder">
        <s:complexType>
          <s:sequence>
            <s:element minOccurs="1" maxOccurs="1"
                       name="newOrder" type="s0:Order" />
          </s:sequence>
        </s:complexType>
      </s:element>
      <s:complexType name="Order">
        <s:sequence>
          <s:element minOccurs="0" maxOccurs="1"
                     name="CustomerEmail" type="s:string" />
          <s:element minOccurs="1" maxOccurs="1"
                     name="ShipVia" type="s0:Shipper" />
          <s:element minOccurs="0" maxOccurs="1"
                     name="ShipName" type="s:string" />
          <s:element minOccurs="0" maxOccurs="1"
                     name="ShipAddress" type="s:string" />
          <s:element minOccurs="0" maxOccurs="1"
                     name="ShipCity" type="s:string" />
          <s:element minOccurs="0" maxOccurs="1"
                     name="ShipState" type="s:string" />
          <s:element minOccurs="0" maxOccurs="1"
                     name="ShipZipCode" type="s:string" />
          <s:element minOccurs="0" maxOccurs="1"
                     name="OrderItems"
                     type="s0:ArrayOfOrderItem" />
        </s:sequence>
      </s:complexType>
      <s:simpleType name="Shipper">
        <s:restriction base="s:string">
          <s:enumeration value="FedEx" />
          <s:enumeration value="UPS" />
```

```xml
        <s:enumeration value="USPS" />
      </s:restriction>
    </s:simpleType>
    <s:complexType name="ArrayOfOrderItem">
      <s:sequence>
        <s:element minOccurs="0" maxOccurs="unbounded"
                   name="OrderItem" type="s0:OrderItem" />
      </s:sequence>
    </s:complexType>
    <s:complexType name="OrderItem">
      <s:sequence>
        <s:element minOccurs="1" maxOccurs="1"
                   name="ProductID" type="s:int" />
        <s:element minOccurs="1" maxOccurs="1"
                   name="Quantity" type="s:int" />
      </s:sequence>
    </s:complexType>
    <s:element name="PlaceOrderResponse">
      <s:complexType>
        <s:sequence>
          <s:element minOccurs="0" maxOccurs="1"
                     name="PlaceOrderResult" type="s:string" />
        </s:sequence>
      </s:complexType>
    </s:element>
    <s:element name="CheckStatus">
      <s:complexType>
        <s:sequence>
          <s:element minOccurs="0" maxOccurs="1"
                     name="OrderId" type="s:string" />
        </s:sequence>
      </s:complexType>
    </s:element>
    <s:element name="CheckStatusResponse">
      <s:complexType>
        <s:sequence>
          <s:element minOccurs="1" maxOccurs="1"
                     name="CheckStatusResult"
                     type="s0:OrderInfo" />
        </s:sequence>
      </s:complexType>
    </s:element>
    <s:complexType name="OrderInfo">
```

```
  <s:sequence>
    <s:element minOccurs="1" maxOccurs="1"
               name="Status" type="s0:OrderStatus" />
    <s:element minOccurs="0" maxOccurs="1"
               name="ShippingType" type="s:string" />
    <s:element minOccurs="1" maxOccurs="1"
               name="DeliveredDate" type="s:dateTime" />
    <s:element minOccurs="0" maxOccurs="1"
               name="DeliveredTo" type="s:string" />
  </s:sequence>
</s:complexType>
<s:simpleType name="OrderStatus">
  <s:restriction base="s:string">
    <s:enumeration value="Pending" />
    <s:enumeration value="Shipped" />
    <s:enumeration value="Delivered" />
  </s:restriction>
</s:simpleType>
<s:element name="GetPriceQuote">
  <s:complexType>
    <s:sequence>
      <s:element minOccurs="1" maxOccurs="1" name="newOrder"
               type="s0:Order" />
    </s:sequence>
  </s:complexType>
</s:element>
<s:element name="GetPriceQuoteResponse">
  <s:complexType>
    <s:sequence>
      <s:element minOccurs="1" maxOccurs="1"
               name="GetPriceQuoteResult"
               type="s0:QuoteInfo" />
    </s:sequence>
  </s:complexType>
</s:element>
<s:complexType name="QuoteInfo">
  <s:sequence>
    <s:element minOccurs="1" maxOccurs="1"
               name="ProductCost" type="s:double" />
    <s:element minOccurs="1" maxOccurs="1"
               name="Tax" type="s:double" />
    <s:element minOccurs="1" maxOccurs="1"
               name="Shipping" type="s:double" />
```

```xml
                    <s:element minOccurs="1" maxOccurs="1"
                          name="TotalCost" type="s:double" />
          </s:sequence>
        </s:complexType>
      </s:schema>
  </types>
  <message name="PlaceOrderSoapIn">
    <part name="parameters" element="s0:PlaceOrder" />
  </message>
  <message name="PlaceOrderSoapOut">
    <part name="parameters" element="s0:PlaceOrderResponse" />
  </message>
  <message name="CheckStatusSoapIn">
    <part name="parameters" element="s0:CheckStatus" />
  </message>
  <message name="CheckStatusSoapOut">
    <part name="parameters" element="s0:CheckStatusResponse" />
  </message>
  <message name="GetPriceQuoteSoapIn">
    <part name="parameters" element="s0:GetPriceQuote" />
  </message>
  <message name="GetPriceQuoteSoapOut">
    <part name="parameters" element="s0:GetPriceQuoteResponse" />
  </message>
  <portType name="ISupplier">
    <operation name="PlaceOrder">
      <documentation>
        Places the order then returns the new order id
      </documentation>
      <input message="s0:PlaceOrderSoapIn" />
      <output message="s0:PlaceOrderSoapOut" />
    </operation>
    <operation name="CheckStatus">
      <input message="s0:CheckStatusSoapIn" />
      <output message="s0:CheckStatusSoapOut" />
    </operation>
    <operation name="GetPriceQuote">
      <input message="s0:GetPriceQuoteSoapIn" />
      <output message="s0:GetPriceQuoteSoapOut" />
    </operation>
  </portType>
  <binding name="ISupplier" type="s0:ISupplier">
```

```
<soap:binding
  transport=
  "http://schemas.xmlsoap.org/soap/http" style="document" />
<operation name="PlaceOrder">
  <soap:operation
    soapAction="http://LearnXmlWS.com/Supplier/PlaceOrder"
    style="document" />
  <input>
    <soap:body use="literal" />
  </input>
  <output>
    <soap:body use="literal" />
  </output>
</operation>
<operation name="CheckStatus">
  <soap:operation
    soapAction="http://LearnXmlWS.com/Supplier/CheckStatus"
    style="document" />
  <input>
    <soap:body use="literal" />
  </input>
  <output>
    <soap:body use="literal" />
  </output>
</operation>
<operation name="GetPriceQuote">
  <soap:operation
      soapAction=
      "http://LearnXmlWS.com/Supplier/GetPriceQuote"
      style="document" />
  <input>
    <soap:body use="literal" />
  </input>
  <output>
    <soap:body use="literal" />
  </output>
</operation>
</binding>
</definitions>
```

8.2 Implementing an Interface

Whether you define the interfaces yourself or you work with interfaces defined by someone else, you'll eventually want to implement them. Although you can read the WSDL document and write all the corresponding VB code from scratch, including the `WebServiceBinding` attribute, something tells me you're not going to want to do this. Instead, you can use wsdl.exe with the /server switch to tell it you want to create a service that implements the specified interface. wsdl.exe takes the WSDL document's URL, the language to use for generated code, and the output file name:

```
wsdl.exe /server http://VBWSServer/vbwsbook/Chapter8/Single-
➥Interface.wsdl /l:VB /out:CSupplier.vb
```

Listing 8.3 shows the interesting part of the resulting code in CSupplier.vb.

Listing 8.3   A Web service implementation generated by wsdl.exe when using /server switch (VBWSBook\Chapter8\InterfaceImpl\CSupplier.vb)

```
'
'This source code was auto-generated by wsdl
'
<WebServiceBindingAttribute(Name:="ISupplier", _
[Namespace]:="http://LearnXmlWS.com/Supplier")> _
Public MustInherit Class ISupplier
    Inherits WebService

    <WebMethodAttribute(), _
     SoapDocumentMethodAttribute( _
     "http://LearnXmlWS.com/Supplier/PlaceOrder", _
     RequestNamespace:="http://LearnXmlWS.com/Supplier", _
     ResponseNamespace:="http://LearnXmlWS.com/Supplier", _
     Use:=Description.SoapBindingUse.Literal, _
     ParameterStyle:=SoapParameterStyle.Wrapped)> _
    Public MustOverride Function PlaceOrder( _
        ByVal newOrder As Order) As String

    <WebMethodAttribute(), _
     SoapDocumentMethodAttribute( _
       "http://LearnXmlWS.com/Supplier/CheckStatus", _
       RequestNamespace:="http://LearnXmlWS.com/Supplier", _
       ResponseNamespace:="http://LearnXmlWS.com/Supplier", _
       Use:=Description.SoapBindingUse.Literal, _
       ParameterStyle:=SoapParameterStyle.Wrapped)> _
    Public MustOverride Function CheckStatus( _
                              ByVal OrderId As String) As _
```

```
        <XmlElementAttribute(IsNullable:=False)> OrderInfo

    <WebMethodAttribute(), _
     SoapDocumentMethodAttribute( _
        "http://LearnXmlWS.com/Supplier/GetPriceQuote", _
        RequestNamespace:="http://LearnXmlWS.com/Supplier", _
        ResponseNamespace:="http://LearnXmlWS.com/Supplier", _
        Use:=Description.SoapBindingUse.Literal, _
        ParameterStyle:=SoapParameterStyle.Wrapped)> _
    Public MustOverride Function GetPriceQuote( _
        ByVal newOrder As Order) As QuoteInfo
  End Class
```

Note that the class name is by default the same as the binding name, that is, `ISupplier`. You'll also see a `WebServiceBinding` attribute applied to `ISupplier` to set the binding's name and namespace. Each method has a `SoapDocumentMethod` attribute that specifies things like the request and response namespaces and the fact that message parts are literal and wrapped.

Notice also that the class is abstract (MustInherit). While you can easily put implementation code in the class itself, it is generally a good idea to put implementation code in a class that inherits from it. This way you will not be confused about which methods are part of the original interface you are implementing and which ones you added yourself. Also, keeping the interface methods in a separate class means there's less chance that you'll accidentally modify one or more of the interface methods as you are implementing the Web service.

Listing 8.4 shows an example Web service that implements the ISupplier interface by inheriting from the ISupplier abstract class that wsdl.exe generated.

Listing 8.4   An example Web service that implements the ISupplier interface (VBWSBook\Chapter8\InterfaceImpl\SingleInterfaceImple.asmx.vb)

```
Imports System.Web.Services
Imports System.Web.Services.Protocols

<WebServiceBinding( _
    Name:="ISupplier", _
    [Namespace]:="http://LearnXmlWS.com/Supplier", _
    Location:= _
"http://vbwsserver/vbwsbook/chapter8/SingleInterface.wsdl"), _
    WebService(Namespace:="somenamespace")> _
```

```vb
Public Class SingleInterfaceImpl
    Inherits ISupplier

    <WebMethodAttribute(), _
    SoapDocumentMethodAttribute( _
    "http://LearnXmlWS.com/Supplier/CheckStatus", _
    RequestNamespace:="http://LearnXmlWS.com/Supplier", _
    ResponseNamespace:="http://LearnXmlWS.com/Supplier", _
    Use:=Description.SoapBindingUse.Literal, _
    ParameterStyle:=Protocols.SoapParameterStyle.Wrapped, _
    Binding:="ISupplier")> _
    Public Overrides Function CheckStatus( _
            ByVal OrderId As String) As OrderInfo

    End Function

    <WebMethodAttribute(), _
    SoapDocumentMethodAttribute( _
    "http://LearnXmlWS.com/Supplier/GetPriceQuote", _
    RequestNamespace:="http://LearnXmlWS.com/Supplier", _
    ResponseNamespace:="http://LearnXmlWS.com/Supplier", _
    Use:=Description.SoapBindingUse.Literal, _
    ParameterStyle:=Protocols.SoapParameterStyle.Wrapped, _
    Binding:="ISupplier")> _
    Public Overrides Function GetPriceQuote( _
            ByVal newOrder As Order) As QuoteInfo

    End Function

    <WebMethodAttribute(), _
    SoapDocumentMethodAttribute( _
        "http://LearnXmlWS.com/Supplier/PlaceOrder", _
        RequestNamespace:="http://LearnXmlWS.com/Supplier", _
        ResponseNamespace:="http://LearnXmlWS.com/Supplier", _
        Use:=Description.SoapBindingUse.Literal, _
        ParameterStyle:=Protocols.SoapParameterStyle.Wrapped, _
        Binding:="ISupplier")> _
        Public Overrides Function PlaceOrder( _
                ByVal newOrder As Order) As String

    End Function
End Class
```

The code in Listing 8.4 is part of a Web project called InterfaceImpl. In this project, you'll find the CSupplier.vb file that was generated by wsdl.exe. The Web service class in Listing 8.4 inherits from ISupplier (which is defined in CSupplier.vb). To implement the Web service interface as defined by ISupplier, you

- Add a WebServiceBinding attribute on your Web service class (the class name is SingleInterfaceImpl in Listing 8.4), set the WebServiceBinding's Name property to ISupplier, and set its Location property to the URL of the interface WSDL. This way you specify that the interface definition should be imported from that URL rather than duplicated in your Web service's WSDL.

- Override each of the ISupplier class methods: CheckStatus, GetQuote and PlaceOrder.

- Set the Binding property of the SoapDocumentMethod attribute to ISupplier on each of these methods. Here you're specifying that each of these methods belongs to the ISupplier interface.

Once you perform these steps and compile your Web service, the resulting WSDL will look like the one in Listing 8.5.

Listing 8.5   WSDL for a Web service that implements the ISupplier interface. This WSDL imports the ISupplier definitions from SingleInterface.wsdl.

```
<definitions xmlns:http="http://schemas.xmlsoap.org/wsdl/http/"
xmlns:soap="http://schemas.xmlsoap.org/wsdl/soap/"
xmlns:s="http://www.w3.org/2001/XMLSchema"
xmlns:soapenc="http://schemas.xmlsoap.org/soap/encoding/"
xmlns:i0="http://LearnXmlWS.com/Supplier"
xmlns:tns="somenamespace"
targetNamespace="somenamespace"
xmlns="http://schemas.xmlsoap.org/wsdl/">
<import namespace="http://LearnXmlWS.com/Supplier"
  location=
"http://vbwsserver/vbwsbook/chapter8/SingleInterface.wsdl" />
 <types />
  <service name="SingleInterfaceImpl">
    <port name="ISupplier" binding="i0:ISupplier">
      <soap:address
       location="http://vbwsserver/vbwsbook/chapter8/
➡InterfaceImpl/SingleInterfaceImpl.asmx" />
    </port>
  </service>
</definitions>
```

The WSDL in Listing 8.5 is lacking most of what you're used to seeing in a WSDL document. It does not contain message, port, portType, or binding definitions. Instead, it imports the SingleInterface.wsdl document that contains the ISupplier interface definition. By having implementations reference the interface in this way, you avoid duplicating the interface definition with all the associated maintenance headaches.

8.3 Implementing Multiple Interfaces

The next logical step is to implement multiple interfaces on the same Web service. You do this by applying multiple WebServiceBinding attributes to the class implementing the Web service. On each Web method you set the Soap-DocumentService or SoapRpcService Binding property to the name of the binding that contains this method. Taking the SupplierIface1 class in Listing 8.1, you might want to factor out its methods into two interfaces: IOrderMgmt and IQuoteMgmt. Listing 8.6 shows the code used to achieve this.

Listing 8.6 Defining multiple bindings (interfaces) (VBWSBook\Chapter8\Supplier2.asmx.vb)

```
<WebServiceBinding( _
Name:="IOrderMgmt", _
[Namespace]:="http://LearnXmlWS.com/Supplier"), _
WebServiceBinding( _
Name:="IQuoteMgmt", _
[Namespace]:="http://LearnXmlWS.com/Supplier"), _
WebService([Namespace]:="http://LearnXmlWS.com/Supplier")> _
Public Class SupplierIface2
    Inherits System.Web.Services.WebService
    <WebMethod( _
    Description:= _
    "Places the order then returns the new order id"), _
    SoapDocumentMethod(Binding:="IOrderMgmt")> _
    Public Function PlaceOrder( _
                    ByVal newOrder As Order) As String
        'returns a new order id
    End Function
    <WebMethod(), _
    SoapDocumentMethod(Binding:="IOrderMgmt")> _
    Public Function CheckStatus( _
```

```
                        ByVal OrderId As String) As OrderInfo
            'returns an orderinfo structure
        End Function

        <WebMethod(), _
        SoapDocumentMethod(Binding:="IQuoteMgmt")> _
        Public Function GetPriceQuote( _
                        ByVal newOrder As Order) As QuoteInfo()
            'returns an orderinfo structure
        End Function
    End Class
```

Note that there are two bindings with different names—both in the same namespace. Also, GetPriceQuote is now part of the IQuoteMgmt binding.

Listing 8.7 shows the bindings defined in the resulting WSDL document.

Listing 8.7   The resulting WSDL document with two bindings (VBWSBook\Chapter8\MultiInterface.wsdl)

```
<binding name="IQuoteMgmt" type="s0:IQuoteMgmt">
 <soap:binding
       transport="http://schemas.xmlsoap.org/soap/http"
        style="document" />
  <operation name="GetPriceQuote">
    <soap:operation
      soapAction="http://LearnXmlWS.com/Supplier/GetPriceQuote"
      style="document" />
    <input>
      <soap:body use="literal" />
    </input>
    <output>
      <soap:body use="literal" />
    </output>
  </operation>
 </binding>

<binding name="IOrderMgmt" type="s0:IOrderMgmt">
  <soap:binding transport="http://schemas.xmlsoap.org/soap/http"
style="document" />
  <operation name="PlaceOrder">
    <soap:operation
      soapAction="http://LearnXmlWS.com/Supplier/PlaceOrder"
      style="document" />
    <input>
```

```
          <soap:body use="literal" />
        </input>
        <output>
          <soap:body use="literal" />
        </output>
      </operation>
      <operation name="CheckStatus">
        <soap:operation
          soapAction="http://LearnXmlWS.com/Supplier/CheckStatus"
          style="document" />
        <input>
          <soap:body use="literal" />
        </input>
        <output>
          <soap:body use="literal" />
        </output>
      </operation>
    </binding>
```

To implement these interfaces you run wsdl.exe with the /server parameter just as you did for the single interface case. However, the output this time is different: You get one file that contains two classes—one for each binding. The first class you get, IQuoteMgmt, has one method called GetPriceQuote. The second class, IOrderMgmt, has two methods called PlaceOrder and CheckStatus. You can add this file to your Web service project and create classes that inherit from each of IQuoteMgmt and IOrderMgmt, and then start implementing each interface's methods. For example, Listing 8.8 shows a Web service that implements IQuoteMgmt.

Listing 8.8   An example Web service that implements IQuoteMgmt (VBWSBook\Chapter8\InterfaceImpl\QuoteMgmtImpl.asmx.vb)

```
Imports System.Web.Services
Imports System.Web.Services.Protocols

<WebServiceBinding( _
 Name:="IQuoteMgmt", _
 Namespace:="http://LearnXmlWS.com/Supplier", _
 Location:= _
 "http://vbwsserver/vbwsbook/chapter8/MultiInterface.wsdl"), _
 WebService(Namespace:="http://tempuri.org/")> _
Public Class QuoteMgmtImpl
```

```
Inherits MultiIface1.IQuoteMgmt

<WebMethodAttribute(), _
SoapDocumentMethodAttribute( _
"http://LearnXmlWS.com/Supplier/GetPriceQuote", _
 RequestNamespace:="http://LearnXmlWS.com/Supplier", _
 ResponseNamespace:="http://LearnXmlWS.com/Supplier", _
 Use:=Description.SoapBindingUse.Literal, _
 ParameterStyle:=SoapParameterStyle.Wrapped, _
 Binding:="IQuoteMgmt")> _
 Public Overrides Function GetPriceQuote( _
        ByVal newOrder As InterfaceImpl.MultiIface1.Order) _
                As InterfaceImpl.MultiIface1.QuoteInfo()

    End Function
End Class
```

Since .NET supports single inheritance, a class cannot inherit from more than one base class. This means you cannot create a Web service that inherits from both classes generated by wsdl.exe (the classes IQuoteMgmt and IOrderMgmt). You will end up with a Web service class for each binding you want to implement.

This is not exactly what comes to mind when I think of multiple interfaces. Ideally, we can have one Web service class that implements both IQuoteMgmt and IOrderMgt. While it's possible to achieve this, you can't do it by inheriting from abstract classes generated by wsdl.exe. Instead, you must create a Web service class, and then manually specify the bindings and the methods. The process is almost identical to the single-interface implementation case except you are not overriding any base class methods. The steps for implementing multiple interfaces on a single Web service class are:

- Create a Web service.

- Add a WebServiceBinding attribute to the Web service class for each interface you want to implement. Specify the binding's name, namespace, and location (the URL of a WSDL document where the binding is defined).

- Create WebMethods on this Web service that correspond to the operations defined in each binding. You can get some help from wsdl.exe by running it with the /server flag then copying the abstract method definitions it creates and pasting them into your Web service. If you do this, be sure to remove the MustOverride keyword from those methods.

- Specify the binding name for each Web method. This name must match one of the binding names defined by SoapServiceBinding attributes on the Web service class.

Listing 8.9 shows an example Web service class that implements both IQuoteMgmt and IOrderMgmt.

Listing 8.9   A single Web service class that implements both IQuoteMgmt and IOrderMgmt interfaces (VBWSBook\Chapter8\InterfaceImpl\ MultipleInterfaceImpl.asmx.vb)

```
Imports System.Web.Services
Imports System.Web.Services.Protocols

<WebService(Namespace:="http://tempuri.org/"), _
WebServiceBindingAttribute(Name:="IQuoteMgmt", _
 [Namespace]:="http://LearnXmlWS.com/Supplier", _
 Location:= _
 "http://vbwsserver/vbwsbook/chapter8/MultiInterface.wsdl"), _
 WebServiceBindingAttribute(Name:="IOrderMgmt", _
 [Namespace]:="http://LearnXmlWS.com/Supplier", _
 Location:= _
 "http://vbwsserver/vbwsbook/chapter8/MultiInterface.wsdl")> _
Public Class MultipleInterfaceImpl
    Inherits WebService

    <WebMethodAttribute(), _
        SoapDocumentMethodAttribute( _
        "http://LearnXmlWS.com/Supplier/GetPriceQuote", _
        RequestNamespace:="http://LearnXmlWS.com/Supplier", _
        ResponseNamespace:="http://LearnXmlWS.com/Supplier", _
        Use:=Description.SoapBindingUse.Literal, _
        ParameterStyle:=SoapParameterStyle.Wrapped, _
        Binding:="IQuoteMgmt")> _
    Public Function GetPriceQuote( _
            ByVal newOrder _
            As InterfaceImpl.MultiIface1.Order) _
            As InterfaceImpl.MultiIface1.QuoteInfo()
    End Function

    <WebMethodAttribute(), _
```

```
        SoapDocumentMethodAttribute( _
        "http://LearnXmlWS.com/Supplier/PlaceOrder", _
        RequestNamespace:="http://LearnXmlWS.com/Supplier", _
        ResponseNamespace:="http://LearnXmlWS.com/Supplier", _
        Use:=Description.SoapBindingUse.Literal, _
        ParameterStyle:=SoapParameterStyle.Wrapped, _
        Binding:="IOrderMgmt")> _
      Public Function PlaceOrder( _
              ByVal newOrder As InterfaceImpl.MultiIface1.Order) _
              As String

      End Function


      <WebMethodAttribute(), _
        SoapDocumentMethodAttribute( _
        "http://LearnXmlWS.com/Supplier/CheckStatus", _
        RequestNamespace:="http://LearnXmlWS.com/Supplier", _
        ResponseNamespace:="http://LearnXmlWS.com/Supplier", _
        Use:=Description.SoapBindingUse.Literal, _
        ParameterStyle:=SoapParameterStyle.Wrapped, _
        Binding:="IOrderMgmt")> _
      Public Function CheckStatus(ByVal OrderId As String) _
              As InterfaceImpl.MultiIface1.OrderInfo

      End Function
    End Class
```

The Web service class in Listing 8.9 has two WebServiceBinding attributes for
IQuoteMgmt and ISupplierMgmt. Inside the class, you'll see the GetPriceQuote
Web method that belongs to the IQuoteMgmt interface. You'll also see the IOrderMgmt interface methods: PlaceOrder and CheckStatus. Listing 8.10 shows
the resulting WSDL.

Listing 8.10   The WSDL for the service in Listing 8.9

```
<?xml version="1.0" encoding="utf-8"?>
<definitions
xmlns:soap="http://schemas.xmlsoap.org/wsdl/soap/"
xmlns:s="http://www.w3.org/2001/XMLSchema"
xmlns:i0="http://LearnXmlWS.com/Supplier"
xmlns:tns="http://tempuri.org/"
targetNamespace="http://tempuri.org/"
```

```
xmlns="http://schemas.xmlsoap.org/wsdl/">
  <import namespace="http://LearnXmlWS.com/Supplier"
  location=
"http://vbwsserver/vbwsbook/chapter8/MultiInterface.wsdl" />
  <types />
  <service name="MultipleInterfaceImpl">
    <port name="IOrderMgmt" binding="i0:IOrderMgmt">
      <soap:address
location="http://vbwsserver/vbwsbook/chapter8/_
InterfaceImpl/MultipleInterfaceImpl.asmx" />
    </port>
    <port name="IQuoteMgmt" binding="i0:IQuoteMgmt">
      <soap:address
location="http://vbwsserver/vbwsbook/chapter8/_
InterfaceImpl/MultipleInterfaceImpl.asmx" />
    </port>
  </service>
</definitions>
```

The most interesting feature of the WSDL in Listing 8.10 is the presence of two `<port>` elements inside the `<service>` element, indicating that the service implements two different interfaces.

8.4 Interfaces in Different Namespaces

Here's an interesting twist on the above scenario: What if we placed the bindings in different namespaces, for example, `IQuoteMgmt` in a namespace called `http://LearnXmlWS.com/QuoteMgmt` and `IOrderMgmt` in another namespace called `http://LearnXmlWS.com/OrderMgmt`? Listing 8.11 shows the code for `SupplierIface3` that has two bindings, each in its own namespace.

Listing 8.11   A Web service with two bindings in two different namespaces (VBWSBook\Chapter8\Supplier3.asmx.vb)

```
<WebServiceBinding( _
Name:="IOrderMgmt", _
[Namespace]:="http://LearnXmlWS.com/OrderMgmt"), _
WebServiceBinding( _
Name:="IQuoteMgmt", _
[Namespace]:="http://LearnXmlWS.com/QuoteMgmt"), _
WebService([Namespace]:="http://LearnXmlWS.com/Supplier")> _
```

```
Public Class SupplierIface3
        Inherits System.Web.Services.WebService
        <WebMethod( _
 Description:="Places the order then returns the new order id"),

 _
        SoapDocumentMethod(Binding:="IOrderMgmt")> _
        Public Function PlaceOrder(ByVal newOrder As Order) _
                        As String
          'returns a new order id
        End Function
        <WebMethod(), _
        SoapDocumentMethod(Binding:="IOrderMgmt")> _
        Public Function CheckStatus(ByVal OrderId As String) _
                        As OrderInfo
          'returns an orderinfo structure
        End Function

        <WebMethod(), _
        SoapDocumentMethod(Binding:="IQuoteMgmt")> _
        Public Function GetPriceQuote(ByVal newOrder As Order) _
                        As QuoteInfo()
          'returns an orderinfo structure
        End Function
     End Class
```

The result is that each binding (interface) is defined in its own WSDL document.
This is because bindings belong to the WSDL document's targetNamespace
and you can have one targetNamepace only per WSDL document. These separate WSDL documents are imported into the main WSDL document using the
<import> element as shown in Listing 8.12.

**Listing 8.12 Each binding is defined in a separate WSDL document that is then
imported into the main WSDL document using** <import>.

```
<definitions targetNamespace="http://LearnXmlWS.com/Supplier"
➥...>
  <import namespace="http://LearnXmlWS.com/QuoteMgmt"
    location="http://vbwsserver/vbwsbook/Chapter8/
➥supplier3.asmx?schema=schema1"/>
  <import namespace="http://LearnXmlWS.com/OrderMgmt"
   location="http://vbwsserver/vbwsbook/Chapter8/
➥supplier3.asmx?schema=schema2"
/>
```

```
    <import namespace="http://LearnXmlWS.com/QuoteMgmt"
      location="http://vbwsserver/vbwsbook/Chapter8/_
  supplier3.asmx?wsdl=wsdl1" />
    <import namespace="http://LearnXmlWS.com/OrderMgmt"
      location="http://vbwsserver/vbwsbook/Chapter8/_
  supplier3.asmx?wsdl=wsdl2" />
    <types />
    <service name="SupplierIface3">
      <port name="IQuoteMgmt" binding="i2:IQuoteMgmt">
        <soap:address
          location="http://vbwsserver/vbwsbook/Chapter8/_
  supplier3.asmx" />
      </port>
      <port name="IOrderMgmt" binding="i1:IOrderMgmt">
        <soap:address location=
          "http://vbwsserver/vbwsbook/Chapter8/supplier3.asmx" />
      </port>
    </service>
  </definitions>
```

To access the `IQuoteMgmt` binding definition, you navigate to the .asmx file with a query string of `wsdl=wsdl1` (for example, `supplier3.asmx?wsdl=wsdl1`). Similarly, `IOrderMgmt` definition is at `supplier3.asmx?wsdl=wsdl2`. Similarly, types used by the methods of each interface, for example, `Order` and `QuoteInfo`, are defined in the schemas located at `supplier3.asmx?schema=schema1` and `supplier3.asmx?schema=schema2`. In this case, the interfaces, type definitions, and implementation definition (the service) are all separated in different locations. For complex Web services that implement many interfaces, separating interface definitions makes them easier to maintain and be independent of one another.

Running wsdl.exe with /server on the WSDL in Listing 8.12 generates two separate classes: one for each binding, as in the previous case where both bindings belonged to the same class. The difference in this case is that class has a `WebServiceBinding` attribute on it with its `Namespace` property set to `http://LearnXmlWS.com/QuoteMgmt` for `IQuoteMgmt` and `http://LearnXmlWS.com/OrderMgmt` for `IOrderMgmt`.

When you run wsdl.exe on the WSDL document in Listing 8.12, it needs to get the other WSDL documents referenced by `<import>` elements. This works fine as long as you tell wsdl.exe to access the main WSDL document using http, (for example

```
wsdl.exe http://localhost/SupplierIface3.asmx?WSDL).
```

If however, you give wsdl.exe a file path instead of a URL, it will not be able to retrieve the imported WSDL documents. So if you save the WSDL document in Listing 8.12 to disk and issue the following command:

```
wsdl.exe D:\documents\SupplierIface3.wsdl
```

you will get an error about undefined types because wsdl.exe cannot read the schema or the WSDL documents referenced by `<import>`s.

8.5 Programming Against Interfaces

The previous section showed you how to define and implement interfaces. This section completes the picture by showing you how to code clients against those interfaces.

8.5.1 *Generating Proxies from Interfaces*

On the client side, a Web service proxy exposes the set of methods that reflects the binding's operations. As far as the client is concerned, this set of methods is considered the Web service's interface.

When you add a Web reference to an interface-only WSDL document, Visual Studio .NET recognizes an interface-only WSDL and generates the proxy class for you (beta versions didn't do this). Since the WSDL document doesn't contain a `<service>` element, the generated proxy class will not have a Web service URL in its constructor. You can also use wsdl.exe to generate the proxy class:

```
wsdl.exe /l:VB /out:MyClass.vb SingleInterface.wsdl
```

Listing 8.13 shows two example proxy classes one for `IOrderMgmt` and one for `IQuoteMgmt`. These proxies were generated using wsdl.exe.

Listing 8.13 Proxy classes generated based on IOrderMgmt and IQuoteMgmt interface definitions (VBWSClientCode\Chapter8\Interfaces\InterfaceClient\ Supplier3.vb)

```vb
<WebServiceBindingAttribute( _
    Name:="IOrderMgmt", _
    [Namespace]:="http://LearnXmlWS.com/OrderMgmt")> _
Public Class COrderMgmt
    Inherits SoapHttpClientProtocol

    Public Sub New()
        MyBase.New()
    End Sub

    <SoapDocumentMethod( _
        "http://LearnXmlWS.com/Supplier/PlaceOrder", _
        RequestNamespace:="http://LearnXmlWS.com/Supplier", _
        ResponseNamespace:="http://LearnXmlWS.com/Supplier")> _
    Public Function PlaceOrder(ByVal newOrder As Order) As String
        Dim results() As Object = Me.Invoke("PlaceOrder", _
                            New Object() {newOrder})
        Return CType(results(0), String)
    End Function


    <SoapDocumentMethod( _
      "http://LearnXmlWS.com/Supplier/CheckStatus", _
      RequestNamespace:="http://LearnXmlWS.com/Supplier", _
      ResponseNamespace:="http://LearnXmlWS.com/Supplier")> _
      Public Function CheckStatus( _
                  ByVal OrderId As String) As OrderInfo
        Dim results() As Object = Me.Invoke("CheckStatus", _
                            New Object() {OrderId})
        Return CType(results(0), OrderInfo)
    End Function

End Class

<WebServiceBinding( _
    Name:="IQuoteMgmt", _
    [Namespace]:="http://LearnXmlWS.com/QuoteMgmt")> _
Public Class CQuoteMgmt
    Inherits SoapHttpClientProtocol
```

```
<SoapDocumentMethod( _
    "http://LearnXmlWS.com/Supplier/GetPriceQuote", _
    RequestNamespace:="http://LearnXmlWS.com/Supplier", _
    ResponseNamespace:="http://LearnXmlWS.com/Supplier")> _
Public Function GetPriceQuote( _
                ByVal newOrder As InterfaceClient.Order) _
        As InterfaceClient.QuoteInfo()
    Dim results() As Object = Me.Invoke("GetPriceQuote", _
                        New Object() {newOrder})
    Return CType(results(0), QuoteInfo())
End Function
End Class
```

I specifically renamed the classes to begin with a "C" to make it clear that these are classes and not interfaces. The first class, COrderMgmt, represents the IOrderMgmt binding as indicated by its WebServiceBinding attribute. The class inherits from SoapHttpClientProtocol and adds two methods, PlaceOrder and CheckStatus, each with a SoapDocumentMethod attribute that defines the request and response namespaces as defined in the WSDL. Similarly, the second class, CQuoteMgmt, represents the IQuoteMgmt binding. It also inherits from SoapHttpClientProtocol and adds a function called GetPriceQuote as defined in the WSDL.

The classes in Listing 8.13 are definitely good enough for the client to call the service based on the two interfaces IOrderMgmt and IQuoteMgmt. However, some developers might want to take it a step further and program against interfaces, instead of classes, on the client side.

Unfortunately, WebServiceBinding cannot be applied to interfaces. One way around this is to define manually two interfaces on the client side called IOrderMgmt and IQuoteMgmt as shown in Listing 8.14.

Listing 8.14 Defining interfaces on the client side and creating a class that implements these interfaces and forwards method calls to the Web service proxy classes (VBWSClientCode\Chapter8\Interfaces\InterfaceClient\ Supplier3.vb)

```
Interface IOrderMgmt
    Function PlaceOrder(ByVal newOrder As Order) As String
    Function CheckStatus(ByVal OrderId As String) As OrderInfo
End Interface
```

```
Interface IQuoteMgmt
    Function GetPriceQuote(ByVal newOrder As Order) As QuoteInfo()
End Interface
Public Class SupplierProxy
    Implements IOrderMgmt
    Implements IQuoteMgmt
    Private _ordermgmt As COrderMgmt
    Private _quotemgmt As CQuoteMgmt

    Public Function CheckStatus( _
                ByVal OrderId As String) As OrderInfo _
        Implements InterfaceClient.IOrderMgmt.CheckStatus
        Return _ordermgmt.CheckStatus(OrderId)
    End Function

    Public Function PlaceOrder(ByVal newOrder As Order) _
        As String _
        Implements InterfaceClient.IOrderMgmt.PlaceOrder
        Return _ordermgmt.PlaceOrder(newOrder)
    End Function

    Public Function GetPriceQuote( _
                ByVal newOrder As Order) As QuoteInfo() _
        Implements InterfaceClient.IQuoteMgmt.GetPriceQuote
        Return _quotemgmt.GetPriceQuote(newOrder)
    End Function

    Public Sub New(ByVal Url As String)
        _ordermgmt = New COrderMgmt()
        _quotemgmt = New CQuoteMgmt()
        _ordermgmt.Url = Url
        _quotemgmt.Url = Url
    End Sub
End Class
```

Each interface includes methods of the corresponding binding as defined in the WSDL document. A class, called SupplierProxy, implements both interfaces and contains instances of COrderMgmt and CQuoteMgmt. You can build the code in Listing 8.14 in a separate .dll and distribute it to client developers as a prepackaged interface-based proxy for your Web service. This is valuable if you are responsible for maintaining the Web service and the proxy classes and you want to abstract client developers from the details of your Web service's interface.

Listing 8.15 shows example client code that is designed to work against the interfaces `IOrderMgmt` and `IQuoteMgmt`.

Listing 8.15   An example client that works against the interfaces not the Web service proxy (VBWSClientCode\Chapter8\Interfaces\InterfaceClient\ Form1.vb)

```
Private Const SERVICE_URL As String = _
    "http://VBWSServer/vbwsbook/Chapter8/Supplier3.asmx"
Private Sub btnPlaceOrder_Click(ByVal sender As System.Object, _
        ByVal e As System.EventArgs) Handles
btnPlaceOrder.Click
    Dim ws As IOrderMgmt
    ws = New SupplierProxy(SERVICE_URL)
    ws.PlaceOrder(MakeOrder())
End Sub
Private Sub btnQuote_Click(ByVal sender As System.Object, _
        ByVal e As System.EventArgs) Handles btnQuote.Click
    Dim ws As IQuoteMgmt
    ws = New SupplierProxy(SERVICE_URL)
    ws.GetPriceQuote(MakeOrder())
End Sub
```

To invoke the methods of the `IOrderMgmt` binding, the client declares a variable of type `IOrderMgmt`, then sets it to a new instance of `SupplierProxy` and proceeds to call `PlaceOrder` or `CheckStatus`. Similarly, to call methods of `IQuoteMgmt`, the client declares a variable of type `IQuoteMgmt` and sets it to a new instance of `SupplierProxy` and calls `GetPriceQuote`.

The code in Listing 8.15 makes it very clear that the client is programmed against an interface and not a specific implementation. However, there's still one glaring problem with this code: The Web service URL, which is the location of a specific implementation of `IOrderMgmt` and `IQuoteMgmt`, is hard-coded as a constant. The next sections deal with determining the Web service URL at runtime based on external configuration settings.

8.6 Choosing Implementations at Runtime

Instead of hard-coding the service URL in client code, you can add it to the application's XML configuration file. For Web applications, this is the web.config file that's in the application's vroot or the folder where your Web form is located. For all other application types, it's a file with the same name as the main application's executable, but with a .config extension. For example, if your Windows application is called myapp.exe, the configuration file is called mayapp.exe.config and resides in the same folder as myapp.exe. The application's configuration file has an `<appSettings>` section where you can add your own configuration information. For example, if you know the Web service's URL, you can add it like this:

```
<appSettings>
    <add key="WSUrl" value="http://hostname/service.asmx" />
</appSettings>
```

At runtime, you use `System.Configuration.ConfigurationSettings` to read the URL from the config file:

```
theProxy.Url= _
    System.Configuration.ConfigurationSettings _
  .AppSettings ("WSUrl")
```

Instead of writing this code yourself, when you run wsdl.exe to generate the proxy class, use the /appsettingurlkey switch like this:

```
wsdl.exe /l:VB /out:proxy.vb http://localhost/service.asmx?wsdl
/➥appsettingurlkey:urlkeyname
```

where `urlkeyname` is the name you used for the Web service URL configuration key, (`WSUrl` in this example). Alternatively, if you add a Web reference with VS .NET, select the Web reference and open its properties. Change the URL Behavior property to Dynamic (default is Static). The resulting proxy class contains the code to read from `AppSettings` as shown in Listing 8.16.

Listing 8.16   The proxy class generated by wsdl.exe reads from AppSettings in the constructor

```
Public Sub New()
    MyBase.New
    Dim urlSetting As String = _
      System.Configuration.ConfigurationSettings.AppSettings( _
                "VBWSServer.DataService")
    If (Not (urlSetting) Is Nothing) Then
        Me.Url = String.Concat(urlSetting, "")
    Else
        Me.Url = _
          "http://vbwsserver/vbwsbook/Chapter8/DataService.asmx"
    End If
End Sub
```

As a rule, you should not leave the Web service URL hard-coded in a production client. By making it configurable, you can avoid client recompilation, testing, and deployment when the Web service URL changes.

8.7   Summary

In this chapter you were introduced to the concept of interface-based programming as it applies to .NET Web services. You learned how to develop Web services based on interfaces by separating the WSDL binding definition from the Web service implementation, then using wsdl.exe to generate Web service implementations from a WSDL document. You also learned how to implement multiple interfaces (bindings) using a single class and what the resulting WSDL looks like. Finally, you saw how clients can program against interfaces and how to dynamically read the Web service's URL from a configuration file rather than hard-coding it in the client.

8.8   Resources

WSDL discussion list http://groups.yahoo.com/group/wsdl/ .

Web Services Description Language (WSDL) 1.1: http://www.w3.org/TR/wsdl.

DevelopMentor's .NET Web discussion list: http://discuss.develop.com/dotnet-web.html.

W3C XML Schema specifications and resources: http://www.w3.org/XML/Schema.

Chapter 9

Handling Data in .NET Web Services

> Why does this applied science, which saves work and makes life easier,
> bring us so little happiness? The simple answer runs: Because we have
> not yet learned to make sensible use of it. —Albert Einstein

Now that you know how to build and invoke Web services, you'll want to do
something useful with them. The most common applications for Web services involve moving data in and out of data sources on the intranet or Internet. This
chapter explains your options for dealing with data in .NET Web services, including how to use ADO.NET DataSets, arrays, and your own custom classes.

9.1 Serialization and Web Services

Chapter 2 introduced you to the process of serializing objects and primitives
to XML. You learned how .NET's serialization attributes can be used to control
this process. Serialization is an important part of Web services because it provides the mapping between the data structures you use in Visual Basic and
XML messages.

It's important to understand that Web services receive and return XML only;
everything else is an illusion performed by the tools you use. So the next time
you create a Web method that returns a DataSet or an array of objects, remember that what you are really returning is XML. This XML is obtained by serializing
the DataSet or the array of objects. The client never sees your array or your
DataSet, it receives XML only. Depending on the tools the client uses, it might

treat the XML as an XML document, or it might deserialize it into an array of objects or a DataSet. For example, Figure 9.1 shows a .NET Web service that exposes a Web method that returns a DataSet. The returned DataSet is serialized to XML and that's all the client receives.

A VB 6 client might handle this XML directly using the Document Object Model. A .NET client might deserialize this XML back into a DataSet, but this is not the same DataSet that was returned by the Web method call; it's another DataSet reconstructed from the received XML.

.NET generally tries to make life easier for client developers by deserializing the received XML into client-side objects such as the DataSet. The exact types of objects used for this deserialization depend on the Web service's WSDL. Therefore, if you want to change how the client sees these types, you must change the Web service's WSDL. You do this by using the serialization attributes discussed in Chapter 2. The following sections examine applications of serialization and serialization attributes within the context of .NET Web services.

9.2   Starting with a Relational Database

A common Web service scenario occurs when you have a relational database and you want to expose some of it to applications over the Web. So you create a Web service with some Web methods that return DataSets. If you are going to al-

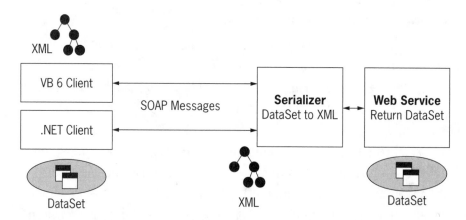

Figure 9.1   Serialization and Web services

low clients to update your database, you might also create some Web methods that take in a DataSet and use it to update the database. Listing 9.1 shows an example Web method called GetCustomersDataSet that returns a DataSet from the Customers table in the Northwind database.

Listing 9.1   A Web method that returns a DataSet (VBWSBook\Chapter9\CustomerOrders.asmx.vb)

```
<WebMethod()> _
Public Function GetCustomersDataSet() As DataSet
    Dim Sql As String = _
        "SELECT CustomerID, CompanyName FROM Customers"
    Dim ds As DataSet
    ds = GetData(Sql, "Customers")
    Return ds
End Function
Private Function GetData( _
        ByVal Sql As String, _
        ByVal TableName As String) As DataSet
        Dim ConnStr As String = _
          ConfigurationSettings.AppSettings.Get("ConnStr")
    Dim cn As New SqlConnection(ConnStr)
    Try
        cn.Open()
        Dim da As New SqlDataAdapter(Sql, cn)
        Dim ds As New DataSet()
        ds.Namespace = _
            "http://www.LearnXmlWS.com/customerorders/ds"
        da.Fill(ds, TableName)
        Return ds
    Finally
        cn.Dispose()·
    End Try
End Function
```

`GetCustomersDataSet` uses `GetData` to create a new DataSet and fill it with a list of customer ids and company names from the Customers table. Then it returns this DataSet to the client. Remember, it just looks like you're returning a DataSet—what's really returned is XML. Listing 9.2 shows an example request message and the corresponding response message with the DataSet. It should be very clear from Listing 9.2 that all the client receives is XML.

HANDLING DATA IN .NET WEB SERVICES   325

Listing 9.2   Example request and response messages for the Web method in Listing 9.1

```xml
<!-- request message -->
<soap:Envelope
    xmlns:soap="http://schemas.xmlsoap.org/soap/envelope/"
    xmlns:xsi="http://www.w3.org/2001/XMLSchema-instance"
    xmlns:xsd="http://www.w3.org/2001/XMLSchema">
  <soap:Body>
    <GetCustomersDataSet
        xmlns="http://www.LearnXmlWS.com/customerorders" />
  </soap:Body>
</soap:Envelope>

<!-- response message -->
<soap:Envelope
xmlns:soap="http://schemas.xmlsoap.org/soap/envelope/"
xmlns:xsi="http://www.w3.org/2001/XMLSchema-instance"
xmlns:xsd="http://www.w3.org/2001/XMLSchema">
  <soap:Body>
    <GetCustomersDataSetResponse
        xmlns="http://www.LearnXmlWS.com/customerorders">
      <GetCustomersDataSetResult>
        <!-- this is the serialized DataSet -->
        <xsd:schema id="NewDataSet"
            targetNamespace=
              "http://www.LearnXmlWS.com/customerorders/ds"
            xmlns="http://www.LearnXmlWS.com/customerorders/ds"
            xmlns:xsd="http://www.w3.org/2001/XMLSchema"
            xmlns:msdata="urn:schemas-microsoft-com:xml-msdata"
            attributeFormDefault="qualified"
            elementFormDefault="qualified">
          <xsd:element name="NewDataSet" msdata:IsDataSet="true">
            <!-- type definition removed -->
          </xsd:element>
        </xsd:schema>
        <diffgr:diffgram
            xmlns:msdata="urn:schemas-microsoft-com:xml-msdata"
            xmlns:diffgr=
            "urn:schemas-microsoft-com:xml-diffgram-v1">
          <NewDataSet
            xmlns="http://www.LearnXmlWS.com/customerorders/ds">
            <Customers diffgr:id="Customers1"
                msdata:rowOrder="0">
```

```
                <CustomerID>ALFKI</CustomerID>
                <CompanyName>Alfreds Futterkiste</CompanyName>
            </Customers>
        <!-- data removed -->
            </NewDataSet>
          </diffgr:diffgram>
        </GetCustomersDataSetResult>
      </GetCustomersDataSetResponse>
    </soap:Body>
  </soap:Envelope>
```

The response message in Listing 9.2 contains the serialized DataSet beginning
with the `<xsd:schema>` element. By default, a serialized DataSet contains an
XSD schema and a DiffGram containing the data. If you take a look at the service's WSDL document, you'll see that the type definitions reflect this as shown
in Listing 9.3.

**Listing 9.3   WSDL defining the response message for the method shown in
Listing 9.1**

```
<s:element name="GetCustomersDataSetResponse">
  <s:complexType>
    <s:sequence>
      <s:element minOccurs="1" maxOccurs="1"
            name="GetCustomersDataSetResult" nillable="true">
        <s:complexType>
         <s:sequence>
           <s:element ref="s:schema" />
           <s:any />
         </s:sequence>
        </s:complexType>
      </s:element>
    </s:sequence>
  </s:complexType>
</s:element>
```

I extracted the schema in Listing 9.3 from the types section of the service's
WSDL. The schema declares an element called `GetCustomersDataSetRe-`
`sult`, which is of a complex type that contains a sequence of two elements.
First, `<s:element ref="s:schema"/>` means that the first element will be a
`<schema>` element that belongs to the XSD namespace denoted here by the `s`

prefix. Second, `<s:any/>` means another element will follow whose name and type are undetermined.

9.2.1 Typed DataSets

Although the type definition in Listing 9.3 describes the serialized DataSet, it doesn't really tell the client much about what the DataSet contains. A developer looking at this WSDL cannot infer much about the structure of the returned XML. To make your service's WSDL more specific about what you are returning, you should return a typed DataSet. A typed DataSet is a class that inherits from the DataSet and defines the DataSet's structure, including tables, columns, and relations at design time. This makes it possible for .NET to emit more specific type definitions in the service's WSDL. Therefore, clients can better understand the data they are getting.

If you have an XML Schema that describes your data, you can easily create a typed DataSet using xsd.exe (more on this later in this chapter). If you have the relational database only, you can use Visual Studio's Schema designer and Server Explorer to create a typed DataSet.

From the project menu, choose Add New Item. Select the DataSet template and enter the name of your typed DataSet (for example, Customers as in Figure 9.2), then click Open. This will add a new schema called Customers.xsd to your project and bring up the Schema designer.

Click on the DataSet tab at the bottom to switch to designer view if you're not already there. Now open the Server Explorer and add a new database connection to your database server if you don't already have one. Expand this connection and find the table you want (for example, Customers). Drag this table and drop it on the Schema designer. You should have an element declaration with a complex type that corresponds to the Customers table. You can repeat this process for all the tables you want to have in the DataSet. For example, drag the Orders table onto the Schema designer to create an Orders element as shown in Figure 9.3.

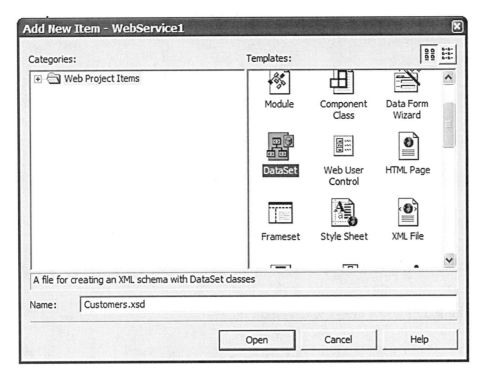

Figure 9.2 Adding a new typed DataSet to the project

You can now set some of the properties of the schema itself by clicking any-where on the designer surface, then opening the properties window, which shows a list of schema properties including `targetNamespace` and `dataSet-Name` as shown in Figure 9.4. Set the `dataSetName` to `CustomerOrders-DataSet` and the `targetNamespace` to `http://www.LearnXmlWS.com/customerorders/schema`.

The schema you created contains the elements Customers and Orders, but they are unrelated. You can create a relation by simply dragging a Relation from the toolbox onto the CustomerID element. You'll see the Edit Relation dia-log as shown in Figure 9.5. This dialog lets you specify the name of the rela-tion and the parent and child elements (tables) and fields (columns) involved in this relation.

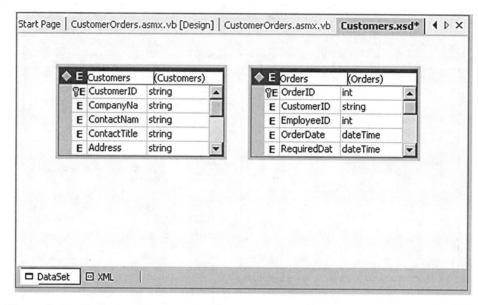

Figure 9.3   Adding tables to the typed DataSet

Figure 9.4   Setting schema properties including targetNamespace

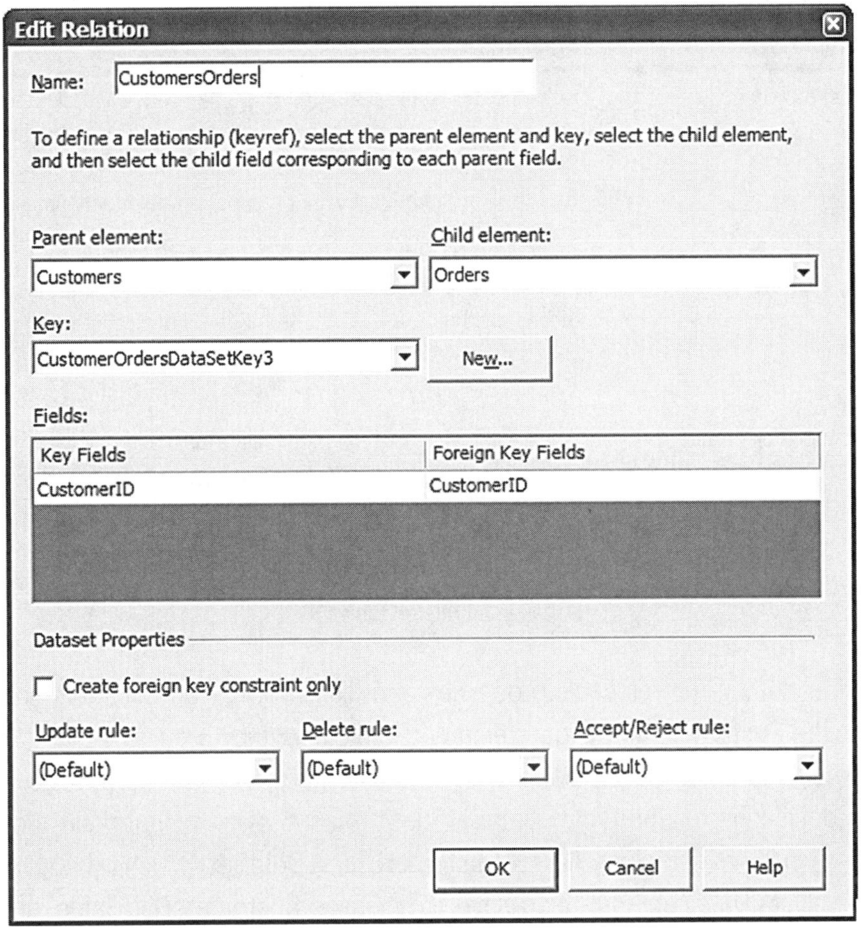

Figure 9.5 Editing a DataSet relation

At the bottom of this dialog you'll see some DataSet-specific properties. These properties affect the structure of a DataSet that reads this schema. For example, checking "Create foreign key constraint only" causes the DataSet to create primary and foreign key constraints but the DataSet tables are not related as parent/child. The remaining three properties affect how changes in primary key value in the parent table affect the corresponding records in the child table. Table 9.1 shows the meaning of these three properties.

Table 9.1 DataSet relation rules

Property	Meaning
Update rule	How updates to the parent table are handled. Cascade (the default) means updates cascade down to records in the child table. SetNull or SetDefault means values in related rows are set to DBNull or the default value, respectively. None means nothing is done to related rows.
Delete rule	How deleted parent records are handled. Cascade (the default) means child records are deleted. SetNull or SetDefault means values in related rows are set to DBNull or the default value respectively. None means nothing is done to related rows.
Accept/Reject rule	When you manipulate the parent DataTable and delete or update parent records, then call AcceptChanges or RejectChanges—this rule is invoked to determine what happens. Cascade is the default and means that updates and/or deletes should be cascaded to the related table(s). None means no action should be taken on related tables.

After setting the relation's properties and clicking OK, you will see a link between the Customers and Orders elements indicating they are related.

When you build the project a .vb file is automatically generated: It contains class definitions for the typed DataSet classes as shown in Figure 9.6. For example, you'll have a class called CustomerOrdersDataSet, which inherits from System.Data.DataSet. You'll also have the classes CustomersDataTable and OrdersDataTable, both of which inherit from System.Data.DataTable.

You can use CustomerOrdersDataSet just as you would a DataSet, including filling it with data using SqlDataAdapter and returning it from a Web method. Listing 9.4 shows an example Web method that returns an instance of CustomerOrdersDataSet.

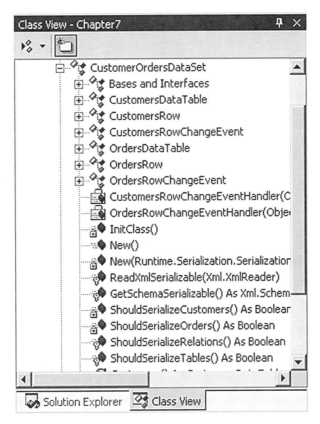

Figure 9.6 Typed DataSet class called CustomerOrdersDataSet

**Listing 9.4 A Web method that returns an instance of the typed DataSet
(VBWSBook\Chapter9\CustomerOrders.asmx.vb)**

```
<WebMethod()> _
Public Function GetCustomerOrdersTypedDataSet() As _
                CustomerOrdersDataSet
    Dim Sql1 As String = "SELECT * FROM Customers"
    Dim Sql2 As String = "SELECT * FROM Orders"
    Dim ds As New CustomerOrdersDataSet()
    Dim ConnStr As String = _
        ConfigurationSettings.AppSettings.Get("ConnStr")
    Dim cn As New SqlConnection(ConnStr)
    Try
        cn.Open()
        Dim da1 As New SqlDataAdapter(Sql1, cn)
        Dim da2 As New SqlDataAdapter(Sql2, cn)
```

```
            da1.Fill(ds, "Customers")
            da2.Fill(ds, "Orders")
        Catch ex As Exception
            Debug.WriteLine(ex.Message)
        Finally
            cn.Dispose()
        End Try
        Return ds
    End Function
```

The code in Listing 9.4 uses two SqlDataAdapters to load data from the Customers and Orders tables into an instance of CustomerOrdersDataSet, then returns that instance. The resulting WSDL imports the typed DataSet's schema as shown in Listing 9.5.

Listing 9.5   Returning a typed DataSet causes the service's WSDL to import the DataSet's schema

```
<!-- import the typed DataSet's schema -->
<import
namespace="http://www.LearnXmlWS.com/customerorders/schema"
location=
"http://localhost/VBWSBook/Chapter9/CustomerOrders.asmx?
➥schema=CustomerOrdersDataSet" />
<types>
<s:schema attributeFormDefault="qualified"
        elementFormDefault="qualified"
<s:element name="GetCustomerOrdersTypedDataSetResponse">
  <s:complexType>
    <s:sequence>
      <s:element minOccurs="1" maxOccurs="1"
          name="GetCustomerOrdersTypedDataSetResult"
          nillable="true">
        <s:complexType>
          <s:sequence>
        <!-- any element from the typed
          DataSet's namespace is allowed -->
          <s:any
           namespace=
           "http://www.LearnXmlWS.com/customerorders/schema" />
          </s:sequence>
        </s:complexType>
      </s:element>
```

```
        </s:sequence>
      </s:complexType>
    </s:element>
  </s:schema>
</types>
```

Listing 9.5 shows a fragment of the Web service's WSDL. Notice that clients can get the typed DataSet's schema from `WebserviceUrl?schema=Customer-OrdersDataSet`. Also note that the Web method's return value is defined as having a sequence of any elements that belong to the namespace `http://www.LearnXmlWS.com/customerorders/schema`, which is the namespace we used for the typed DataSet's schema. A client can look at this WSDL and the typed DataSet's schema and understand the structure of XML returned from `GetCustomerOrdersTypedDataSet`. This is the primary benefit of using typed DataSets versus ordinary DataSets.

9.2.2 Nested Elements

If you open the typed DataSet's schema in XML view, you'll see that the Customers and Orders elements are not nested. That is, an instance document would look something like this:

```
<CustomerOrdersDataSet>
    <Customers></Customers>
    <Customers></Customers>
    <Orders></Orders>
    <Orders></Orders>
    <Orders></Orders>
</CustomerOrdersDataSet>
```

Suppose you wanted Orders elements to be nested within Customers elements instead, like this:

```
<CustomerOrdersDataSet>
    <Customers>
        <Orders></Orders>
    </Customers>
    <Customers>
        <Orders></Orders>
    </Customers>
</CustomerOrdersDataSet>
```

To get this format, you must change the Customers element's complex type in the DataSet schema to indicate that it will contain Orders elements. You do this by editing the schema directly or by using the designer to drag the Orders element onto the Customers element. The resulting typed DataSet has two relations: one based on the nesting of Customers and Orders and the other based on the unique/keyref constraints. In most cases, what you want is one relation based on the unique/keyref constraints; that is, you want to relate the two tables based on the primary key/foreign key constraints. To eliminate the extra relation, you need to edit the schema and add a `msdata:IsNested="true"` attribute on the `<xsd:keyref>` element like this:

```
<xsd:keyref name="CustomersOrders"
  refer="NestedCustomersKey1"
  msdata:IsNested="true">
```

`IsNested` is one of the annotations you can use to affect how a DataSet is constructed from a schema. Other annotations will be covered in detail later in this chapter. There's an example nested DataSet in this chapter's Web service project. Listing 9.6 shows the modified schema for this nested DataSet.

Listing 9.6 Part of the modified schema for Orders nested within Customers (VBWSBook\Chapter9\Customers.xsd)

```
<xsd:schema ...>
  <xsd:element msdata:IsDataSet="true" name="NestedCustomers">
    <xsd:complexType>
      <xsd:choice maxOccurs="unbounded">
        <xsd:element name="Customers">
          <xsd:complexType>
            <xsd:sequence>
              <xsd:element name="CustomerID" type="xsd:string" />
              <xsd:element name="CompanyName" type="xsd:string" />
      <!-- other elements removed -->
                <xsd:element minOccurs="0"
                  maxOccurs="unbounded" name="Orders">
                <xsd:complexType>
                  <xsd:sequence>
                    <xsd:element name="OrderID"
                                 msdata:ReadOnly="true"
                      msdata:AutoIncrement="true"
```

```
                    type="xsd:int" />
        <xsd:element name="CustomerID"
            minOccurs="0" type="xsd:string" />
        <xsd:element name="EmployeeID"
            minOccurs="0" type="xsd:int" />
        <xsd:element name="OrderDate"
            minOccurs="0" type="xsd:dateTime" />
    <!-- other elements removed -->
            </xsd:sequence>
          </xsd:complexType>
        </xsd:element>
      </xsd:sequence>
    </xsd:complexType>
  </xsd:element>
 </xsd:choice>
 </xsd:complexType>
 </xsd:element>
</xsd:schema>
```

When you serialize the resulting typed DataSet, it will nest `<Orders>` elements inside the parent `<Customers>` element as specified by the modified schema.

9.3   Round-Triping DataSets

Now that you know how to create typed DataSets, let's look at a Web service and a Windows Forms client that use typed DataSets to send data back and forth over the Internet. Listing 9.7 shows a Web method called `SaveCustomer-OrdersTypedDataSet` that receives a DataSet, uses it to update the Customers and Orders tables, and returns the refreshed DataSet. This method complements the `GetCustomerOrdersTypedDataSet` method in Listing 9.4.

Listing 9.7   A method to save changes to the database (VBWSBook\Chapter9\CustomerOrders.asmx)

```
<WebMethod()> _
Public Function SaveCustomerOrdersTypedDataSet( _
        ByVal ds As CustomerOrdersDataSet) _
        As CustomerOrdersDataSet
    Dim Sql1 As String = _
        "SELECT CustomerID, CompanyName FROM Customers"
    Dim Sql2 As String = "SELECT * FROM Orders"
```

```
        Dim ConnStr As String = _
          ConfigurationSettings.AppSettings.Get("ConnStr")
        Dim cn As New SqlConnection(ConnStr)
        Try
            cn.Open()
            Dim da1 As New SqlDataAdapter(Sql1, cn)
            Dim da2 As New SqlDataAdapter(Sql2, cn)
            Dim cb1 As New SqlCommandBuilder(da1)
            Dim cb2 As New SqlCommandBuilder(da2)
            da1.Update(ds, "Customers")
            da2.Update(ds, "Orders")
            cn.Close()
        Catch ex As Exception
            Debug.WriteLine(ex.Message)
            Throw New Exception(ex.Message)
        Finally
            cn.Dispose()
        End Try
        Return ds
    End Function
```

To update a database from a DataSet, you need to create a SqlDataAdapter (or an OleDbDataAdapter) for each database table that you want to update. Then you create Select, Update, Insert, and Delete commands for the adapter. When there's a one-to-one correspondence between the tables in your DataSet and the tables in the database, you can create the Select command only, and then use a SqlCommandBuilder, which builds the remaining commands for you.

After you've created the data adapters, you call Update on each adapter and pass it the DataSet and the name of the table to update. In addition to updating the database table, the adapter also refreshes the DataSet with the current database table's content.

After updating both Customers and Orders tables, `SaveCustomerOrders-TypedDataSet` returns the refreshed DataSet. This is only necessary if the client needs to display the current content of the database, which is usually the case. Listing 9.8 shows an example Windows Forms client code.

Listing 9.8   A client invoking GetCustomerOrdersTypedDataSet and SaveCustomerOrdersTypedDataSet (VBWSClientCode\Chapter9\ frmRndTrip.vb)

```
Public Class frmRndTrip
    Inherits System.Windows.Forms.Form
    Private _UseProxy As Boolean
    Private ds As vbwsserver.CustomerOrdersDataSet
    Dim ws As vbwsserver.CustomerOrders
    Private Sub frmRndTrip_Load(ByVal sender As System.Object, _
                ByVal e As System.EventArgs) _
                Handles MyBase.Load
        ws = New vbwsserver.CustomerOrders()
        SetProxy(ws)
        GetData()
    End Sub
    Private Sub btnRefresh_Click(ByVal sender As System.Object, _
            ByVal e As System.EventArgs) Handles btnRefresh.Click
        lblStatus.Text = "Refreshing ..."
        Me.Refresh()
        GetData()
        lblStatus.Text = "Refresh completed successfully"
    End Sub
    Private Sub GetData()
        ds = ws.GetCustomerOrdersTypedDataSet()
        dgOrders.DataSource = ds
    End Sub
    Private Sub btnSave_Click(ByVal sender As System.Object, _
            ByVal e As System.EventArgs) Handles btnSave.Click
        lblStatus.Text = "Saving ..."
        Me.Refresh()
        Dim newDS As New vbwsserver.CustomerOrdersDataSet()
        newDS = ws.SaveCustomerOrdersTypedDataSet _
            (ds.GetChanges())
        ds.Merge(newDS)
        lblStatus.Text = "Save completed successfully"
    End Sub
End Class
```

This Windows Forms client consists of a form with a data grid, a button for saving changes, and a button for refreshing the data. The client has added a Web reference to the Customers Web service on VBWSServer. As part of adding a

Web reference, the generated proxy code includes a typed DataSet called `Cus-tomerOrdersDataSet` that mirrors the one used by the service.

Listing 9.8 declares a member variable called ds of type `CustomerOrder-sDataSet` (which belongs to the `VBWSServer` namespace). This variable is declared as a class member variable because it will be used to hold the data returned from the Web service and all updates made by the user.

When the form is loaded, the code in `frmRndTrip_Load` instantiates a Web service proxy and calls `GetCustomerOrdersTypedDataSet` to retrieve the DataSet. Then it binds the data grid called `dgOrders` to the returned DataSet. The grid displays a hierarchy of customers and their orders as shown in Figure 9.7.

The user can edit the data and click Save, which executes btnSave_Click in Listing 9.8. This procedure calls ds.GetChanges to get a new DataSet that contains changed rows. Then it calls the Web service's `SaveCustomerOrders-`

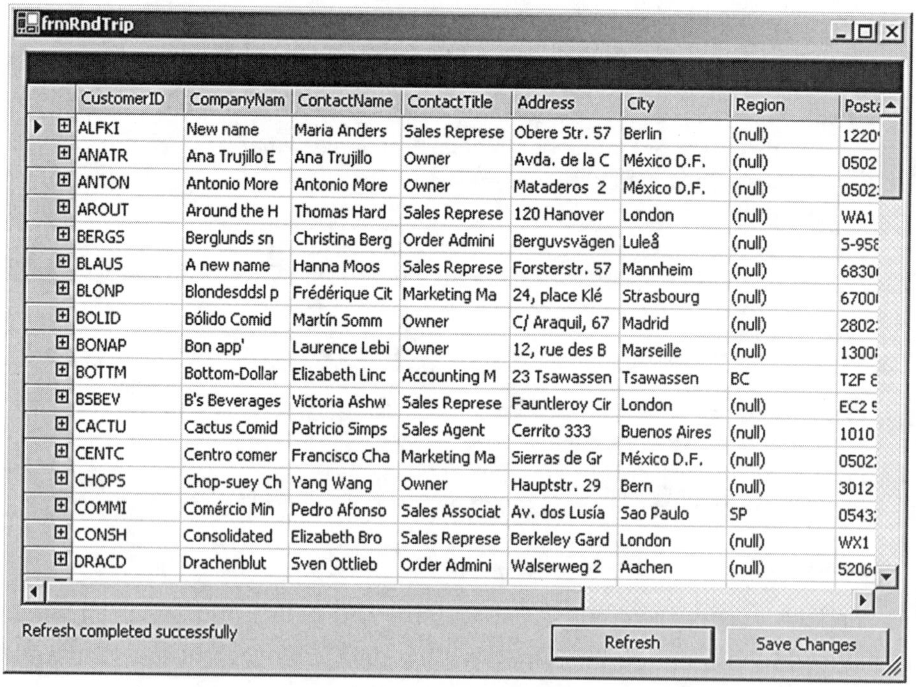

		CustomerID	CompanyNam	ContactName	ContactTitle	Address	City	Region	Posta
▶	⊞	ALFKI	New name	Maria Anders	Sales Represe	Obere Str. 57	Berlin	(null)	1220'
	⊞	ANATR	Ana Trujillo E	Ana Trujillo	Owner	Avda. de la C	México D.F.	(null)	0502
	⊞	ANTON	Antonio More	Antonio More	Owner	Mataderos 2	México D.F.	(null)	0502:
	⊞	AROUT	Around the H	Thomas Hard	Sales Represe	120 Hanover	London	(null)	WA1
	⊞	BERGS	Berglunds sn	Christina Berg	Order Admini	Berguvsvägen	Luleå	(null)	S-958
	⊞	BLAUS	A new name	Hanna Moos	Sales Represe	Forsterstr. 57	Mannheim	(null)	68300
	⊞	BLONP	Blondesddsl p	Frédérique Cit	Marketing Ma	24, place Klé	Strasbourg	(null)	67000
	⊞	BOLID	Bólido Comid	Martín Somm	Owner	C/ Araquil, 67	Madrid	(null)	2802:
	⊞	BONAP	Bon app'	Laurence Lebi	Owner	12, rue des B	Marseille	(null)	1300:
	⊞	BOTTM	Bottom-Dollar	Elizabeth Linc	Accounting M	23 Tsawassen	Tsawassen	BC	T2F 8
	⊞	BSBEV	B's Beverages	Victoria Ashw	Sales Represe	Fauntleroy Cir	London	(null)	EC2 5
	⊞	CACTU	Cactus Comid	Patricio Simps	Sales Agent	Cerrito 333	Buenos Aires	(null)	1010
	⊞	CENTC	Centro comer	Francisco Cha	Marketing Ma	Sierras de Gr	México D.F.	(null)	0502:
	⊞	CHOPS	Chop-suey Ch	Yang Wang	Owner	Hauptstr. 29	Bern	(null)	3012
	⊞	COMMI	Comércio Min	Pedro Afonso	Sales Associat	Av. dos Lusía	Sao Paulo	SP	0543:
	⊞	CONSH	Consolidated	Elizabeth Bro	Sales Represe	Berkeley Gard	London	(null)	WX1
	⊞	DRACD	Drachenblut	Sven Ottlieb	Order Admini	Walserweg 2	Aachen	(null)	52060

Refresh completed successfully   [Refresh]   [Save Changes]

Figure 9.7   Customers and their orders displayed in a data bound grid

`TypedDataSet` method, passing it the changes DataSet and receiving a refreshed DataSet. To display any new data in the returned DataSet, it calls `ds.Merge`, and passes it the returned DataSet.

The code you write for sending and receiving DataSets on the Web service side is concise and straightforward. Similarly, .NET clients can leverage DataSets to write equally concise code. Remember that other clients, such as VB 6 and Java, have to work with the DataSet as XML. Using XML technologies such as the Document Object Model (DOM), XML Path (XPath), and Extensible Stylesheet Language Transformation (XSLT), non-.NET clients have rich programming models that allow extensive manipulation of a DataSet represented as XML. However, these clients require more code to manipulate the DataSet compared to .NET clients. In Chapter 12 you will see a Java client that calls this Web service, manipulates the returned dataset, and sends it back to the Web service for saving.

9.4 Starting with a Schema

The previous section covered the process of exposing/updating data when you start with a relational database. In many cases, especially business-to-business integration scenarios, you'll start with an XML schema that describes the business documents to be exchanged.

The next sections explain some of the tasks you'll perform when starting with a schema, such as creating DataSets from the schema and importing/exporting data according to the schema.

9.4.1 DataSets from Schemas

Starting with a schema, you have the option to create the DataSet structure at runtime or at design time. To create the DataSet structure at runtime, you instantiate a DataSet and tell it to read an XML schema, causing it to create tables, columns, constraints, and relations based on the schema. You can fill this DataSet with data from a relational database or from an XML document. The role of the schema here is simply to tell the DataSet about the table structure.

Consider, for example, the invoice schema in Listing 9.9. This simple schema declares an invoice element that contains the usual information like `invoiceNumber` and `invoiceDate`. The invoice also contains item elements whose type is defined by `ItemType`.

Listing 9.9   An example invoice schema (VBWSBook\Chapter9\Invoice.xsd)

```
<xsd:schema
targetNamespace="http://www.LearnXmlWS.com/Invoicing/schema"
xmlns:xsd="http://www.w3.org/2001/XMLSchema" xmlns:ws="http://
www.LearnXmlWS.com/Invoicing/schema"
elementFormDefault="qualified">
    <xsd:element name="invoice">
        <xsd:complexType>
            <xsd:sequence>
                <xsd:element name="invoiceNumber"
                            type="xsd:string" />
                <xsd:element name="supplierID" type="xsd:int" />
                <xsd:element name="invoiceDate"
                            type="xsd:date" />
                <xsd:element name="poNumber" type="xsd:string" />
                <xsd:element name="subTotal" type="ws:money" />
                <xsd:element name="salesTax" type="ws:money" />
                <xsd:element name="paymentReceived"
                            type="ws:money" />
                <xsd:element name="amtDue" type="ws:money" />
                <xsd:element name="terms" type="xsd:string"
                            minOccurs="0" />
                <xsd:element name="contactName"
                            type="xsd:string" minOccurs="0" />
                <xsd:element name="contactNumber"
                            type="xsd:string" minOccurs="0" />
                <xsd:element name="promotion" type="xsd:string"
                            minOccurs="0" />
                <xsd:element name="item" type="ws:ItemType"
                            maxOccurs="unbounded" />
            </xsd:sequence>
        </xsd:complexType>
    </xsd:element>
    <xsd:simpleType name="money">
        <xsd:restriction base="xsd:decimal">
            <xsd:fractionDigits value="2" />
        </xsd:restriction>
```

```
        </xsd:simpleType>
        <xsd:complexType name="ItemType">
            <xsd:sequence>
                <xsd:element name="partNum" type="xsd:string" />
                <xsd:element name="quant" type="xsd:int" />
                <xsd:element name="unitPrice" type="ws:money" />
                <xsd:element name="total" type="ws:money" />
            </xsd:sequence>
        </xsd:complexType>
    </xsd:schema>
```

XML lets you define parent-child documents with nested elements like this invoice, but relational databases need explicit columns (primary and foreign key) to establish parent-child relations. For example, according to this schema, each document contains exactly one invoice element and that element contains its child item element. Therefore, the schema does not need to define a primary key (`<xsd:key>` or `<xsd:unique>`) for the invoice because there's only one invoice per document. Also, the schema does not need to define a foreign key (`<xsd:keyref>`) for the items, because items are nested inside their parent invoice so you know exactly which invoice these items belong to.

If you take this schema and load it into a DataSet by calling ReadXmlSchema, the DataSet creates tables called invoice and item corresponding to the invoice and item elements. Listing 9.10 shows the code for reading the schema into a DataSet, then reporting the table structure created within the DataSet.

Listing 9.10 Reading the invoice schema into a DataSet and reporting the resulting tables and relations (VBWSClientCode\Chapter9\XmlDataEngine\ SqlMetaDataAdapter.vb)

```
Public Function GetDSStructureFromSchema( _
                ByVal xsd As XmlDocument) As String
    Dim ds As New DataSet()
    ds.ReadXmlSchema(New XmlNodeReader(xsd))
    Return GetDSStructure(ds)
End Function
Public Function GetDSStructure(ByVal ds As DataSet) As String
    Dim tbl As DataTable
    Dim col As DataColumn
    Dim constr As Constraint
    Dim uq As System.Data.UniqueConstraint
```

```
Dim fk As System.Data.ForeignKeyConstraint
Dim needsComma As Boolean = False
Dim res As New StringWriter()
'Load the schema into the DataSet
For Each tbl In ds.Tables
    res.WriteLine(" Table: " + tbl.TableName)
    For Each col In tbl.Columns
        res.WriteLine("   --- Column name: " + _
            col.ColumnName + ", type: " + _
            col.DataType.ToString())
    Next
    res.WriteLine("   --- Constraints --- ")
    For Each constr In tbl.Constraints
        If constr.GetType() Is GetType(UniqueConstraint) Then
            uq = constr
            If uq.IsPrimaryKey Then
                res.WriteLine("    -- Primary Key constraint")
            Else
                res.WriteLine("    -- Unique constraint")
            End If
            res.WriteLine("        Constraint name: " + _
                constr.ConstraintName)
            For Each col In uq.Columns
                res.WriteLine("        Constraint column: " + _
                    col.ColumnName)
            Next
        ElseIf constr.GetType Is _
                GetType(ForeignKeyConstraint) Then
            fk = constr
            res.WriteLine("    -- Foreign Key constraint")
            res.WriteLine("        Parent table: " + _
                fk.RelatedTable.TableName)
            For Each col In fk.Columns
                res.WriteLine("        Constraint column: " + _
                    col.ColumnName)
            Next
            For Each col In fk.RelatedColumns
                res.WriteLine("        Related column: " + _
                    col.ColumnName)
            Next
        Else
            res.WriteLine("        Unknown constraint type!!!")
        End If
```

```
      Next
   Next
   Dim rel As DataRelation
   res.WriteLine("====== Relations ======")
For Each rel In ds.Relations
    res.WriteLine("Relation name: " + rel.RelationName)
    res.WriteLine(" -- Parent table: " + _
          rel.ParentTable.TableName + _
          " -- Child table: " + rel.ChildTable.TableName)
    For Each col In rel.ChildColumns
        res.WriteLine(" --- Relation column: " + col.ColumnName)
    Next
Next
Return res.ToString()


End Function
```

GetDSStructureFromSchema begins by creating a DataSet object and calling its
ReadXmlSchema method to load the specified schema into the DataSet. Note
that the schema is passed in as an XmlDocument so an XmlNodeReader is used
to read the schema into the DataSet. The call to GetDSStructure is where the interesting work is done. This function loops through each table of the input
DataSet and gets the table's name. Then for each column in that table, it gets
the column name and type. Next, it gets the constraints on that table and determines whether each constraint is a unique, primary key, or foreign key constraint. After finishing all tables, it examines the DataSet Relations collection
and reads the parent and child table and the relation columns of each relation.
Figure 9.8 shows the result of running this code on the example invoice schema
shown in Listing 9.9.

Each complex type in the XSD schema results in a table in the DataSet. The
columns reported in Figure 9.8 reflect the invoice schema with their types translated from the XML Schema type to the corresponding .NET Framework type.
For your reference, Appendix A lists the built-in XML Schema types and their corresponding .NET data and SQL Server types.

Looking at the table structure reported in Figure 9.8, you'll notice two additional columns that were not in the original schema: invoice_Id on both the invoice and item tables. These are the primary key and foreign key columns

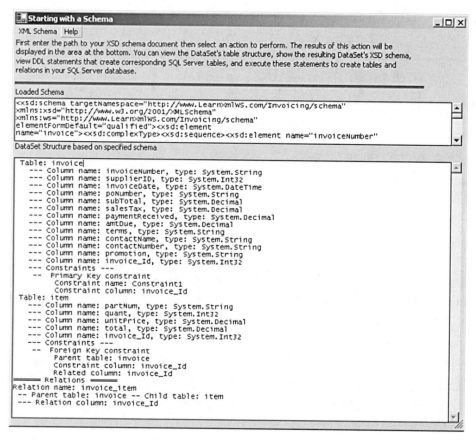

Figure 9.8   Running XmlData on the invoice schema

needed to establish the relation as explained. You'll notice a primary key constraint on the invoice table based on invoice_Id and a foreign key constraint on the items table based on invoice_Id. You'll also notice that the parent-child relation is based on the invoice_Id column.

To obtain the schema from the DataSet, you call GetXmlSchema (see Listing 9.11).

Listing 9.11 The DataSet's schema obtained by calling DataSet.GetXmlSchema after loading the invoice schema by calling ReadXmlSchema

```xml
<?xml version="1.0" encoding="utf-16"?>
<xs:schema id="NewDataSet"
targetNamespace="http://www.LearnXmlWS.com/Invoicing/schema"
xmlns:mstns="http://www.LearnXmlWS.com/Invoicing/schema"
xmlns="http://www.LearnXmlWS.com/Invoicing/schema"
xmlns:xs="http://www.w3.org/2001/XMLSchema"
xmlns:msdata="urn:schemas-microsoft-com:xml-msdata"
attributeFormDefault="qualified"
elementFormDefault="qualified">
  <xs:simpleType name="money">
    <xs:restriction base="xs:decimal" />
  </xs:simpleType>
  <xs:complexType name="ItemType">
    <xs:sequence>
      <xs:element name="partNum" type="xs:string" />
      <xs:element name="quant" type="xs:int" />
      <xs:element name="unitPrice" type="money" />
      <xs:element name="total" type="money" />
    </xs:sequence>
  </xs:complexType>
  <xs:element name="invoice">
    <xs:complexType>
      <xs:sequence>
        <xs:element name="invoiceNumber" type="xs:string" />
        <xs:element name="supplierID" type="xs:int" />
        <xs:element name="invoiceDate" type="xs:date" />
        <xs:element name="poNumber" type="xs:string" />
        <xs:element name="subTotal" type="money" />
        <xs:element name="salesTax" type="money" />
        <xs:element name="paymentReceived" type="money" />
        <xs:element name="amtDue" type="money" />
        <xs:element name="terms" type="xs:string"
        minOccurs="0" />
        <xs:element name="contactName" type="xs:string"
                    minOccurs="0" />
        <xs:element name="contactNumber" type="xs:string"
                    minOccurs="0" />
        <xs:element name="promotion" type="xs:string"
                    minOccurs="0" />
        <xs:element name="item" type="mstns:ItemType"
                             maxOccurs="unbounded"
```

```
                    minOccurs="0" />
        </xs:sequence>
      </xs:complexType>
    </xs:element>
    <xs:element name="NewDataSet" msdata:IsDataSet="true">
      <xs:complexType>
        <xs:choice maxOccurs="unbounded">
          <xs:element ref="invoice" />
        </xs:choice>
      </xs:complexType>
    </xs:element>
  </xs:schema>
```

Comparing the schema in Listing 9.11 to the original one (in Listing 9.9), you'll notice an interesting difference. The schema in Listing 9.11 declares an element called NewDataSet that was not in the original schema. This element represents the DataSet itself and serves as a container for the elements that represent the individual tables.

The schema can also be annotated with attributes from the `urn:schemas-microsoft-com:xml-msdata` namespace. These attributes convey additional information about the DataSet's table structure. For example, msdata:Ordinal specifies the ordinal position of a column within the table. Table 9.2 lists the commonly used msdata annotations and their meanings.

Table 9.2   MS Data schema annotations

Annotation	Applies to	Meaning
IsDataSet	`<xsd:element>` representing DataSet	This element represents the DataSet.
TableName	`<xsd:element>` representing a table	The name of the table if different from the name of the element. Use this to override element name if it is an invalid database name. For example, you can create a table called CustomerOrder from an element called Order.

Table 9.2 **(continued) MS Data schema annotations**

Annotation	Applies to	Meaning
ColumnName	\<xsd:element\>or \<xsd:attribute\> representing a column	The name of the column if different from the name of the element/attribute. Use this to override element/attribute name if it is an invalid database name. For example, you can create a column called OrderTime from an element called Time.
Ordinal	\<xsd:element\>or \<xsd:attribute\> representing a column	The ordinal position of the column within the table.
ReadOnly	\<xsd:element\>or \<xsd:attribute\> representing a column	Whether or not the column value can be edited. For example, an auto-increment column would be read-only.
AllowDBNull	\<xsd:element\>or \<xsd:attribute\> representing a column	Whether or not to allow nulls. You need to set this to false if the column is a primary key.
AutoIncrement	\<xsd:element\>or \<xsd:attribute\> representing a column	If set to true, it indicates that the column value should be incremented automatically. Column type must be xsd:int.
ConstraintName	\<xsd:unique\>, \<xsd:key\> or \<xsd:keyref\> elements	The name of the corresponding constraint that's created within the DataSet. Default is the value of the name attribute.
PrimaryKey	\<xsd:unique\> or \<xsd:key\> elements	If set to true, then a primary key is created in the DataSet. Otherwise, a unique constraint is created.

Table 9.2   (continued) MS Data schema annotations

Annotation	Applies to	Meaning
ConstraintOnly	\<xsd:keyref> elements	If set to true, the DataSet will have a constraint corresponding to this keyref but will not have a parent-child relation between the two tables.
IsNested	\<xsd:keyref> elements	If set to true, it indicates that the parent and child tables are nested in the XML document similar to the example invoice document where items are nested within the invoice.
UpdateRule	\<xsd:keyref> elements	How updates to parent records are handled. See the section titled Typed DataSets above.
DeleteRule	\<xsd:keyref> elements	How deleted parent records are handled. See the section titled Typed DataSets above.
AcceptRejectRule	\<xsd:keyref> elements	How changes are handled when you call AcceptChanges or RejectChanges. See the section titled Typed DataSets above.
Relationship	Unlike all other annotations, this one is an element. Use it inside an \<xsd:appinfo> element.	Use \<msdata:Relationship> to explicitly define a relationship between two tables independent of any unique, key, or keyref definitions.

9.4.2   Typed DataSets from Schemas

To create the DataSet structure at design time, you use a tool such as xsd.exe, to read the XML Schema and generate a set of classes that represent a typed DataSet. As you saw in Chapter 2, xsd.exe is a command line tool that can create classes from XML Schemas and vice versa. In total, xsd.exe can do four different but related things:

- Create typed DataSets in VB, C#, or JScript from an XML Schema
- Create VB, C#, or JScript classes from an XML Schema
- Create a schema from types in a compiled assembly
- Infer a schema from an instance XML document

Before you create a typed DataSet, you might want to make a copy of the schema and annotate it with msdata attributes to control the typed DataSet. For example, you don't want the typed DataSet to be called NewDataSet, which is the default you saw when you loaded the invoice schema into the DataSet. Instead you want the DataSet to be called Invoices and you want the invoiceNumber element to map to a column called invoiceNum. To do this you edit the schema and add an `<Invoices>` element with `msdata:IsDataSet="true"`. You also add `msdata:ColumnName="invoiceNum"` on the invoiceNumber element declaration and `msdata:TableName` on both invoice and item element declarations. Listing 9.12 shows the annotated schema.

Listing 9.12 Annotating the invoice schema to specify table and column names (VBWSBook\Chapter9\AnnotatedInvoice.xsd)

```
<xsd:schema ...>
   <xsd:element name="Invoices" msdata:IsDataSet="true">
      <xsd:complexType>
         <xsd:sequence>
            <xsd:element name="invoice"
                         msdata:TableName="Invoice">
               <xsd:complexType>
                  <xsd:sequence>
                     <xsd:element name="invoiceNumber"
                        msdata:ColumnName="invoiceNum"
                        type="xsd:string" />
                   <!-- other elements removed -->
                        <xsd:element name="item"
                           msdata:TableName="InvoiceItem"
                           type="ws:ItemType"
                           maxOccurs="unbounded" />
                  </xsd:sequence>
               </xsd:complexType>
```

```
          </xsd:element>
        </xsd:sequence>
      </xsd:complexType>
    </xsd:element>
  </xsd:schema>
```

To generate a type DataSet from the annotated schema, you issue the command (assuming xsd.exe is in your path):

```
xsd.exe AnnotatedInvoice.xsd /DataSet /l:VB
```

You'll get a message indicating that a file called `AnnotatedInvoice .vb` has been created.

```
Microsoft (R) Xml Schemas/DataTypes support utility
[Microsoft (R) .NET Framework, Version 1.0.3705.0]
Copyright (C) Microsoft Corporation 1998-2001. All rights
➥reserved.

Writing file 'D:\VBWSBook\Chapter9\AnnotatedInvoice.vb'.
```

You can add this new file to your project[1] and begin using the typed DataSet. Listing 9.13 shows a Web service with a simple method that receives invoices; Listing 9.14 shows the relevant part of the service's WSDL.

Listing 9.13   A Web method that receives an instance of the invoice typed DataSet (VBWSBook\Chapter9\Invoicing.asmx.vb)

```
<WebService([Namespace]:= _
"http://www.LearnXmlWS.com/invoicing")> _
Public Class Invoicing
    Inherits System.Web.Services.WebService

    <WebMethod()> _
    Public Sub SubmitInvoice( _
        ByVal ds As Invoices)
        'validate and save the invoices
    End Sub

End Class
```

---

[1]When you try to add a .vb file to a Web project, make sure you point to it using a path (for example, D:\files\invoice.vb) rather than a URL (for example, http://localhost/projects/invoice.vb). For security reasons, ASP.NET will, by default, always return a 404 error when you request a .vb file. This is designed to protect your source code from being publicly available on the Web.

The Web method in Listing 9.13 takes in one parameter of type Invoices, which is the typed DataSet created from AnnotatedInvoice.xsd. The corresponding WSDL in Listing 9.14 is very similar to the WSDL in Listing 9.5, which also imported the schema for a typed DataSet.

Listing 9.14   The service's WSDL imports the invoice typed DataSet's schema

```
<import
namespace="http://www.LearnXmlWS.com/Invoicing/schema"
location=
"http://vbwsserver/vbwsbook/chapter9/
➥Invoicing.asmx?schema=Invoices"
/>
<types>
  <s:schema
         attributeFormDefault="qualified"
         elementFormDefault="qualified"
         targetNamespace="http://www.LearnXmlWS.com/invoicing">
    <s:import
        namespace="http://www.LearnXmlWS.com/Invoicing/schema" />
    <s:import namespace="http://www.w3.org/2001/XMLSchema" />
    <s:element name="SubmitInvoice">
      <s:complexType>
        <s:sequence>
          <s:element minOccurs="0" maxOccurs="1" name="ds">
            <s:complexType>
              <s:sequence>
                <s:any
                 namespace=
                 "http://www.LearnXmlWS.com/Invoicing/schema" />
              </s:sequence>
            </s:complexType>
          </s:element>
        </s:sequence>
      </s:complexType>
    </s:element>
    <s:element name="SubmitInvoiceResponse">
      <s:complexType />
    </s:element>
  </s:schema>
</types>
```

Note that because of the added annotations, the typed DataSet's schema (the one imported by the service's WSDL) is slightly different from the original schema: It has different element names such as invoiceNum instead of invoice-Number and InvoiceItem instead of item.

9.5 Handling XML Documents

While it's easy to return and receive DataSets from Web services, sending and receiving XML documents provides the most control over message format. In this section, I will show you how to return an XML document with a specific structure, perhaps based on a schema, like the SOAP message in Listing 9.15.

Listing 9.15 The desired SOAP message. The payload is an XML document fragment based on a predefined schema.

```
<soap:Envelope ...>
  <soap:Body>
    <CustomerData xmlns="http://www.LearnXmlWS.com/
➥customerorders">
      <Customers CustomerID="ALFKI"
       CompanyName="Alfreds Futterkiste" />
        ...
      <Customers CustomerID="WOLZA"
              CompanyName="Wolski  Zajazd" />
    </CustomerData>
  </soap:Body>
</soap:Envelope>
```

There are several steps you must take on the server side to return an XML document as in Listing 9.15. First, you have to add the right attributes to your Web method to make sure your XML document gets serialized directly inside `<soap:Body>` with no wrapper elements (see Chapter 6). Then you have to get the data from the data source (database), get it into the right XML format, and return it. Listing 9.16 shows an example Web method that returns the XML document in Listing 9.15.

Listing 9.16   A Web method that returns the SOAP message shown in Listing 9.15 (VBWSBook\Chapter9\CustomerOrders.asmx.vb)

```
<WebMethod(), _
SoapDocumentMethod( _
ParameterStyle:=SoapParameterStyle.Bare)> _
Public Function GetCustomersXml() As _
     <XmlAnyElement()> XmlElement

   Dim Sql As String = _
 "SELECT CustomerID, CompanyName FROM Customers FOR XML AUTO"
   Dim ConnStr As String = _
     ConfigurationSettings.AppSettings.Get("ConnStr")
   Dim cn As New SqlConnection(ConnStr)
   Dim doc As New XmlDocument()
   Const NS As String = _
          "http://www.LearnXmlWS.com/customerorders"
   Try
       cn.Open()
       Dim cmd As New SqlCommand(Sql, cn)
       Dim xr As XmlTextReader = cmd.ExecuteXmlReader
       doc.LoadXml("<CustomerData xmlns='" + NS + "'>" + _
           xr.GetRemainder().ReadToEnd() + _
           "</CustomerData>")
       xr.Close()
   Catch ex As Exception
       Debug.WriteLine(ex.Message)
       Throw New SoapException(ex.Message, _
               SoapException.ServerFaultCode)
   Finally
       cn.Dispose()
   End Try
   Return doc.DocumentElement
 End Function
```

The Web method in Listing 9.16 has a `SoapDocumentMethod` attribute with the `ParameterStyle` property set to `Bare`. The default value for this property is `Wrapped`, which means the returned XML element will be wrapped inside an element called `GetCustomersXmlResponse` which is not what we want.

The method returns an XML document which, by default, will be serialized in an element called `GetCustomersXmlResult` (this element is in addition to `GetCustomersXmlResponse`), for example:

```
<GetCustomersXmlResult>
  <CustomerData xmlns="http://www.LearnXmlWS.com/customerorders">
    <Customers CustomerID="ALFKI"
               CompanyName="Alfreds Futterkiste" />
    ...
  </CustomerData>
</GetCustomersXmlResult>
```

You can control this element's name by applying an `XmlElement` attribute like this:

```
Public Function GetCustomersXml() As _
 <XmlElement(ElementName:= "DataElement")> XmlElement
```

This would cause the XML document to be serialized inside an element called DataElement:

```
<DataElement>
  <CustomerData xmlns="http://www.LearnXmlWS.com/customerorders">
    <Customers CustomerID="ALFKI"
               CompanyName="Alfreds Futterkiste" />
    ...
  </CustomerData>
</DataElement>
```

But that's not exactly what we want because it still has a wrapper element around `<CustomerData>`. To serialize the document contents directly into `<soap:Body>`, you need to add an `XmlAnyElement` attribute to the method's return value as in Listing 9.16. This tells the serializer to serialize the returned element and all its children directly into `<soap:Body>`.

In this example, the customer data is in a SQL Server table named Customers. To get this data out in the correct format, you can use SQL Server's `FOR XML` clause, which returns the results as an XML document fragment. You can control the exact format of this XML using `FOR XML EXPLICIT`. If you use `FOR XML AUTO` as in Listing 9.16, each record will be returned as an element with the record's data as attributes.

If your SQL statement returns XML, you use the SqlCommand's `Exe-cuteXmlReader` method, which returns the XML data in an XmlReader. You can get an XML string out of this reader and load it into an XML document. Because the returned XML is a document fragment containing an element for each record, you need to make it a well-formed XML document by enclosing it in a document element, (for example, `<CustomerData>`). Then you return the document's `DocumentElement`, which is the topmost or root element in the document.

Now that you've implemented a Web method that returns an XML document, you'll want to let clients know the exact contents of the document. If you look at the service's WSDL, you'll find that the output message from `GetCustomerXml` contains one part that can have any element. This doesn't tell the client much about the XML document your Web method returns.

Unfortunately, you can't directly specify a schema for the XML document that you return. As a workaround, you can edit the service's WSDL and add your own complex type definition. To do this, save the WSDL document to a file on your Web site, then edit the document and add an element declaration describing the returned CustomerData element. Change the `GetCustomerXml-SoapOut` message part to point to this new element declaration. Listing 9.17 shows the edited portions of the WSDL document.

Listing 9.17 Editing GetCustomerXmlSoapOut in the service's WSDL to define the XML structure returned by the Web method (VBWSBook\Chapter9\EditedCustomerOrders.wsdl)

```
<!-- other elements removed -->
<s:schema>
<!-- other elements removed -->
<!-- the CustomerData element -->
      <s:element name="CustomerData">
    <s:complexType>
       <s:choice maxOccurs="unbounded">
         <s:element name="Customers">
           <s:complexType>
             <s:attribute name="CustomerID"
                      form="unqualified" type="s:string" />
             <s:attribute name="CompanyName"
                      form="unqualified" type="s:string" />
```

```
            </s:complexType>
          </s:element>
        </s:choice>
      </s:complexType>
    </s:element>
  </s:schema>

  <!-- other elements removed -->

    <message name="GetCustomersXmlSoapOut">
      <part name="parameters" element="s0:CustomerData" />
    </message>
```

When a .NET client adds a Web reference using this WSDL, the generated code includes a class called CustomerDataCustomers. This class has two public fields: `CustomerID` and `CompanyName`, which correspond to the Customers element declaration in Listing 9.17. Listing 9.18 shows the generated proxy method for `GetCustomersXml`.

Listing 9.18   An auto-generated proxy method for GetCustomersXml

```
<System.Web.Services.Protocols.SoapDocumentMethodAttribute( _
"http://www.LearnXmlWS.com/customerorders/GetCustomersXml", _
Use:=System.Web.Services.Description.SoapBindingUse.Literal,_
 ParameterStyle:= _
 System.Web.Services.Protocols.SoapParameterStyle.Bare)> _
Public Function GetCustomersXml() As _
 <System.Xml.Serialization.XmlArrayAttribute("CustomerData", _
[Namespace]:="http://www.LearnXmlWS.com/customerorders", _
IsNullable:=False), _
System.Xml.Serialization.XmlArrayItemAttribute("Customers", _
 [Namespace]:="http://www.LearnXmlWS.com/customerorders", _
 IsNullable:=False)> CustomerDataCustomers()
    Dim results() As Object = Me.Invoke("GetCustomersXml", _
                              New Object(-1) {})
    Return CType(results(0), CustomerDataCustomers())
End Function
```

Note that the method's return type is an array of CustomerDataCustomers objects instead of an XML element. Here .NET is trying to be helpful by deserializing the returned XML into an array of objects for you. The assumption is that you'd rather work with objects and their properties than use the DOM or an

XmlReader to process the returned XML. This assumption may be correct in many cases, but certainly not all. There are many times when you'll simply want to get the returned XML and work with it. For example, you might want to apply an XSLT transformation to render the XML as HTML or any other format. You might also need to search for nodes using XPath. The point is that XML technologies offer a rich programming model that you're likely to want to use at some point.

A client can easily override this default behavior to receive the returned XML as an XML element. To do this, edit GetCustomersXml on the client and change the return type to XmlElement, adding to it an XmlAnyElement attribute as shown in Listing 9.19. You'll need to change the last line to convert the return value to an XmlElement instead of an array of CustomerDataCustomers.

Listing 9.19   Modified client code. Note the XmlAnyElement attribute

```
<System.Web.Services.Protocols.SoapDocumentMethodAttribute( _
"http://www.LearnXmlWS.com/customerorders/GetCustomersXml",_
 Use:=System.Web.Services.Description.SoapBindingUse.Literal, _
 ParameterStyle:= _
 System.Web.Services.Protocols.SoapParameterStyle.Bare)> _
Public Function GetCustomersXml() As _
<System.Xml.Serialization.XmlAnyElement()> Xml.XmlElement
    Dim results() As Object = Me.Invoke("GetCustomersXml", _
                              New Object(-1) {})
    Return CType(results(0), Xml.XmlElement)
End Function
```

Listing 9.20 shows an example client that uses this technique to retrieve the customer's XML and report the number of customers using the DOM.

Listing 9.20   An example client that receives customer data as XML (VBWSClientCode\Chapter9\Form1.vb)

```
Dim ws As New vbwsserver.CustomerOrders()
If chkProxy.Checked Then
    ws.Proxy = New System.Net.WebProxy("http://localhost:8080")
End If
Dim el As XmlElement
el = ws.GetCustomersXml
Dim num As Integer = _
    el.GetElementsByTagName("Customers", _
```

```
                "http://www.LearnXmlWS.com/customerorders").Count
        Debug.WriteLine("Number of elements: " + num.ToString())
        Debug.WriteLine("XML Data: ")
        Debug.WriteLine(el.OuterXml)
```

9.6 Handling Object Arrays

Chapter 2 covered XML serialization and showed you examples of serializing custom objects and arrays to XML. In this section, we'll take it one step further and build a Web method that returns an array of objects. Then we'll build a client that calls this method and binds a data grid to the returned array.

Listing 9.21 shows a Customer class that has two properties: `CompanyName` and `CustomerID`.

Listing 9.21   An example Customer class (VBWSBook\Chapter9\Customer.vb)

```
<XmlType([Namespace] := _
"http://www.LearnXmlWS.com/customerorders/")> _
Public Class Customer
    Private mCompanyName As String
    Private mCustomerID As String
    <XmlAttributeAttribute()> _
    Public Property CompanyName() As String
        Get
            Return mCompanyName
        End Get
        Set(ByVal Value As String)
            mCompanyName = Value
        End Set
    End Property
    <XmlAttributeAttribute()> _
    Public Property CustomerID() As String
        Get
            Return mCustomerID
        End Get
        Set(ByVal Value As String)
            mCustomerID = Value
        End Set
    End Property
End Class
```

The class itself has an `XmlType` attribute that specifies that the generated XSD type should belong to the namespace `http://www.LearnXmlWS.com/`

customerorders/. Both `CompanyName` and `CustomerID` properties have an `XmlAttribute` attribute indicating that they will be serialized as attributes of the Customer element rather than elements. Listing 9.22 shows a Web method that returns an array of Customer objects.

Listing 9.22 An example Web method returning an array of Customer objects. Note the use of XmlInclude and XmlArrayItem (VBWSBook\Chapter9\ CustomerOrders.asmx.vb)

```
<WebMethod(), _
SoapDocumentMethod( _
ParameterStyle:=SoapParameterStyle.Bare), _
XmlInclude(GetType(Chapter9.Customer))> _
Public Function GetCustomersArray() As _
    <XmlArray(ElementName:= "Customers"), _
     XmlArrayItem(GetType(Chapter9.Customer), _
     IsNullable:=False, ElementName:= "Customer")> ArrayList

    Dim Sql As String = _
    "SELECT CustomerID, CompanyName FROM Customers"
    Dim ConnStr As String = _
        ConfigurationSettings.AppSettings.Get("ConnStr")
    Dim cn As New SqlConnection(ConnStr)
    Dim Customers As New ArrayList()
    Dim Acustomer As Customer
    Try
        cn.Open()
        Dim cmd As New SqlCommand(Sql, cn)
        Dim dr As SqlDataReader = cmd.ExecuteReader()
        While (dr.Read())
            Acustomer = New Customer()
            Acustomer.CustomerID = dr.GetString(0)
            Acustomer.CompanyName = dr.GetString(1)
            Customers.Add(Acustomer)
        End While
        Return Customers
    Catch ex As Exception
        Debug.WriteLine(ex.Message)
        Throw New SoapException(ex.Message, _
                SoapException.ServerFaultCode)
    Finally
        cn.Dispose()
    End Try
End Function
```

The method in Listing 9.22 returns an ArrayList that can contain any object. By default, the service's WSDL will not have a specific definition for the return type. Also, by default, the serializer will not be able to serialize this ArrayList because it doesn't know what type of objects the ArrayList contains. To solve both problems, there are two serialization attributes applied in Listing 9.22. First, the `XmlInclude` attribute tells the serializer to expect objects of type `Chapter9.Customer` in the return value. Second, `XmlArrayItem` is used to emit the `Customer` XSD type definition in the service's WSDL. This way clients know what to expect from this method. There's also a third serialization attribute used in Listing 9.22: `XmlArray` is used to indicate that the XML element that represents the array should be called Customers.

The method's implementation retrieves customer data from a database into a `SqlDataReader`. The `While` loop goes through records in this reader, creating a new Customer object for each record and adding it to the `ArrayList` called Customers. When the loop is finished, the Customers `ArrayList` is returned.

When a client adds a reference to this Web service, the generated code will include a Customer class that has two public fields: `CompanyName` and `CustomerID`. It's possible for the client to replace this class with another class that better fits its needs. For example, I replaced this class with another one called Company that has public properties instead of the public fields as shown in Listing 9.23.

Note: The Web service proxy in `VBWSClientCode\Chapter9\Web References\VBWSServer\Reference.vb` has been modified to return an array of Company objects from the `GetCustomerArray` method. If you regenerate this proxy, you have to manually redo this modification.

Listing 9.23   The client uses a class called Company to deserialize customer data (VBWSClientCode\Chapter9\Company.vb)

```
Imports System.Xml.Serialization
<XmlType( _
"Customer", [Namespace]:="http://www.LearnXmlWS.com/
➥customerorders")> _
Public Class Company
    Private mCustomerID As String
```

```
    Private mCompanyName As String
    <System.Xml.Serialization.XmlAttributeAttribute()> _
    Public Property CustomerID() As String
        Get
            Return mCustomerID
        End Get
        Set(ByVal Value As String)
            mCustomerID = Value
        End Set
    End Property
    <System.Xml.Serialization.XmlAttributeAttribute()> _
    Public Property CompanyName() As String
        Get
            Return mCompanyName
        End Get
        Set(ByVal Value As String)
            mCompanyName = Value
        End Set
    End Property
End Class
```

Listing 9.24 shows an example client that calls `GetCustomersArray` and binds a data grid to the returned array of Company objects. Figure 9.9 shows the data bound grid as a result of running this client code.

Listing 9.24 An example client that binds a grid to the array of Company objects (VBWSClientCode\Chapter9\frmArrayBind.vb)

```
Private Sub frmArrayBind_Load(ByVal sender As Object, _
        ByVal e As System.EventArgs) Handles MyBase.Load
    Dim customers As Company()
    Dim ws As New localhost.CustomerOrders()
    customers = ws.GetCustomersArray()
    dgCustomers.DataSource = customers
End Sub
```

9.7 Summary

In this chapter, you learned about the many options available for handling various types of data depending on where the data originates. Using XML Schemas and a combination of ADO.NET and the XML Framework, you have a rich programming model for manipulating relational and hierarchical data.

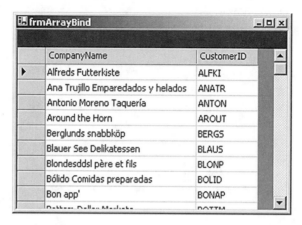

Figure 9.9   A datagrid bound to the returned array of Company objects

9.8   Resources

.NET Web services discussion list: http://www.asplists.com/asplists/aspngweb-services.asp.

DevelopMentor's .NET Web discussion list: http://discuss.develop.com/dotnet-web.html.

.NET data discussion list: http://www.asplists.com/asplists/aspngdata.asp.

.NET XML discussion list: http://www.asplists.com/asplists/aspngxml.asp.

Chapter 10

Reusable Infrastructure with SOAP Extensions

> Everything should be made as simple as possible, but not simpler.
> —Albert Einstein

A typical Web service requires substantial infrastructure. If you are building services mainly for application integration, you'll probably need to implement security and error handling. Commercial Web services require at least an additional usage tracking system. Instead of implementing this infrastructure as part of the service itself, you should consider implementing it as reusable components that can be used with any Web service. This gives you all the traditional benefits of code reuse, including less development time and testing for subsequent projects. But it also has an especially important benefit in the rapidly changing world of Web services: When new standards emerge (and they will), you can replace your existing infrastructure component with one that implements the new standard, thereby minimizing change to the Web service code itself. In this chapter, you will learn how to leverage a powerful .NET feature named SOAP extensions to implement such reusable infrastructure components.

10.1 Web Service Request Processing

It's important to understand how Web service requests are processed and responses returned in order to understand where SOAP extensions fit within the big picture. First, I'll explain how request processing works, then I'll explain the details of SOAP extensions and how they can help to implement reusable infrastructure.

```
<httpHandlers>
    <add verb="*" path="*.aspx"
        type="System.Web.UI.PageHandlerFactory"/>
    <add verb="*" path="*.asmx"
        type=
        "System.Web.Services.Protocols.WebServiceHandler
➡Factory,
        System.Web.Services, version=1.0.3300.0,
➡Culture=neutral,
        PublicKeyToken=b03f5f7f11d50a3a"
        validate="false"/>
</httpHandlers>
```

Each `<add>` element maps requests for a specific file extension and HTTP verb to a specific class that will handle those requests. In this example, all requests for .aspx files (regardless of the HTTP verb used) are handled by the class System.Web.UI.PageHandlerFactory. Similarly, requests for .asmx files are handled by System.Web.Services.Protocols.WebServiceHandlerFactory, which is in the System.Web.Services.dll assembly.

When a Web service request arrives, ASP.NET instantiates a System.Web.Services.WebServiceHandlerFactory and calls its GetHandler method, which returns an HttpHandler object (an object that implements IHttpHandler). This returned object is responsible for handling the incoming request. The type of this object depends on the options you configure on your Web methods. If the Web method being requested uses ASP.NET sessions, then the returned object is a System.Web.Services.Protocols.SyncSessionHandler; otherwise, it's a System.Web.Services.Protocols.SyncSessionlessHandler as shown in Figure 10.1. This HttpHandler object eventually instantiates your Web service class, invokes the requested method, and returns the result as part of the HTTP response.

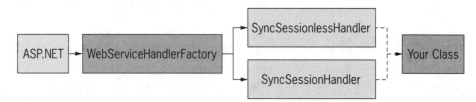

Figure 10.1   Web service request processing with HttpHandlers

REAL WORLD XML WEB SERVICES

10.2   Extending Web Service Request Processing

If you take another look at the request processing diagram in Figure 10.1, you'll notice dashed lines indicating additional processing between the HttpHandlers and your Web service class. In fact, you can perform your own custom request processing by creating classes that inherit System.Web.Services.Protocols.SoapExtension and inserting them along the request processing path between the HttpHandler and your Web service. Such classes, called SOAP extensions, allow you to perform pre- and post-processing by operating directly on the SOAP request/response message at various stages during request/response processing. Their ability to process SOAP messages outside of your Web service implementation makes SOAP extensions a good choice for implementing many infrastructure services such as security and usage accounting (also known as metering).

Architecturally, SOAP extensions are fairly sophisticated because of their lifecycle and how they are initialized. Instead of exposing the entire architecture at once, I'll peel it off one layer at a time making it easier to digest. This means you won't have the complete picture until I've peeled all the layers and you have read all the following sections.

10.2.1   SOAP Extension Processing

```
Public MustOverride Sub ProcessMessage( _
       ByVal message As _
       System.Web.Services.Protocols.SoapMessage)
```

This method is actually called four times for each Web method invocation: twice for the request and twice for the response. Each time ProcessMessage is called, the current request or response processing stage is indicated by the Stage property of the SoapMessage parameter. The first ProcessMessage is called before the incoming XML is deserialized into the corresponding types. At this time, the SoapMessage's Stage property is set to BeforeDeserialize. After incoming data is deserialized, ProcessMessage is called again with the Stage property set to AfterDeserialize. Next, the requested Web method is invoked and ProcessMessage is called for the third time *before* returned data (the return value and any ByRef parameters) is serialized into the response message. In this third time, Message.Stage is set to BeforeSerialize. Finally, after returned data is serialized, ProcessMessage is called for the fourth time with Message.Stage set to AfterSerialize.

Note that there's one new instance of your SOAP extension class for the entire request/response process, so for each incoming request, ProcessMessage is called four times *on the same instance* of your SOAP extension.

So what can you do in ProcessMessage? Through the SoapMessage class, you have access to all request and response information including SOAP headers, SOAP Action, and the entire SOAP message stream. You also have access to the information about the Web method used to service the request. SoapMessage has a MethodInfo property that returns a LogicalMethodInfo object. With this object you learn pretty much anything about the Web method, including its name, parameters, and any .NET attributes applied to it.

There are different things you can do at the various stages. For example, you can read input parameters (using SoapMessage.GetInParameterValue) only in the AfterDeserialize stage. Similarly, you can read the return value and ByRef parameters only in the BeforeSerialize stage.

Although SoapMessage exposes all this information as read-only properties, it's sufficient for many tasks where you don't need to alter the message itself. If you need to alter the message (perhaps you want to compress or decompress SOAP messages), you must override one other method, which I'll explain later in this section.

Another interesting thing about SoapExtensions is that you can throw a SoapException from ProcessMessage, which causes request processing to be aborted and a <Fault> to be sent back to the client. We'll use this feature when implementing security to prevent unauthorized access to Web methods.

10.2.2 Per-Instance Initialization

Since one instance of your SOAP extension is created and called four times for each Web method request, you will probably need a way to initialize this instance with information that will be used when you are processing the message. For example, you might want to capture the time that the request arrived and store it in a member variable. One of the SoapExtensions methods that you override, Initialize, is the correct place to do this kind of initialization. Initialize takes one parameter of type Object, which I'll explain in a later section. Generally speaking, Initialize is the place to do per-instance initialization. For example, this implementation creates a new GUID and stores it in a member variable named _RequestId for use in subsequent calls to ProcessMessage:

```
Public Overrides Sub Initialize(ByVal initializer As Object)
    _RequestId = System.Guid.NewGuid().ToString()
End Sub
```

10.2.3 Applying SOAP Extensions

After you've built your SOAP extension, you need to insert it in the request processing stream between the HttpHandler and your Web service. You have two options for doing this. To apply a SOAP extension to all Web methods on all Web services in a particular vroot, you can simply edit the vroot's web.config and add a reference to the SOAP extension by adding the following to the webServices section:

```
<soapExtensionTypes>
    <add type="YourExtensionTypeName,YourExtensionAssemblyName"
     priority="1" group="0"/>
</soapExtensionTypes>
```

The type attribute references the fully qualified name of your SOAP extension class including the namespace it's in—for example, MyCompany.MyExtensions.TheExtension followed by a comma and then the name of the assembly. For example, if your extension class is called MyNS.MyExtension and it's in an assembly called Infrastructure.dll, then the configuration would be:

```
<soapExtensionTypes>
    <add type="MyNS.MyExtension,Infrastructure"
     priority="1" group="0"/>
</soapExtensionTypes>
```

The priority attribute indicates the relative priority of the extension within the request/response processing sequence. For example, if you have a security SOAP extension and a usage accounting SOAP extension, you will want the security extension to process the request first. That way, if the request is denied, it will not show up in the usage log. To do this, you'd give the security extension a lower sequence number (by setting the priority attribute) than the accounting extension. Finally, the group attribute is also a priority-related setting with two possible values: 0 and 1. Extensions configured with group = 0 belong to a higher-priority group than extensions with group = 1. When determining the sequence of running extensions, ASP.NET first sorts them by group, then by priority within each group. Therefore, the priority setting affects the extension's relative priority compared to other extensions within its group.

10.2.4 Applying SOAP Extensions with CLR Attributes

In many cases, you'll want to apply your SOAP extension to specific methods of the Web service rather than to all methods. You can do this by applying custom CLR (Common Language Runtime) attributes much like the XML serialization attributes you've seen throughout this book. First, the SOAP extension creator must create a custom attribute specific to this extension. Then developers who want to use this SOAP extension apply the custom attribute to one or more Web methods on their services.

To create a custom attribute, you create a class that inherits from System.Web.Services.Protocols.SoapExtensionAttribute and you override its two properties: ExtensionType and Priority. ExtensionType is a read-only property used to tell ASP.NET the SOAP extension's class type. Priority is a read-write property used to tell ASP.NET the extension's priority and, because it's writable, lets the developer using your SOAP extension specify the extension's priority. Listing 10.1 shows an example attribute implementation.

Listing 10.1 An example custom attribute for applying a SOAP extension (VBWSBook\Chapter10\Infrastructure\Accounting.vb)

```
Imports System.Web.Services.Protocols
...
<AttributeUsage(AttributeTargets.Method)> _
Public Class AccountingAttribute
    Inherits SoapExtensionAttribute
    Private _Priority As Integer
    Private _LogResponse As Boolean
```

```
Public Sub New()
    'default priority is low
    _Priority = 9
End Sub

Public Overrides ReadOnly Property ExtensionType() _
        As System.Type
    Get
        Return GetType(Accounting)
    End Get
End Property
Public Overrides Property Priority() As Integer
    Get
        Return _Priority
    End Get
    Set(ByVal Value As Integer)
        _Priority = Value
    End Set
End Property
Public Property LogResponse() As Boolean
    Get
        Return _LogResponse
    End Get
    Set(ByVal Value As Boolean)
        _LogResponse = Value
    End Set
End Property
End Class
```

The AttributeUsage attribute indicates that this custom attribute can be applied to methods (not classes, parameters, and so forth). The default priority is set in the constructor to 9 (low). ExtensionType returns the type of a class named Accounting, which is the actual SOAP extension class.

To apply the Accounting extension, a Web service developer adds a reference to the assembly that contains the extension class and then adds the AccountingAttribute to the Web methods like this:

```
<WebMethod(), AccountingAttribute()> _
Public Function GetTemperature(ByVal ZipCode As String) As Single
```

Recall that VB .NET lets you omit the Attribute suffix when specifying attributes. Therefore, instead of specifying AccountingAttribute(), you can just specify Accounting() for short. Now when ASP.NET receives a request for the GetTemperature method, it will instantiate the Accounting SOAP extension and invoke its Initialize and ProcessMessage methods as previously explained.

10.2.5 Per-Service Intialization

I explained how you can use the Initialize method to perform per-instance initialization. Sometimes, however, this is not efficient. Consider, for instance, the usage accounting extension that needs to log each request to a database. It is inefficient to have to read the database's connection string with each request. Therefore, there's a need to initialize certain variables once, then cache these variables and use their values with each subsequent request. When you use web.config to apply a SOAP extension, you have the opportunity to perform a one-time initialization for each Web service in the vroot where web.config resides. When the Web service is invoked for the first time, ASP.NET instantiates your SOAP extension and calls its overloaded GetInitializer method, passing it the type of the Web service being invoked as shown in Figure 10.2. This is an opportunity for you to perform initialization work that needs to be done only once per Web service rather than once per Web method invocation. For example, you can read a database connection string from a configuration file such as web.config.

But there's one slight problem: This instance of the SOAP extension won't stay around for long; it's only used to call GetInitializer. ASP.NET will create new instances of the SOAP extension to process incoming requests. Therefore, if you read a connection string from web.config, you cannot store it in a member variable because it will be lost when this instance of the extension is destroyed. So where do you cache this connection string for use in subsequent requests?

The solution to this problem is to return the connection string as the return value from GetInitializer. When the next request comes in and ASP.NET creates new instances of your extension, it calls Initialize on this new instance, passing it whatever you returned from GetInitializer as shown in Figure 10.2. Note that you

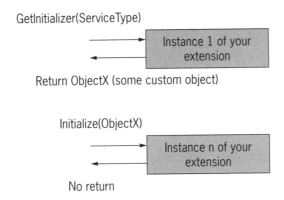

GetInitializer(ServiceType)

Instance 1 of your extension

Return ObjectX (some custom object)

Initialize(ObjectX)

Instance n of your extension

No return

Figure 10.2 How per-service initialization works

don't have to return a string from GetInitializer, you can return a System.Object, that is, anything you like.

In general, if your SOAP extension needs to read configuration information that does not change between Web method invocations, you should read this information and return it in GetInitializer, then read it again with each request from the input object parameter in Initialize. Listing 10.2 shows an example extension that does this.

Listing 10.2 An example extension using GetInitializer and Initialize

```
Imports System.Web.Services.Protocols
...
Public Class SoapSecurity
    Inherits SoapExtension

    Private _ConnStr As String

    Public Overloads Overrides Function GetInitializer( _
                ByVal serviceType As System.Type) As Object
        Dim ConnStr As String

        ConnStr = System.Configuration. _
ConfigurationSettings.AppSettings.Item("SoapSecurityConnStr")

Return Config
```

```
    End Function

    Public Overrides Sub Initialize(ByVal initializer As Object)
        _ConnStr = CType(initializer,String)
    End Sub
...
```

The GetInitializer method in Listing 10.2 will be called once for each Web service that this extension is applied to (assuming the extension is applied using web.config as explained earlier). When GetInitializer is called, a connection string is read from the web.config file and returned.

With each incoming request to the Web service, a new instance of the SoapSecurity class is created and Initialize is called. The initializer parameter (the only parameter to Initialize) will be the connection string that was originally returned from GetInitializer. The example in Listing 10.2 stores this connection string in the member variable _ConnStr for use during the four calls to Process-Message (not shown in this listing).

10.2.6 Per-Method Intialization

There are some cases when the initialization or configuration data you read will vary for each Web method. For example, a usage accounting service might need to know whether it should log the time that the request completed (in addition to the time when the request came in). You can hard code this information in the SOAP extension itself but that would severely limit its reusability. Since we are trying to implement reusable Web services infrastructure, such information ought to be provided through external configuration.

When you apply a SOAP extension using custom CLR attributes (rather than web.config), the extension gets a chance to perform an initialization for each Web method that it applies to. When the Web method is invoked for the first time, ASP.NET creates an instance of your Web service and calls the overloaded GetInitializer method, this time passing it a LogicalMethodInfo object and a ServiceAttribute. LogicalMethodInfo gives you access to the method's metadata, such as its name and a list of parameters. ServiceAttribute is an instance of your custom attribute that was used to apply the extension to the Web method. Similar to per-service initialization, you return some object from GetInitialize and this

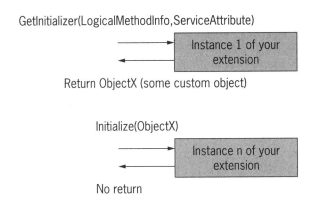

GetInitializer(LogicalMethodInfo,ServiceAttribute)

Instance 1 of your extension

Return ObjectX (some custom object)

Initialize(ObjectX)

Instance n of your extension

No return

Figure 10.3 How per-Web method initialization works

object is passed back to Initialize for each new instance of your extension as shown in Figure 10.3.

Receiving the custom attribute as a parameter allows the developer using your extension to easily pass you configuration information. Consider, for example, the SoapSecurityAttribute in Listing 10.3.

Listing 10.3 The SoapSecurityAttribute is used to apply a SOAP extension to Web methods (VBWSBook\Chapter10\Infrastructure\SoapSecurity.vb)

```vb
<AttributeUsage(AttributeTargets.Method)> _
Public Class SoapSecurityAttribute
    Inherits SoapExtensionAttribute

    Private _Priority As Integer
    Private _Permissions As String

    Public Sub New(ByVal RequestedPermissions As String)
        _Permissions = RequestedPermissions
        _Priority = 1
    End Sub

    Public Property Permissions() As String
        Get
            Return _Permissions
        End Get
        Set(ByVal Value As String)
            _Permissions = Value
```

```
            End Set
        End Property
        Public Overrides Property Priority() As Integer
            Get
                Return _Priority
            End Get
            Set(ByVal Value As Integer)
                'ingore this
            End Set
        End Property
        Public Overrides ReadOnly Property ExtensionType() As
    System.Type
            Get
                Return GetType(SoapSecurity)
            End Get
        End Property
    End Class
```

The interesting aspect of SoapSecurityAttribute is that its constructor takes in a string parameter and stores it in the _Permissions request variable. This means a developer using your extension can specify the permission that a Web method requires like this:

```
<WebMethod(), SoapSecurity("Temperature")> _
Public Function GetTemperature(...) ...
```

When a GetInitializer is called, an instance of SoapSecurity is passed in with its Permissions property set to "Temperature." Using this combination of custom attributes and per-Web method initialization, developers using your extension can pass it configuration information specific to each Web method.

10.2.7 Modifying Message Streams

So far, our discussion of SOAP extensions has focused on extensions that do not modify the request/response stream. Some types of SOAP extensions require the ability to modify request/response messages—for example, a compression/decompression extension needs to read a compressed message and replace it with the decompressed equivalent and vice versa.

To do this in SOAP extensions, you use streams. A request or response message is represented as a stream from which you can read and process message content. Then you write out the new content (for example, the compressed message) to a new stream as shown in Figure 10.4.

So where do you get the input stream and how do you return the output stream? The answer lies in the fourth method of the SoapExtension class: Chain-Stream. This method takes in a stream object that represents the input stream and returns a stream object that represents the output stream. ChainStream is called twice per Web method invocation: once for the request and once for the response. When this method is called on your extension, you want to save a reference to the input stream in a member variable. You also want to create a new stream and save it in a member variable and return a reference to it. For example:

```
Dim _InStrm As System.IO.Stream
Dim _OutStrm As System.IO.Stream
...
Public Overrides Function ChainStream( _
        ByVal stream As System.IO.Stream) As System.IO.Stream
    _InStrm = stream
    _OutStrm = New System.IO.MemoryStream()
    Return _OutStrm
End Function
```

Input Stream

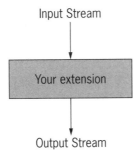

Your extension

Output Stream

Figure 10.4 SOAP extensions can read request/response messages from an input stream and write modified messages to an output stream. Streams are chained: The output stream from the first SOAP extension becomes the input stream to the second SOAP extension.

In this example, I create a new System.IO.MemoryStream and use that as my output stream. Here _InStrm corresponds to the Input Stream in Figure 10.4 and _Outstrm corresponds to the Output Stream.

It's important to understand that you don't do any stream reading or writing in ChainStream, you just set up the input and output streams and use them later when ProcessMessage is called. Once you implement ChainStream and provide an output stream as in this example, you are responsible for writing the message out to this output stream.

Not all extensions need to modify request/response messages; therefore, ChainStream is Overridable rather than MustOverride—that is, you should not implement it unless you plan to modify request and/or response messages.

10.2.8 SOAP Extension Lifetime Summary

I've peeled off the many layers of SOAP extension architecture and explained the four base class methods and how they work. Figure 10.5 shows a sequence diagram that summarizes the life and sequence of methods of a SOAP extension.

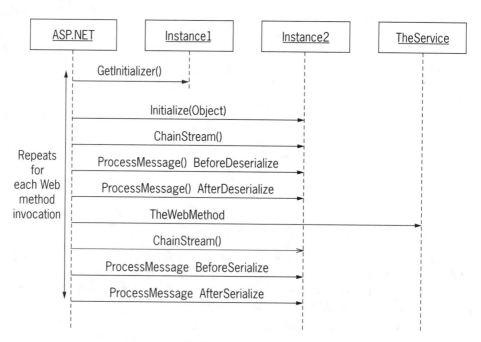

Figure 10.5   Summary of SOAP extension lifetime and sequence of events

REAL WORLD XML WEB SERVICES

First, an instance of the extension is created and GetInitializer is called to obtain your custom initialization object (which can be anything you want). There are two overloaded versions of GetInitializer; which one called depends on how the extension was applied (via web.config or via a custom attribute).

Next, another instance of the extension is created to process a specific incoming request. Initialize is called on this instance, passing it the object that was returned from GetInitialize. Then ChainStream is called to set up the input stream (this method is optional). Then ProcessMessage is called before the request message is deserialized and again after the request message is deserialized. At this point, the service's Web method is invoked and the return value and any out parameters are obtained. ChainStream is called again to set up the output stream. Next, ProcessMessage is called again (still on instance2) before data is serialized into the response message and again after it's serialized.

The next incoming request will result in a new instance of the SOAP extension being created (for example, instance3) and the sequence repeats starting with the call to Initialize as shown in Figure 10.5.

10.2.9 Client-Side SOAP Extensions

In addition to using SOAP extensions on the server to provide Web service infrastructure, you can also use them on the client. Later in this chapter, I'll show an example compression/decompression SOAP extension that can be applied on the client to compress request messages and decompress response messages. On the server, the same extension can be used to decompress request messages and compress response messages. SOAP extensions work the same way on the client with the following exceptions:

- The SoapMessage parameter received by ProcessMessage is actually one of SoapServerMessage or SoapClientMessage (both inherit from SoapMessage) depending on whether the extension is being used on the client or the server.

- Because the client initiates the request and receives the response, the four stages of ProcessMessage are reversed on the client. The order on the client is: BeforeSerialize, AfterSerialize, BeforeDeserialize, and AfterDeserialize. The SOAP request message is sent to the Web service between AfterSerialize and BeforeDeserialize.

Now that you understand how SOAP extensions work, you are ready to implement reusable authorization, usage tracking, and compression infrastructure.

10.3 Authorization SOAP Extension

The WS-Security specification defines standards for using SOAP headers to communicate credentials, digitally sign and encrypt messages. In most cases, you're still pretty much on your own for implementing authorization (controlling access to resources based on user credentials).

Usually, authentication and authorization are insufficient because they don't protect your service from threats such as compromised data integrity/confidentiality or replay attacks. If you are transmitting sensitive data, you're also likely to need digital signature and encryption mechanisms. Although you can use SSL for data encryption, WS-Security recommends XML Signature and XML Encryption to digitally sign and encrypt SOAP messages. See www.LearnXmlws.com/wssecurity for more information on WS-Security.[1]

The following sections show you how to leverage SOAP extensions to build an infrastructure for authorization. It's not my intention to create a security framework for Web services. I'm merely using authorization as an example to explain SOAP extensions. I recommend that you use off-the-shelf security implementations whenever possible and implement your own authorization only if there's no off-the-shelf implementation that suites your needs.

10.3.1 Database Schema

To understand how the security extension handles authentication and authorization, you need to understand the underlying database tables shown in Figure 10.6. The Users table contains a userid and password for each registered user. UserPermissions contains a record for each permission that each user is allowed. For example, if user01 is allowed both GetWeather and GetTemperature, UserPermissions will contain two records. The first record will contain user01, Weather and the second will contain user01, Temperature.

---

[1]There were no implementations of WS-Security at the time of this writing. Therefore, it didn't make sense to write too much about it in this book because it's subject to change. I'll update the online WS-Security section as implementations become available.

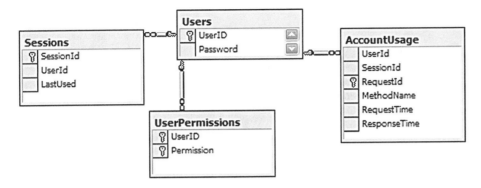

Figure 10.6 Database schema used by the weather Web service

The Sessions table is used to track currently logged-on users. When the service authenticates a user, a new record is inserted in this table with a unique SessionId (a GUID). The LastUsed field indicates the date and time that the last request was received in the session. This is useful for identifying and removing stale sessions. Finally, AccountUsage holds a record for each incoming request, as a way to track Web service usage.

10.3.2 Overall Architecture

Figure 10.7 shows the overall security architecture applied to a weather Web service. The Web service itself implements a LogOn and LogOff method that delegates the real work to the SecurityMgr class (explained in the next section). The Security SoapExtension intercepts all requests (except those to LogOn and LogOff) and checks that the client is currently logged on and has the required permission (again the real work is delegated to SecurityMgr).

10.3.3 LogOn/LogOff and Permissions Checking

A class called SessionMgr is used to handle all database activities. This class exposes methods named LogOn and LogOff, which handle creating and removing records from the Sessions table. LogOn checks the supplied user id and password against the Users table and calls CreateSession if the credentials are correct. LogOff simply deletes the session record. Listing 10.4 shows the implementation of LogOn, LogOff, and CreateSession.

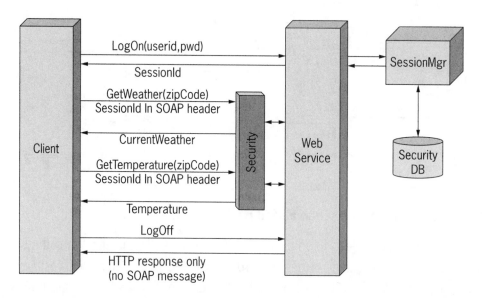

Figure 10.7 How the security SoapExtension fits in with other components to implement security

Listing 10.4 Authentication functions of the SessionMgr class: LogOn, LogOff, and CreateSession (VBWSBook\Chapter10\Infrastructure\SessionMgr.vb)

```
Imports System.Web.Services.Protocols
Imports System.Data.SqlClient
Imports System.Configuration.ConfigurationSettings
Public Class SessionMgr
    Private Const SESSION_NOT_FOUND As Integer = -1
    Private Const NOT_ALLOWED As Integer = -2
    Private Const ALLOWED As Integer = 1

    Public Shared Function LogOn(ByVal UserId As String, _
                    ByVal pwd As String) As String
        UserId = UserId.ToLower()
        Dim cn As New _
            SqlConnection(AppSettings("SoapSecurityConnStr"))
        Dim Sql As String = _
        "SELECT LOWER(UserID) As LUser,Password FROM_
         Users WHERE UserId='" + _
            UserId + "' AND Password='" + pwd + "'"

        Dim dr As SqlDataReader
```

```vb
    Try
        cn.Open()
    Catch ex As SqlException
        ErrMgr.LogAndThrowEx(ex.Message, _
                SoapException.ServerFaultCode, _
                "SessionMgr.LogOn", "Try again later")
    End Try
    Dim IsValid As Boolean = False
    Dim sessId As String = ""
    Try
        Dim cmd As New SqlCommand(Sql, cn)
        dr = cmd.ExecuteReader()
        If dr.Read() AndAlso _
                UserId = dr("LUser") AndAlso _
                pwd = dr("Password") Then
            dr.Close()

            sessId = CreateSession(cn, UserId)
            IsValid = True
        Else
            IsValid = False
        End If
    Catch ex As SqlException
        ErrMgr.LogAndThrowEx(ex.Message, _
                SoapException.ServerFaultCode, _
                "SessionMgr.LogOn", "Try again later")
    Finally
        cn.Close()
    End Try
    If IsValid Then
        Return sessId
    Else
      ErrMgr.ThrowCustomEx( _
      "Invalid userid and/or password", _
         SoapException.ClientFaultCode, "SessionMgr.LogOn", _
         "Retry with different userid and password")

    End If
End Function
Public Shared Sub LogOff(ByVal SessionId As String)
    Dim cn As New SqlConnection(System.Configuration. _
      ConfigurationSettings.AppSettings.Item( _
        "SoapSecurityConnStr"))
```

```
        Try
            cn.Open()
        Catch ex As Exception
            ErrMgr.LogEx("An error in SessionMgr.LogOff: " + _
            ex.Message)
        End Try
        Try
            Dim cmdCheck As New SqlCommand( _
                "DELETE FROM SESSIONS WHERE SESSIONID='" + _
                SessionId + "'", cn)
            cmdCheck.ExecuteNonQuery()
        Catch ex As Exception
            ErrMgr.LogEx("An error in SessionMgr.LogOff: " + _
             ex.Message)
        Finally
            cn.Close()
        End Try
    End Sub
    Public Shared Function CreateSession( _
            ByRef cn As SqlConnection, _
            ByVal userId As String) As String
        Dim SessionId As String = System.Guid.NewGuid().ToString
        'create a session for this logon
        Dim cmdKey As SqlCommand = New SqlCommand( _
                "CreateSession '" + SessionId + "', '" + _
                userId + "'", cn)
        cmdKey.ExecuteNonQuery()
        Return SessionId
    End Function
End Class
```

I chose to make all of SessionMgr's methods shared because it doesn't need
to retain any state information across method calls and shared methods are easier to call because you don't need to instantiate an object first. In Listing 10.4,
LogOn reads the security database connection string from the application's config file (you will need to modify this connection string in web.config to point to
your SQL Server database). Then it connects to the database and executes a
SELECT statement to find out whether the supplied user id and password exist in
the Users table.

The code checks that at least one record was returned and that the user id and password in that record are equal to what the user entered.[2] If everything checks, the code calls CreateSession, passing it the database connection and the user id. CreateSession does two things: It creates a new GUID that becomes the session id and it calls a stored procedure named CreateSession to insert a new record in the Sessions table. CreateSession then returns the new session id, which is returned to the caller of LogOn. Although you can create a new GUID within the stored procedure, I choose to do it in code to allow for additional future processing, such as digitally signing the session id.

If the supplied user id and password do not exist, LogOn uses the ErrMgr's ThrowCustomEx method to throw a SOAP exception. ErrMgr is an infrastructure component (implemented in ErrMgr.vb) that exposes shared methods for throwing SoapExceptions and logging errors. ThrowCustomEx throws a SoapException (see Chapter 7 for more information) while LogAndThrowEx logs the exception to the application event log,[3] then throws a SoapException. LogEx logs the exception without throwing it. The LogOff method simply deletes the session row from the Sessions table using the supplied SessionId.

SessionMgr also exposes an overloaded CheckPermission method (shown in Listing 10.5) that checks the supplied session id against the Sessions table and checks that the corresponding user has the requested permission.

---

[2] I do this check to protect against users entering a'or'b='b as the user id, which will always return all records in the Users table, making it insufficient to check whether there were records returned.

[3] ASP.NET applications (including Web services) run by default under a Windows account called ASP-NET that has limited privileges. Specifically, it lacks the ability to write to the registry under HKEY_LOCAL_MACHINE (HKLM). When a Web service tries to write to the event log with a new event source name, a new event source must be created, which means the Web service needs to write to HKLM. By default, this results in an access denied exception and the Web service will not work. To work around this, either create your event log sources when you deploy your Web services, or make sure the ASPNET account has the permissions to write to the registry. Alternatively, you can replace the ASPNET account with a more powerful account for development purposes only. You do this in machine.config by changing the <processModel> element like this:

```
<processModel userName="system" password="AutoGenerate" .../>
```

For more information on the ASP.NET process identity, see http://go.microsoft.com/fwlink/?LinkId=5903.

Listing 10.5 CheckPermission overloaded method (VBWSBook\Chapter10\Infrastructure\SessionMgr.vb)

```
Public Shared Sub CheckPermission(ByVal DBConnStr As String, _
ByVal SessionId As String, ByVal ReqPermission As String)
        Dim cn As New SqlConnection(DBConnStr)
        Dim TimeOut As Integer = 59 'timeout in minutes
        Try
            cn.Open()
        Catch ex As Exception
            ErrMgr.LogAndThrowEx(ex.Message, _
                    SoapException.ServerFaultCode, _
                    "SessionMgr.CheckPermission", _
                    "Try again later")
        End Try
        Try
            Dim cmdCheck As New SqlCommand("CheckPermission '" + _
            SessionId + "','" + ReqPermission + _
            "'," + TimeOut.ToString(), cn)
            Dim results As Integer = cmdCheck.ExecuteScalar()
            If results = SESSION_NOT_FOUND Then
                'this is a header issue, no detail
                Throw New SoapHeaderException("Session key " + _
            SessionId + _
            " is invalid. Your session may have timed out", _
                    SoapException.ClientFaultCode)
                ElseIf results = NOT_ALLOWED Then
                ErrMgr.ThrowCustomEx( _
"Your profile does not allow you to perform this function", _
            SoapException.ClientFaultCode, _
"SessionMgr.CheckPermission", "Choose another function")
                ElseIf results = ALLOWED Then
                'nothing to do here

            Else
                'this should never occur
                ErrMgr.ThrowCustomEx( _
            "An error occurred while checking permissions: " + _
                results.ToString() + _
" is an invalid return value from CheckPermission", _
                SoapException.ServerFaultCode, _
                "SessionMgr.CheckPermission", "Try again later")
```

```
            End If
        Catch ex As SqlException
            ErrMgr.LogAndThrowEx(ex.Message, _
                    SoapException.ServerFaultCode, _
                    "SessionMgr.CheckPermission", _
                    "Try again later")
        Finally
            cn.Close()
        End Try
    End Sub
```

10.3.4 Using SOAP Headers

After logging on and obtaining a session id, a client must send the session id
with each subsequent request. A good way to do this is through a SOAP header
that the client sends with each request. Although you can use HTTP cookies to
get back the session id with each request, a SOAP header is preferable because
it is independent of the transport protocol—which means you can continue to
use this architecture even if you decide HTTP is no good and you switch to TCP
or some other transport.

The security extension relies on a specific SOAP header class named SessionHeader, which is defined in SoapSecurity.vb (part of the infrastructure
project). A Web service that uses the security SOAP extension will need to declare a member of type SessionHeader to represent the SOAP header that will
be sent by the client with each request. Then each secure method will need to
have the SoapHeader attribute applied to it like this:

```
Public Class Weather
    'The session id
    Public sessHdr As SessionHeader
<WebMethod(), _
  SoapHeader("sessHdr", _
  Required:=True, _
  Direction:=SoapHeaderDirection.In) > _
Public Function GetTemperature(...)
```

10.3.5 The Authorization SOAP Extension

The SoapSecurity extension is shown in Listing 10.6.

Listing 10.6   The SoapSecurity SOAP extension
(VBWSBook\Chapter10\Infrastructure\SoapSecurity.vb)

```vb
Public Structure SoapSecurityConfig
    Public ConnStr As String
    Public ReqPermission As String
End Structure

Public Class SoapSecurity
    Inherits SoapExtension
    Private _RequestedPermissions As String
    Private _ConnStr As String

    Public Overloads Overrides Function GetInitializer( _
            ByVal methodInfo As LogicalMethodInfo, _
            ByVal attribute As SoapExtensionAttribute) As Object
        'this method is called once
        'for each WebMethod that has the extension
        Dim config As SoapSecurityConfig
        config.ReqPermission = _
            CType(attribute,SoapSecurityAttribute).Permissions
        config.ConnStr = _
            System.Configuration. _
                ConfigurationSettings.AppSettings.Item( _
                "SoapSecurityConnStr")

        Return config

    End Function

    Public Overrides Sub Initialize(ByVal initializer As Object)
        Dim config As SoapSecurityConfig = _
                CType(initializer, SoapSecurityConfig)
        _RequestedPermissions = config.ReqPermission
        _ConnStr = config.ConnStr
    End Sub

    Public Overrides Sub ProcessMessage( _
        ByVal message As
➡System.Web.Services.Protocols.SoapMessage)
            'we don't want to catch the exception, just let it go back
            If message.Stage = SoapMessageStage.AfterDeserialize Then
                SessionMgr.CheckPermission( _
                    _ConnStr, _
```

```
            SessionMgr.GetSessionId(message.Headers), _
            _RequestedPermissions)
        End If
    End Sub

    Public Overloads Overrides Function GetInitializer( _
                ByVal serviceType As System.Type) As Object
        'this method will not be called
    End Function
End Class
```

The SoapSecurity extension is applied to each Web method using the SoapSecurityAttribute that was shown in Listing 10.3. When GetInitializer (in Listing 10.6) is called, it gets as input the SoapSecurityAttribute that was used on the specific Web method being requested. The GetInitializer implementation reads the SoapSecurityAttribute.Permissions property and stores it in config.ReqPermission. Here, config is a structure called SoapSecurityConfig with two members to hold the connection string and required permissions. GetInitializer also reads the connection string and stores it in config.ConnStr, then returns config.

When Initialize is called, it gets the config structure as its input parameter. It reads the ReqPermission and ConnStr members and stores them in the _RequesterPermissions and _ConnStr members.

Next, ProcessMessage is called four times. This method is interested only in one particular stage—AfterDeserialize. I picked this stage because I wanted to check permissions before the Web method is invoked, so I had to use either BeforeDeserialize or AfterDeserialize. Since the incoming SOAP header is needed to get the session id and perform the authorization check, BeforeDeserialize doesn't work because at this stage the headers are not yet deserialized.

In AfterDeserialize stage, ProcessMessage calls SessionMgr.CheckPermission, passing it the database connection string, session id (extracted from the message.Headers collection by a call to SessionMgr.GetSessionId), and the requested permissions. If all is well, processing continues normally; otherwise, if the session id is invalid or if the user doesn't have the requested permission, CheckPermission will throw an exception that causes request processing to be aborted.

Let's take a look at how this extension would be applied to a Web service.

10.3.6 Using The SOAP Extension

Listing 10.7 shows an example Web service with a member variable named sessHdr of type SessionHeader. The Web service contains a copy of the GetCustomersDataSet and GetCustomersXml methods from Chapter 9. I added the SoapHeaderAttribute to each of the Web methods and made it required (see Chapter 7 for more information on implementing SOAP headers). To apply the SOAP extension, I added the SoapSecurity attribute to each method. To specify the requested permission, I pass the SoapSecurity constructor the string "Manager" for GetCustomersDataSet method and the string "User" in the GetCustomersXml method. These strings must match the Permission field of the UserPermissions table or the user will not be allowed access to the method.

Listing 10.7 Adding SoapHeader attribute to GetTemperature and GetWeather as part of implementing authorization (VBWSBook\Chapter10\CustomerOrders.asmx.vb)

```
Imports LearnXmlWS.Web.Services.Infrastructure
<WebService([Namespace]:= _
"http://www.LearnXmlWS.com/customerorders")> _
Public Class CustomerOrders
    Inherits System.Web.Services.WebService

Public sessHdr As SessionHeader

'You need Manager permission to access this method
 <WebMethod(), _
 SoapSecurity("Manager"), _
 SoapHeader("sessHdr", _
    Required:=True, Direction:=SoapHeaderDirection.In), _
    Accounting(LogResponse:=True)> _
 Public Function GetCustomersDataSet() As DataSet
    'code omitted for brevity
 End Function

'You need User permission to access this method
<WebMethod(), _
SoapSecurity("User"), _
SoapHeader("sessHdr", _
```

```
        Required:=True, Direction:=SoapHeaderDirection.In), _
      Accounting(LogResponse:=True), _
    SoapDocumentMethod(ParameterStyle:=SoapParameterStyle.Bare)> _
    Public Function GetCustomersXml() As <XmlAnyElement()> XmlElement
          'code omitted for brevity
    End Function
```

Note that LogOn and LogOff Web methods (not shown here) do not have the SoapSecurity extension applied to them. This is because a user must first call LogOn to get the session id; therefore, you can't require the LogOn request to already have a valid session id! LogOff could require a valid SessionId header but it already takes the SessionId as a parameter, so that would be redundant.

Combining this SOAP extension with the LogOn and LogOff methods gives you an infrastructure that provides authentication and authorization for Web services. Some of the ways you can improve on this include writing a SQL Server job to clean out old sessions and adding more sophisticated authorization logic to suit your needs. You can also implement some extra safety mechanisms such as digitally signing the session id. This allows you to check the authenticity of the session id that you receive with each request *before* you hit the database to check that the session is valid.

To give you the big picture of what we just did, Figure 10.8 shows a class diagram of the Weather service implementing security. The Web service itself needs to expose LogOn and LogOff Web methods; these are not part of the infrastructure. A client must first call LogOn and supply a user id and password to get a new session id.

10.4 Usage Accounting

The next SOAP extension we'll build is for usage accounting or metering. The idea is to intercept each incoming request and log it to the AccountUsage database table with the userid, method name, and request time. It would also be nice if the extension could optionally log the time that the response was sent back to the client. That way you also get an idea of how long each method invocation took. Listing 10.8 shows the Accounting SOAP extension implementation.

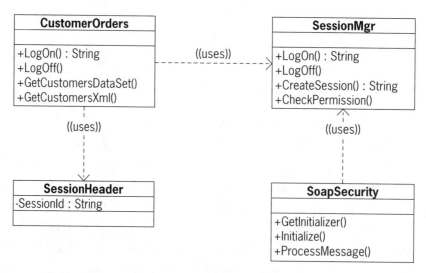

Figure 10.8 The main classes used to implement authentication and authorization for a Web service

Listing 10.8 The usage accounting SOAP extension (VBWSBook\Chapter10\Infrastructure\Accounting.vb)

```
Public Structure AccountingExtensionConfig
    Public ConnStr As String
    Public LogResponse As Boolean
End Structure

Public Class Accounting
    Inherits System.Web.Services.Protocols.SoapExtension

    Private _RequestId As String
    Private _ConnStr As String
    Private _LogResponse As Boolean

    Public Overloads Overrides Function GetInitializer( _
                   ByVal serviceType As System.Type) As Object
        'if configured in web.config, this
        'method is called just once
        Return Nothing
    End Function

    Public Overloads Overrides Function GetInitializer( _
           ByVal methodInfo As LogicalMethodInfo, _
```

```vbnet
            ByVal attribute As SoapExtensionAttribute) As Object
        'if configured with attribute,
        'this method is called once for each
        'WebMethod that has the extension
        'get the DB connection string
        Dim config As AccountingExtensionConfig
        config.LogResponse = CType(attribute, _
            AccountingAttribute).LogResponse
        config.ConnStr = _
            System.Configuration. _
                ConfigurationSettings.AppSettings.Item( _
            "AccountingConnStr")

        'return Config because that's
        'what we need with each request
        Return config
End Function

Public Overrides Sub Initialize(ByVal initializer As Object)
        'this is called once per WebMethod invocation
        Dim config As AccountingExtensionConfig = _
                    CType(initializer, AccountingExtensionConfig)
        _ConnStr = config.ConnStr
        _LogResponse = config.LogResponse
        _RequestId = System.Guid.NewGuid().ToString()
End Sub

Public Overrides Sub ProcessMessage( _
            ByVal message As _
            System.Web.Services.Protocols.SoapMessage)
        'this is called once per stage per webmethod invocation
        Try
            Select Case message.Stage
                Case SoapMessageStage.BeforeDeserialize
                Case SoapMessageStage.AfterDeserialize
                    Dim params As LogRequestParams
                    params.DBConnStr = _ConnStr
                    params.RequestTime = System.DateTime.Now()
                    params.RequestId = Me._RequestId
                    params.MethodName = message.MethodInfo.Name
                    params.SessionId = _
                        SessionMgr.GetSessionId(message.Headers)
                    ThreadPool.QueueUserWorkItem( _
                        New WaitCallback( _
```

```
                        AddressOf AccountLog.LogRequest), params)

            Case SoapMessageStage.BeforeSerialize
            Case SoapMessageStage.AfterSerialize
                If Me._LogResponse Then
                    Dim params As LogResponseParams
                    params.DBConnStr = _ConnStr
                    params.RequestId = Me._RequestId
                    Params.ResponseTime = _
                        System.DateTime.Now()
                    ThreadPool.QueueUserWorkItem( _
                        New WaitCallback( _
                        AddressOf _
                        AccountLog.LogResponse), params)
                End If
        End Select
    Catch ex As Exception
        ErrMgr.LogEx( _
        "Error in Accounting.ProcessMessage: " + _
        ex.Message)
    End Try
    End Sub
End Class
```

This SOAP extension is applied with the AccountingAttribute you saw in Listing 10.1. When GetInitializer is called, the extension reads out the LogResponse property from the input AccountingAttribute object to determine whether it should log the response time. It also reads the usage accounting database connection string from web.config. Note that this connection string can be different from the one used by the security SOAP extension; that is, you can have different databases for security and usage accounting. Both pieces of configuration information are stored in an AccountingExtensionConfig structure and returned from GetInitializer.

When Initializer is called, it reads out the connection string and LogResponse from the input configuration object. It also creates a new GUID and stores it in the member variable named _RequestId. This unique request id will be used later to correlate a response with the corresponding request.

When ProcessMessage is called in the AfterDeserialize stage, it needs to insert a new record in the AccountUsage database table. To do this, it relies on a class named AccountLog, which exposes two shared methods: LogRequest and LogResponse. These methods encapsulate the code that connects to the database and execute the stored procedures LogRequest and LogResponse for logging the request and response.

10.4.1 Using the Thread Pool

There's one slight problem: If ProcessMessage were to call AccountLog.LogRequest directly, it would block execution until the database insert operation completes. Since the request logging function performed by this extension does not affect the normal message processing, there's no need to block execution. Instead, ProcessMessage uses the System.Threading.ThreadPool object to queue the call to AccountLog.LogRequest. The ThreadPool object manages a pool of threads on your application's behalf, taking care of things such as creating new threads and dispatching new work on available threads. Note that the Thread-Pool object is not specifically related to Web services; it is part of the .NET Framework class library.

When you queue a work item, (function call), on the thread pool, this work item enters a first-in-first-out queue that is served by the pool of threads managed by ThreadPool. When a thread becomes available, the next work item in this queue gets dispatched on the thread. This is an efficient way to log requests to a database without unnecessarily delaying Web service request processing.

The work item you queue must be in the form of a WaitCallback delegate:

```
Public Delegate Sub WaitCallback(ByVal state As Object )
```

The state parameter is a generic way to pass information to the function that will be executed by the thread pool. In this example, AccountLog.LogResponse and AccountLog.LogRequest are both declared according to the WaitCallback declaration (except they are shared):

```
Public Shared Sub LogRequest(ByVal Params As Object)
Public Shared Sub LogResponse(ByVal Params As Object)
```

The parameter to LogRequest is a LogRequestParams structure defined as:

```
Public Structure LogRequestParams
    Public DBConnStr As String
    Public RequestTime As DateTime
    Public SessionId As String
    Public RequestId As String
    Public MethodName As String
End Structure
```

And the parameter to LogResponse is a LogResponseParams structure defined as:

```
Public Structure LogResponseParams
    Public DBConnStr As String
    Public ResponseTime As DateTime
    Public RequestId As String
End Structure
```

To pass the necessary parameters to LogRequest, ProcessMessage declares a variable of type LogRequestParams, sets its individual members, and passes it to the WaitCallback constructor. The new WaitCallback is added to the thread pool using ThreadPool.QueueUserWorkItem.

Similarly, in the AfterSerialize stage, if _LogResponse is True, a call to AccountLog.LogResponse is queued to the threadpool. Note that the unique request id (_RequestId) is passed to LogResponse so that it can update the ResponseTime field for that record in the AccountUsage table. Listing 10.7 shows the AccountingAttribute applied to both GetCustomersDataSet and GetCustomersXml.

10.5 An Example Client

To show you how a client would interact with a Web service that uses the security and accounting extensions, I wrote a very simple client shown in Listing 10.9.

Listing 10.9 A simple client calling the Web service (VBWSClientCode\Chapter10\SecurityTestClient\Form1.vb)

```
Private Sub btnCall_Click( _
    ByVal sender As System.Object, _
    ByVal e As System.EventArgs) Handles btnCall.Click
```

```
        Dim ws As New vbwsserver.CustomerOrders()
        Dim sessionId As String
        'call LogOn
        sessionId = ws.LogOn(txtUid.Text, txtpwd.Text)
        'create a new sessionHeader
        ws.SessionHeaderValue = New vbwsserver.SessionHeader()
        'set the SessionId member of the session header
        ws.SessionHeaderValue.SessionId = sessionId
        'now call the Web service
        Dim ds As DataSet
        ds = ws.GetCustomersDataSet()
        MessageBox.Show("Table contains " + _
            ds.Tables(0).Rows.Count.ToString() + _
            " records.")
        '...
        'now we're done
        ws.LogOff(sessionId)
    End Sub
```

The client begins by instantiating a Web service proxy. Then it declares a string variable called SessionId and uses it to hold the returned session id from LogOn (try calling LogOn with a different password and watch the exception you'll get). To pass this session id back with subsequent requests, the client creates a new SessionHeader object and sets the ws.SessionHeaderValue property. Then it sets the SessionId member of this new SessionHeader to the SessionId that was returned from LogOn.

From this point on, any calls to the Web service will automatically receive the SessionHeader SOAP header with the correct SessionId. When finished calling the service, I call LogOff just to clean up the session (this is not required but I'm trying to be a good citizen).

You'll notice that to call one method (GetCustomersDataSet), I first had to call LogOn, then LogOff. This is definitely significant overhead so you don't want to do it with every call. Instead, you should instantiate a Web service proxy and call LogOn when the application starts, then cache this instance of the proxy for use throughout the application. You also need to handle the situation where the session expires (because the user went to get coffee) requiring LogOn again. If your client is an ASP.NET application, it can store the session id it gets from LogOn in the ASP.NET data cache or in the Application cache.

10.6 A Compression SOAP Extension

The preceding SOAP extensions read the request message and take the appropriate actions based on what's in the message and how they are configured. Now I'll show you a SOAP extension that modifies the message stream on both the client and service sides. Listing 10.10 shows the CompressExtension SOAP extension class.

Listing 10.10 The compression SOAP Extension (VBWSBook\Chapter10\Infrastructure\Compress.vb)

```vb
Imports System.Web.Services
Imports System.Web.Services.Protocols
Imports System.Configuration
Imports System.IO
Public Enum CompressionTypes
    GZip
    None
End Enum
Public Class CompressExtension
    Inherits System.Web.Services.Protocols.SoapExtension

    Private _CompressionType As CompressionTypes
    Private _workStream As CompressDecompressStream

    Public Overloads Overrides Function GetInitializer( _
                ByVal serviceType As System.Type) As Object
        Dim compressionType As String = ""
        compressionType = _
            ConfigurationSettings.AppSettings.Get( _
            "CompressionType")
        If Not (compressionType Is Nothing) Then
            Select Case compressionType.ToLower
                Case "gzip"
                    Return CompressionTypes.GZip
                Case Else
                    Return CompressionTypes.None
            End Select
        Else
            'GZip is default
            Return CompressionTypes.GZip
        End If
    End Function
```

```
Public Overloads Overrides Function GetInitializer( _
        ByVal methodInfo As LogicalMethodInfo, _
        ByVal attribute As SoapExtensionAttribute) As Object

    Return CType(attribute, CompressAttribute).CompressionType

End Function

Public Overrides Sub Initialize(ByVal initializer As Object)
    _CompressionType = CType(initializer, CompressionTypes)
End Sub
Public Overrides Function ChainStream( _
    ByVal stream As System.IO.Stream) As System.IO.Stream
    _workStream = New CompressDecompressStream(stream)
    _workStream.CompressionType = _CompressionType
    Return _workStream
End Function

Public Overrides Sub ProcessMessage(ByVal message As _
System.Web.Services.Protocols.SoapMessage)
    If message.Stage = SoapMessageStage.AfterSerialize Then
        _workStream.Close()
    End If
End Sub
End Class
```

I wanted users to be able to apply this SOAP extension to an entire vroot via web.config as well as to specific Web methods via a custom attribute. Therefore, I needed to implement initialization code in both overloads of GetInitializer.

The first GetInitializer in Listing 10.10 is called if the extension is applied via Web.config. In this case, I read the configuration setting called Compression-Type from web.config. There are two possible values for this setting: GZip and None. This allows users to turn compression on/off without actually removing the SOAP extension. It also allows future extensibility by implementing new compression algorithms and adding them to the set of possible values of the CompressionType setting. If CompressionType is not found in web.config, the default is GZip.

Similarly, the second implementation of GetInitializer in Listing 10.10 converts the attribute parameter to an instance of CompressAttribute (see Listing 10.11), then returns the CompressionType property of the attribute. This allows developers to apply the extension by applying the CompressAttribute attribute to Web methods.

Regardless how the SOAP extension was applied, when Initialize is called it receives the configured compression type in its initializer parameter. Initialize simply converts initializer to the CompressionTypes and stores it in the _CompressionType private field.

Since this SOAP extension modifies message streams, it overrides ChainStream. When ChainStream is called, I create a new instance of CompressDecompressStream, which is a custom stream class that does the compression/ decompression. I'll explain this class shortly. Before returning this instance of CompressDecompressStream, I set its CompressionType property to the specified compression type.

Finally, in ProcessMessage, I ignore all message stages except for AfterSerialize. When ProcessMessage is called in the AfterSerialize stage, our stream has already compressed the response message. To flush out the stream and close it, I call _workStream.Close(). Without this important step you'd see weird behavior where sometimes the extension works fine and other times you get only a fraction of the response message back to the client.

Listing 10.11   CompressAttribute is used to apply the compression extension to specific methods (VBWSBook\Chapter10\Infrastructure\Compress.vb)

```
<AttributeUsage(AttributeTargets.Method)> _
Public Class CompressAttribute
    Inherits SoapExtensionAttribute

    Private _Priority As Integer = 0
    Private _CompressionType As CompressionTypes

    Public Sub New()
        MyBase.New()
        'GZip is default
        _CompressionType = CompressionTypes.GZip
    End Sub
    Public Sub New(ByVal compressType As CompressionTypes)
        MyBase.New()
        _CompressionType = compressType
```

```
    End Sub
    Public Overrides ReadOnly Property ExtensionType() _
          As System.Type
        Get
            Return GetType(CompressExtension)
        End Get
    End Property
    Public Overrides Property Priority() As Integer
        Get
            Return _Priority
        End Get
        Set(ByVal Value As Integer)
            _Priority = Value
        End Set
    End Property
    Public Property CompressionType() As CompressionTypes
        Get
            Return _CompressionType
        End Get
        Set(ByVal Value As CompressionTypes)
            _CompressionType = Value
        End Set
    End Property
End Class
```

Listing 10.12 shows the CompressDecompressStream which inherits from System.IO.Stream and performs compression when writing and decompression when reading.

Listing 10.12 CompressDecompressStream does the real compression/ decompression work (VBWSBook\Chapter10\Infrastructure\ CompressDecompressStream.vb)

```
Imports System.IO

Public Class CompressDecompressStream
    Inherits System.IO.Stream

    Private _OutStrm As Stream
    Private _InStrm As Stream
    Public CompressionType As CompressionTypes
    Public Sub New(ByVal InStrm As Stream)
        _InStrm = InStrm
    End Sub
```

```vb
Public Overrides Function Read(ByVal buffer() As Byte, _
        ByVal offset As Integer, _
        ByVal count As Integer) As Integer
    If _OutStrm Is Nothing Then
        Select Case Me.CompressionType
            Case CompressionTypes.GZip
                _OutStrm = _
                New NZlib.GZip.GZipInputStream(_InStrm)
            Case CompressionTypes.None
                _OutStrm = _InStrm
        End Select
    End If

    Dim readcount As Integer = _OutStrm.Read( _
        buffer, offset, count)
    If readcount < 0 Then readcount = 0
    Return readcount
End Function

Public Overrides Sub Write(ByVal buffer() As Byte, _
        ByVal offset As Integer, ByVal count As Integer)
    If _OutStrm Is Nothing Then
        Select Case Me.CompressionType
            Case CompressionTypes.GZip
                _OutStrm = New NZlib.GZip.GZipOutputStream( _
                    _InStrm)
            Case CompressionTypes.None
                _OutStrm = _InStrm
        End Select

    End If
    _OutStrm.Write(buffer, offset, count)
End Sub

Public Overrides Sub Flush()
    _OutStrm.Flush()
End Sub
Public Overrides Sub Close()
    _OutStrm.Close()
End Sub
Public Overrides ReadOnly Property CanRead() As Boolean
    Get
        Return True
    End Get
```

```
        End Property
        Public Overrides ReadOnly Property CanWrite() As Boolean
            Get
                Return True
            End Get
        End Property
    'Stub methods removed
    End Class
```

When CompressDecompressStream is instantiated, its constructor receives a Stream object that acts as the underlying stream. This means when Read is called, CompressDecompressStream reads from this underlying stream and decompresses the data as it reads it. Similarly, when Write is called, CompressDecompressStream compresses the data, then writes it to this underlying stream. So the underlying stream is sometimes a read-only stream (when decompressing) and sometimes a write-only stream (when compressing).

When Read is called, I check if _OutStrm is nothing. If it is, then I check the value of the CompressionType public field. If CompressionType is GZip, I set _OutStrm to a new instance of GZipInputStream that is part of the NZipLib library, which is downloadable free from http://www.icsharpcode.net/Open-Source/NZipLib/default.asp (it's also on the book's CD). GZipInputStream reads compressed data from the underlying stream and returns the decompressed data.

If CompressionType is set to None, I simply set _OutStrm to _InStrm, which effectively makes this a transparent, pass-through stream.

I then read from _OutStream and return the readcount that is the number of bytes read from the stream. Note that GZipInputStream.Read returns _1 when there's no more data to read. This results in an exception being thrown with a message indicating that Read should return a non-negative number. As a workaround, I check if readcount is less than zero and set it to zero.

The Write method is similar but uses a GZipOutputStream instead of a GZipInputStream. First, I check if _OutStrm is nothing. If it is and if CompressionType is GZip, I set _OutStrm to a new instance of GZipOutputStream; otherwise, I set _OutStrm to _InStrm. Then I call Write, passing it the three input parameters.

Flush and Close are simply wrapper methods around _OutStrm.Flush and _OutStrm.Close methods, respectively. I also implemented CanRead and Can-Write and return True from both properties.

To test this SOAP extension, I created a new Web method called GetCustomersDataSetCompressed in the CustomerOrders Web service. I then added to it the CompressAttribute attribute as shown in Listing 10.13.

Listing 10.13 GetCustomersDataSetCompressed with the CompressAttribute applied (VBWSBook\Chapter10\Infrastructure\CustomerOrders.asmx.vb)

```
<WebMethod(), _
    SoapHeader("sessHdr", _
    Required:=True, Direction:=SoapHeaderDirection.In), _
    SoapSecurity("Manager"), _
    Compress(CompressionTypes.GZip)> _
    Public Function GetCustomersDataSetCompressed() As DataSet
        Return GetCustomersDataSet()
End Function
```

To send a compressed request message, the client must also be configured to use this SOAP extension. To do this, I opened the SecurityTestClient project and added a reference to infrastructure.dll (the DLL that contains the SOAP extension). I then updated the Web reference to CustomerOrders and manually added the CompressAttribute to the GetCustomerDataSetCompressed in the Web service proxy class as shown in Listing 10.14.

Listing 10.14 Adding CompressAttribute to the GetCustomersDataSet-Compressed on the proxy class (VBWSClientCode\Chapter10\SecurityTestClient\WebReferences\vbwsserver\Reference.vb)

```
<LearnXmlWS.Web.Services.Infrastructure.CompressAttribute( _
LearnXmlWS.Web.Services.Infrastructure.CompressionTypes.GZip), _
System.Web.Services.Protocols.SoapHeaderAttribute( _
        "SessionHeaderValue"), _
System.Web.Services.Protocols.SoapDocumentMethodAttribute( _
"http://www.LearnXmlWS.com/customerorders/_
GetCustomersDataSetCompressed", _
RequestNamespace:="http://www.LearnXmlWS.com/customerorders", _
ResponseNamespace:="http://www.LearnXmlWS.com/customerorders", _
Use:=System.Web.Services.Description.SoapBindingUse.Literal, _
```

```
        ParameterStyle:= _
        System.Web.Services.Protocols.SoapParameterStyle.Wrapped)> _
        Public Function GetCustomersDataSetCompressed() As _
                    System.Data.DataSet
                Dim results() As Object = _
                Me.Invoke("GetCustomersDataSetCompressed", _
                New Object(-1) {})
                Return CType(results(0), System.Data.DataSet)
        End Function
```

I then added code to the client that invokes the GetCustomersDataSetCompressed method. Using proxyTrace, I captured the request and response messages as shown in Figure 10.9.

Finally, I wanted to test applying the compression extension via web.config. So I created a new Web service named CustomerOrdersCompressed and placed it in VBWSBook\Chapter10\CompressedService\CustomerOrdersCompressed.asmx.vb. The code in this Web service is simply a complete copy of the CustomerOrders Web service code. I then added a web.config file to the CompressedService folder and added to it a soapExtensionTypes section as well as a compressionType key as shown in Listing 10.15.

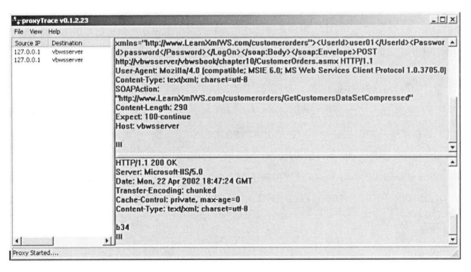

Figure 10.9   The request and response messages with compressed data

Listing 10.15 Applying the compression SOAP extension via Web.config (VBWSBook\Chapter10\CompressedService\web.config)

```
<configuration>
<appSettings>
   <add key="CompressionType" value="gzip"/>
</appSettings>
<system.web>
   <webServices>
      <soapExtensionTypes>
      <add
type="LearnXmlWS.Web.Services.Infrastructure.CompressExtension,
➥Infrastructure"
         priority="0" group="0"/>
      </soapExtensionTypes>
   </webServices>
</system.web>
</configuration>
```

On the client, I added a Web reference to this service, manually edited the proxy class, and added the CompressAttribute to each of LogOn, LogOff, Get-CustomersDataSet, and GetCustomerXml methods. The updated proxy is in VB-WSClientCode\Chapter10\SecurityTestClient\vbwsserver1\Reference.vb). Since the extension is applied to the entire Web service, all calls to this service (for example, LogOn, LogOff, and GetCustomersDataSet) will be compressed as shown in Figure 10.10.

10.7 Summary

SOAP Extensions provide an extensibility mechanism for adding custom behavior to Web service request/response processing. By encapsulating infrastructure services such as security and usage accounting in SOAP extensions, you can build reusable and flexible infrastructure components. Developers can apply such components to their Web services using web.config files or CLR custom attributes.

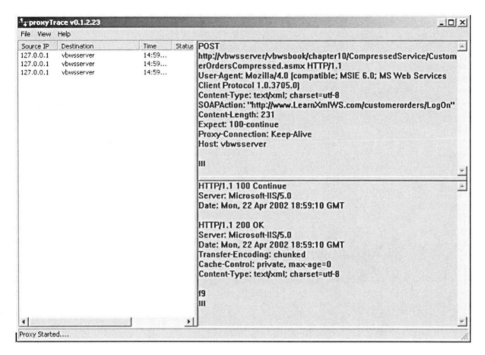

Figure 10.10 Calls to all methods, (for example, LogOn, LogOn, and GetCustomersDataSet) are compressed

10.8 Resources

DevelopMentor's .NET Web discussion list: http://discuss.develop.com/dotnet-web.html.

NZLib compression library: http://www.icsharpcode.net/OpenSource/NZipLib/default.asp.

WS-Security overview: http://www.LearnXmlws.com/wssecurity.

Chapter 11

UDDI: A Web Service

Discovery consists in seeing what everyone else has seen and thinking
what no one else has thought. —Albert Szent-Gyorgi

In a world full of Web services, Universal Description Discovery and Integration
(UDDI) becomes an extremely valuable component. As a service built into Windows .NET server, UDDI is also likely to become the de-facto standard Web services catalog *within* the enterprise. Therefore, to complete the Web services
story, I will explain what UDDI is and the scenarios where applications can benefit
from private and public UDDI implementations. I will focus on writing UDDI-
enabled applications that communicate with UDDI as a SOAP-based Web service.

11.1 What is UDDI?
On the surface, UDDI is a directory where businesses can register and search
for Web services. However, digging a little deeper, you'll find that there's more to
UDDI than simply directory information. UDDI is centered on the concept of a
Web service interface that is typically described by a WSDL document.

As Web services become popular, it is likely that industries will define standard Web service interfaces that businesses can implement. The travel industry
might publish standard interfaces for hotel rate-checking and reservations, then
register those interfaces with UDDI. Hotels would then expose Web services that
implement those interfaces and register their services with UDDI as shown in
Figure 11.1. A travel agency can search UDDI to see if Hilton Hotels exposes a
Web service that implements the standard room reservation interface. When the
travel agency finds the desired Web service in UDDI, it begins to communicate

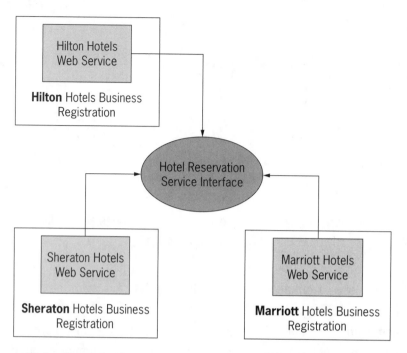

Figure 11.1 Organizations expose Web services that implement an industry-standard interface

with that service immediately because the service implements a well-known hotel reservations interface. Hence business applications can be more easily integrated through implementing and programming against well-known standard interfaces.

Ideally, a business application finds the Web services it needs and begins using them. This does not require intervention from the end user, except possibly to define some criteria that the Web services must meet, such as business name or geographic location. For this to happen, applications must be able to programmatically search a directory such as UDDI. In fact, UDDI is not designed to be searched by end users at runtime. Instead, UDDI exposes its data through a set of operations known as the inquiry API. UDDI also exposes the publishing API that can be used to register businesses and services with UDDI.

To ensure maximum interoperability, UDDI exposes its APIs as Web service operations. Therefore, you can think of the UDDI API as a live, production Web service that you can program against for publishing to and searching UDDI's registry.

To summarize, there are two distinct features of UDDI that differentiate it from ordinary Web directories such as Yahoo! First, every Web service registered with UDDI implements an interface that is also registered with UDDI. The interface might be defined by the same developer who built the Web service or by a standards organization. Second, not only can people (specifically developers) use UDDI at design time to find Web services and publish their services, applications can also use UDDI at runtime to programmatically locate and publish Web services.

11.2 What UDDI Is Made Of

Most people think of UDDI as a Web site or a Web service end point but there are several things that make up UDDI. This section breaks down UDDI into distinct parts and explains the role of each.

11.2.1 UDDI Specifications

UDDI is a set of specifications with private and public implementations. UDDI provides two Web services: inquiry and publishing. The inquiry Web service provides operations such as find_business and get_businessDetail. Similarly, the publishing Web service provides operations like save_business and delete_business. The operations provided by the inquiry and publishing Web services use document/literal SOAP messages. These messages are documented and explained in the UDDI Programmer's API Specification. The UDDI Data Structure Specification explains the input and output XML data structures used by the UDDI Web service operations. These data structures are also defined in the UDDI XML Schema.

11.2.2 UDDI Operators

UDDI operators are organizations that implement a UDDI registry and expose it via Web services according to the UDDI specifications. At the time of this writing, four organizations provide public UDDI V2 implementations: Hewlett-Packard, IBM, Microsoft, and SAP.

Each operator implements his/her own UDDI registry store which is replicated with other operator nodes so that the information you enter at one operator's site can be *queried* from any other site. Each operator also exposes one or more Web service end points that provide the standard UDDI APIs as documented in the Programmer's Specification. For example, Microsoft's beta implementation of UDDI V2 inquiry APIs is exposed at http://uddi.rte.microsoft.com/inquire and the corresponding UDDI publishing APIs implementation is at https://uddi.rte.microsoft.com/publish.

Operators might also expose a Web user interface for humans to register with and search UDDI. Such operators Web UI's are simply HTML front ends for a subset of the UDDI APIs and typically add no features beyond what's available through the API.

You can see two examples of search user interfaces at Microsoft's UDDI site (http://uddi.rte.microsoft.com/search/frames.aspx) and IBM's site (https://www-3.ibm.com/services/uddi/v2beta/protect/find). All sites require registration in order to *publish* your business and Web services.

To register your business and services with UDDI, you pick an operator site, such as Microsoft, and register with that operator to obtain user credentials in the form of a user id and password. These credentials apply only to the particular operator site with which you register; credentials are not shared or replicated across operator sites. You use these credentials to register your business and Web services. Later, you can edit your business and service registration at the *same operator site* where you registered. The changes you make will be replicated to other sites so that applications and users querying UDDI at any of the operator sites can view your information.

11.2.3 UDDI Registrars

Using UDDI's publishing APIs, companies can set up public Web sites for registering with UDDI. These Web sites are known as UDDI registrars and typically add some value over the standard operator sites. For example, a registrar might specialize in registering businesses within a specific industry. A list of UDDI registrars can be found at http://www.uddi.org/solutions.html#registrars.

11.2.4 Private Implementations

Perhaps the most interesting aspect of UDDI is the availability of implementations that you can download and install for use within your intranet. A typical large organization with dozens of departments might have tens or hundreds of Web services scattered in various locations. Such an organization can benefit from a private, internal directory of Web services. Instead of reinventing the wheel, the organization might install a private version of UDDI. For example, IBM provides a private UDDI implementation that you can download and install and Windows .NET Server includes a built-in UDDI registry that organizations can use on their intranets. Whether you program against a private UDDI implementation or the public UDDI registry, the APIs (in the form of SOAP messages) you use are the same.

11.3 UDDI Usage Scenarios

This section explains at a high level some of the common UDDI usage scenarios. The objective is to give you the big picture of how and when UDDI can be used. Once you conceptually understand these scenarios, the following sections explain the details of programming UDDI. Please note that the diagrams in this section are not proper UML sequence diagrams. Instead of objects and operations, they show the interaction between client application, UDDI, and a third-party Web service.

11.3.1 Finding Closest Business

Occasionally I go to the local Kinko's store to reproduce course manuals or other documents. When I first moved to my current house, I went to Kinko's Web site and used their store locator to find the nearest store by zip code. Most people in the U.S. use the Web or their Yellow Pages to find the closest branch of a business. In many cases, the business itself is already known to users (I used Kinko's for many years before I moved to my current house), and they just want to find the nearest branch.

In the world of connected applications, you might start seeing Windows applications that let you print *directly* to the nearest printing/copying store (call it Printers R Us) by sending the print file to the store's Web service.

One of the issues posed by this scenario is that of finding the closest Printers R Us store. This is where UDDI can be useful. A client application can send a message to UDDI asking for a list of the closest Printers R Us businesses as shown in Figure 11.2. UDDI sends back a list of businesses and Web services that satisfy the client's search criteria. The client application then shows this list to the end user and asks him or her to choose the specific branch to which to print. Once a branch is chosen, the client begins to interact with that branch's Web service and sends it the print file.

In this context, UDDI is acting as a smart Yellow Pages directory that can be used by applications rather than directly by end users. Notice that this scenario applies to Windows, Web, and any other types of client applications that can invoke a Web service. Applications on hand-held devices, for example PocketPC, can also benefit from this smart Yellow Pages scenario.

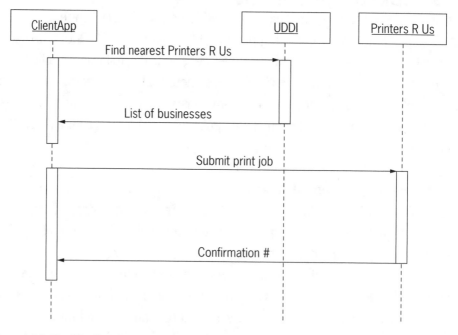

Figure 11.2   Finding businesses that match certain search criteria

11.3.2 The Invocation Pattern

This powerful usage scenario is straight from the UDDI V2.0 API Specification. Here, UDDI is used to solve the problem of invoking a relocated Web service. Potentially, commercial Web services can have thousands of client applications that rely on the service's availability. If the service's end point moves, all clients must be notified ahead of time to make sure they point to the new end point location when it's ready. Coordinating such a move can be a logistical nightmare and things are likely to go wrong.

Alternatively, the Web service operator might create a locator Web service just to tell clients about the location of the real Web service. Client applications query this locator service at runtime to get the end point URL of the real service. However, this solution doesn't work because now you have to worry about the locator Web service and what happens if you need to move it. What you need is a highly-available directory such as UDDI that can be used as a locator for your Web services.

Before moving your Web service, you edit the service's UDDI registration to point to the new end point URL. At runtime, a client application calls your Web service, which might have been relocated. After receiving an error (404 not found), the client sends a message to UDDI asking for the current service location as shown in Figure 11.3.

UDDI responds with the new end point URL that the client uses to invoke the Web service. Assuming the invocation works and the service responds, the client can cache the new URL locally (for example, in a config file) for future use.

In this scenario, UDDI acts as a readily-accessible, highly-available directory that can save you from a potential logistical nightmare.

11.3.3 Finding Trading Partners' Services

Let's say your company purchases a new business accounting application that supports electronic invoicing. The application is designed to send XML invoice documents to Web services that implement a hypothetical standard invoicing interface called Xinvoice. After installing the application, an accountant begins entering a list of current customers, their names, and contact information. When entering a customer called Acme Autos, the accountant sees a button labeled

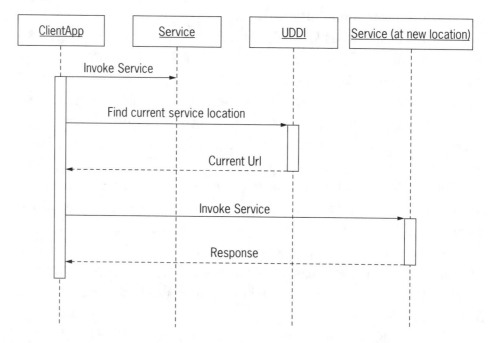

Figure 11.3   The UDDI Invocation Pattern

"Send electronic invoices" and clicks it. The application then initiates a UDDI query asking for a business named Acme Autos that implements the standard Xinvoice interface as shown in Figure 11.4.

Assuming Acme Autos has registered a service that implements Xinvoice, UDDI responds with some information about the business and the service. The accounting application then issues another message asking for the details of the invoicing service (for example, the end point URL) and UDDI responds with the details. The accounting application stores Acme Autos' invoicing Web service end point URL in its local database for future use. At this point, the accounting application is ready to begin sending electronic invoices to Acme Autos.

Although the accountant could have obtained Acme Autos' end point URL through other means (calling them or getting it from their Web site), UDDI makes it more convenient and eliminates some of the friction involved in setting up e-commerce. Note that for this scenario to work, the accounting application must be programmed to invoke the Xinvoice interface and Acme Autos must implement it. The area of industry standard e-commerce messages and interfaces

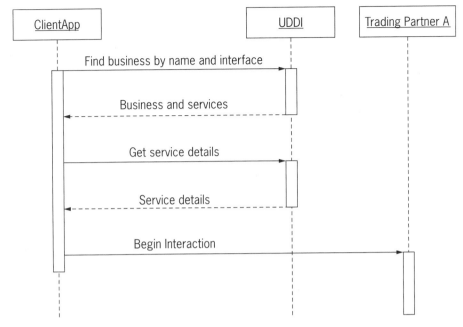

Figure 11.4 Finding trading partners' services

is still evolving and has a long way to go. In the short term, the above scenario is more likely to work if both trading partners install the same or compatible accounting packages.

11.3.4 Registering Services

Going back to the electronic invoicing scenario, let's examine how Acme Autos might have registered its services with UDDI. Acme Autos purchases and installs a commercial accounting application and proceeds to configure it. One of the configuration options is to receive invoices electronically. When the user chooses this option, the accounting application configures a Web service that implements the hypothetical Xinvoice interface. The client application then asks whether or not this service should be known to the public. Assuming the user answers "yes," the application sends a message to UDDI asking to register Acme Autos as a business (assuming it was not already registered). The invoicing service can be registered as part of the same request message or can be registered in a subsequent request as shown in Figure 11.5.

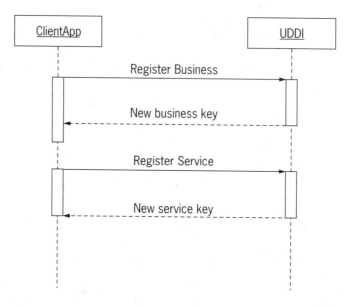

Figure 11.5   Registering a business and a service with UDDI

A common objection to this model is one that I frequently hear from my students—publicly exposing business services. The objection centers on the security threat that this might pose. Personally, I don't believe that security by obscurity is a good long-term strategy. Instead, we must think about security risks and address them via a combination of technologies and procedures. Today, the Web is routinely used for sensitive transactions such as e-commerce and bank-account management. As recently as 1996, most people did not feel the Web would ever be sufficiently secure for banks to post customers' account statements or stores to accept credit card numbers. A lot has changed since then and it's likely the same will happen with Web services.

11.3.5   Publish/Subscribe Pattern

When you think of a typical Web service, you think of one Web service and many clients invoking it. This is certainly the most common scenario, but turning this scenario on its head makes for an interesting model that is useful in many applications.[1] Consider a retail company that has many stores spread across the

---

[1]Thanks to Chris Kurt, Microsoft's UDDI Program Manager, for pointing out this scenario.

country and possibly, the world. The company's headquarters wants to send current merchandise prices daily to each store location. In a real-world scenario, the stores might have different applications (perhaps some stores were acquired in a business merger) or different versions of the same application. In most cases, communicating with all stores, including new ones as they open, is not an easy task.

Web services can help by easing the application integration aspect of the problem. Headquarters defines a Web service interface called RetailPricing. Each store then exposes a Web service that implements this interface. To push information out to stores, headquarters writes a client application that invokes each store's Web service sending it current pricing information as shown in Figure 11.6.

For the client application to find all store Web services, it consults UDDI. At runtime, the client asks UDDI for a list of services that implement the RetailPricing interface (assuming HQ already registered this interface with UDDI). As each new store comes online, it simply registers its interface with UDDI. The next time the client runs UDDI, it automatically finds the new store and pushes pricing information to it as shown in Figure 11.7.

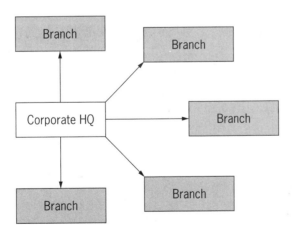

Figure 11.6 The publish/subscribe Web services scenario. Branches subscribe by exposing a Web service that implements a predefined interface.

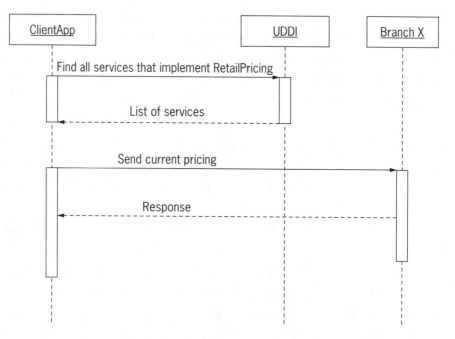

Figure 11.7 UDDI and the publish/subscribe scenario

This pattern is effective in many scenarios where an application needs to push content to many "subscribing" applications. Instead of managing subscriptions yourself, you rely on UDDI to manage them for you.

11.4 Main Data Structures

Information registered with UDDI is represented by XML documents containing structures described in UDDI's XML Schema.[2] There are four key data structures central to most UDDI usage scenarios. Figure 11.8 shows these four structures, two additional structures, and the relations between them.

The businessEntity data structure is used to represent a business or, more generally, a service provider. Each businessEntity may contain services represented by businessService structures. A businessService contains bindingTemplates that point to tModel structures (more on this later). Businesses might be

---

[2]For your convenience, a UDDI XML schema is included on the book's CD in a file named uddi_v2.xsd.

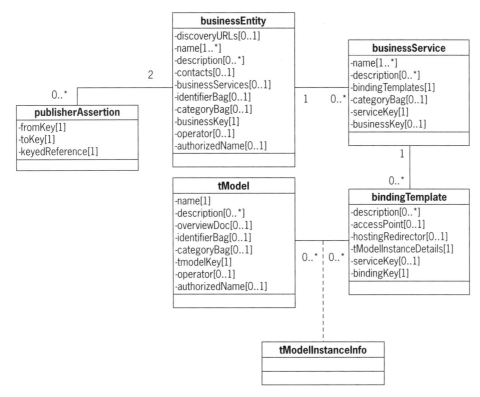

Figure 11.8   The main UDDI data structures

related (for example, a parent-child business relation) using publisherAssertion
structure. Listing 11.1 shows part of the UDDI XML Schema that contains the
formal definitions of the above XML structures.

**Listing 11.1   XML Schema types and element declarations for the main UDDI
data structures (VBWSClientCode\Chapter11\UDDISchemas\uddi_v2.xsd)**

```
<!-- businessEntity structure -->
<element name="businessEntity" type="uddi:businessEntity"/>
<complexType name="businessEntity">
  <sequence>
    <element ref="uddi:discoveryURLs" minOccurs="0"/>
    <element ref="uddi:name" maxOccurs="unbounded"/>
    <element ref="uddi:description"
                minOccurs="0" maxOccurs="unbounded"/>
    <element ref="uddi:contacts" minOccurs="0"/>
    <element ref="uddi:businessServices" minOccurs="0"/>
```

```
      <element ref="uddi:identifierBag" minOccurs="0"/>
      <element ref="uddi:categoryBag" minOccurs="0"/>
    </sequence>
    <attribute name="businessKey"
                        use="required" type="uddi:businessKey"/>
    <attribute name="operator" use="optional" type="string"/>
    <attribute name="authorizedName" use="optional"
                 type="string"/>
</complexType>

  <!-- businessService structure -->
  <element name="businessService" type="uddi:businessService"/>
  <complexType name="businessService">
    <sequence>
      <element ref="uddi:name" maxOccurs="unbounded"/>
      <element ref="uddi:description" minOccurs="0"
                                    maxOccurs="unbounded"/>
      <element ref="uddi:bindingTemplates"/>
      <element ref="uddi:categoryBag" minOccurs="0"/>
    </sequence>
    <attribute name="serviceKey"
                        use="required" type="uddi:serviceKey"/>
    <attribute name="businessKey"
                        use="optional" type="uddi:businessKey"/>
</complexType>

<!-- bindingTemplate structure -->
  <element name="bindingTemplate" type="uddi:bindingTemplate"/>
  <complexType name="bindingTemplate">
    <sequence>
      <element ref="uddi:description" minOccurs="0"
                                    maxOccurs="unbounded"/>
      <choice>
        <element ref="uddi:accessPoint" minOccurs="0"/>
        <element ref="uddi:hostingRedirector" minOccurs="0"/>
      </choice>
      <element ref="uddi:tModelInstanceDetails"/>
    </sequence>
    <attribute name="serviceKey" use="optional"
                                    type="uddi:serviceKey"/>
    <attribute name="bindingKey" use="required"
                                    type="uddi:bindingKey"/>
</complexType>
```

```
<!-- tModel structure -->
  <element name="tModel" type="uddi:tModel"/>
  <complexType name="tModel">
    <sequence>
      <element ref="uddi:name"/>
      <element ref="uddi:description" minOccurs="0"
               maxOccurs="unbounded"/>
      <element ref="uddi:overviewDoc" minOccurs="0"/>
      <element ref="uddi:identifierBag" minOccurs="0"/>
      <element ref="uddi:categoryBag" minOccurs="0"/>
    </sequence>
    <attribute name="tModelKey" use="required"
               type="uddi:tModelKey"/>
    <attribute name="operator" use="optional" type="string"/>
    <attribute name="authorizedName" use="optional"
               type="string"/>
</complexType>
```

11.4.1 businessEntity

Each business registered with UDDI is represented via a businessEntity data structure. Think of this entity as the starting point for your relationship with UDDI: When you publish your services to UDDI, you start by publishing a new businessEntity. Similarly, when searching UDDI, many of the inquiry APIs search a specific businessEntity.

Figure 11.8 shows the businessEntity structure and its contents. Listing 11.1 showed the corresponding XML Schema complex type definition. Listing 11.2 shows an example businessEntity structure from Microsoft's UDDI v2 implementation.

Listing 11.2 An example businessEntity structure

```
<businessEntity
  businessKey="677cfa1a-2717-4620-be39-6631bb74b6e1"
  operator="Microsoft Corporation"
  authorizedName=" Yasser Shohoud : 86">
  <discoveryURLs>
    <discoveryURL useType="businessEntity">
    http://uddi.rte.microsoft.com/discovery?_
     businessKey=677cfa1a-2717-4620-be39-6631bb74b6e1
    </discoveryURL>
  </discoveryURLs>
```

```xml
<name xml:lang="en">
    LearnXmlWS: The Resource for Web Service Developers
</name>
<description
xml:lang="en">An online community for developers of
Web services and Web service applications. Read articles,
download code, and ask questions pertaining to Web services.
Created by Yasser Shohoud.
</description>
<businessServices>
  <businessService
  serviceKey="d8091de4-0a4a-4061-9979-5d19131aece5"
  businessKey="677cfa1a-2717-4620-be39-6631bb74b6e1">
  <name xml:lang="en">The Weather service</name>
  <description xml:lang="en">
    Returns the current weather conditions for a given zip code
  </description>
  <bindingTemplates>
    <bindingTemplate
        bindingKey="942595d7-0311-48b7-9c65-995748a3a8af"
        serviceKey="d8091de4-0a4a-4061-9979-5d19131aece5">
      <accessPoint URLType="http">
      http://www.LearnXmlWS.com/services/weatherRetriever.asmx
      </accessPoint>
      <tModelInstanceDetails>
       <tModelInstanceInfo
          tModelKey= _
          "uuid:42fab02f-300a-4315-aa4a-f97242ff6953">
        <instanceDetails>
         <overviewDoc>
           <overviewURL>
http://www.learnxmlws.com/services/weatherretriever.asmx?WSDL
           </overviewURL>
         </overviewDoc>
        </instanceDetails>
       </tModelInstanceInfo>
      </tModelInstanceDetails>
    </bindingTemplate>
  </bindingTemplates>
 </businessService>
</businessServices>
</businessEntity>
```

Each businessEntity is uniquely identified by a Universally Unique Identifier (UUID) called a businessKey. The operator assigns this businessKey to the businessEntity when it's published. The publisher also optionally saves the name of the person who published the businessEntity in the authorizedName attribute.

A businessEntity may have one or more discoveryURL elements that contain URLs that point to discovery documents. In this context, the name "discovery document" has nothing to do with Web services; it's simply a document that provides information about the business itself. When you register a new business, the operator automatically adds a discoveryURL to it that points to the businessEntity information on that operator's node. For example, if you open Internet Explorer and navigate to the discoveryURL from Listing 11.2, http://uddi.rte.microsoft.com/discovery?businessKey=677...e1,[3] you will get back an XML document that contains the LearnXmlWS businessEntity definition like the one in Listing 11.2. You can also add your own discovery URLs, a link to your company's home page, or some other document that provides more information about the business. To help differentiate the types of URLs, the useType attribute can be set to a value that identifies the type of document returned by the discovery URL. UDDI defines only two useType values: businessEntity and businessEntityEx. When useType is businessEntity, it means that navigating to the discovery URL gets you an XML document that contains a UDDI businessEntity structure. Similarly, when useType is businessEntityEx, the discovery URL gets you an XML document that contains a UDDI businessEntityEx structure. businessEntityEx is similar to businessEntity but allows third parties to extend it by adding their own XML elements to the structure.

Each businessEntity has one or more name and zero or more descriptions. Multiple names and descriptions are allowed to support multiple languages. If multiple names are specified, each must have an xml:lang attribute indicating the language used and each must be in a unique language; you cannot specify two names in the same language. The same language rules apply to description. Note that businessEntity names do not have to be unique across all

---

[3]This URL points to the Microsoft beta implementation of UDDI V2. It is likely that this URL will change when the V2 implementation is released. For updates to this chapter, including current UDDI URLs, see the book's support Web site at www.LearnXmlws.com/book.

businessEntities, so it's likely that some businesses registered with UDDI will have the same name. businessKey is considered the only unique identifier for a businessEntity.

A businessEntity may optionally contain a contacts structure used to hold contact information such as mailing address, phone, and email.[4] A contacts structure can contain multiple contact structures for different uses such as technical support, sales, investors, and so forth.

identifierBag and categoryBag are two data structures used to add identification and categorization information to a businessEntity. I will explain these structures in more detail later in this chapter. For now, keep in mind that identifierBag is a structure used to add identification information such as a Federal Tax Id or a D-U-N-S number to the business. Similarly, categoryBag is used to categorize or classify the business; for example, a categoryBag might categorize the business as being a retail or travel business. Both identifierBag and categoryBag are optional. The example in Listing 11.2 does not have either.

11.4.2 businessService

A businessEntity may contain zero or more businessService structures that are used to describe services provided by the businessEntity. In this context, the word service does not necessarily mean Web service; it can be anything. If you browse UDDI, you'll find services ranging from SOAP-based Web services, to HTML Web pages, to fax and telephone numbers. Although UDDI does not stipulate that a businessService must be a Web service, for the purpose of this chapter, I will focus only on businessServices that are SOAP-based Web services.

A businessService is uniquely identified by a serviceKey that is an auto-assigned UUID. Each businessService has one or more names and zero or more descriptions that work in the same way as the businessEntity's name and description. An optional categoryBag may be included to categorize the businessService.

---

[4] It's only a matter of time until professional spammers discover that they can scrape email addresses from public UDDI registries. Whatever email address you enter in the businessEntity contacts, be sure the email's owner doesn't mind getting spammed!

11.4.3 bindingTemplate

To describe the technical aspects of the Web service, each businessService contains zero or more bindingTemplate structures. A bindingTemplate defines such technical information as the service's interface and end point URL. Each bindingTemplate is uniquely identified by an auto-generated UUID stored in bindingKey. The optional description elements work in the same way as description elements in other UDDI structures.

Each bindingTemplate must contain *either* an accessPoint *or* a hostingRedirector element as indicated by the `<choice>` element in Listing 11.1. An accessPoint element contains the URL where the service can be accessed with the type of URL indicated by the URLType attribute. URLType values can be mailto, http, https, ftp, fax, phone, or other. For SOAP-over-HTTP services, you care about http and https only. Note that you must include the protocol prefix (for example, http://) in the URL contained in accessPoint. Omitting the http:// prefix is a common error when registering services with UDDI.

If a bindingTemplate does not contain an accessPoint element, it must contain a hostingRedirector element that points to another bindingTemplate. For example:

```
<hostingRedirector
bindingKey="86e46ccd-82a5-454f-8957-381c2f724d6f"/>
```

A bindingTemplate that contains a hostingRedirector is essentially saying "don't use me, rather go find the bindingTemplate identified by this bindingKey and use that instead." This feature is useful when you want the technical information of one service to be utilized by other services that "link" to it via the hostingRedirector. The name hostingRedirector indicates one scenario where this feature might be useful: If the service is hosted for you by some other organization, you might want to allow that organization to control the bindingTemplate information such as accessPoint. When you register your service, you add to it a bindingTemplate with a hostingRedirector that contains the bindingKey for the appropriate bindingTemplate maintained by your host.

11.4.4 tModel

UDDI's tModel reminds me of XML namespaces: both are equally simple and equally confusing to many developers. It is not clear what the word tModel stands for; it could be technical model or type model. But that's not important; what's important is what tModel is and how it's used.

A tModel is a general purpose data structure for linking to meta data outside of UDDI. The most important content of a tModel structure is a URL to a document that provides more information on this meta data. This document can be anything—an HTML page, a Word document, or a WSDL document—depending on what exactly the tModel describes. I know this is not a concrete definition, but the abstract nature of the tModel is what makes it so versatile that it is used in various places in UDDI today and is extensible to meet future needs.

11.4.5 tModels as Service Types

Making tModels concrete always helps people understand them better, so I will explain the specific use of tModels for defining service types. Listing 11.3 shows an example tModel I registered with UDDI to describe the interface of my WeatherRetriever Web service.

Listing 11.3 An example tModel that represents the WeatherRetriever service type (service interface)

```
<tModel
   tModelKey="uuid:42fab02f-300a-4315-aa4a-f97242ff6953"
   operator="Microsoft Corporation"
   authorizedName=" Yasser Shohoud : 86">
 <name>Weather Service Interface</name>
 <description xml:lang="en">
     Standard interface for Web services providing
     current weather information
    </description>
 <overviewDoc>
 <description xml:lang="en">
        The Weather service's WSDL document
    </description>
  <overviewURL>
 http://www.learnxmlws.com/services/ifaces/weatherretriever.wsdl
    </overviewURL>
```

```
  </overviewDoc>
  <categoryBag>
    <keyedReference
        tModelKey=
          "uuid:c1acf26d-9672-4404-9d70-39b756e62ab4"
        keyName=
          "Specification for a web service described in WSDL"
        keyValue="wsdlSpec"/>
    <keyedReference
        tModelKey="uuid:c0b9fe13-179f-413d-8a5b-5004db8e5bb2"
        keyName="On-Line Information Services"
        keyValue="514191"/>
  </categoryBag>
</tModel>
```

tModels are top-level data structures in UDDI, meaning that they are not contained in a businessEntity. Each tModel is uniquely identified by its tModelKey, which is an auto-assigned UUID. A tModel also has a name and zero or more description elements with different languages. The overviewURL element contains a URL pointing to a document that describes the Web service's interface. When I registered this tModel, I entered the URL to a WSDL document that describes the WeatherRetriever's service interface. overviewURLs don't have to point to WSDL documents; anything that describes the Web service interface is allowed. Practically, however, you should point to a WSDL document since WSDL is becoming increasingly popular and many development tools, including Visual Studio .NET, rely on WSDL documents to create Web service proxies. Note that the WSDL document you point to here does not need to have a `<service>` or `<port>` definition. That is, it is only used to define an interface, not to specify where implementations of that interface are located. The bindingTemplate's accessPoint can be used to specify the actual service location.

The tModel in Listing 11.3 contains a categoryBag that is used to categorize the tModel. I'll defer explanation of the categoryBag contents until after the section on categorization later in this chapter.

Ignoring the categoryBag for now, the tModel in Listing 11.3 becomes just a way to point to the WeatherRetriever's WSDL document that describes the service interface. Again, please note that the weatherretriever.wsdl document does not need to contain the Web service location, only the interface definition.

11.4.6 tModel As Meta Data

Besides their use as service types, tModels are also used to hold meta data about business and services registered with UDDI. Imagine you are designing a relational database to store business information. You might create a business table with name, description, and other columns. If you want the database to be extensible so that any other business properties can be stored, you might create a table called keyedReference with two columns called keyName and keyValue as shown in Figure 11.9. Database users can then use this table to store additional information about their businesses. For example, to store the business's Federal Tax Id, I can add a row in keyedReference with the following values:

```
keyName = Federal Tax Id
keyValue = 999-99999
```

This approach allows flexibility but has a serious issue. It relies on all persons or applications entering data to use consistent names. For example, another user might enter their business's Federal Tax Id like this:

```
keyName = Id
keyValue = 8811-888888
```

Looking at this record you'd have no idea that this was a Federal Tax Id. To solve this problem, you might create a table called tModel with columns called name, description, overviewDoc, and tModelKey, which is a unique identifier (the primary key). This table would hold a record for each unique property type that us-

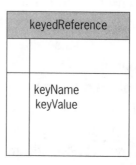

Figure 11.9 An example keyedReference table in a relational database

ers want to add to the database. For example, it would hold a record for the Federal Tax Id property type:

```
name = Federal Tax Id
description = The business's federal tax identifier
tModelKey = 4771063B-2499-41f0-BE59-786DCE3E42F4
overviewDoc = link to the IRS web site where they explain tax ids
```

To describe records in the keyedReference table as holding Federal Tax Ids, you would add a foreign key to keyedReference and point to the above tModel record. Figure 11.10 shows the resulting keyedReference and tModel tables.

In this context, the tModel table is used to hold meta data about records in the keyedReference table. This is exactly how UDDI uses tModels for meta data. To ensure UDDI can be extended to hold information beyond what's defined in the standard data structures, UDDI uses a data structure called keyedReference. This structure contains keyName, keyValue, and tModelKey attributes exactly like the keyedReference table in Figure 11.10. keyedReference is used in places where extensibility is needed; for example, in publisherAssertions, categoryBag, and identifierBag—all of which will be covered in later sections.

This usage of tModels is similar to how XML namespaces are used in XML documents: A tModel provides context to a piece of information and an XML namespace provides context to an XML element or attribute. Since UDDI information is exposed as XML, the question is: Why not provide context by using XML namespaces as qualifiers for the key names? tModels are better for this application because they can contain rich information such as name, description,

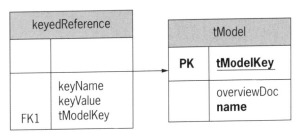

Figure 11.10 A tModel table and a keyedReference table with a one-to-many relation

and a link to an overview document that provides the reader with more information about what that tModel describes. In addition, because each tModel has an auto-assigned tModelKey, it's easier to ensure that tModelKeys are unique than to try to ensure that user-entered XML namespaces are unique.

11.4.7   tModelInstanceInfo

Returning to the diagram in Figure 11.8, you'll see that each bindingTemplate may be associated with zero or more tModels and a tModel may be associated with zero or more bindingTemplates. To manage this many-to-many relation, a data structure called tModelInstanceInfo is used. Listing 11.4 shows the XML Schema for tModelInstanceInfo and instanceDetails.

Listing 11.4   tModelInstanceInfo and instanceDetails schema (VBWSClientCode\Chapter11\UDDISchemas\uddi_v2.xsd)

```
<element name="tModelInstanceInfo"
         type="uddi:tModelInstanceInfo"/>
<complexType name="tModelInstanceInfo">
  <sequence>
    <element ref="uddi:description"
                    minOccurs="0" maxOccurs="unbounded"/>
    <element ref="uddi:instanceDetails" minOccurs="0"/>
  </sequence>
  <attribute name="tModelKey" use="required"
          type="uddi:tModelKey"/>
</complexType>
  <element name="instanceDetails"
          type="uddi:instanceDetails"/>
<complexType name="instanceDetails">
  <sequence>
    <element ref="uddi:description"
                    minOccurs="0" maxOccurs="unbounded"/>
    <element ref="uddi:overviewDoc" minOccurs="0"/>
    <element ref="uddi:instanceParms" minOccurs="0"/>
  </sequence>
</complexType>
```

A tModelInstanceInfo points to a tModel using that tModel's tModelKey. For example, the tModelInstanceInfo in Listing 11.2 has a tModelKey with the same value as the tModelKey of the WeatherRetriever tModel in Listing 11.3.

Referencing a tModel from a tModelInstanceInfo is like saying "this service implements the interface defined by that tModel."

The tModelInstanceInfo in Listing 11.2 contains an instanceDetails element that points to the Web service's WSDL document. This is not strictly required since the tModel already points to another WSDL document that defines the service's interface, and the bindingTemplate's accessPoint element provides the location of the Web service. So all the information a client needs to invoke this Web service is provided by the tModel and accessPoint. However, there might be cases where you want to specify an overview document for a specific implementation of an interface. Perhaps you've created a WSDL document with extensibility elements that specify the Web service's response time and availability guarantees. Such information is implementation-specific so it wouldn't be part of the interface's overview document and therefore needs to be specified in an instance-specific overview document.

Looking at Listing 11.2, you'll notice that tModelInstanceInfo is contained within tModelInstanceDetails. This is because a service may implement several interfaces, in which case there would be a tModelInstanceInfo structure with the appropriate tModelKey for each implemented interface.

I will show you several code examples later in this chapter that will help reinforce your understanding of tModels and tModelInstanceInfos.

11.4.8   publisherAssertion

While UDDI defines a structure called businessEntity, in reality, this structure represents an entity that provides one or more services. This entity need not be a business, it can be a department within a business or for a multi-national corporation; it can be a business branch in a specific country. The result is that, practically, different parts or branches of a multi-national corporation or a government will be represented by different UDDI businessEntity structures and create the need to link those businessStructures to indicate that they all belong to the same organization. This is one scenario where UDDI businessEntity structures need to be related to one another.

To relate two business entities A and B, the publisher of each business entity must create a publisherAssertion structure that contains A's businessKey and

B's businessKey. The two businesses are related only if both publishers create the same publisherAssertion structures. To prevent others from randomly associating their businesses with yours, having just one publisherAssertion structure is not sufficient to establish a relation.

The publisherAssertion structure contains three elements: fromKey, toKey, and keyedReference. fromKey and toKey are the business keys of the two related businesses. keyedReference contains a name-value pair that describes the relation along with a reference to a tModel. For example, if A and B are the East Coast and West Coast branches of a business, the publisherAssertion from A to B might look like this:

```
<publisherAssertion>
  <fromKey>this would be A's businessKey</fromKey>
  <toKey>this would be B's businessKey</toKey>
  <keyedReference
      tModelKey='uuid:807a2c6a-ee22-470d-adc7-e0424a337c03'
      keyName='Branch' keyValue='peer-peer'/>
</publisherAssertion>
```

The tModel referenced by the tModelKey attribute of keyedReference is one of the UDDI standard tModels. It is called uddi-org:relationships and is used to indicate that data referencing this tModel defines a relationship between organizations.

This is an example of a tModel used to provide meta data other than a Web service's interface. The uddi-org:relationships tModel is simply a way to indicate that the keyName and keyValue specify a relation between the two businesses. If the keyName and keyValue specified the Dun and Bradstreet D-U-N-S number for business A instead, you would reference the tModel called dnb-com:D-U-N-S, which is another standard UDDI tModel that indicates the data used is a D-U-N-S number.

In this case, the tModelKey is that of the uddi-org:relationships tModel so we know that keyName and keyValue define the relation between the two businesses. keyName can be anything you like; when you use the uddi-org:relationships tModel, keyValue must be one of parent-child, peer-peer, or identity. These three values are defined in the UDDI specification as the only allowable values when using uddi-org:relationships tModel. The suggested way to provide more information about the business relation is by using keyName. You can set key-Name to whatever value you like, including a phrase that explains the relation in more detail.

11.5 A Real-World Example

To show you a real-world example that applies the key data structures explained above, I extracted the businessService structure for a Web service named Galapagos. This service is a commercial Web service that provides financial information such as real time and delayed stock quotes.[5] Listing 11.5 shows the entire businessService structure that contains four bindingTemplates.

Listing 11.5 A real-world example of a commercial Web service registered with UDDI

```
<!-- The service itself -->
<businessService
    serviceKey="ec5c6fd5-7724-440f-9bf7-d8b89ff69402"
    businessKey="cba3f867-fc0e-4d3c-bc76-4a64f4b79398">
  <name>Galapagos</name>
  <description xml:lang="en">
Financial XML Web Services (beta)</description>
  <bindingTemplates>
  <!-- first binding: For Logon part of service -->
    <bindingTemplate
        serviceKey="ec5c6fd5-7724-440f-9bf7-d8b89ff69402"
        bindingKey="5d01bf89-2456-4b31-9f44-215e6eb8ffdd">
      <description xml:lang="en">Galapagos Logon Service</
➡description>
<!-- access point points to service's end point URL -->
        <accessPoint URLType="http">
            http://beta.earthconnect.net/logon/2001/01/logon.asmx
        </accessPoint>
        <tModelInstanceDetails>
<!-- reference to the tModel describing
     the logon service interface -->
            <tModelInstanceInfo
            tModelKey="uuid:51890f8b-eac5-45fe-8aaa-59ca745f0fc3">
```

---

[5]At the time of this writing, the Galapagos service is still registered with the Microsoft UDDI V1 production registry at http://uddi.microsoft.com. However, the service itself is no longer online.

```xml
          <description
            xml:lang="en">Galapagos Logon tModel</description>
          <instanceDetails>
            <description
            xml:lang="en">SDK document</description>
            <overviewDoc>
              <description xml:lang="en"/>
              <overviewURL/>
            </overviewDoc>
    <!-- point developers to the SDK documentation -->
            <instanceParms>
            http://earthconnect.net/galapagos/SDK
            </instanceParms>
          </instanceDetails>
        </tModelInstanceInfo>
      </tModelInstanceDetails>
    </bindingTemplate>
  <!-- second binging: delayed market data -->
    <bindingTemplate
        serviceKey="ec5c6fd5-7724-440f-9bf7-d8b89ff69402"
        bindingKey="f583c31b-9ab4-4890-a0ff-f75792bb86aa">
      <description xml:lang="en">
        Galapagos MarketDataDelayed Service
      </description>
      <!-- The service's endpoint URL -->
      <accessPoint URLType="http">http://beta.earthconnect.net/_
marketdatadelayed/2001/01/marketdatadelayed.asmx
      </accessPoint>
      <tModelInstanceDetails>
  <!-- reference to the tModel describing the delayed market
  data service interface -->
        <tModelInstanceInfo
          tModelKey="uuid:f0ee3b46-5797-4d81-95ca-c3141c76739e">
          <description xml:lang="en">
            Galapagos MarketDataDelayed tModel
          </description>
          <instanceDetails>
            <description
            xml:lang="en">SDK document</description>
            <overviewDoc>
              <description xml:lang="en"/>
              <overviewURL/>
            </overviewDoc>
            <instanceParms>
```

```
                http://earthconnect.net/galapagos/SDK
              </instanceParms>
            </instanceDetails>
          </tModelInstanceInfo>
        </tModelInstanceDetails>
      </bindingTemplate>
<!-- third binding: real time market data -->
      <bindingTemplate
          serviceKey="ec5c6fd5-7724-440f-9bf7-d8b89ff69402"
          bindingKey="66560d4a-d5b2-42a4-9bb9-50e7ea66ab6e">
        <description xml:lang="en">
          Galapagos MarketDataRealTime Service
        </description>
<!-- The service's endpoint URL -->
        <accessPoint URLType="http">http://beta.earthconnect.net/_
marketdatarealtime/2001/01/marketdatarealtime.asmx</accessPoint>
          <tModelInstanceDetails>
  <!-- reference to the tModel describing the real time market
    data service interface -->
            <tModelInstanceInfo
              tModelKey=
              "uuid:2db65006-7f6b-4ccc-a2d0-a0214d2ea192">
            <description xml:lang="en">
                Galapagos MarketDataRealTime tModel
            </description>
            <instanceDetails>
              <description
              xml:lang="en">SDK document</description>
              <overviewDoc>
                <description xml:lang="en"/>
                <overviewURL/>
              </overviewDoc>
              <instanceParms>
                http://earthconnect.net/galapagos/SDK
              </instanceParms>
            </instanceDetails>
          </tModelInstanceInfo>
        </tModelInstanceDetails>
      </bindingTemplate>
<!-- fourth binding: administration -->
      <bindingTemplate
          serviceKey="ec5c6fd5-7724-440f-9bf7-d8b89ff69402"
          bindingKey="2dd692a9-7d89-4aa0-9bf6-441b63ae5e05">
        <description xml:lang="en">
```

```
                Galapagos UserAdmin Service
            </description>
    <!-- The service's endpoint URL -->
            <accessPoint URLType="http">
    http://beta.earthconnect.net/useradmin/2001/01/useradmin.asmx
            </accessPoint>
            <tModelInstanceDetails>
                <!-- reference to the tModel describing the
                    administration service interface -->
                <tModelInstanceInfo
                tModelKey="uuid:8e162a3b-ae05-4b9e-b159-8e1ebd8b6a8e">
                    <description xml:lang="en">
                        Galapagos UserAdmin tModel
                    </description>
                    <instanceDetails>
                        <description
                        xml:lang="en">SDK document</description>
                        <overviewDoc>
                            <description xml:lang="en"/>
                            <overviewURL/>
                        </overviewDoc>
                        <instanceParms>
                            http://earthconnect.net/galapagos/SDK
                        </instanceParms>
                    </instanceDetails>
                </tModelInstanceInfo>
            </tModelInstanceDetails>
        </bindingTemplate>
    </bindingTemplates>
</businessService>
```

Galapagos is an example of a composite service made up of several end points that work together to deliver a set of functionality. There are four distinct end points, each described with its own bindingTemplate. The interface exposed at each end point is described by a service type tModel.

The first binding is for the Logon part of the service called Galapagos Logon Service. Its end point URL, http://beta.earthconnect.net/logon/2001/01/ logon.asmx, is contained in the `<accessPoint>` element. The tModelInstance-Info references the service type tModel by its unique tModelKey. The instanceDetails uses instanceParms to point developers to an online SDK that provides more information about the service. It would have been more appropriate to use the overviewURL field to point to this SDK, but there are no set rules.

The same pattern repeats for each of the remaining three bindings. Each binding has a description and points to the service's end point URL within `<accessPoint>`. Also within each binding, tModelInstanceInfo references the corresponding service type tModel and points to the SDK documentation.

11.6 How Categorization Works

UDDI is expected to hold hundreds of thousands of business entities and services. With such a large volume of data, it's necessary to categorize businesses, services, and other UDDI data items based on a meaningful categorization scheme. For example, businesses might be categorized by geographic region or industry type.

In general, categorization (sometimes called classification), is the process of adding information to a UDDI data structure, such as a business entity, making this data structure a member of one or more predefined categories.

To categorize a business entity, you add keyedReference elements to the entity's categoryBag, which acts as a collection of keyedReferences. Listing 11.6 shows the categoryBag schema and Listing 11.7 shows an example category-Bag from the LearnXmlws businessEntity.

Listing 11.6 categoryBag schema
(VBWSClientCode\Chapter11\UDDISchemas\uddi_v2.xsd)

```
<element name="categoryBag" type="uddi:categoryBag"/>
<complexType name="categoryBag">
  <sequence>
    <element ref="uddi:keyedReference"
             minOccurs="0" maxOccurs="unbounded"/>
  </sequence>
</complexType>
```

Listing 11.7 A categoryBag within a businessEntity

```
<businessEntity
  businessKey="677cfa1a-2717-4620-be39-6631bb74b6e1"
  operator="Microsoft Corporation"
  authorizedName="Yasser Shohoud : 86">
```

```
. . .
<categoryBag>
 <keyedReference
    tModelKey="uuid:c0b9fe13-179f-413d-8a5b-5004db8e5bb2"
   keyName="Educational Services" keyValue="61" />
 <keyedReference
    tModelKey="uuid:c0b9fe13-179f-413d-8a5b-5004db8e5bb2"
   keyName="Other Information Services" keyValue="51419" />
</categoryBag>
</businessEntity>
```

The example in Listing 11.7 has two categories both referencing the same tModel as indicated by tModelKey. The tModel referenced here is part of the North American Industry Classification System (NAICS) taxonomy, which is one of four categorization tModels or taxonomies built into UDDI. Note that an application or operator site might choose to display the taxonomy name instead of the tModelKey. Microsoft's UDDI site does in fact display the name ntis-gov:naics:1997 as shown in Figure 11.11.

The values in keyName and keyValue refer to predefined NAICS classifications. Having standard classifications such as NAICS enables applications to search for businesses that belong to one or more of those standard classifications. For example, an application can be designed to search for all companies that provide educational services, or companies that sell office supplies, and so forth.

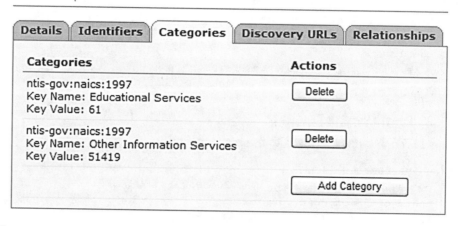

Figure 11.11 Viewing a provider's (businessEntity's) categories

REAL WORLD XML WEB SERVICES

The built-in taxonomies include an Other Taxonomy that can be used to store general keywords that might be used when searching. A UDDI registrar might use Other Taxonomy to store keywords that are meaningful for users of that registrar. The registrar can then provide a specialized UDDI search feature that searches for businesses using specified keywords. You'll see examples of this later in this chapter.

11.7 How Identifiers Work

Beyond Categorization, there's also the need to identify a business uniquely by a well-known identifier such as a Federal Tax Id. Following the extensibility theme, UDDI businessEntity structures can be assigned unique ids using a collection of keyedReferences inside an identifierBag. Listing 11.8 shows the identifierBag schema.

Listing 11.8   identifierBag schema

```
<element name="identifierBag" type="uddi:identifierBag"/>
<complexType name="identifierBag">
  <sequence>
    <element ref="uddi:keyedReference"
             minOccurs="0" maxOccurs="unbounded"/>
  </sequence>
</complexType>
```

An identifier bag is simply a collection of keyedReference elements. Within an identifierBag, a keyedReference element points to a tModel that defines an identifier. For example, there are two built-in tModels that represent identifiers. The tModel called dnb-com:D-U-N-S represents Dun & Bradstreet D-U-N-S numbers, and the tModel called thomasregister-com:supplierID represents Thomas Register supplier IDs.

Looking back at the data structures in Figure 11.8, you'll notice that the tModel itself contains a categoryBag and identifierBag. This means a tModel, just like a businessEntity, can be assigned categories and/or unique ids. I point this out because it may not be obvious that a tModel can be a powerful tool when searching for Web services, provided, of course, the tModel itself is appropriately categorized.

11.8 WSDL and UDDI

WSDL is used to define a Web service's interface and its end point URL. WSDL also allows the use of arbitrary extensibility elements to provide other information outside the scope of the WSDL specification. UDDI overlaps with WSDL in two areas: A bindingTemplate's accessPoint element provides a service's end point URL, and the instanceParms element can be used to provide arbitrary information needed to invoke the service, similar to WSDL's extensibility elements.

This overlap has created much confusion among Web service developers and Web service tools developers. For example, from where should a service's end point be obtained, UDDI's `<accessPoint>` or the service's WSDL `<port>` element? There are several views for how UDDI and WSDL should be combined. Here's one of those views based on a UDDI draft document.

11.8.1 WSDL in UDDI Best Practices View

There's a UDDI document titled "Using WSDL in a UDDI Registry" that attempts to answer some of these questions by providing best practices for registering WSDL-based services in UDDI. However, because there are many options for constructing WSDL documents, there are many possible combinations for registering WSDL-based services. The UDDI best practices document covers only a specific scenario where a WSDL document contains interface-only information and the service's end point URL is registered in UDDI's accessPoint.

The best practices view assumes that the WSDL document is divided into two parts: the interface definition (everything except the `<service>` element) and the implementation definition (the service element and its child elements). The best practices view cares only about the interface definition part and ignores the implementation definition part. Although the general tendency is to edit the service's auto-generated WSDL document and break it into two distinct documents, it's not necessary to do this. The division can be more of a logical one.

Under the best practices view, the process of registering interfaces (service types) is separate from that of registering services. First, the interface is registered by creating a tModel that acts as a service type definition. The rules for creating this tModel are as follows:

- The tModel's overviewDoc points to the WSDL document that contains the *interface* definition.

- The tModel must be categorized as an interface definition for a WSDL-based service. A special categorization tModel has been defined for this purpose. This tModel is called wsdlSpec and is part of the uddi-org:types taxonomy.

Listing 11.3 shows an example tModel that satisfies these rules. As you know, each tModel is uniquely identified by its tModeKey. For a service type tModel, the tModelKey becomes the unique interface identifier.

After the interface is registered, services that implement this interface can be registered. Each service that implements an interface has a bindingTemplate that points to the interface's tModel using that tModel's key. The binding will also contain an `<accessPoint>` element that contains the service's end point URL. Any other details needed to invoke the service can be contained in the instance-Parms element.

Once a service is registered according to the best practices, developers or applications that need to invoke the service use the service's bindingTemplate to find out the service's access point and the service's interface id (tModelKey). Then they look up the interface tModel and retrieve its WSDL document from the location pointed to in the overviewDoc field.

Because of the inherent separation of interface and implementation, this scenario is a good fit for services that implement industry-standard interfaces. For example, the accounting software industry can define a standard invoicing interface and register it with UDDI as a service type. Customers can deploy Web services that implement this interface and register each service as a businessService with the appropriate binding information.

11.9 Visual Studio .NET and UDDI

Visual Studio .NET (VS .NET) integrates UDDI in two different places letting you easily register your services with UDDI and search for services within UDDI.

11.9.1   Add Web Reference Dialog

Using Visual Studio's Add Web Reference dialog, you can search the production and test UDDI registries for Web services. This dialog searches for businesses that satisfy two criteria:

- The business name that you typed in.
- At least one of the business's services must point to a tModel categorized as a wsdlSpec as outlined in the UDDI best practices document explained above.

Assuming you find the service you're looking for, when you click on it, VS .NET retrieves the service interface's WSDL document and uses it to generate a proxy class. If the interface's WSDL document is a *pure interface definition* (no implementation definition), the generated proxy class will not point to the service's end point. You can easily edit this class's constructor and add the line Me.Url = *web service Url* or set its Url property at runtime.

11.9.2   Getting Services to Appear in the Add Web Reference Dialog

If you know a Web service is registered with UDDI but you can't get it to show in the Add Web Reference dialog, it's because the service wasn't registered according to the best practices document. I'll show you the UDDI messages used to register service interfaces and implementations later in this chapter. If you just want a quick way to get your service to show up (even without creating a UDDI user id), visit http://www.qUDDI.com and register your service there. If you've already created a UDDI user id, you can use VS .NET's Start page to register your service as I will explain next.

11.9.3   Searching UDDI from the Start Page

The XML Web Services link on VS .NET's start page takes you to a page where you can search for services and register your own service as shown in Figure 11.12.[6]

---

[6]This page is actually retrieved from http://msdn.microsoft.com/vsdata/SP2xmlwebsvcs.xml in the form of an XML file which is then rendered as HTML within Visual Studio's shell.

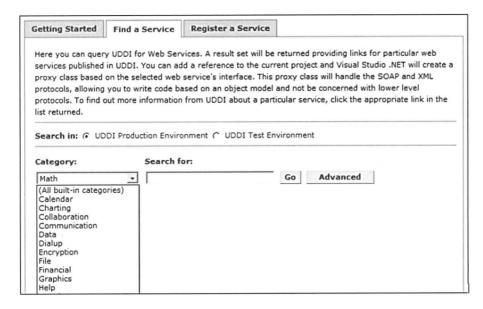

Getting Started | **Find a Service** | **Register a Service**

Here you can query UDDI for Web Services. A result set will be returned providing links for particular web services published in UDDI. You can add a reference to the current project and Visual Studio .NET will create a proxy class based on the selected web service's interface. This proxy class will handle the SOAP and XML protocols, allowing you to write code based on an object model and not be concerned with lower level protocols. To find out more information from UDDI about a particular service, click the appropriate link in the list returned.

Search in: ⦿ UDDI Production Environment ◯ UDDI Test Environment

Category: **Search for:**

| Math ▾ |

[_____] [Go] [Advanced]

(All built-in categories)
Calendar
Charting
Collaboration
Communication
Data
Dialup
Encryption
File
Financial
Graphics
Help

Figure 11.12 VS .NET's Start Page lets you find and publish services

The search page lets you search by category using a list of built-in categories such as Calendar, Data, and Weather as shown in the drop down in Figure 11.6. These categories are part of a categorization scheme created specifically for VS .NET search purposes. The tModel that describes this categorization scheme is called "VS Web Service Search Categorization" and is shown in Listing 11.9.

Listing 11.9 VS Web Service Search Categorization tModel

```
<tModelDetail generic="1.0"
    operator="Microsoft Corporation"
   truncated="false" xmlns="urn:uddi-org:api">
  <tModel
        tModelKey="uuid:4c1f2e1f-4b7c-44eb-9b87-6e7d80f82b3e"
        operator="Microsoft Corporation"
        authorizedName="Brigette Krantz">
    <name>VS Web Service Search Categorization</name>
    <description xml:lang="en">
    This service type determines how a service is
    categorized within the VS Web Service Search Page
        </description>
    <overviewDoc>
      <description xml:lang="en"/>
```

```
        <overviewURL/>
      </overviewDoc>
    </tModel>
  </tModelDetail>
```

When you select a category or enter a keyword and click Go, you get a list of services with a link below each service to add a Web reference to the current project as shown in Figure 11.13. Clicking on this link will generate a proxy class and add it to your project. The proxy's URL will be set to the URL contained in the `<accessPoint>` element, which is compliant with UDDI's WSDL best practices document.

To categorize your service type into one of these categories, you need to add a tModelBag with a keyedReference to the VS categorization tModel, as explained above in the section How Categorization Works. VS .NET lets you do this as part of the Web service registration process when you use the built-in Register a Service page.

This page walks you through the process of first logging on to UDDI, then selecting one of the businesses that you have registered with UDDI (most people will have only one business registered with UDDI). Then you reach a page where you specify your service name, description, access point, WSDL document URL, and a category for your service as shown in Figure 11.14.

Visual Studio's start page is great for searching and registering services at design time. However, many UDDI usage scenarios require querying UDDI at runtime or programmatically registering services as they come online. The next sections explain how to program UDDI using the SOAP message-based API.

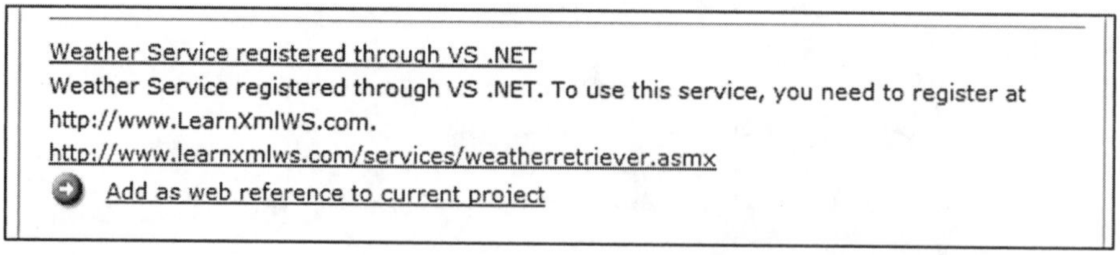

Weather Service registered through VS .NET
Weather Service registered through VS .NET. To use this service, you need to register at http://www.LearnXmlWS.com.
http://www.learnxmlws.com/services/weatherretriever.asmx
⊙ Add as web reference to current project

Figure 11.13 Results of searching the UDDI registry for services in the Weather category

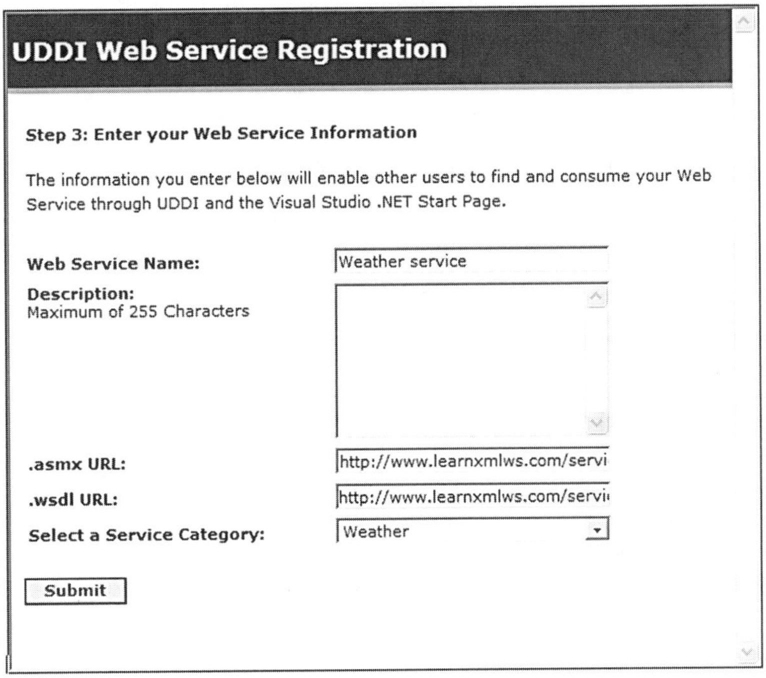

UDDI Web Service Registration

Step 3: Enter your Web Service Information

The information you enter below will enable other users to find and consume your Web Service through UDDI and the Visual Studio .NET Start Page.

Web Service Name: Weather service

Description:
Maximum of 255 Characters

.asmx URL: http://www.learnxmlws.com/servi

.wsdl URL: http://www.learnxmlws.com/servi

Select a Service Category: Weather

Submit

Figure 11.14   Registering your Web service from VS .NET's Start Page

11.10   Programming UDDI

UDDI APIs are exposed as Web service operations and invoked via SOAP messages. To invoke a UDDI API, the client forms a SOAP message and sends it via HTTP POST to one of the UDDI nodes' end point URL. UDDI processes the request message and sends back a response in the form of another SOAP message.

You can use a variety of tools to invoke UDDI APIs, including the UDDI SDK available from Microsoft. This SDK provides a nice object model that wraps UDDI's SOAP messages and exposes them as objects with properties and methods. The SDK is available in different versions, including a COM implementation for VB 6 and other COM-capable languages and a .NET implementation for clients using the CLR.

Although the SDK gives you a convenient object model, you still have to learn the UDDI API to use the SDK. After you've learned the parts of the API that you need to use, you can then use the SDK's object model to invoke those APIs. By first learning the APIs, then using the SDK, you get the best of both worlds: You understand exactly which SDK objects and data structures to use and you don't have to deal with low-level SOAP messages and XML.

The best way to learn a Web service's API is to program directly against it by forming and sending request messages yourself and parsing response messages. The next few sections show you examples of programming against the API directly. This knowledge is then used as the foundation for the subsequent sections that show you how to use the UDDI SDK.

11.10.1 UDDI Message Types

UDDI APIs tend to fall into four broad categories. First, there are messages used to search for things such as businesses or services. These messages start with find_xxx where xxx is the name type of object you're searching for, (for example, find_business and find_service). Like any search mechanism, find messages let you specify search criteria such as names, categories, and identifiers. When searching by names, you can specify a percent sign as a wild card character.

The second group of messages is the detail messages that follow the naming convention get_xxxDetail where xxx is the type of object for which you want detailed information. For example, get_businessDetail and get_tModelDetail return the details of a business and a tModel, respectively. A get_xxxDetail message contains the unique identifier of the object for which you want detailed information. For example, get_businessDetail contains a businessKey while get_tModelDetail contains a tModelKey.

The third group is the save messages—for example, save_business and save_binding. These APIs can be used to save new objects or to replace existing objects. When saving new objects, the response message contains the newly saved object key.

Finally, the delete messages such as delete_business and delete_publisherAssertions delete specified objects. Similar to get_xxxDetail messages, most delete messages also require a key that uniquely identifies the object to be deleted.

11.10.2   A UDDI API Learning Aid

To help you learn the UDDI API, I created an application that sends and receives SOAP messages over HTTP. This application is written in VB .NET but does not use any of the .NET Web services stack. Instead, it simply forms the SOAP message as an XML document and uses classes in System.Net to post the request and receive the response. The application code is included in this chapter's folder (VBWSBook\Chapter11\UDDIAPIs.aspx) and is also live at http://www.LearnXmlws.com/UDDI/UDDIAPIs.aspx.

Figure 11.15 shows the application's Web-based user interface, which consists of a simple page with a series of text areas and buttons. There is a text area for the request message and another for the response message for each of the APIs. For your convenience, the request messages have been already formed with the string ***** used as a data placeholder. The application's HTML is generated by applying an XSLT transformation (VBWSBook\Chapter11\UDDIMessages.xsl) to an XML document containing UDDI message templates (VBWSBook\Chapter11\UDDIMessages.xml). This HTML generation is done statically at design time and the generated HTML is saved to the file UDDIAPIs.aspx.

To invoke an API, replace data placeholders in the request message with your own data and click Submit. The result will show the response message in the response text area. You can use this application to follow through the next sections as I explain the commonly used UDDI APIs.

All the code in this chapter points to Microsoft's UDDI V2 registry at http://uddi.rte.microsoft.com/inquire and https://uddi.rte.microsoft.com/publish. If at the time you read this, the Microsoft UDDI end point URLs have changed, you can simply modify these URLs in the code to point to the current ones. I've defined these URLs as constants in the code examples to make it easy for you to modify them. For updates to this chapter's code, see the book's support site at http://www.LearnXmlws.com/book.

11.11   Querying UDDI

Instead of repeating the API reference information which is readily available in UDDI's API Specification, I will show you how to use the APIs to accomplish

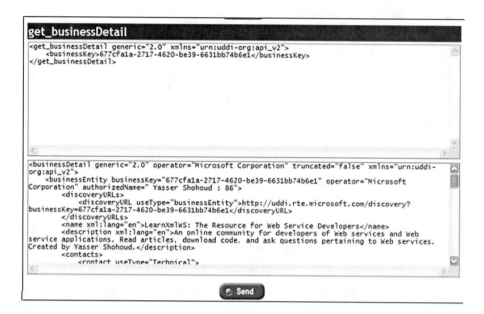

Figure 11.15   The UDDI Test Application. The top text area shows the request message and the bottom one shows the response message.

common tasks. The examples in this section coupled with the UDDI learning aid explained above will have you writing your own UDDI applications in no time.

11.11.1   Finding a Business by Name

The simplest UDDI search is finding a business by name. This is a good starting example because it is simple and easy to learn. Listing 11.10 shows example request and response messages without the SOAP Envelope and Body elements.

Listing 11.10   Example find_business request and response messages

```
<!-- find business by name request -->
<find_business generic="2.0" maxRows="50"
             xmlns="urn:uddi-org:api_v2">
    <name>LearnXmlWS</name>
</find_business>

<!-- find business response -->
<businessList generic="2.0" operator="Microsoft Corporation"
             truncated="false" xmlns="urn:uddi-org:api_v2">
```

```
    <businessInfos>
        <businessInfo
            businessKey="677cfa1a-2717-4620-be39-6631bb74b6e1">
            <name xml:lang="en">
                LearnXmlWS: The Resource for Web Service Developers
            </name>
        <description xml:lang="en">An online community for
developers of Web services and Web service applications.
Read articles, download code, and ask questions pertaining to
Web services. Created by Yasser Shohoud.</description>
            <serviceInfos>
                <serviceInfo
                    serviceKey=
                    "d8091de4-0a4a-4061-9979-5d19131aece5"
                    businessKey=
                    "677cfa1a-2717-4620-be39-6631bb74b6e1">
                    <name xml:lang="en">The Weather service</name>
                </serviceInfo>
            </serviceInfos>
        </businessInfo>
    </businessInfos>
</businessList>
```

The request message begins with the `<find_business>` element that contains a `<name>` element. The default namespace, urn:uddi-org:api_v2, is the namespace used for all UDDI version 2.0 request and response messages. The attribute named `generic` is used on all UDDI messages to indicate the UDDI version number. Allowed values are "1.0" or "2.0" depending on which UDDI version you are querying. maxRows is an optional attribute used to indicate the maximum number of businesses that should be returned.

The text content of `<name>` is the string you want to search for. You can use the percent sign as wild cards in this string. For example, %Corporation matches business entities whose names end with Corporation. By default, the string you specify is used to match the beginning of the business name, not the entire name. Therefore in this example, I only specified "LearnXmlWS" when the business name is "LearnXmlWS: The Resource for Web Service Developers." You can specify up to five names by repeating the `<name>` element.

The response message is a businessList message. All response messages have an operator attribute containing the name of the operator that sent this response. In addition, some response messages include a truncated attribute that is set to True if there are more results than those returned in the response message. This is useful if your search returned thousands of businesses, but you specified maxRows = 50. You would get back 50 businesses and truncated would be true.

businessInfos contains zero or more businessInfo structures each containing the businessKey, name, description, and a list of services for a particular business. Each serviceInfo structure provides you with the serviceKey and the service name as well as the businessKey of the business to which this service belongs. If you wanted to get more information about a particular service, you would then call get_serviceDetail and pass it the serviceKey. get_serviceDetail returns a complete businessService structure with all the service information.

11.11.2 Finding Businesses by Categories

In addition to searching by name, you can also find businesses that belong to one or more categories. The find_business API lets you specify a list of categories in a categoryBag structure. By default, businesses that belong to all specified categories (logical AND) are returned. You can also specify a findQualifiers structure to control how categories are searched. For example, if you specify the combineCategoryBags findQualifier, the search will look for the specified categories in the businessEntity's categoryBag and in the categoryBag of each businessService within the businessEntity, in effect combining business and service category bags for search purposes. This might be handy if you are interested in businesses and services connected with a particular category—for example, Educational Services.

```
<!-- find business using categories -->
<find_business generic="2.0" maxRows="50"
            xmlns="urn:uddi-org:api_v2">
    <categoryBag>
        <keyedReference
            tModelKey="uuid:c0b9fe13-179f-413d-8a5b-5004db8e5bb2"
            keyName="Educational Services"
```

```
                keyValue="61" />
        </categoryBag>
</find_business>
<!-- response to find business with categories -->
<businessList generic="2.0"
            operator="Microsoft Corporation"
            truncated="false" xmlns="urn:uddi-org:api_v2">
    <businessInfos>
        <businessInfo
            businessKey="677cfa1a-2717-4620-be39-6631bb74b6e1">
            <name xml:lang="en">
                LearnXmlWS: The Resource for Web Service Developers
            </name>
            <description xml:lang="en">
An online community for developers of Web services
and Web service applications. Read articles, download code,
 and ask questions pertaining to Web services.
Created by Yasser Shohoud.</description>
            <serviceInfos>
                <serviceInfo
                serviceKey="d8091de4-0a4a-4061-9979-5d19131aece5"
                businessKey=
                "677cfa1a-2717-4620-be39-6631bb74b6e1">
                    <name xml:lang="en">The Weather service</name>
                </serviceInfo>
            </serviceInfos>
        </businessInfo>
    </businessInfos>
</businessList>
```

The response message contains a businessInfos structure with a businessInfo structure for each business that matches the search criteria.

11.11.3 Finding Service Interfaces

UDDI makes it possible to search for tModels using the find_tModel API. You can search by tModel name, identifier, and category. Like all UDDI searches, you can control the logical grouping of search criteria using a findQualifiers structure (default is logical AND).

As an example, consider the scenario where you want to find all tModels that have been categorized as Web service interfaces. As you now know, the appropriate category for Web service interfaces is wsdlSpec, which is part of the uddi-org:types taxonomy. Listing 11.11 shows an example find_tModel message that is equivalent to asking: "Give me all WSDL-based Web service interfaces." Needless to say, this search can return a large result set, especially if you run it against a production registry. However, running it against Microsoft's test registry produces a small result set (at least for now).

Listing 11.11 find_tModel message with response

```
<!-- find all WSDL Web service interfaces -->
<find_tModel generic="2.0" xmlns="urn:uddi-org:api_v2">
    <categoryBag>
        <keyedReference
        tModelKey="uuid:C1ACF26D-9672-4404-9D70-39B756E62AB4"
        keyName="Specification for a web service described in WSDL"
        keyValue="wsdlSpec" />
    </categoryBag>
</find_tModel>
<!-- find web service interfaces response -->
<tModelList generic="2.0"
    operator="Microsoft Corporation" truncated="false"
    xmlns="urn:uddi-org:api_v2">
    <tModelInfos>
        <tModelInfo
            tModelKey=
            "uuid:7f30bebd-35cc-4873-8f91-f53f779d92fd">
            <name>Server Time Web Service</name>
        </tModelInfo>
        <tModelInfo
            tModelKey=
            "uuid:42fab02f-300a-4315-aa4a-f97242ff6953">
            <name>Weather Service Interface</name>
        </tModelInfo>
    </tModelInfos>
</tModelList>
```

The request message in Listing 11.11 includes a categoryBag with one reference to the wsdlSpec tModel. Note that keyName is an optional attribute; however, if you include it, its value must be exactly as shown.

The response message returns a list of tModelInfo structures, one for each tModel that matches the search criteria. To get more information about the returned tModels, you'd take one or more of the returned tModelKeys and pass them to a call to get_tModelDetails.

Once you have a list of registered Web service interfaces, you might want to find all businesses with services that implement one or more of those interfaces. You can do this by passing the interface's tModelKey to a find_business call as shown in the next section.

11.11.4 Finding Businesses by Service Interface

A common scenario is when you know a specific service type or interface and want to find a list of businesses that expose services that implement this interface. For example, if you write a client application that invokes the Weather Web service interface, you might want to know which businesses support this interface so that you can choose where to point your client application.

You can do this at design time (possibly using the operator's Web user interface), or you might do it at runtime, possibly letting your application's user pick from a list of service providers (businesses).

To find businesses with services that expose a particular interface, you send a find_business message with a tModelBag containing one tModelKey for each interface you're searching by. Listing 11.12 shows example request and response messages.

Listing 11.12 Example find_business message with response

```
<!-- finding a business that implements an interface -->
<find_business generic="2.0" maxRows="50"
     xmlns="urn:uddi-org:api_v2">
    <tModelBag>
        <tModelKey>
          uuid:42fab02f-300a-4315-aa4a-f97242ff6953
        </tModelKey>
    </tModelBag>
</find_business>

<!-- response -->
<businessList generic="2.0"
    operator="Microsoft Corporation"
    truncated="false" xmlns="urn:uddi-org:api_v2">
    <businessInfos>
```

```
        <businessInfo
            businessKey="1030973b-c87d-4e00-bc16-f3a815f2d883">
            <name xml:lang="en">DevXpert</name>
            <description xml:lang="en">
    XML Web Services Training and Consulting
            </description>
            <serviceInfos>
                <serviceInfo
                serviceKey="7c19ab87-1bc5-4fb6-841b-a4149a802a71"
                businessKey="1030973b-c87d-4e00-bc16-f3a815f2d883">
                    <name xml:lang="en">Weather service</name>
                </serviceInfo>
            </serviceInfos>
        </businessInfo>
        <businessInfo
            businessKey="677cfa1a-2717-4620-be39-6631bb74b6e1">
            <name xml:lang="en">
                LearnXmlWS: The Resource for Web Service Developers
            </name>
            <description xml:lang="en">
    An online community for developers of Web services
    and Web service applications. Read articles, download code,
    and ask questions pertaining to Web services. Created by Yasser
    Shohoud.
            </description>
            <serviceInfos>
                <serviceInfo
                    serviceKey=
                    "d8091de4-0a4a-4061-9979-5d19131aece5"
                    businessKey=
                    "677cfa1a-2717-4620-be39-6631bb74b6e1">
                    <name xml:lang="en">
                        The Weather service
                    </name>
                </serviceInfo>
            </serviceInfos>
        </businessInfo>
    </businessInfos>
</businessList>
```

In Listing 11.12, the tModelKey in the request message references the Weather Service Interface tModel that I registered with UDDI. This message is in effect asking the question "Give me a list of businesses with services that implement the Weather Interface." The response message contains a list of businessInfo structures, one for each business with a service that implements the specified interface. Assuming you have a client application programmed to invoke the Weather Interface, this client can pick any of the returned services and automatically invoke it.

11.11.5 Finding Services by Name

UDDI lets you search for services by name using a find_service message. This message has a businessKey attribute used to indicate the business within which to search for services. If you want to search the entire UDDI registry (not within a specific business), you set businessKey to an empty string as shown in Listing 11.13. You can search for services by name, category, and tModel (businessService structure does not have an identifierBag so you cannot search by identifiers).

Listing 11.13   find_service message and response

```
<!-- finding services by name (globally) -->
<find_service businessKey=""
    generic="2.0" xmlns="urn:uddi-org:api_v2">
   <name>Weather</name>
</find_service>
<!-- response -->
<serviceList generic="2.0"
 operator="Microsoft Corporation"
 truncated="false" xmlns="urn:uddi-org:api_v2">
   <serviceInfos>
      <serviceInfo
          serviceKey="7c19ab87-1bc5-4fb6-841b-a4149a802a71"
          businessKey="">
         <name xml:lang="en">Weather service</name>
      </serviceInfo>
   </serviceInfos>
</serviceList>
```

The example in Listing 11.13 searches for all services whose names begin with Weather. The result is a list of serviceInfo structures that match the search criteria. In this example, the Weather service is returned.

11.11.6   Getting Service Details

Once you have a serviceKey, you can get the service's details including binding information by calling get_serviceDetail and passing it the serviceKey. Listing 11.14 shows an example request and response message for retrieving the Weather service's details.

Listing 11.14   Retrieving service details using get_serviceDetail message

```
<!-- get service detail -->
<get_serviceDetail generic="2.0" xmlns="urn:uddi-org:api_v2">
    <serviceKey>7c19ab87-1bc5-4fb6-841b-a4149a802a71</serviceKey>
</get_serviceDetail>
<!-- get service detail response -->
<serviceDetail generic="2.0" operator="Microsoft Corporation"
                truncated="false" xmlns="urn:uddi-org:api_v2">
    <businessService
            serviceKey="7c19ab87-1bc5-4fb6-841b-a4149a802a71"
            businessKey="1030973b-c87d-4e00-bc16-f3a815f2d883">
        <name xml:lang="en">Weather service</name>
        <description xml:lang="en">
           Current weather service
        </description>
        <bindingTemplates>
            <bindingTemplate
              bindingKey="c2d99cd6-e6b9-4819-96b4-f392ceed3a4e"
              serviceKey="7c19ab87-1bc5-4fb6-841b-a4149a802a71">
                <accessPoint URLType="http">
        http://www.LearnXmlWS.com/services/weatherRetriever.asmx
                </accessPoint>
                <tModelInstanceDetails>
                    <tModelInstanceInfo
                      tModelKey=
                      "uuid:42fab02f-300a-4315-aa4a-
➥f97242ff6953">
                        <instanceDetails>
                            <overviewDoc>
                                <overviewURL>
        http://www.learnxmlws.com/services/weatherretriever.asmx?WSDL
                                </overviewURL>
                            </overviewDoc>
                        </instanceDetails>
                    </tModelInstanceInfo>
                </tModelInstanceDetails>
```

```
            </bindingTemplate>
        </bindingTemplates>
    </businessService>
</serviceDetail>
```

The request message contains one `<serviceKey>` element with the requested service's key. The response message contains zero or more businessService structures that contain a bindingTemplates structure (see the section on UDDI data structures). Each bindingTemplate structure contains a service's access-Point URL, which is useful when you want to invoke that service.

There's a similar scenario where you need to get the details of a specific service binding rather than the entire service. To do this, you'll need to know the binding's key, which you then send in a get_bindingDetail request as in Listing 11.15.

Listing 11.15 Calling get_bindingDetail and the corresponding response message

```
<!-- get binding detail -->
<get_bindingDetail generic="2.0" xmlns="urn:uddi-org:api_v2">
    <bindingKey>c2d99cd6-e6b9-4819-96b4-f392ceed3a4e</bindingKey>
</get_bindingDetail>
<!-- get binding detail response -->
<bindingDetail generic="2.0"
            operator="Microsoft Corporation"
            truncated="false" xmlns="urn:uddi-org:api_v2">
    <bindingTemplate
        bindingKey="c2d99cd6-e6b9-4819-96b4-f392ceed3a4e"
        serviceKey="7c19ab87-1bc5-4fb6-841b-a4149a802a71">
        <accessPoint URLType="http">
        http://www.LearnXmlWS.com/services/weatherRetriever.asmx
        </accessPoint>
        <tModelInstanceDetails>
            <tModelInstanceInfo
            tModelKey="uuid:42fab02f-300a-4315-aa4a-f97242ff6953">
                <instanceDetails>
                    <overviewDoc>
                        <overviewURL>
    http://www.learnxmlws.com/services/weatherretriever.asmx?WSDL
                        </overviewURL>
                    </overviewDoc>
                </instanceDetails>
```

```
            </tModelInstanceInfo>
          </tModelInstanceDetails>
      </bindingTemplate>
  </bindingDetail>
```

The response contains a bindingTemplate structure with the requested binding's information. get_bindingDetail is a more specific query and should be preferred over get_serviceDetail when you want a specific binding and its bindingKey.

11.12 Publishing Your Web Services with UDDI

11.12.1 UDDI Security

To ensure only authorized persons can modify a business's UDDI registration, the publishing API requires authentication. UDDI's authentication model is based on the client application submitting user information in the form of a userID and a credential (password) via the get_authToken API. If successful, the return message contains an authInfo element that has an authentication token represented as a string. All subsequent publishing messages must include this authInfo element with its text content. UDDI uses this authentication token to determine if the client application has been previously authenticated. When the client application is finished with the publishing API, it calls discard_authToken and passes it the authInfo element. This instructs UDDI to invalidate the authentication token, which means the client application must call get_authToken to get a new, valid token before using the publishing API again. To protect the user's credentials and the authentication token from being tampered with, all publishing messages must be sent over HTTPS (SSL). Listing 11.16 shows example get_authToken and discard_authToken and their responses. All examples in this section assume you have already called get_authToken and have an authentication token that you will pass with each API call.

Listing 11.16   calling get_authToken and discard_authToken and the corresponding response messages

```
<!-- get auth token -->
<get_authToken generic="2.0"
  userID="*****" cred="*****" xmlns="urn:uddi-org:api_v2" />
```

```
<!-- auth token response -->
<authToken operator="Microsoft Corporation"
    generic="2.0" xmlns="urn:uddi-org:api_v2">
    <authInfo>1BAAAAAAH!...9vt0GicSyOws5</authInfo>
</authToken>

<!-- discard auth token -->
<discard_authToken generic="2.0" xmlns="urn:uddi-org:api_v2">
    <authInfo>1BAAAAAAH!...9vt0GicSyOws5</authInfo>
</discard_authToken>

<!-- discard auth token response -->
<dispositionReport generic="2.0"
    operator="Microsoft Corporation" xmlns="urn:uddi-org:api_v2">
    <result errno="0">
        <errInfo errCode="E_success" />
    </result>
</dispositionReport>
```

11.12.2 Publishing a Service Interface

If you create a Web service that does not implement an already-registered interface, you'll need to register the Web service's interface before registering the service itself. Registering a Web service interface is a top-level operation, meaning that you can do it as the first operation in the process of registering a service.

As you now know, an interface is registered with UDDI by creating a new tModel. Listing 11.17 shows an example of saving an interface for a service that returns the server time (not very exciting, but useful as a learning aid as you'll see later in this chapter).

Listing 11.17 Calling save_tModel to register a service interface and the corresponding response message

```
<!-- publishing a Web service interface -->
  <save_tModel generic="2.0" xmlns="urn:uddi-org:api_v2">
    <authInfo>*****</authInfo>
    <tModel tModelKey="">
      <name>Server Time Web Service</name>
      <description xml:lang="en">
This interface is to be implemented by services that
return server time. It is used for demonstration and
education purposes
```

```
      </description>
      <overviewDoc>
        <description xml:lang="en">
          WSDL document describing the interface
        </description>
        <overviewURL>
      http://www.learnxmlws.com/services/ifaces/serverTime.wsdl
        </overviewURL>
      </overviewDoc>
      <categoryBag>
        <keyedReference
      tModelKey="uuid:c1acf26d-9672-4404-9d70-39b756e62ab4"
      keyName="Specification for a web service described in WSDL"
      keyValue="wsdlSpec"/>
      </categoryBag>
    </tModel>
  </save_tModel>

  <!-- response to saving a Web service interface -->
  <tModelDetail generic="2.0" operator="Microsoft Corporation"
                truncated="false" xmlns="urn:uddi-org:api_v2">
    <tModel tModelKey=
          "uuid:7f30bebd-35cc-4873-8f91-f53f779d92fd"
            operator="Microsoft Corporation"
            authorizedName=" Yasser Shohoud">
      <name>Server Time Web Service</name>
      <description xml:lang="en">
This interface is to be implemented by services that
return server time. It is used for demonstration and
education purposes
      </description>
      <overviewDoc>
        <description xml:lang="en">
          WSDL document describing the interface
        </description>
        <overviewURL>
     http://www.learnxmlws.com/services/ifaces/serverTime.wsdl
        </overviewURL>
      </overviewDoc>
      <categoryBag>
        <keyedReference
          tModelKey="uuid:c1acf26d-9672-4404-9d70-39b756e62ab4"
          keyName=
            "Specification for a web service described in WSDL"
```

```
            keyValue="wsdlSpec"/>
      </categoryBag>
    </tModel>
  </tModelDetail>
```

The request message includes the tModel name, description, overviewDoc, and categoryBag. The categoryBag contains one category that references the wsdl-Spec tModel as required to properly classify Web service interfaces.

The response message contains a tModel structure for the newly registered tModel. The returned tModelKey is the unique identifier automatically assigned to the new tModel. You'll use this tModeKey later when registering services that implement this interface.

11.12.3   Publishing a Business

To publish a business, you send a save_business message with a businessEntity structure. This structure can be a complete businessEntity structure including one or more businessService structures that may, in turn, include bindingTemplate structures. In essence, you can publish a business along with all the services it implements in one API call. If you don't specify a value for businessKey, the business is saved as a new one. If a businessKey is specified, the information you send replaces the business with the specified key, assuming you have permission to do so. Listing 11.18 shows an example save_business message that saves only the business information without any services.

Listing 11.18   An example save_business message and the corresponding response

```
<save_business generic="2.0" xmlns="urn:uddi-org:api_v2">
    <authInfo>1BAAAAAAAH!...</authInfo>
    <businessEntity businessKey="">
        <discoveryURLs>
            <discoveryURL useType="Home Page">
        http://www.devxpert.com/training/
            </discoveryURL>
        </discoveryURLs>
        <name xml:lang="en">DevXpert</name>
        <description xml:lang="en">
          XML Web Services Training and Consulting
        </description>
```

```
                <contacts>
                    <contact useType="Business">
                        <personName>Yasser Shohoud</personName>
                        <phone>703-626-6822</phone>
                    </contact>
                    <contact useType="Technical">
                        <personName>Yasser Shohoud</personName>
                        <phone>703-626-6822</phone>
                    </contact>
                </contacts>
        </businessEntity>
</save_business>
<!-- response from save_business -->
<businessDetail generic="2.0"
                operator="Microsoft Corporation"
                truncated="false" xmlns="urn:uddi-org:api_v2">
    <businessEntity
        businessKey="1030973b-c87d-4e00-bc16-f3a815f2d883"
        operator="Microsoft Corporation"
        authorizedName=" Yasser Shohoud : 86">
        <discoveryURLs>
            <discoveryURL useType="Home Page">
             http://www.devxpert.com/training/
            </discoveryURL>
            <discoveryURL useType="businessEntity">
http://uddi.rte.microsoft.com/discovery?_
businessKey=4dedd794-4582-4aea-a156-a4c0b0e5bac4
            </discoveryURL>
        </discoveryURLs>
        <name xml:lang="en">DevXpert</name>
        <description xml:lang="en">
          XML Web Services Training and Consulting
         </description>
        <contacts>
            <contact useType="Business">
                <personName>Yasser Shohoud</personName>
                <phone>703-626-6822</phone>
            </contact>
            <contact useType="Technical">
                <personName>Yasser Shohoud</personName>
                <phone>703-626-6822</phone>
```

```
            </contact>
          </contacts>
      </businessEntity>
  </businessDetail>
```

The request message includes a discovery URL that points to a Web page. discoverURL is an optional element as discussed in the data structures section. It is specified here only to illustrate its usage. The request message also contains two contact structures that specify business and technical contacts.

The response message echoes back the business information with two additional pieces of information. The first is the business as a newly assigned businessKey. This key is important for query APIs that operate within the scope of a business—for example, find_service within a business. It is also important for updating the business content—for example, adding services to the business. The second piece of information is the new discoveryURL automatically assigned by the operator. Issuing an HTTP GET request with this URL (navigating to this URL with a browser), will return the businessEntity information.

11.12.4 Publishing a Service

If you want to add services to a business or update published services, you issue a save_service API passing it a businessService structure. As shown in Listing 11.19, the request message contains a complete businessService structure with the businessKey of LearnXmlWS. It also contains a tModelInstanceInfo that references the Server Time Web service interface that I registered earlier by using the interface's tModelKey. The request message includes two URLs: accessPoint is the service's end point URL and overviewDoc points to the service's WSDL document.

Listing 11.19 Saving a service using save_service and the response message

```
<!-- saving a service to an existing business -->
<save_service generic="2.0" xmlns="urn:uddi-org:api_v2">
    <authInfo>1BAAAAAA...</authInfo>
    <businessService
          businessKey="677cfa1a-2717-4620-be39-6631bb74b6e1"
          serviceKey="">
        <name xml:lang="en">Time service</name>
```

```
            <description xml:lang="en">
Server time service
            </description>
            <bindingTemplates>
                <bindingTemplate bindingKey="">
                    <accessPoint URLType="http">
http://www.learnxmlws.com/services/serverTime.asmx
                    </accessPoint>
                    <tModelInstanceDetails>
                        <tModelInstanceInfo
                            tModelKey=
                            "uuid:7f30bebd-35cc-4873-8f91-f53f779d92fd">
                            <instanceDetails>
                                <overviewDoc>
                                    <overviewURL>
http://www.learnxmlws.com/services/serverTime.asmx?WSDL
                                    </overviewURL>
                                </overviewDoc>
                            </instanceDetails>
                        </tModelInstanceInfo>
                    </tModelInstanceDetails>
                </bindingTemplate>
            </bindingTemplates>
        </businessService>
</save_service>


<!-- response -->
<serviceDetail generic="2.0" operator="Microsoft Corporation"
                truncated="false" xmlns="urn:uddi-org:api_v2">
    <businessService
        serviceKey="8267329b-535e-4366-9059-d5c3124460cd"
        businessKey="677cfa1a-2717-4620-be39-6631bb74b6e1">
        <name xml:lang="en">Time service</name>
        <description
            xml:lang="en">Server time service</description>
        <bindingTemplates>
            <bindingTemplate
                bindingKey="0f694b511-5852-451c-8b03-5b91330dff83"
                serviceKey="8267329b-535e-4366-9059-d5c3124460cd">
                <accessPoint URLType="http">
                http://www.learnxmlws.com/services/serverTime.asmx
                </accessPoint>
                <tModelInstanceDetails>
```

```
                    <tModelInstanceInfo
                        tModelKey=
                        "uuid:7f30bebd-35cc-4873-8f91-f53f779d92fd">
                            <instanceDetails>
                                <overviewDoc>
                                    <overviewURL>
            http://www.learnxmlws.com/services/serverTime.asmx?WSDL
                                    </overviewURL>
                                </overviewDoc>
                            </instanceDetails>
                        </tModelInstanceInfo>
                    </tModelInstanceDetails>
                </bindingTemplate>
            </bindingTemplates>
        </businessService>
    </serviceDetail>
```

The returned businessService structure contains newly assigned serviceKey and bindingKey. Later, other applications can use these keys with get_serviceDetails and get_bindingDetails to get service and binding details, respectively. To update this service, you send another save_service message with the new information and the serviceKey to indicate you want to update an existing service versus create a new one.

11.12.5 Specifying Business Relations

To associate two businesses, you send a set_publisherAssertions message with the keys of the two businesses that you want to associate and a keyedReference indicating the relation type (see the section on publisherAssertion data structure). The example in Listing 11.20 sends a message to associate the business entities DevXpert and LearnXmlWS, specifying parent-child as the relation type.

Listing 11.20   Relating business entities with set_publisherAssertions and the corresponding response message

```
<!-- set publisher assertions -->
<set_publisherAssertions generic="2.0"
                        xmlns="urn:uddi-org:api_v2">
    <authInfo>1BAAAAAAAH!...</authInfo>
    <publisherAssertion>
```

```
        <fromKey>1030973b-c87d-4e00-bc16-f3a815f2d883</fromKey>
        <toKey>677cfa1a-2717-4620-be39-6631bb74b6e1</toKey>
        <keyedReference
            tModelKey="uuid:807a2c6a-ee22-470d-adc7-e0424a337c03"
            keyName="BusinessRelation"
            keyValue="parent-child" />
    </publisherAssertion>
</set_publisherAssertions>
<!-- set publisher assertions response -->
<publisherAssertions
        operator="Microsoft Corporation"
        authorizedName=" Yasser Shohoud"
        generic="2.0" xmlns="urn:uddi-org:api_v2">
    <publisherAssertion>
        <fromKey>1030973b-c87d-4e00-bc16-f3a815f2d883</fromKey>
        <toKey>677cfa1a-2717-4620-be39-6631bb74b6e1</toKey>
        <keyedReference
            tModelKey="uuid:807a2c6a-ee22-470d-adc7-e0424a337c03"
            keyName="BusinessRelation"
            keyValue="parent-child" />
    </publisherAssertion>
</publisherAssertions>
```

The response message returns a list of all assertions made by the publisher who's identified by authInfo. Since the publisher in this case is the authorized owner of both businesses, one set_publisherAssertions message is sufficient to establish the relation. Otherwise, if the two businesses are managed by different publishers, each publisher must submit a set_publisherAssertions message with the same content for the relation to be established.

11.13   An Inquiry Example

11.13.1   Choosing Services That Implement a Specific Interface

Here's a sample application that searches for services implementing a specific interface and lets the user choose which service to invoke. This application uses the UDDI APIs directly by forming and sending SOAP messages.

The application is Web-based using ASP.NET. You can access this application on your server using the URL http://VBWSServer/VBWSBook/Chapter11/WeatherChooser.aspx. The first page, weatherchooser.aspx, sends a find_business message with a tModelBag that contains the tModelKey of the Weather service interface. To form the message, the application uses an XmlTextWriter and a StringWriter as shown in Listing 11.21. Then it uses an instance of UDDIAPI to call SendInquiryMsg, passing it the find_business message. UDDIAPI is a class I wrote to send messages to the UDDI registry. You pass it the message, it wraps it in a SOAP envelope, and then uses HttpWebRequest and HttpWebResponse to send and receive the HTTP POST request. Then it returns the response as a string.

Listing 11.21 Finding services that implement the weather interface (VBWSBook\Chapter11\WeatherChooser.aspx.vb)

```
Private Sub lnkView_Click(ByVal sender As System.Object, _
        ByVal e As System.EventArgs) Handles lnkView.Click
    Dim sw As New StringWriter()
    Dim xw As New XmlTextWriter(sw)
    'form the message
    xw.WriteStartElement("find_business", UDDI_NS)
    xw.WriteAttributeString("generic", "2.0")
    xw.WriteStartElement("tModelBag")
    xw.WriteElementString("tModelKey", KEY)
    xw.WriteEndElement()
    xw.WriteEndElement()
    reqMsg.Text = sw.ToString()

    Dim listsw As New StringWriter()
    Dim uddi As New UDDIAPI()
    Dim resp As String
    'send the message
    resp = uddi.SendInquiryMsg(sw.ToString(), False)
    respMsg.Text = resp

    'parse the response using the DOM
    Dim doc As New XmlDocument()
    Dim nl As XmlNodeList
    Dim bus As XmlNode
    Dim nsmgr As XmlNamespaceManager = _
        New XmlNamespaceManager(doc.NameTable)
    nsmgr.AddNamespace("u", UDDI_NS)
    doc.LoadXml(resp)
    nl = doc.SelectNodes("//u:businessInfo", nsmgr)
    If nl.Count = 0 Then
```

```
                            'no businesses found
                   Else
                       'display the list of businesses
                       For Each bus In nl
                    'note: the following line contained HTML
                    'that was too long
                    'to print, please see the code
                    'file weatherchooser.aspx.vb
                    listsw.WriteLine( _
                    "see code file for HTML that goes here…" _
                    bus.SelectSingleNode("u:name", nsmgr).InnerText, _
                    bus.SelectSingleNode( _
                    "u:serviceInfos/u:serviceInfo/u:name", _
                    nsmgr).InnerText, _
                    bus.SelectSingleNode( _
                    "u:serviceInfos/u:serviceInfo/@serviceKey", _
                    nsmgr).InnerText)
                       Next
                   End If
                   serviceList.InnerHtml = listsw.ToString()
             End Sub
```

To parse the returned list of businesses, the code in Listing 11.21 loads this string into a DOM document and uses XPath queries with SelectNodes and SelectSingleNode to find the business name, service name, and service key. The service key is particularly important as it is passed to the next page when the user chooses a service to invoke. The parsed information is formatted with HTML and added to the output stream that gets sent to the browser. Each service listed has a hyperlink that points to weather.aspx with the service id in the query string, for example:

```
http://VBWSServer/VBWSBook/Chapter11/Weather.aspx?id=7c19ab87-
➥1bc5-4fb6-841b-a4149a802a71
```

As an added bonus, I display the find_business message and its response at the bottom of the page so you can see what message was sent to UDDI and the response returned. Figure 11.16 shows an example weatherchooser.aspx page.

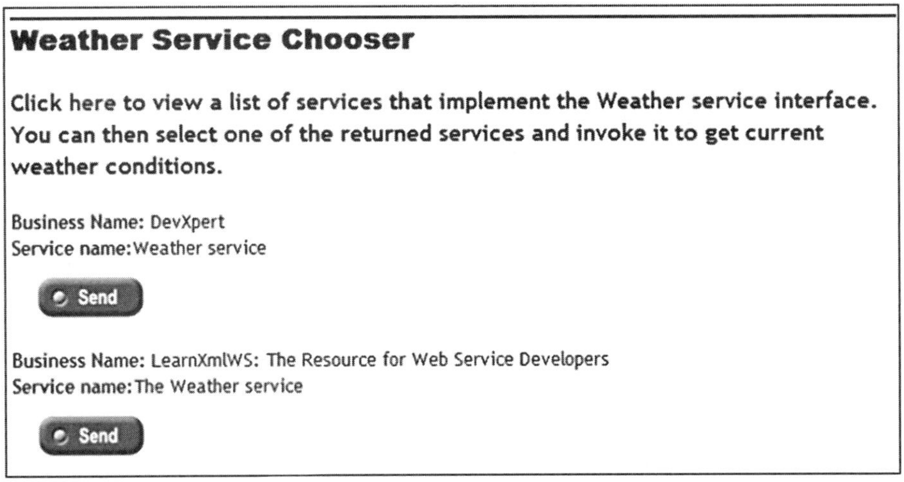

Weather Service Chooser

Click here to view a list of services that implement the Weather service interface.
You can then select one of the returned services and invoke it to get current
weather conditions.

Business Name: DevXpert
Service name: Weather service

Business Name: LearnXmlWS: The Resource for Web Service Developers
Service name: The Weather service

**Figure 11.16   The WeatherChooser page lists services that implement the
weather interface**

When the user clicks on one of the services, weather.aspx is loaded, which
takes the selected service key and sends a get_serviceDetail message to get
the service's end point URL as shown in Listing 11.22. It uses the same techniques to send the message: XmlTextWriter with a StringWriter to form the message and an instance of UDDIAPI to send the message. It then uses the DOM to
retrieve the accessPoint element's text out of the returned response document
and saves this URL in a hidden form field called Info.

**Listing 11.22   Getting the selected service's URL
(VBWSBook\Chapter11\Weather.aspx.vb)**

```
Private Function GetServiceUrl(ByVal serviceKey As String) As
➡String
        Dim sw As New StringWriter()
        Dim xw As New XmlTextWriter(sw)
        xw.WriteStartElement("get_serviceDetail", UDDI_NS)
        xw.WriteAttributeString("generic", "2.0")
        xw.WriteElementString("serviceKey", serviceKey)
        xw.WriteEndElement()
        reqMsg.Text = sw.ToString()

        Dim listsw As New StringWriter()
        Dim uddi As New UDDIAPI()
```

```
                Dim resp As String
                resp = uddi.SendInquiryMsg(sw.ToString(), False)
                respMsg.Text = resp.ToString()
                Dim doc As New XmlDocument()
                Dim service As XmlNode
                Dim nsmgr As XmlNamespaceManager = New _
                    XmlNamespaceManager(doc.NameTable)
                nsmgr.AddNamespace("u", UDDI_NS)
                doc.LoadXml(resp)
                service = doc.SelectSingleNode("//u:accessPoint", nsmgr)
                If Not (service Is Nothing) Then
                    Return service.InnerText
                Else
                    Info.InnerHtml = "<b>No service URL returned</b>"
                    Return ""
                End If
        End Function
```

When the user enters a zip code and clicks Send, the code in Listing 11.23 is invoked. The code first does some validation to ensure a numeric zip code was passed, then instantiates a WeatherService proxy. For convenience, I created this proxy by adding a reference to the Weather service, then I took out the service's URL from the proxy's constructor so the proxy acts as an interface proxy. To invoke the Web service, you must first set the proxy's Url property to the Url that was retrieved earlier from UDDI and stored in the hidden form field.

The service returns an instance of CurrentWeather that contains information like temperature, humidity, and sky conditions. This information is then displayed in various HTML elements such as labels and divs with the result as shown in Figure 11.18.

Listing 11.23 Invoking the selected weather service (VBWSBook\Chapter11\Weather.aspx.vb)

```
    Private Sub imgSend_Click(ByVal sender As System.Object, _
       ByVal e As System.Web.UI.ImageClickEventArgs) _
       Handles imgSend.Click
            If txtZipCode.Text.Length = 0 _
               OrElse Not IsNumeric(txtZipCode.Text) Then
                Info.InnerHtml = _
                   "<b>Please enter a valid zip code</b>"
                Exit Sub
```

```
          End If
          Dim ws As New WeatherService.WeatherRetriever()
          'set the url to the one retrieved earlier from UDDI
          ws.Url = lblServiceUrl.Text
         'invoke the Web service
          Dim cw As WeatherService.CurrentWeather = _
                  ws.GetWeather(txtZipCode.Text)
          lblTemp.Text = cw.CurrentTemp.ToString()
          lblConditions.Text = cw.Conditions
         'display the returned information as html
          Dim sw As New StringWriter()
          sw.WriteLine("<b>Barometer</b> " + _
            cw.Barometer.ToString() + _
             " and " + cw.BarometerDirection)
          sw.WriteLine("<br><b>Humidity</b> at " + _
            (cw.Humidity * 100).ToString() + "%")
          sw.WriteLine("<br><b>Last updated</b> on " + _
                      cw.LastUpdated)
          Info.InnerHtml = sw.ToString()
          imgConditions.ImageUrl = cw.IconUrl
     End Sub
```

Current Weather Conditions

Enter a zip code below and click on Send to get current weather
conditions using the service you selected.

Zip code 20171   ⊙ Send

30.9 clear

Barometer 30.38 and Falling
Humidity at 88%
Last updated on Dec 09, 2001 - 11:51 PM EST

Figure 11.17   Weather information returned from a weather service

This example application shows you how to get a list of businesses that implements a specific interface and how to find a selected service's end point URL and proceed to invoke this service. You can build this model into your application to dynamically bind to services at runtime, either based on user selection or some other selection criteria.

11.14   Using the UDDI SDK

The previous two examples showed you how to invoke UDDI APIs directly by sending and receiving SOAP messages. This is great for learning but once you've learned the API you'll want a library that handles all the details of SOAP messaging and lets you focus on the UDDI API itself. Microsoft's UDDI SDK provides such a library. The SDK comes in two flavors: A .NET class library and a COM component.

Both SDKs provide a nice object model that wraps the underlying UDDI APIs and data structures. The purpose of these objects is to free you from directly manipulating SOAP messages and XML documents. However, they are not intended to absolve you from knowing the UDDI API and data structures. Therefore, the object model is a close mapping of UDDI APIs into objects.

The .NET SDK breaks out its functionality into seven namespaces shown in Figure 11.18. Table 11.1 shows what's in each namespace.

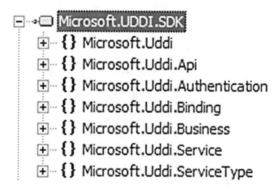

Figure 11.18   The UDDI SDK contains seven namespaces

Table 11.1   The UDDI SDK Namespaces and What They Contain

Namespace	Contains
Microsoft.Uddi	Classes that represent the UDDI APIs, (for example, FindBusiness)
Microsoft.Uddi.Api	Classes and types supporting the UDDI APIs, (for example, FindQualifier and KeyedReference)
Microsoft.Uddi.Authentication	Classes that represent GetAuthToken and DiscardAuthToken APIs and the AuthToken itself
Microsoft.Uddi.Binding	Classes related to binding data structures
Microsoft.Uddi.Business	Classes related to businessEntity data structures
Microsoft.Uddi.Service	Classes related to businessService data structures
Microsoft.Uddi.ServiceType	Classes related to tModel data structures

There is a set of core steps you must follow to invoke UDDI APIs via the SDK:

1. Prepare the data structures you want to send. Instantiate the corresponding objects and set their properties.
2. Create an instance of the class that corresponds to the API, for example, the FindBusiness class, and set its properties.
3. Call the Send method on the API class. This sends the SOAP message and receives the response.
4. Retrieve returned data using the return value from the Send method.

To show you an example of this, I implemented the UDDI invocation pattern using the SDK as shown in Listing 11.24.

Listing 11.24   The invocation pattern implemented with the UDDI SDK. Only GetCurrentUrl is different from the previous implementation (VBWSClientCode\Chapter11\TimeWSClient_SDK\Uddi.vb)

```
Public Shared Function GetCurrentUrl( _
   ByVal bindingKey As String) As String
   Try
       Microsoft.Uddi.Inquire.Url = UDDI_INQUIRE_URL
       Dim getBindingDet As New _
           Microsoft.Uddi.GetBindingDetail()
       getBindingDet.BindingKeys.Add(bindingKey)
```

```
        Dim bd As Microsoft.Uddi.BindingDetail = _
                getBindingDet.Send()
        If Not (bd Is Nothing) AndAlso _
            bd.BindingTemplates.Count > 0 Then
            Return bd.BindingTemplates.Item(0).AccessPoint.Text
        Else
            Return ""
        End If
    Catch ex As Exception
        Debug.WriteLine(ex.Message)
    End Try
End Function
```

GetCurrentUrl uses the SDK to compose the get_bindingDetail SOAP message and get the response. First, I set Microsoft.Uddi.Inquire.Url to the UDDI inquiry URL. This tells the SDK where to send all inquiry messages. If you were publishing to UDDI, you would set Microsoft.Uddi.Publish.Url instead.

The API I want to call is get_bindingDetail, so I instantiate an object from the Microsoft.Uddi.GetBindingDetail class. Next, I add a key to its BindingKeys collection using the bindingKey parameter that was passed into this method. Now the API call is ready to be sent. I call Send and capture the return value in a new variable called bd of type Microsoft.Uddi.BindingDetail (recall that the get_bindingDetail API returns a bindingDetail data structure. The BindingDetail class corresponds to this data structure).

If this return value is not nothing, and if it contains at least one BindingTemplate, I go ahead and get the AccessPoint out of the first BindingTemplate, then return the AccessPoint's Text property that is the URL I'm looking for. Otherwise, I just return an empty string.

Looking at the code in Listing 11.24, you realize how much work the SDK saves you by handling all SOAP messaging. You also realize that the SDK object model is almost a one-to-one mapping to the UDDI APIs and data structures. So once you learn the UDDI APIs and data structures, using the SDK will be a matter of adding a reference to the SDK .dll and programming against its objects.

11.15   Private UDDI Implementations

As organizations rely on Web services to integrate business applications, there will be a need to maintain a catalog of all Web services available within an organization and to search this catalog both at design and runtime. Instead of reinventing the wheel, organizations can use private implementations of UDDI to act as this internal catalog of Web services. This provides a standards-based catalog that allows different departments or divisions to use different development tools while still interoperating with the same catalog. In addition, because the private catalog exposes the same API as the public UDDI registry, whatever code you write to interact with the private catalog can be easily changed to interact with the public UDDI if needed.

11.15.1   Windows .NET Server

Windows .NET Server has a built-in version of UDDI named UDDI Services for Windows .NET. This is an implementation of the V1 and V2 UDDI specifications built on the .NET Framework. This implementation uses SQL Server 2000 or MSDE as the back end data store and integrates with Active Directory for authentication and authorization.

You interact with UDDI Services via a Web-based user interface similar to the one at http://uddi.rte.microsoft.com. In addition to searching and publishing, this user interface lets you administer your UDDI installation.

From the administration section, you can import existing categorization schemes contained in an xml file. This is useful if you want to copy categorization schemes from one private registry to another or if you want to import new categorization schemes from the public UDDI registry to your private one.

11.16   Summary

UDDI provides a catalog of Web service interfaces and implementations that can be searched and manipulated via SOAP messages. Using UDDI, you can create Web service clients that dynamically locate Web services at runtime and implement many scenarios that require a centralized Web services catalog. While UDDI is not required for building or consuming Web services, there are many scenarios where applications can benefit from using UDDI.

Within an organization, private UDDI implementations can make it easy to catalog and find Web services for application integration purposes. Because the UDDI API is based on SOAP messages, departments within an organization can choose different development tools while still communicating with the private UDDI implementation.

11.17 Resources

UDDI's home page: http://www.uddi.org.

Editors: B. McKee, D. Ehnebuske, D. Rogers. Contributors: T. Bellwood, D. Bryan, J. Burinda, T. Clement, V. Draluk, B. Eisenberg, T. Glover, A. Harris, A. Hately, D. Ho, Y-L. Husband, A. Karp, K. Kibakura, C. Kurt, J. Lancelle, S. Lee, S. MacRoibeaird, A. Thomas Manes, J. Munter, T. Nordan, C. Reeves, J. Rodriguez, C. Tomlinson, C. Tosun, C. von Riegen, P. Yendluri, UDDI V2.0 API Specification: http://www.uddi.org/pubs/ProgrammersAPI-V2.00-Open-20010608.pdf, © 2001 by Accenture, Ariba Inc., Commerce One Inc., Compaq Computer Corporation, Equifax Inc., Fujitsu Limited, Hewlett-Packard Company, i2 Technologies Inc., Intel Corporation, International Business Machines Corporation, Microsoft Corporation, Oracle Corporation, SAP AG, Sun Microsystems, Inc., and VeriSign Inc. All rights reserved.

Editors: B. McKee, D. Ehnebuske, D. Rogers. Contributors: T. Bellwood, D. Bryan, J. Burinda, T. Clement, V. Draluk, B. Eisenberg, T. Glover, A. Harris, A. Hately, D. Ho, Y-L. Husband, A. Karp, K. Kibakura, C. Kurt, J. Lancelle, S. Lee, S. MacRoibeaird, A. Thomas Manes, J. Munter, T. Nordan, C. Reeves, J. Rodriguez, C. Tomlinson, C. Tosun, C. von Riegen, P. Yendluri, UDDI V2.0 Data Structure Reference: http://www.uddi.org/pubs/DataStructure-V2.00-Open-20010608.pdf, © 2001 by Accenture, Ariba Inc., Commerce One Inc., Compaq Computer Corporation, Equifax Inc., Fujitsu Limited, Hewlett-Packard Company, i2 Technologies Inc., Intel Corporation, International Business Machines Corporation, Microsoft Corporation, Oracle Corporation, SAP AG, Sun Microsystems, Inc., and VeriSign Inc. All rights reserved.

F. Curbera, D. Ehnebuske, D. Rogers, Using WSDL in a UDDI Registry: V1.05 http://www.uddi.org/pubs/wsdlbestpractices-V1.05-Open-20010625.pdf,

Y. Shohoud, UDDI API test page: www.LearnXmlws.com/uddi/UDDIAPIs.aspx.

UDDI Search page: http://www.LearnXmlws.com/wssearch.

UDDI Technical mailing list: http://groups.yahoo.com/group/uddi-technical.

UDDI programming news group:

news://msnews.microsoft.com/microsoft.public.uddi.programming.

UDDI specifications news group:

news://msnews.microsoft.com/microsoft.public.uddi.specification.

General UDDI questions news group:

news://msnews.microsoft.com/microsoft.public.uddi.general.

Chapter 12

Other SOAP Toolkits

Just because I don't care doesn't mean I don't understand.
—Homer Simpson

So far this book has focused on showing you how to build and invoke Web services with VB .NET and VB 6. Being platform-independent, Web services are all about interoperability (interop for short). In fact, the true value of Web services is enabling easy integration of heterogeneous applications. Therefore, real-world Web services will likely have a variety of clients written in various languages. This chapter has two objectives that will prepare you for real-world Web services:

- Familiarize you with other SOAP toolkits that you might encounter in client or service implementations
- Point out some potential interop problems and suggest workarounds

It's not possible to cover every SOAP implementation (there are 81 by some counts), so I've chosen three diverse, popular implementations with broad platform coverage. They are: PocketSOAP for the PocketPC, Apache SOAP for Java, and DHTML Web Service Behavior for Internet Explorer clients.

12.1 Defining Interop

Is Web Services interop possible? Absolutely. Is it easy? It depends on how you define interop. The term interop is sufficiently vague that it warrants a definition. I define interop as:

A client and service written in different languages successfully communicating data.

If you think this definition is too simple, maybe I don't expect as much as you do. My view is that this definition is the minimum acceptable level of interop; anything beyond this is nice to have but not required. But there are other views on the meaning of interop.

Most developers expect interop between their Web service development tools. As a VB developer, you might expect that VS .NET should be able to add a Web reference to a Java service and auto-generate the right proxy code. You want to call this proxy and not worry about what's happening under the covers. If VS .NET fails to do this for a specific service, you might think that VB .NET cannot interoperate with that service. But it's really the tools that are failing here, not the underlying Web service technologies. Maybe you can edit the Java service's WSDL and fix it so that VS .NET can read it. Or you can read the WSDL and write the proxy code yourself. The point is, if you understand the root of the problem you can solve it and make interop happen.

I cannot stress this enough: If you want to master Web services development, especially interop, you must clearly distinguish between Web service development tools (for example, VS .NET) and Web service technologies (for example, SOAP and WSDL). If you don't, you'll be bound by the capabilities of the tools you use, which are often lagging those of the underlying technologies.

So why are there interop problems? After all, don't we have specifications that define everything needed to interoperate? Not exactly. In their effort to be simple, and sometimes by mistake, specifications leave out important implementation details or make contradicting recommendations. The result is possible and probable interop problems between different implementations of the same specification. Here's an overview of some interop problems you might encounter.

12.2   Interop Problems

In his MSDN article,[1] Keith Ballinger outlined common Web services interop problems broken down by the layer at which they occur. In this section, I will describe various interop issues I encountered while building Web service applica-

---

[1] See Resources at end of this chapter.

tions. Following Ballinger's lead, I'll categorize these issues by the layer at which they occur.

12.2.1 HTTP

Although HTTP is a relatively simple protocol, there are specific requirements for using HTTP to invoke a Web service. Some service tools are more stringent than others about these requirements and some client tools are better than others at meeting them.

For example, an HTTP SOAP request should contain a Content-Type header with the character set used:

```
Content-Type: text/xml; charset=utf-8
```

Some clients do not send the character set as part of Content-Type and many Web service implementations don't know how to handle such requests.

Another required HTTP header is the SOAPAction that is a quote-enclosed string, for example, "urn:myservice-action." Most Web service implementations require that incoming requests contain the appropriate SOAPAction header for the requested operation. Some implementations let you turn this off, for example, .NET lets you do this with the RoutingStyle attribute, which eliminates dependency on the value of SOAPAction (although the SOAPAction header itself is still required), as explained in Chapter 6. A client that doesn't send this SOAPAction header or sends an incorrect value is likely to fail in invoking the required operation. Interestingly, some Web service tools do not take this into account when auto-generating a client proxy, so you have to edit the generated proxy manually to send the correct SOAPAction. We'll see an example of this later in this chapter.

Finally, some services keep track of client sessions through the use of HTTP cookies. This works the same as a Web site with sessions: The service sends an HTTP cookie to the client and the client is expected to send this cookie back with subsequent requests to the service. If a particular service implementation relies on HTTP cookies, there might be interop issues with clients that do not support this feature.

12.2.2 WSDL

WSDL is a fairly complex specification with many possible scenarios and combinations that leads to highly potential interop problems. For example, some client toolkits do not support non-SOAP bindings in WSDL and fail to read WSDL documents with such bindings. This is a problem, particularly for .NET Web services which, by default, have HTTP GET and POST bindings in their WSDL.

Some service toolkits generate WSDL that is simply incorrect—the most common problem being lack of qualified names in references to WSDL items such as binding and operation names.

Some service tools generate WSDL documents broken out into interface and implementation with `<import>` to import the interface part into the implementation part. Meanwhile, some client tools don't support the WSDL `<import>` element making them unable to read such WSDL documents.

What does all this mean? It depends on the tool you're using. As mentioned in Chapter 4, some Web service client tools use WSDL at design time to generate proxy code and others use WSDL at runtime to dynamically generate a proxy. For example, .NET uses WSDL to generate a proxy for you. If for some reason the WSDL is bad (for example, missing namespace prefixes), you can write the proxy code yourself and proceed to call the service. In this case, the incorrect WSDL is a design-time issue and has no effect on runtime operation. If, however, you are using the SOAP Toolkit's high level API you need a correct WSDL document at runtime. In this scenario, the WSDL document is an issue at runtime rather than design time. To fix this, you can either make a local copy of the WSDL or you can switch to using the low level API, which does not use a WSDL document at runtime.

12.2.3 SOAP

The SOAP message itself is the source of most interop problems and is the focus of current interop efforts. As simple as SOAP is, it specifies four different message formats and an optional encoding style. To date, most interop efforts have focused on RPC/section 5 encoded messages. Within this message format, most interop issues center on Section 5 encoding and that's where most of the interop efforts have focused.

However, document/literal messages are easier to interoperate because, by definition, the contents of the SOAP Body are application-specific so there are fewer things the tools have to agree on. Today, many popular SOAP tools support document/literal messages in one way or another (for example, a low level API) so you should not run into many problems at the SOAP level when using document/literal messages. However, typically you have to do a lot more work to use document/literal compared to RPC/encoded. But doing more work is not an issue if document/literal becomes your only choice for interoperability in a specific scenario.

In addition to Section 5 encoding, one of the SOAP-related interop issues is support for SOAP headers: Some SOAP implementations simply do not support SOAP headers and others do not support header attributes, such as mustUnderstand and actor. Services that rely on these SOAP features should ensure that target client tools provide necessary support.

The good news is that development tools are getting better at interop and many of them already interoperate quite well. In addition, many tools provide a low level API where you take full control over request/response messages to do whatever is necessary for interop. But it wasn't easy getting where we are today; it took much effort from SOAP toolkit builders to enable today's level of interop. And things are improving with each new toolkit release.

12.3 Interop Efforts

Over the past few years there have been numerous Web services interop efforts. The most successful organized effort was started by Tony Hong of xmethods.net, who created an online forum for builders of SOAP toolkits to test interop and communicate and resolve issues. This forum is known as the SOAP-Builders email list at http://groups.yahoo.com/group/soapbuilders/.[2] The actual interop testing is being done in rounds with each round progressively

---

[2]The SOAPBuilders list is intended for developers building SOAP implementations (for example, people building the SOAP Toolkit) to hammer out interoperability issues. It is not intended for developers building Web services. There are other lists dedicated to helping developers building Web services, such as aspngwebservices at aspfriends.com and the SOAP list at discuss.develop.com.

covering more sophisticated features and specifications than the preceding round. Just for your information, here's how interop testing works:

- A list of Web service operations is specified. The operations are chosen to satisfy certain interop scenarios or requirements. For example, echo-String is a simple operation that receives a string and echoes it back. This simple operation uncovers basic interop issues, that is, whether or not the client and service can communicate. echoStringArray is a similar operation that echoes a string array that uncovers basic array interop issues. This list of operations along with some additional information (SOAPAction, encoding style, and so forth) becomes the proposed set of interop tests. For example, round 1 proposal is at http://www.xmethods.net/soapbuilders/proposal.html and round 2-A proposal is at http://www.whitemesa.com/interop/proposal2.html.

- A WSDL document is created to describe the tests. This WSDL document acts as a test specification; however, the tools being tested may not be WSDL aware. Both round one and two tests focus on SOAP interop, not WSDL.

- Builders of SOAP implementations create Web services (using their own SOAP implementations) that implement the test specifications. For example, the SOAP Toolkit's implementation of round two tests is at http://mssoapinterop.org/stkV3/Interop.wsdl.

- Builders of SOAP implementations create clients (using their SOAP implementations) that invoke other Web services implementing the test suite. Invocation results (success or failure and error message) are usually documented on the Web. For example, test results for .NET Web service clients are at http://mssoapinterop.org/results/resaspx.xml.

- The client and service builders work together on the SOAPBuilders list to resolve any interop issues.

Once a test specification is agreed upon, steps three through five are ongoing as SOAP tool builders update their tools and fix interop issues. When the tools achieve sufficient interop success within a test spec (as determined by members of SOAPBuilders), the group moves on to another round of interop testing.

Thanks to these efforts, we now have a decent level of interop among diverse tools. Let's examine some of the more popular tools and see examples of interop in action.

12.4 PocketSOAP Clients

I've attended several talks and read numerous articles that claim to show you how to "develop applications for mobile devices." In fact, they show you how to build *Web* applications accessible to mobile devices. That's not the same thing. A mobile application resides and executes on the mobile device and leverages the capabilities of that device. Many such applications will also need to retrieve or send information from/to the Web. This is an area where Web services really shine: You expose your existing or new applications via Web services and you program mobile clients to access those Web services. That way, your back-end applications are device independent: Any device can communicate with those Web services given a SOAP stack for that device.

PocketSOAP is the de facto standard SOAP implementation for the PocketPC that offers pretty good SOAP support, which interoperates with most popular SOAP implementations including the SOAP toolkit and .NET Web services. PocketSOAP exposes a COM-based API that makes it easy to program in Embedded Visual Basic or Embedded Visual C++. In addition, PocketSOAP comes in a Win32 implementation that you can use from any COM-aware language (including script languages) on Win32 platforms (even Windows 95). Both the Win32 and PocketPC implementations expose nearly identical object models making it easy to learn and program PocketSOAP using VB 6, then moving your skills and code to Embedded VB.

Figure 12.1 shows the essential PocketSOAP classes. I left out classes and interfaces that have to do with custom serialization. I will not explain how to do custom serialization with PocketSOAP, but note: PocketSOAP supports a serialization model very similar to the SOAP Toolkit. You can create a custom serializer to serialize application-specific objects by implementing ISoapSerializer.

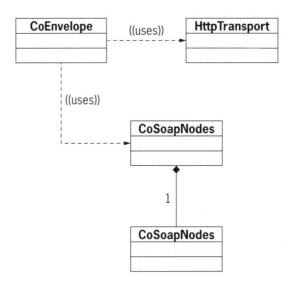

Figure 12.1   The essential PocketSOAP classes

To send a SOAP request, you begin by creating a CoEnvelope object. CoEnvelope exposes properties that let you set various parts of the physical SOAP Envelope including MethodName (name of the Web service operation) and URI (namespace of the Web service operation). CoEnvelope also exposes Web service operation parameters as a collection of CoSoapNode objects. Each CoSoapNode represents an XML element inside the message's Body. Using CoSoapNode, you can set/read all aspects of the corresponding XML element including the element's name, namespace, and text content (value).

Instead of using custom serializers, you can create new CoSoapNode objects and set their name, namespace, and value yourself. This is very similar to using the SOAP Toolkit's low level API.

HTTPTransport is responsible for sending the HTTP request and receiving the response. In addition to HTTP, PocketSOAP also supports custom transports as COM classes that implement ISOAPTransport. For example, a downloadable TransportPak provides support for several other transports including raw TCP.

12.4.1 RPC/Encoded Messages with PocketSOAP

To demonstrate interoperability, I built a client (shown in Listing 12.1) that invokes the VB .NET Weather service using PocketSOAP 1.2.

Listing 12.1 A PocketSOAP client invoking a .NET Weather service (VBWSClientCode\PocketSoapClient\frmWeather.frm)

```
Private Sub cmdGet_Click()
    Dim envReq As PocketSOAP.CoEnvelope

    Set envReq = New PocketSOAP.CoEnvelope
    envReq.MethodName = "GetWeather"
    envReq.URI = "http://tempuri.org/"
    envReq.Parameters.Create "zipCode", txtZip.Text
    Dim http As PocketSOAP.HTTPTransport
    Set http = New PocketSOAP.HTTPTransport

    'change this to point to your proxy if you have one
    'http.SetProxy "pluto", 8080
    http.SOAPAction = "http://tempuri.org/GetWeather"
    Call http.Send( _
"http://www.learnxmlws.com/services/WeatherRetriever.asmx", _
    envReq.Serialize)
    Dim envResp As PocketSOAP.CoEnvelope
    Set envResp = New PocketSOAP.CoEnvelope
    Call envResp.Parse(http)
    Call DisplayData(envResp)

End Sub
Private Sub DisplayData(response As PocketSOAP.CoEnvelope)
    Dim result As CoSoapNode
    Set result = response.Body.Item(1)
    lblConditions.Caption = _
      result.Nodes.ItemByName("Conditions").Value
    lblCurrentTemp.Caption = _
      result.Nodes.ItemByName("CurrentTemp").Value
    lblInfo.Caption = "Barometer at " & _
    result.Nodes.ItemByName("Barometer").Value & " and " & _
    result.Nodes.ItemByName("BarometerDirection").Value & _
    vbCrLf _
    "Humidity is " & result.Nodes.ItemByName("Humidity").Value _
    * 100 & "%"

End Sub
```

To invoke the GetWeather operation, I create a CoEnvelope object and set its MethodName to GetWeather and its URI to http://tempuri.org/. To send the zip code, I need to create a new CoSoapNode and set its name to zipCode and its value to the user-entered zip code. I do this by accessing the envelope's parameters collection and calling its Create method. This method creates the CoSoapNode and adds it to the collection in one step.

To send the message, I create an HTTPTransport object, set its SOAPAction property, and call its Send method, passing it the service's end point URL and the serialized envelope. Note that calling envReq.Serialize serializes the SOAP envelope along with any parameters you've added to it and returns the serialized SOAP message as a string.

To retrieve the response, I create a new CoEnvelope, named envResp, and call its Parse method and pass it the HTTPTransport object. This new envelope contains the response message. DisplayData handles reading out information from the response message using the result.Nodes collection that contains Co-SoapNode objects. As a point of reference, Listing 12.2 shows a template response SOAP Body.

Listing 12.2   A template response message from the Weather service

```
<soap:Body
soap:encodingStyle="http://schemas.xmlsoap.org/soap/encoding/">
  <tns:GetWeatherResponse>
    <GetWeatherResult href="#id1" />
  </tns:GetWeatherResponse>
  <types:CurrentWeather id="id1" xsi:type="types:CurrentWeather">
    <LastUpdated xsi:type="xsd:string">string</LastUpdated>
    <IconUrl xsi:type="xsd:string">string</IconUrl>
    <Conditions xsi:type="xsd:string">string</Conditions>
    <CurrentTemp xsi:type="xsd:float">float</CurrentTemp>
    <Humidity xsi:type="xsd:float">float</Humidity>
    <Barometer xsi:type="xsd:float">float</Barometer>
    <BarometerDirection
    xsi:type="xsd:string">string</BarometerDirection>
  </types:CurrentWeather>
</soap:Body>
```

DisplayData first declares a variable-named result and sets it to the item corresponding to the GetWeatherResult element. Using this result variable, I can get its contents using its Nodes property, which returns a collection of Co-SoapNode objects. This collection contains a CoSoapNode object for each element in the CurrentWeather structure shown in Listing 12.2. For example, to get the text content of the Conditions element, I call result.Nodes.Item-ByName("Conditions").Value. By using CoSoapNode and CoSoapNodes, I do not need to write a custom deserializer for the CurrentWeather structure. Figure 12.2 shows the PocketSOAPClient in action.

12.4.2   Document/Literal Messages with PocketSOAP

In addition to RPC/encoded messages, PocketSOAP also supports document/literal messages. To show you an example of this, I built a PocketSOAP client that invokes the GetCustomersDataSet operation explained in Chapter 9. Running this sample invokes the operation and displays the returned data in a list-view as shown in Figure 12.3. Listing 12.3 shows the sample client code.

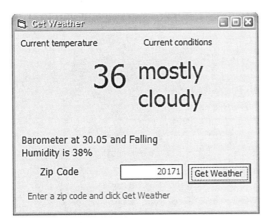

Figure 12.2   The PocketSOAP client displaying current weather information

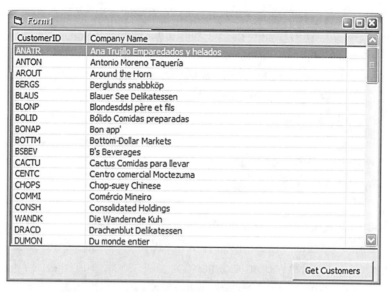

Figure 12.3 Using PocketSOAP to invoke a document/literal service and displaying the results

Listing 12.3 PocketSOAP client code for invoking a document/literal Web service (VBWSClientCode\PocketSoapClient\frmDocument.frm)

```
Private Sub cmdGetCustomers_Click()
    Dim envReq As PocketSOAP.CoEnvelope
    Set envReq = New PocketSOAP.CoEnvelope
    envReq.EncodingStyle = ""
        Dim node As CoSoapNode
    Set node = New CoSoapNode
    node.Name = "GetCustomersDataSet"
    node.Namespace = "http://www.LearnXmlWS.com/customerorders"
    Call envReq.Body.Append(node)
    Dim http As PocketSOAP.HTTPTransport
    Set http = New PocketSOAP.HTTPTransport

    'change this to point to your proxy if you have one
    'http.SetProxy "pluto", 8080
    http.SOAPAction = _
      "http://www.LearnXmlWS.com/customerorders/
►GetCustomersDataSet"
    Call http.Send( _
      "http://VBWSServer/vbwsbook/Chapter9/CustomerOrders.asmx", _
      envReq.Serialize)
```

```
        Dim envResp As PocketSOAP.CoEnvelope
        Set envResp = New PocketSOAP.CoEnvelope
        Call envResp.Parse(http)
        Call ShowCustomers(envResp)

End Sub
Private Sub ShowCustomers(response As CoEnvelope)
lvw.ListItems.Clear
    Dim li As ListItem
    Dim result As CoSoapNode
    Set result = _
        response.Body.ItemByName("GetCustomersDataSetResponse") _
        .Nodes.ItemByName("GetCustomersDataSetResult")
    Dim theData As CoSoapNode
    Set theData = result.Nodes.ItemByName("diffgram") _
                    .Nodes.ItemByName("NewDataSet")
    Dim aCustomer As CoSoapNode
    For Each aCustomer In theData.Nodes
        Set li = lvw.ListItems.Add(, , _
            aCustomer.Nodes.ItemByName("CustomerID").Value)
        Call li.ListSubItems.Add(, , _
            aCustomer.Nodes.ItemByName("CompanyName").Value)
    Next
End Sub
```

To send a document/literal message, I create a CoEnvelope and set its EncodingStyle property to an empty string. The default encoding style is Section 5
encoding that is used with RPC. By definition, there is no encoding for literal
messages, hence the empty string.

Then I create a new CoSoapNode that represents the literal contents of the
request's Body. In this case, all I need to send is an element called GetCustomersDataSet with the namespace URI "http://www.LearnXmlWS.com/
customerorders." I then append this node to the Body before sending the message with an HTTPTransport object.

A procedure named ShowCustomers (in Listing 12.3) is responsible for pulling data out of the response and filling the listview. To do this, it first extracts the
GetCustomersDataSetResult element, then uses it to extract the NewDataSet element (see Chapter 9 for a description of the response document). It enumer-
ates each child element within NewDataSet and extracts CustomerID and
CompanyName information from it and displays this information in the listview.

The code in Listing 12.3 reminds me of using the SOAP Toolkit's low level API: It seems like a lot of code but it is actually fewer lines than you would have to write and maintain if you decided to create custom serializers. It is also a consistent programming model that you have to learn only once and can use for any future Web service you want to invoke.

12.5 Java Clients

Owing to the relatively recent popularity of Java and J2EE, many businesses have Java applications that need to be integrated with VB/COM applications. For this reason, I consider interop with Java clients/services an important element of successful Web service implementations.

There are many SOAP implementations in the Java world ranging from free, open-source implementations to productized, fully supported tools. Some of the tools participating in interop testing include Apache SOAP, Apache Axis, WASP Developer (from Systinet) and GLUE (from The Mind Electric).

Apache SOAP is one of the original, early-on SOAP implementations. It started as an IBM SOAP stack named SOAP4J and was then turned over to the Apache Software Foundation (www.apache.org) and became an open-source project.

In addition to Apache SOAP, there's a newer open-source implementation named Apache Axis. Axis is considered a follow-on project to Apache SOAP with a complete rearchitecture aiming at tighter WSDL integration and better EJB support. However, at the time of this writing, Apache Axis is still in the beta stage and there are far more Web services and clients using Apache SOAP than Apache Axis.

12.5.1 IBM's Web Services Toolkit

Apache SOAP is just a SOAP implementation. It lacks some of the additional tools typically needed for Web service development, most notably a WSDL generation and consumption tool. IBM provides a Web Services Toolkit (WSTK Version 2.4) that comes with Apache SOAP and several other Web service-related tools including a WSDL generation wizard, a WSDL-based Java proxy generator, and a UDDI SDK.

You can download the WSTK free at http://www.alphaworks.ibm.com/tech/webservicetoolkit. To install the SDK, you'll need to download and install JDK 1.3 from http://java.sun.com/j2se/1.3/download-windows.html. After you've installed the WSTK (a typical install is fine), you'll need to perform various configuration steps depending on which parts of the WSTK you need to use. To run the examples in this section, you'll need to perform only four configuration steps (none of the other WSTK configuration is required):

1. Make sure the PATH environment variable includes the JDK's bin folder. For example, if you installed the JDK to E:\JDK1.3 make sure you add E:\JDK1.3\bin to the PATH environment variable. You can do this by opening the properties for My Computer, clicking on the Advanced tab, then clicking on Environment Variables. Look for the Path variable (either under your list of environment variables or the System's list) and double-click on it to edit it.

2. Make sure the JAVA_HOME environment variable is defined and points to the folder where you installed the JDK. For example, if you installed the JDK in E:\JDK1.3 make sure JAVA_HOME is defined and points to E:\JDK1.3. You can do this in the same way you configured the PATH variable in Step 1.

3. SET the WSTK_HOME environment variable to point to the location where you installed the WSTK. For example, if you installed the WSTK in D:\WSTK, then set WSTK_HOME to D:\WSTK. Do not add a backslash at the end of the path. You can set this environment variable the same way you set the PATH and JAVA_HOME variables.

4. Each example in the following two sections includes two batch files: build.bat and run.bat. For these batch files to work, you need to define an environment variable named VBWSCLIENTCODE and set it to the path where you copied the book's client code (without a backslash at the end). For example, if you copied the book's client code to D:\VBWSClientCode, then you need to define the environment variable VBWSCLIENTCODE and set it to D:\VBWSClientCode. You can set this environment variable the same way you set the other environment variables.

The toolkit provides three WSDL tools that handle generating code from WSDL and WSDL from code. The first tool, WSDLGen, plays a role similar to that of the SOAP Toolkit's WSDL wizard: It generates WSDL from a Java Class file, an EJB jar file, or a COM interface. The generated WSDL is interesting in that it is separated into two files: One file contains the interface elements, namely every-thing except the `<service>` element. The second file imports the interface file and contains the `<service>` element (implementation details). This separation can be useful for many things including registering the service interface with UDDI (see Chapter 11) and handing it to other developers who will build services that implement this interface.

The other two tools, proxygen and servicegen, play the role of .NET's wsdl.exe. Proxygen generates client-side proxies from WSDL documents and servicegen generates service skeleton implementations or templates from WSDL documents.

Each of these tools has a corresponding batch file that you use to run the tool. These batch files are all located in the bin folder under the folder where you installed the WSTK. To run a tool, simply run the batch file with the same name.

In the next two sections, I'll show you two examples of using the WSTK to invoke an RPC/encoded and a document/literal Web service, respectively.

12.5.2 RPC/Encoded Messages

As an example of RPC/encoded interop, we'll call our trusty Weather service on learnxmlws.com. To generate a Java proxy class, you need to run proxygen.bat on the service's WSDL document. Proxygen does not currently support HTTP GET and HTTP POST bindings that are in the weather service's WSDL document. But don't worry, proxygen will simply ignore bindings it doesn't understand, so you should get a couple of warnings but no real errors. When you are ready to generate the client-side proxy, type the following command:

```
%WSTK_HOME%\bin\proxygen -outputdir TheOutputLocation http://
➡www.learnxmlws.com/services/weatherretriever.asmx?wsdl
```

where TheOutputLocation is where you want output files to go. Proxygen will create a directory structure based on the service's namespace. For example, the weather service's namespace is http://tempuri.org/ so the resulting directory structure is org\tempuri. Within the tempuri directory proxygen creates a file named WeatherRetrieverSoap.java, which is the Web service proxy class that clients use to invoke the service. It also creates a CurrentWeather.java file that contains the CurrentWeather class. This class corresponds to the CurrentWeather complex type returned from the service's GetWeather operation. To deserialize the returned XML into an instance of CurrentWeather, proxygen creates a (de)serializer class in a file named CurrentWeatherSerializer.java. Proxygen also compiles all generated .java files resulting in .class files with the same names.

I ran into one problem with the generated proxy: It does not specify the correct SOAPAction for each Web service operation. Instead, the generated WeatherRetrieverSoap class has a private member variable named SOAPActionURI that is set to "http://tempuri.org/GetWeather" in the class's constructor. This is easy enough to fix; simply open WeatherRetrieverSoap.java and add the following line to GetTemperature function:

```
this.SOAPActionURI = "http://tempuri.org/GetTemperature";
```

And add this line to the GetWeather function:

```
this.SOAPActionURI = "http://tempuri.org/GetWeather";
```

Note that you don't need the extra double quotes around the SOAPAction value; those are added by Apache SOAP. The book's example code includes an already-edited WeatherRetrieverSoap.java file. In addition to the above two lines, the supplied file also includes a SetProxy function that you can use to set an HTTP proxy (for example if you want to use ProxyTrace with these examples) by uncommenting two lines of code.

Now you are ready to write client code that uses the generated proxy to invoke the weather service. Listing 12.4 shows an example client that invokes GetTemperature.

Listing 12.4   A Java client using Apache SOAP to invoke a .NET Web service, RPC/encoded messages
(VBWSClientCode\Chapter12\java\org\tempuri\TempClient.java)

```
package org.tempuri;

public class TempClient
{
  public static void main(String[] args) throws Exception {

    WeatherRetrieverSoap wr=
```

```
      new WeatherRetrieverSoap(
           new java.net.URL(
      "http://www.learnxmlws.com/services/
➥weatherretriever.asmx"));
    float t= wr.GetTemperature(args[0]);
    System.out.println("\r\nTemperature for zipCode " +
                          args[0] + "...\r\n");
    System.out.println(t);
  }
}
```

The first line tells the compiler that this class belongs to the org.tempuri package. Think of a Java package as the equivalent of a .NET namespace. The generated proxy class, WeatherRetrieverSoap, belongs to org.tempuri so I put this client class in the same package. Although this is not necessary, it makes it sightly easier to build and run the client.

The client class is named TempClient (temperature client); it has one static method named main that is the class's entry point. Inside this method, I create a new WeatherRetrieverSoap object passing its constructor a URL object initialized with the service's URL. Then I call the proxy's GetTemperature function, passing it the first argument that the user passed to the class. Then I print out the returned temperature using System.out.println.

To build this example, open a command prompt and change the current drive to the drive where you copied the books code, for example, D:, then run %VBWSCLIENTCODE%\Chapter12\Java\org\tempuri\build.bat. After running build.bat, run runTemp.bat, passing it a zip code, for example:

```
%VBWSCLIENTCODE%\Chapter12\Java\org\tempuri\runTemp 20171
```

The resulting output should look like (hopefully it'll be warmer where you live):

```
Temperature for zipCode 20171...

36.0
```

The preceding example used only simple types: It took in a string and returned a float. Let's take a look at an example that uses complex types. Listing 12.5 shows an example client that invokes GetWeather.

Listing 12.5 Invoking GetWeather and handling the complex return type from Java (VBWSClientCode\Chapter12\java\org\tempuri\GetWeather.java)

```
package org.tempuri;
public class WeatherClient
{
  public static void main(String[] args) throws Exception {
    WeatherRetrieverSoap wr=
          new WeatherRetrieverSoap(new java.net.URL(
      "http://www.learnxmlws.com/services/
►weatherretriever.asmx"));
    org.tempuri.CurrentWeather cw= wr.GetWeather(args[0]);
    System.out.println("\r\nTemperature for zipCode " + args[0] +
                      "...");
    System.out.println(cw.CurrentTemp);
    System.out.println("\r\nCurrent conditions for zipCode " +
                      args[0] +
                      "...");
    System.out.println(cw.Conditions);

  }

}
```

This client is very similar to the Temperature one except it calls GetWeather instead of GetTemperature. GetWeather returns an instance of the CurrentWeather class that was generated by proxygen, so this client captures the returned object in a variable named cw, then reads data out of the object's public fields and displays it using System.out.println. The heavy lifting (as far as deserializing the returned XML into a CurrentWeather object) is done by the generated CurrentWeatherSerializer class.

To run this client, first build it by running build.bat, then run Weather.bat, passing it the zip code:

```
%vbwsclientcode%\chapter12\java\org\tempuri\runWeather.bat 20171

Temperature for zipCode 20171...
36.0

Current conditions for zipCode 20171...
clear
```

As you can see, using the WSTK for Java clients is fairly straightforward as long as your service uses RPC/encoded and if you remember to set the appropriate SOAPAction in the generated proxy class.

You can make it easier for developers using the WSTK to call your Web services by not relying on SOAPAction. To do this, set the RoutingStyle property of SoapRpcService to RequestElement. See Chapter 6 for more information.

12.5.3 Document/Literal Messages

Apache SOAP also supports document/literal message, although proxygen cannot handle WSDL documents with document/literal messages. Instead, you have to write the client proxy yourself using the Apache SOAP object model. This is similar to using the SOAP Toolkit's low level API.

To demonstrate document/literal interop I created a Java client that invokes the CustomerOrders Web service from Chapter 9. The client first calls GetCustomerOrdersTypedDataSet to retrieve the customer order data. Using XML DOM, it edits this DataSet and changes the first customer's company name to the user-specified name. Then it invokes SaveCustomerOrdersTypedDataSet and sends it the modified data to be saved. This sample's code is divided among three classes.

CustomerData is the Web service proxy class. It exposes three public methods, GetCustomerOrdersTypedDataSet, SaveCustomerOrdersTypedDataSet, and GetCustomersXml, which invoke the corresponding Web service operations. We won't use GetCustomersXml in this example but I implemented it as a reference for you to invoke an operation that returns an XML document.

To manipulate the DataSet in Java, CustomerData relies on a class called JDataSet. You might think JDataSet is an implementation of the ADO.NET DataSet for Java. That would be great, however, JDataSet is a simple class I created to manipulate the CustomerOrders typed dataset and create a diffgram (a dataset copy with the changes) to be sent back to the service. JDataSet does this manipulation using the XML DOM.

The third class, CustomerClient, is the Java client that uses CustomerData and CustomerData.JDataSet. It is a rather simple console application that takes in the new company name, invokes GetCustomerOrdersTypedDataSet, updates the first company name to the new name you supplied, and calls SaveCustomer-OrdersTypedDataSet with the updated JDataSet. Listing 12.6 shows the relevant part of the CustomerData proxy class that is where the Apache SOAP action is.

Listing 12.6   A Java proxy class for a .NET document/literal service (VBWSClientCode\Chapter12\java\document\CustomerData.java)

```
public class CustomerData
{

private URL _endPointUrl;
private static final String GetCustomerXmlAction=
      "http://www.LearnXmlWS.com/customerorders/GetCustomersXml";
private static final String GetCustomersDSAction=
   "http://www.LearnXmlWS.com/customerorders/_
 GetCustomerOrdersTypedDataSet";
private static final String
SaveCustomersDSAction=
      "http://www.LearnXmlWS.com/customerorders/_
      SaveCustomerOrdersTypedDataSet";

public CustomerData(URL endPointURL)
{
      this._endPointUrl= endPointURL;
}
public JDataSet GetCustomerOrdersTypedDataSet() throws Exception
{
   Envelope env=new Envelope();
   Document doc= new DocumentImpl();
      Element bodyEntry= doc.createElementNS(
      "http://www.LearnXmlWS.com/customerorders",
      "ns1:GetCustomerOrdersTypedDataSet");
   Vector inDoc=new Vector(1);
   inDoc.addElement(bodyEntry);
   Body body=new Body();
   body.setBodyEntries(inDoc);
      env.setBody(body);
      Message msg=new Message();
   this.setProxy(msg);
   msg.send(_endPointUrl,GetCustomersDSAction,env);
      JDataSet jds=new JDataSet(msg);
      return jds;
```

```
    }
    public void SaveCustomerOrdersTypedDataSet(JDataSet jds)
        throws Exception {
      Envelope env=new Envelope();
      Document doc= new DocumentImpl();
      Element bodyEntry= doc.createElementNS(
        "http://www.LearnXmlWS.com/customerorders",
        "ns1:SaveCustomerOrdersTypedDataSet");
      bodyEntry.setAttribute(
            "xmlns","http://www.LearnXmlWS.com/customerorders");
      bodyEntry.appendChild(doc.importNode(jds.diffGram,true));
      Vector inDoc=new Vector(1);
      inDoc.addElement(bodyEntry);
      Body body=new Body();
      body.setBodyEntries(inDoc);
      env.setBody(body);
      Message msg=new Message();
      this.setProxy(msg);
      msg.send(_endPointUrl,SaveCustomersDSAction,env);
    }
```

The code in Listing 12.6 begins by defining a few private members that represent the end point URL and the various SOAP action values. The constructor takes in the service's end point URL and stores it in the _endPointUrl member variable. GetCustomerOrdersTypedDataSet acts as a wrapper for the Web service's GetCustomerTypedDataSet except it returns a JDataSet object. To invoke this document/literal service, I need to send a SOAP message like the one in Listing 12.7.

Listing 12.7   The document/literal request message

```
<soap:Envelope
xmlns:xsi="http://www.w3.org/2001/XMLSchema-instance"
xmlns:xsd="http://www.w3.org/2001/XMLSchema" xmlns:soap="http://
schemas.xmlsoap.org/soap/envelope/">
  <soap:Body>
    <GetCustomerOrdersTypedDataSet
        xmlns="http://www.LearnXmlWS.com/customerorders" />
  </soap:Body>
</soap:Envelope>
```

To do this, I first create a new Envelope object that represents the message's Envelope. Then I create a new XML document object, which I use to create an XML Element named GetCustomerOrdersTypedDataSet. Note that you can't create an XML element directly; you must first create an XML document, then use its createElementNS method to create an element in a namespace. To add this element to the message Body, I create a Vector object and add this XML element to the Vector. Then I create a new Body object that represents the message Body and attach the entire Vector object to it by calling body.setBodyEntries. Next, I attach this Body to the Envelope by calling Envelope.setBody.

To send the message, I create a new Message object named msg and call this.setProxy. setProxy is a private function that tells Apache SOAP to use an HTTP proxy. If you want to use an HTTP proxy (for example, ProxTrace), edit setProxy and uncomment the two commented lines. Next, I call msg.send, passing it the Web service's URL, the SOAPAction value, and the envelope I created. To parse out the returned XML, I create a new JDataSet object, passing msg to its constructor. JDataSet's constructor extracts the returned XML from the SOAP response message and stores it in a member variable named ds, which is actually an XML Element. I then return this JDataSet to the caller.

SaveCustomerOrdersTypedDataSet is equally straightforward. It creates the request message in much the same way as GetCustomerOrdersTypedDataSet. The main difference is the way it appends the diffGram to the request message by calling bodyEntry.appendChild.

This is basically using standard DOM methods to prepare the request document. JDataSet.diffGram returns an XML DOM Element that contains the diffGram (the updated DataSet) to be sent back to the service. The call to appendChild appends this diffGram element with all its contents into the request element thereby forming the literal document that will be sent to the Web service. This literal document is then appended to the body the same way as in the previous listing and the message is sent off to the service with the appropriate SOAPAction.

Listing 12.8 shows the client using this proxy to retrieve, update, and save the DataSet.

**Listing 12.8   A Java client using the proxy class in Listing 12.6
(VBWSClientCode\Chapter12\java\document\CustomerClient.java)**

```
public class CustomerClient
{
        private static final String SERVICE_URL=
            "http://vbwsbook/vbwsbook/Chapter9/
➥CustomerOrders.asmx";
    public static void main(String[] args) throws Exception {
            if(args.length ==1) {

    CustomerData cd= new CustomerData(new
    java.net.URL(SERVICE_URL));
    System.out.println("retrieving customers DataSet ...");
    JDataSet jds=cd.GetCustomerOrdersTypedDataSet();
    System.out.println("updating company name ...");
    jds.UpdateCompanyName(0,args[0]);
    cd.SaveCustomerOrdersTypedDataSet(jds);
    System.out.println("Updated company name");
      }
    else
       System.out.println("Please specify a new company name");
   }
}
```

The client first defines a private static member to hold the service end point
URL (you'll want to modify this URL to point to your service's location). Then it
creates a new CustomerData object and calls GetCustomerOrdersTyped-
DataSet, capturing the returned JDataSet in a variable named jds. It calls UpdateCompanyName, passing it the record number to update (0 is the first
record) and the user-specified new company name. UpdateCompanyName uses
XML DOM to find the specified record, update it, and create a new diffGram XML
element. Then it stores it in a member variable named diffGram. The code in UpdateCompanyName does not use any Apache SOAP features: It is strictly XML
DOM code. So if you've programmed XML DOM (for example, using MSXML and/
or System.Xml), this code will be easy to understand.

At this point, the data has been retrieved and updated. To save this data, we need to send it to the Web service. The next line calls SaveCustomerOrders-TypedDataSet and passes it the JDataSet object.

To run this client, first run build.bat to build the Java classes. Then run run.bat with a new company name. Be sure to use quotes around the name if it contains spaces. For example:

```
run.bat "this is a new name"

retrieving customers DataSet ...
updating company name ...
Updated company name
```

This example shows that invoking document/literal Web services with Apache SOAP is a straightforward process that corresponds logically to the SOAP request/response message. Most of the code will be in forming/manipulating the request/response XML documents, which is usually the case with document/literal messages. The good news is: This code can use standard APIs such as SAX or DOM, so whoever is developing the client (you or someone else) will probably already have the necessary skills to create these XML documents.

12.6   The Web Service Behavior

There's no doubt that browsers are now the standard application client for both intranet and Internet applications. Given that Internet Explorer is the most popular browser, you might want to leverage IE features when building intranet applications. One of IE's interesting features is the Web service DHTML behavior, which lets you invoke Web services directly from client-side script code. Being a DHTML behavior, there's nothing to install on the client, except of course IE 5.0 or later. In this section I will show you how to use the Web service behavior to invoke RPC/encoded and document/literal services.

12.6.1   Setting Up the Behavior

To get started with the Web service behavior, you first need to copy Webservice.htc to a location on your Web server. This file is on the book's CD (in the extras folder) and you can also get it from http://msdn.microsoft.com/work-shop/author/webservice/webservice.htc. To use the behavior on a page, you must attach it using the BEHAVIOR CSS style, for example:

```
<DIV id=ws
  style="BEHAVIOR: url(webservice.htc)"
    onresult=onWeatherResult();>
</DIV>
```

When using the behavior, the default programming model is asynchronous: You invoke a Web service asynchronously and the behavior informs you via a callback or event handler when the call returns. The onresult attribute hooks up an event handler to be executed when the service call returns. You are now ready to use the Web service behavior from your DHTML page.

12.6.2 Invoking Web Services

To invoke a Web service, you first call the behavior's useService method, pass-ing it the service's WSDL URL and a friendly name for the service. The friendly name is any string that you will use later to refer to this service. One Web ser-vice behavior can handle multiple Web services, so the friendly name you assign for each service needs to be unique.

A good place to call useService is upon page load. You do this by hooking up a function to the body's onload event. This function can call the behavior's us-erService method to set up all the services you plan to call using this behavior.

Listing 12.9 shows an example function called Init that associates a weather service with the friendly name Weather.

Listing 12.9   Calling the Weather .NET service from the DHTML Web service behavior (VBWSBook\Chapter12\WSBehavior.html)

```
<script language=JScript>
function Init() {
      ws.useService(
        "http://vbwsserver/vbwsbook/chapter12/weather.asmx?wsdl",
        "Weather");
}
function GetTemp() {
  errInfo.innerHTML="";
```

```
        conds.innerHTML="";
        temp.innerText="";
        var objCall=new Object();
        objCall.async=false;
        objCall.funcName="GetTemperature";
        objCall.params=new Array();
        objCall.params.zipCode=txtZipCode.value;
        var objResult= ws.Weather.callService(objCall);
        if(!handleError(objResult))
        temp.innerText="temperature is: " + objResult.value;
    }
</script>
```

Note: For security reasons, when using the Web service behavior, IE will let you invoke services that reside on the same Web server from which the page was served. If you want to call a Web service that's not on your server, you'll need to build a wrapper Web service that forwards requests to the real Web service. For example, I wrote a wrapper Web service for the Weather service on LearnXmlWS.com. This wrapper service is in the chapter's Web code folder in the files Weather.asmx and Weather.asmx.vb.

The function GetTemp in Listing 12.9 is executed when the user clicks on a Get Temperature button. The function first initializes some display elements, then creates a new object called objCall. objCall represents the Web service behavior's call object that contains information about the operation you want to call. For example, funcName is the Web service's operation name while params is an associative array (similar to a dictionary object) of parameters. In this example, funcName is GetTemperature and the only parameter in params is called zipCode and is set to the user-entered zip code.

You can also use objCall to set the async property to False as I do in this example. This causes the Web service call to be synchronous, thereby blocking the user interface thread until the call returns. You normally don't want to do this unless you are sure the Web service call will return immediately or when you intentionally want the UI to be frozen until the call returns.

To invoke the Web service, you call the behavior's callService function, passing it the call object. The way you call callService is interesting. First, you access a property of the behavior with the same name as the Web service's friendly name that you assigned in useService. This property returns an object that acts as the Web service proxy. In this example, I used the friendly name "Weather" so ws.Weather is the Web service proxy. I then call ws.Weather.callService, passing it the call object. This call returns a result object from which you can get the call status (success or failure), any error information, and of course the returned data.

If you are just using the call object to set the operation's name and parameters, you can pass those directly to the callService method. However, the call object lets you specify options such as async.

To check for errors, Listing 12.9 calls a function named handleError that returns True if there was an error. If there wasn't an error, the temperature is retrieved using objResult.value, then displayed on the page.

The handleError function is shown in Listing 12.10. handleError displays the error information on the page itself. The code in Listing 12.9 displays the returned temperature using the results object's errorDetail property.

Listing 12.10 Checking for errors when using the DHTML Web service behavior (VBWSBook\Chapter12\WSBehavior.html)

```
function handleError(objResult) {
    if((objResult.error))
    {
        alert("There was an error!");
        errInfo.innerHTML="An error occurred: <br>Fault code" +
      objResult.errorDetail.code + "<br>Fault string: " +
      objResult.errorDetail.string;

        return true;
    }
    else
    {
     return false;
    }
}
```

The errorDetail property returns an object roughly equivalent to the SOAP Fault element. errorDetail has three properties: string returns the faultstring; code returns the faultcode; the property named raw returns an XML DOMDocument object that contains the response SOAP envelope. You can use standard DOM properties and methods on this document to read out information from it or even transform it using XSLT.

12.6.3 Handling Complex Types

Now that you know the basics of using the Web service behavior, the next step is to call a more sophisticated operation that returns a complex type. Listing 12.11 shows an example that calls the GetWeather operation that returns richer weather information.

Listing 12.11 Handling complex types with the Web service behavior (VBWSBook\Chapter12\WSBehavior.html)

```
function GetWeather() {
  errInfo.innerHTML="";

  conds.innerHTML="<b>Retrieving weather information ...</b>";
  var objCall=new Object();
  objCall.async=true;
  objCall.funcName="GetWeather";
  objCall.params=new Array();
  objCall.params.zipCode=txtZipCode.value;
  ws.Weather.callService(objCall);
}
function onWeatherResult() {
  if(!handleError(event.result))
  {
    var doc=event.result.raw;
    temp.innerText=doc.selectSingleNode("//CurrentTemp").text;
    conds.innerHTML="Current conditions: " +
         doc.selectSingleNode("//Conditions").text +
      "<br>" + "Humidity: " +
     doc.selectSingleNode("//Humidity").text;
    icon.src=doc.selectSingleNode("//IconUrl").text;
  }
}
```

The function named GetWeather uses the same Web service behavior as the function named GetTemperature. After initializing a couple of display elements, GetWeather creates a call object, sets the funcName to GetWeather, and adds a parameter named zipCode. This time, the async property is set to true, indicating that the Web service call will be asynchronous and the behavior will fire the onresult event when the call returns. This is why GetWeather does not attempt to read the returned weather information.

When onresult is fired, the event handler function is called. In this example, onWeatherResult is the event handler for the onresult event. Within the event handler, you get access to the result object by calling event.result.

First, onWeatherResult checks for errors by calling handleError. Assuming no errors occurred, it calls event.result.raw to get back the returned SOAP message as a DOMDocument object. This is an easy way to handle complex types: You just read them as XML documents. In this example, I use XPath with selectSingleNode to read out the current temperature, conditions, and humidity from the returned document. I also read the IconUrl and use it as the src for the HTML img tag called icon. The result is displayed in Figure 12.4.

Once you know how to handle complex types with the Web service behavior, invoking document/literal services is no different: You access the returned message using result.raw. As an example, I wrote some code to invoke the GetCustomersXml operation from Chapter 9. Since the client is browser-based, it's

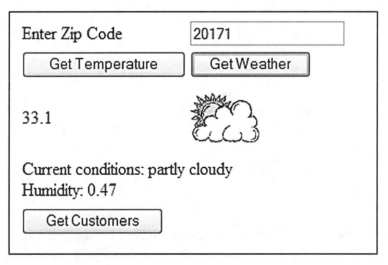

Figure 12.4 A document/literal example

likely you'll want to transform the returned XML to HTML for display. To do this, I used an XSLT stylesheet and the MSXML2.DOMDocument object. Listing 12.12 shows the example code.

Listing 12.12   Calling a document/literal Web service and transforming the response using an XSLT stylesheet

```
function GetCustomers() {
customerWS.useService(
 "http://VBWSServer/vbwsbook/Chapter9/CustomerOrders.asmx?wsdl",
 "Customers");
 var objCall=new Object();
 objCall.async=true;
 objCall.funcName="GetCustomersXml";
 customers.innerText="calling service ...";
 customerWS.Customers.callService(displayCustomers,objCall);


}
function displayCustomers(objResult) {
  if(!handleError(objResult))
  {
    var xsldoc=new ActiveXObject("MSXML2.DOMDocument.3.0");
    xsldoc.async=false;
    xsldoc.load("customers.xsl");
            try {
    customers.innerHTML=objResult.raw.transformNode(xsldoc);
            }
            catch(ex)
              {
                alert( "Error transforming XML. " +
                    "Do you have MSXML3 installed?\n" +
                "Click OK to display the returned XML");
                customers.innerText=objResult.raw.xml;
              }


  }
}
```

The function GetCustomers uses another Web service behavior named customerWS (you can have many Web service behaviors on the same page). It first initializes the behavior by calling useService and passing it the service's URL and a service-friendly name. Then it creates a call object and sets funcName to GetCustomersXml. This time, there is no event handler for the onresult event. Instead, when calling the service, the name of a callback function (displayCustomers in this example), is passed as the first parameter. The advantage of using callbacks rather than an event handler is that you can have a different callback for every Web service operation that you call.

The displayCustomers callback function is also shown in Listing 12.12. After checking for errors, it creates a new MSXML2.DOMDocument object named xsldoc. This object is then used to load the customers.xsl stylesheet. Note that xsldoc.async is set to false before loading the document. Otherwise, the document will be loaded asynchronously, which means the code will have to check if the document has been loaded before actually using it. The returned customer information is accessible as an XML DOMDocument object via the result.raw property. You can transform this XML to HTML by calling transformNode on this DOMDocument and passing it an XSLT stylesheet. transformNode applies the XSLT transformation and returns the result as a string that you can display using the innerHTML property of a UI element, as in this example. The result is a list of customer ids and their company names formatted as an HTML table.

12.7 VB 6 Clients

So far this chapter has focused on invoking VB services from other clients. Starting with this section, we turn things around and look at invoking Web services from VB 6 clients and VB .NET. This section covers VB 6 clients; the next section covers VB .NET clients.

The Microsoft SOAP Toolkit team is an active participant in the SOAP interop efforts outlined earlier in this chapter. As a result, clients using the toolkit can call just about any Web service out there. In some cases, the Web service you want to call will have some quirky aspects that make it difficult or impossible to call with the high level API. For example, the service might have a bad WSDL document or none at all. In these cases, you can use the toolkit's low level API to call the service as explained in Chapter 5.

As an interop example, I wrote a VB 6 client (in Listing 12.13) that uses the low level API to invoke a Web service written in PHP. This example was inspired by a C# example written by my friend Dan Wahlin.[3]

Listing 12.13   A VB 6 client that calls a Web service written in PHP (VBWSClientCode\Chapter12\VB6Client\frmMain.frm)

```
Private Const OPERATION_NAME As String = "getheaders"
Private Const OPERATION_NS = "nntp.xsd"
Private Const OPERATION_PREFIX = "m"
Private Const XSD_NS As String = _
        "http://www.w3.org/2001/XMLSchema"
Private Const XSI_NS As String = _
        "http://www.w3.org/2001/XMLSchema-instance"
Private Const SOAP_ENC As String = _
        "http://schemas.xmlsoap.org/soap/encoding/"
Private Const SERVICE_URL = _
        "http://www.codecraze.com/soap/nntp.php"
Private Const SOAP_ACTION = _
        """http://www.codecraze.com/soap/nntp.php"""
Private Sub cmdPHP_Click()
On Error GoTo eh

    Dim Serializer As SoapSerializer30
    Dim Connector As SoapConnector30
    Dim Rdr As SoapReader30

    Set Connector = New HttpConnector30
    Connector.Property("EndPointURL") = SERVICE_URL
    Connector.Property("SoapAction") = SOAP_ACTION
    If chkPrxy.Value Then
        Connector.Property("ProxyServer") = "localhost"
        Connector.Property("ProxyPort") = "8080"
        Connector.Property("UseProxy") = True
    End If
    'establish connection
    Connector.Connect
    Connector.BeginMessage
    'SoapSerializer uses the Connector
```

---

[3]I learned about this service through a C# client that Dan Wahlin wrote to demonstrate .NET interop with non-.NET Web services. Dan's example is available on his site at http://www.xmlforasp.net/content.aspx?content=codebank&codeType=webservices#MSNewsWebServiceClient.

```
        Set Serializer = New SoapSerializer30
        Serializer.Init Connector.InputStream
        'write the SOAP message
        Serializer.StartEnvelope
        Serializer.StartBody
        Serializer.StartElement OPERATION_NAME, _
                OPERATION_NS, _
                SOAP_ENC, _
                OPERATION_PREFIX
        'declare the xsi and xsd namespaces
        Serializer.SoapNamespace "xsi", XSI_NS
        Serializer.SoapNamespace "xsd", XSD_NS
        'write group name
        Serializer.StartElement "newsgroup"
        'add the xsi:type attribute
        Serializer.SoapAttribute "type", XSI_NS, "xsd:string", "xsi"
        Serializer.WriteString "microsoft.public.webservices"
        Serializer.EndElement
        'write password
        Serializer.StartElement "numitems"
        'add the xsi:type attribute
         Serializer.SoapAttribute "type", XSI_NS, "xsd:int", "xsi"
        Serializer.WriteString "10"
        Serializer.EndElement
        'end the operation element
        Serializer.EndElement
        Serializer.EndBody
        Serializer.EndEnvelope
        Serializer.Finished
        'send the message
        Connector.EndMessage

        'get the response
        Set Rdr = New SoapReader30
        Rdr.Load Connector.OutputStream

        MsgBox Rdr.RpcResult.xml
        Exit Sub
eh:
        MsgBox Err.Description, vbCritical, "Error calling service"
    End Sub
```

This example calls a news Web service on codecraze.com. Specifically, it calls an operation named getheaders that takes in the name of a newsgroup and the maximum number of items to return and returns a list of nntp message headers from that group. The problem with this service is that it requires specific namespace prefixes. That is, it requires that the SOAP envelope prefix be "SOAP-ENV" and the operation element's prefix be "m." Of course this should not be the case: XML namespace prefixes should not matter as long as the namespace URIs they point to are correct.

The code in Listing 12.13 starts with a few constant declarations for things like the operation name, service URL, and SOAP Action. The rest of the code in Listing 12.13 uses the now-familiar low level API. It first creates an HttpConnector30 object and sets its EndPointURL and SoapAction properties. Then it connects to the service and creates a new SoapSerializer30 with the connector's input stream. After calling StartEnvelope[4] and StartBody, it calls StartElement to write the operation's element. Note that in this example, the prefix "m" is specified as the operation's prefix because the Web service expects this particular prefix. Next, two more elements are written to the request message: newsgroup is the newsgroup name and numitems is the maximum number of items to return.

Finally, the message is sent and the response message is loaded into a SoapReader30 object. The returned list of news items is read using the SoapReader30's RpcResult property, which returns an IXMLDOMNode.

There's really nothing too different about this example compared to other low level API examples in Chapter 5. You just need to understand what the Web service looks for in a request message and use the toolkit's API to form the message and send it.

12.8   .NET Clients

.NET Web services framework creators are also active in the interop community, which means it is generally possible to call any Web service from a .NET client.

---

[4]The toolkit's default SOAP envelope prefix is SOAP-ENV, which is what the Web service wants, so we don't need to do anything special with the envelope prefix.

In fact, most of the time this is easy unless there are problems with the Web service or the Web service's WSDL.

12.8.1   Bad WSDL, No Problem

When interoperating with non .NET Web services, it's common to run into Web services that have no WSDL or whose WSDL cannot be read by VS .NET or wsdl.exe. When this happens, you have to write the proxy code yourself. As an example of this scenario, we'll call a Web service that returns sunrise/sunset times given longitude/latitude and a date. The Web service's WSDL document was originally located at http://www.armyaviator.com/cgi-bin/astro.exe/wsdl/ IAstro but has since been taken offline. There's a copy of this WSDL in this chapter's client code folder in a subfolder named Astro. While the service is no longer online, having a copy of this WSDL allows us to learn how to manually create proxies from an invalid WSDL document.

There are several errors in the service's WSDL that prevent VS .NET from generating the proxy class for us. Listing 12.14 shows a shortened version of the service's WSDL where I removed the operations we won't call.

Listing 12.14   A WSDL document for a live Web service. This document doesn't use fully qualified names for WSDL elements and cannot be read by VS .NET or wsdl.exe (VBWSClientCode\Chapter12\Astro\Astro.wsdl).

```
<definitions xmlns="http://schemas.xmlsoap.org/wsdl/"
xmlns:xs="http://www.w3.org/2001/XMLSchema" name="IAstroservice"
targetNamespace="http://www.borland.com/soapServices/"
xmlns:soap="http://schemas.xmlsoap.org/wsdl/soap"
xmlns:soapenc="http://schemas.xmlsoap.org/soap/encoding/">
  <message name="GetSunriseInfoRequest">
    <part name="Latitude" type="xs:double"/>
    <part name="Longitude" type="xs:double"/>
    <part name="Year" type="xs:int"/>
    <part name="Month" type="xs:int"/>
    <part name="Day" type="xs:int"/>
    <part name="TimeBiasMinutes" type="xs:int"/>
  </message>
  <message name="GetSunriseInfoResponse">
    <part name="return" type="xs:string"/>
  </message>
  <portType name="IAstro">
```

```
      <operation name="GetSunriseInfo">
        <input message="GetSunriseInfoRequest"/>
        <output message="GetSunriseInfoResponse"/>
      </operation>
  </portType>
  <binding name="IAstrobinding" type="IAstro">
    <soap:binding style="rpc"
    transport="http://schemas.xmlsoap.org/soap/http"/>
    <operation name="GetSunriseInfo">
      <soap:operation
        soapAction="urn:AstroIntf-IAstro#GetSunriseInfo"/>
      <input>
        <soap:body use="encoded"
          encodingStyle=
          "http://schemas.xmlsoap.org/soap/encoding/"
          namespace="urn:AstroIntf-IAstro"/>
      </input>
      <output>
        <soap:body use="encoded"
          encodingStyle=
          "http://schemas.xmlsoap.org/soap/encoding/"
          namespace="urn:AstroIntf-IAstro"/>
      </output>
    </operation>
    <operation name="GetSunsetInfo">
      <soap:operation
        soapAction="urn:AstroIntf-IAstro#GetSunsetInfo"/>
      <input>
        <soap:body use="encoded"
          encodingStyle=
          "http://schemas.xmlsoap.org/soap/encoding/"
          namespace="urn:AstroIntf-IAstro"/>
      </input>
      <output>
        <soap:body use="encoded"
          encodingStyle=
          "http://schemas.xmlsoap.org/soap/encoding/"
          namespace="urn:AstroIntf-IAstro"/>
      </output>
    </operation>
  </binding>
  <service name="IAstroservice">
    <port name="IAstroPort" binding="IAstrobinding">
      <soap:address location=
```

```
"http://www.armyaviator.com/cgi-bin/astro.exe/soap/IAstro"/>
    </port>
  </service>
</definitions>
```

If you look at the binding attribute of the `<port>` element, you'll notice it is set to `IAstrobinding` with no namespace prefix. Of course, the binding belongs to the targetNamespace that is defined as `http://www.borland.com/soapServices/` so any reference to the binding should use a fully qualified name with a prefix. This is one of the reasons why VS .NET cannot read this WSDL document but we can just ignore this error and extract the information we need. Listing 12.15 shows the method I wrote to invoke `GetSunriseInfo`. This method is in the `CustomProxy` class that we used to invoke `GetServerTime` earlier.

Listing 12.15   A method to invoke GetSunriseInfo

```
Imports System.Web.Services.Protocols
Imports System.Web.Services
<WebServiceBinding("SomeBindingName", "SomeBindingNS")> _
Public Class CustomProxy
    Inherits SoapHttpClientProtocol

    <SoapRpcMethod( _
        Action:="urn:AstroIntf-IAstro#GetSunriseInfo", _
        RequestNamespace:="urn:AstroIntf-IAstro", _
        ResponseNamespace:="urn:AstroIntf-IAstro" _
        )> _
    Public Function GetSunriseInfo(ByVal Latitude As Double, _
    ByVal Longitude As Double, _
    ByVal Year As Integer, _
    ByVal Month As Integer, _
    ByVal Day As Integer, _
    ByVal TimeBiasMinutes As Integer) As String
        Me.Url = _
"http://www.armyaviator.com/cgi-bin/astro.exe/soap/IAstro"
        Dim ret() As Object
        ret = Me.Invoke("GetSunriseInfo", _
 New Object() _
{Latitude, Longitude, Year, Month, Day, TimeBiasMinutes})
```

```
      Return CType(ret(0), String)
    End Function
End Class
```

Looking at the IAstro portType in Listing 12.15, you'll see that the operation name is GetSunsetInfo. Following the input message, you'll see that it has five parts. We begin by defining a function called GetSunsetInfo that takes in the five parameters as defined in the input message and returns a string as defined in the output message. Looking at the <soap:binding> element in Listing 12.14, you'll see that the style is rpc. Then looking at <soap:body>, you'll find that it is encoded. So we apply a SoapRpcMethod attribute to the proxy method. Returning to the WSDL document, we get the soapAction value from <soap:operation> and use it to set SoapRpcMethod's Action property. We also get the <input> namespace attribute from <soap:body> and use it to set the RequestNamespace property. Finally, we get the <output> namespace and use it to set ResponseNamespace.

Now for the method implementation: We get the Web service URL from `<soap:address>` in the WSDL document and use it to set the proxy class's `Url` property. Then we call `Invoke`, passing it the method name and an array of objects that contains the five parameters. Then we take the returned value, convert it to string, and return it. That's it! Listing 12.16 shows an example request message that invokes `GetSunriseInfo`. Also in Listing 12.16 is an example response message from the Web service before it was taken offline.

Listing 12.16 Example SOAP request and response messages for GetSunriseInfo

```
<!-- request message -->
<soap:Envelope
xmlns:soap="http://schemas.xmlsoap.org/soap/envelope/"
xmlns:soapenc="http://schemas.xmlsoap.org/soap/encoding/"
xmlns:tns="http://tempuri.org/"
xmlns:types="http://tempuri.org/encodedTypes"
xmlns:xsi="http://www.w3.org/2001/XMLSchema-instance"
xmlns:xsd="http://www.w3.org/2001/XMLSchema">
  <soap:Body soap:encodingStyle=
        "http://schemas.xmlsoap.org/soap/encoding/">
    <q1:GetSunriseInfo xmlns:q1="urn:AstroIntf-IAstro">
```

```
        <Latitude xsi:type="xsd:double">0</Latitude>
        <Longitude xsi:type="xsd:double">0</Longitude>
        <Year xsi:type="xsd:int">2001</Year>
        <Month xsi:type="xsd:int">11</Month>
        <Day xsi:type="xsd:int">1</Day>
        <TimeBiasMinutes xsi:type="xsd:int">0</TimeBiasMinutes>
      </q1:GetSunriseInfo>
    </soap:Body>
  </soap:Envelope>

  <!-- response message -->
  <SOAP-ENV:Envelope
  xmlns:SOAP-ENV="http://schemas.xmlsoap.org/soap/envelope/"
  xmlns:xsd="http://www.w3.org/1999/XMLSchema"
  xmlns:xsi="http://www.w3.org/1999/XMLSchema-instance"
  xmlns:SOAP-ENC="http://schemas.xmlsoap.org/soap/encoding/">
    <SOAP-ENV:Body>
      <NS1:GetSunriseInfoResponse
       xmlns:NS1="urn:AstroIntf-IAstro"
       SOAP-ENV:encodingStyle=
         "http://schemas.xmlsoap.org/soap/encoding/">
        <NS1:return xsi:type="xsd:string">05:40:09</NS1:return>
      </NS1:GetSunriseInfoResponse>
    </SOAP-ENV:Body>
  </SOAP-ENV:Envelope>
```

12.8.2 Deeper Issues

Some services are so picky about the request message, that you simply need more control than you get from the .NET Web services framework. An example of this is the CodeCraze news service used in the VB 6 client example earlier in this chapter. This service requires a specific namespace prefix for the SOAP envelope. How would you do this in a .NET client? You basically have to create the SOAP request message and send it yourself without relying on SoapHttpClient-Protocol.

While this is not difficult, it would be nice if there were a framework that took care of the common, tedious tasks such as creating the envelope and body. It would be even nicer if such a framework could handle Section 5 serialization for arrays and objects to save you some work. Of course you could build such a framework yourself, but why do that when I already built it for you?

I created a library of classes named SOAP.NET. This library exposes a simple object model for easily sending SOAP requests and receiving responses. It supports both RPC/encoded and document/literal messages and uses the .NET serialization framework to serialize types according to SOAP Section 5 encoding rules. Listing 12.17 shows an example of using SOAP.NET to invoke a Web service written in a Java SOAP implementation called Spheon Jsoap. The Web service's WSDL is bad (unqualified names again) so adding a Web reference doesn't create a proxy class.

Listing 12.17   A .NET client calling a Java Web service (VBWSClientCode\Chapter12\DotNetClient\Form1.vb)

```
Private Sub btnSpheon_Click(ByVal sender As System.Object, _
            ByVal e As System.EventArgs) Handles btnSpheon.Click
'create an operation
Dim op As New LearnXmlWS.SoapNET.WSOperation()
'call open to create a message
Dim msg As LearnXmlWS.SoapNET.SoapMessage = _
    op.Open("http://213.23.125.181:8080/RPC", _
    """""""")
If chkProxy.Checked Then
    'this line sets an HTTP proxy
    op.HttpConnection.SetProxy("http://localhost:8080", False)
End If


'Begin an RPC/encoded message
msg.BeginMessage(LearnXmlWS.SoapNET.MessageStyle.RPCEncoded)
'the operation element
msg.AddRPCOperationElement("ns", _
    "getElementBySymbol ", _
     "urn:SpheonJSOAPChemistry")
'the parameters or parts
msg.AddRPCPart("name", "na")
msg.EndMessage()
Dim resp As LearnXmlWS.SoapNET.SoapMessage = op.Send()
ShowResults(resp)
End Sub
Private Sub ShowResults(ByVal msg As _
        LearnXmlWS.SoapNET.SoapMessage)
    'check for fault
    If msg.HasFault Then
        MessageBox.Show(msg.Fault.Message(), "error", _
```

```
                MessageBoxButtons.OK, MessageBoxIcon.Error)
    Else
        'this is the result xml
        MessageBox.Show(msg.BodyItems.Item(0).OuterXml, _
        "success", _
                MessageBoxButtons.OK, MessageBoxIcon.Information)
    End If
End Sub
```

The two main SOAP.NET objects you'll use are the WSOperation and SoapMessage objects. The WSOperation handles creating a request message object and sends it using an HttpTransport object. SoapMessage exposes methods and properties that help you create the request message and parse the response message including Faults, if any.

The example in Listing 12.17 creates a WSOperation object, then calls its Open method, which takes the Web service URL and the SOAP Action. Calling WSOperation.Open returns a SoapMessage object that represents the request message. The WSOperation also exposes an HttpConnection property, which can be used to set an HTTP proxy as in this example.

To create a SOAP request message, you first call BeginMessage, indicating whether the message is RPC/encoded or document/literal. Assuming the message is RPC/encoded as in this example, you call AddRPCOperationElement and specify the operation's name, namespace prefix, and namespace URI. In this example, the operation is called getElementBySymbol (it returns an element from the periodic table given its symbol). For each operation part (method parameter), you call AddRPCPart and specify the part name and value. In this example, the part's name is "name" and its value is the string "na." In addition to simple types such as strings and integers, AddRPCPart also accepts objects and arrays and serializes them according to Section 5 encoding rules.

When you have finished writing the message, you call SoapMessage.EndMessage. When you call WSOperation.Send, the request message is sent and the response message is parsed into another SoapMessage object that is returned from the Send method.

To determine whether the operation succeeded, you check the SoapMessage.HasFault property, which returns True if there was an error. The procedure named ShowResults in Listing 12.17 first checks for errors. If there was a SOAP Fault returned, it will be accessible to you as the response message's Fault property, which is simple a SoapException.

If there are no errors, you can read the returned information using the response message's BodyItems property that returns an XmlNodeList. In the case of RPC/encoded messages, this list contains all XmlNode objects returned by the remote method call (the nodes inside the `<methodCallResponse>` element). In the case of document/literal messages, this list contains all XmlNode objects inside the response Body element.

That's all fine, but how does this help when the service requires a specific envelope namespace prefix like the CodeCraze newsgroup service? The SoapMessage class exposes fields that let you set all namespace prefixes used in SOAP messages, including the SOAP envelope namespace prefix. Listing 12.18 shows how to invoke the CodeCraze newsgroup service with SOAP.NET.

Listing 12.18 Invoking a PHP Web service using SOAP.NET (VBWSClientCode\Chapter12\DotNetClient\Form1.vb)

```
Private Sub btnPhp_Click(ByVal sender As System.Object, _
    ByVal e As System.EventArgs) Handles btnPhp.Click
  'create an operation
  Dim op As New LearnXmlWS.SoapNET.WSOperation()
  'call open to create a message
  Dim msg As LearnXmlWS.SoapNET.SoapMessage = _
      op.Open("http://www.codecraze.com/soap/nntp.php", _
      """http://www.codecraze.com/soap/nntp.php""")
  If chkProxy.Checked Then
      'this line sets an HTTP proxy
      op.HttpConnection.SetProxy("http://localhost:8080", _
➡False)
  End If
  'specify the SOAP envelope prefix
  'This service needs a specific prefix!!
  msg.SOAPEnvPrefix = "SOAP-ENV"
  'Begin an RPC/encoded message
  msg.BeginMessage(LearnXmlWS.SoapNET.MessageStyle.RPCEncoded)
  'the operation element
  msg.AddRPCOperationElement("m", "getheaders", "nntp.xsd")
  'the parameters or parts
  msg.AddRPCPart("newsgroup", _
```

```
                    "microsoft.public.dotnet.framework.aspnet.webservices")
            msg.AddRPCPart("numitems", 10)
            msg.EndMessage()
            'send it
            Dim resp As LearnXmlWS.SoapNET.SoapMessage = op.Send()
            ShowResults(resp)
        End Sub
```

The code in Listing 12.18 follows the same sequence as the preceding example. It starts with creating an operation and opening a connection to the Web
service's end point URL. Then it sets the envelop prefix in the line

```
    msg.SOAPEnvPrefix = "SOAP-ENV"
```

SOAP.NET can give you this level of control because it creates the request
message itself without relying on SoapHttpClientProtocol. Next, the example in
Listing 12.18 begins an RPC/encoded message and sets the operation name to
getheaders (which returns nntp message headers from the specified newsgroup). This operation takes two parameters: the name of the newsgroup and
the maximum number of headers to return. In this example, the newsgroup is mi-
crosoft.public.dotnet.framework.aspnet.webservices and the number of headers
is ten.

SOAP.NET can also be used to invoke document/literal Web services. To do
this, you do not call AddRPCOperationElement or AddRPCPart; instead, you call
AddLiteralXml, passing it the literal XML document fragment that you want to
send to the service. This fragment must adhere to the rules for carrying XML in
SOAP messages. Specifically, it cannot contain the XML declaration, a doctype
declaration, or processing instructions. Also, the document fragment itself cannot contain a SOAP message. This chapter's DotNetClient project includes an example of calling the GetCustomersXml operation (from Chapter 9) using
SOAP.NET.

12.9 Summary

Web services interop is here today as demonstrated by the many examples in
this chapter, while ongoing efforts show vendors' dedication to improved interop
in the future. Web services can be used today to integrate applications across

platforms and programming languages with relatively little programming effort. This capability represents the true value of Web services since it has a huge potential for integrating applications both within and across organizations.

12.10 Resources

MSDN's Interoperability page: http://msdn.microsoft.com/library/default.asp?url=/library/en-us/dnsvcinter/html/globalxmlwebsrvinterop.asp?frame=true.

Microsoft's interoperability newsgroup news://msnews.microsoft.com/microsoft.public.webservices.gxa-interop.

Web Services Interoperability Organization: http://www.ws-i.org/.

Round 2 interop home: http://www.whitemesa.com/interop.htm, © 2000 by Robert Cunnings.

Round 2A Specs: http://www.whitemesa.com/interop/proposal2.html, © 2000 by Robert Cunnings.

Round 2B Specs: http://www.whitemesa.com/interop/proposalB.html, © 2000 by Robert Cunnings.

Round 2C (headers) Specs: http://www.whitemesa.com/interop/proposalC.html, © 2000 by Robert Cunnings.

A list of issues with the WSDL 1.1 spec: http://wsdl.soapware.org/, © 2002 WSDL Issues.

Ballinger, Keith, "Web Services Interoperability and SOAP", MSDN article, May 2001 http://msdn.microsoft.com/library/en-us/dnsoap/html/soapinterop-bkgnd.asp, © Microsoft Corporation, All rights reserved.

Scott, Seely, "Interoperability Testing", MSDN article, August 2001 http://msdn.microsoft.com/library/en-us/dn_voices_webservice/html/service08152001.asp, © Microsoft Corporation, All rights reserved.

Paul Kulchenko's list of SOAP implementations: http://soaplite.com/#TOOLKITS, ©2000–2001, Paul Kulchenko, All rights reserved.

Chapter 13

A Web Service Walkthrough

The only source of knowledge is experience. —Albert Einstein

To wrap up the book and summarize much of what has been covered, this chapter walks you through the process of building a live Web service. You will learn to design Web service messages, to form those messages with .NET attributes, and to apply the authentication and authorization infrastructure to a new Web service. You'll benefit the most by building the Web service in this chapter and following along as I explain each step.

13.1   Introduction and Requirements

Consider the Weather service I've used throughout this book. Imagine the need to build a new version of this service with some changes and additional features. This section explains the core requirements for this new version.

It is based on messaging, rather than RPC, so the SOAP message format is different. Specifically, the new service uses document/literal messages rather than RPC/encoded, and it will ignore SOAPAction HTTP headers.

Like the old version, the new version exposes two primary operations: GetTemperature and GetWeather. However, not everyone has access to both operations. Instead, the service is secured so that only registered users can invoke its operations (they must logon to the service first). In addition, each registered user has a profile that lists which operations he or she can access. For example, a user might have access to GetTemperature but not GetWeather.

Since users are now registered and each user must logon to invoke an operation, I want to keep track of the Web service usage by each user. This concept of usage accounting is common for public Web services and enables us to bill for future Web service usage (I don't intend to charge people for using the Weather service, but you might build a service and charge for using it).

Finally, the service should be registered with UDDI so that clients may implement the UDDI Invocation pattern (see Chapter 11). When registered with UDDI, the service's interface is registered as a new tModel. This tModel must point to a WSDL document that contains interface-only elements, that is, no `<service>` element.

13.2   Designing Web Service Messages

The first step in implementing a document/literal Web service is to design the messages exchanged between client and service. To do this, you create an XSD schema describing each message. You can use a specialized XSD editor or any text editor, including Notepad. I used VS .NET's Schema editor because it provides an easy GUI for building the base schema structure and gives you access to the schema's text in case you want to do some manual editing. To use VS .NET's Schema editor, go to the File menu and choose New, File. In the New File dialog, select XML Schema as shown in Figure 13.1.

This gives you the Schema Designer with its toolbox and properties window as shown in Figure 13.2. The properties window is useful for changing things like the schema's targetNamespace, elementFormDefault, and attributeFormDefault settings (see Chapter 2 for more information on these settings). I changed the schema targetNamespace to http://www.learnxmlws.com/WeatherService and set the id property to WeatherMessages.

The toolbox contains the building blocks you use when creating a schema: element and attribute declarations, complex and simple type definitions, facets, and keys (see Chapter 2 for more information on XML Schema).

To create a schema, you drag objects from the toolbox to the designer surface and set their properties. For example, to add an element called Temperature, you drag an element option from the toolbox to the designer surface. By default, the element will be called element1 and its type will be (element1). Then

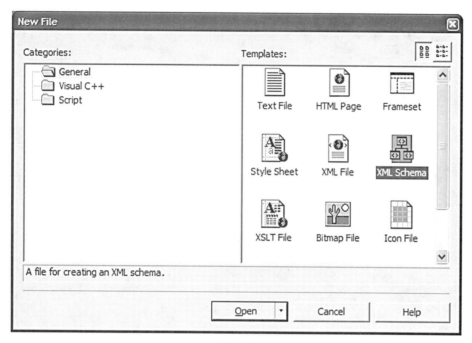

Figure 13.1   Creating a new schema

you can change the element name to Temperature and its type to float. The resulting element box as it will appear on the designer surface is shown in Figure 13.3.

To create an element that has an anonymous complex type, you simply start adding child elements and attributes inside the element box. See Figure 13.4 for an example of what you get in the designer if you create an element called CurrentWeather and then add a Temperature element of type float and a Conditions element of type string.

Note: To change a child element to an attribute, click on the E next to the element and select attribute from the dropdown list as shown in Figure 13.5.

Figure 13.6 shows the designer view for the request and response messages and Listing 13.1 shows the schema (text) view.

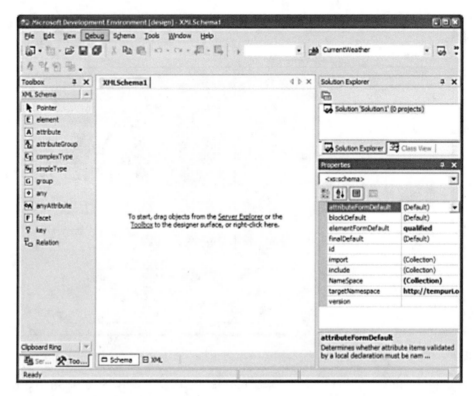

Figure 13.2　The Visual Studio Schema Designer

Figure 13.3　A simple element in the schema designer

**Listing 13.1　A schema defining Web service messages
(VBWSBook\Chapter13\WeatherMessages.xsd)**

```
<xs:schema id="WeatherMessages"
targetNamespace="http://www.learnxmlws.com/WeatherService"
elementFormDefault="qualified"
xmlns="http://www.learnxmlws.com/WeatherService"
xmlns:xs="http://www.w3.org/2001/XMLSchema">
    <!-- the GetTemperature request with the zipcode -->
    <xs:element name="TemperatureRequest" type="xs:string"/>
    <!-- response with temperature -->
```

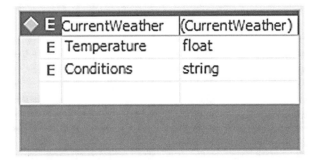

Figure 13.4   An element with an anonymous complex type

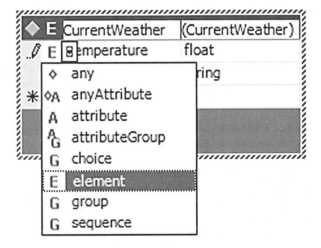

Figure 13.5   Changing a child element to an attribute

```xml
<xs:element name="Temperature" type="xs:float"/>
<!-- GetWeather request with zipcode -->
<xs:element name="WeatherRequest" type="xs:string"/>
<!-- GetWeather response with CurrentWeather -->
<xs:element name="CurrentWeather">
    <xs:complexType>
        <xs:sequence>
            <xs:element name="Temperature" type="xs:float" />
            <xs:element name="Conditions" type="xs:string" />
            <xs:element name="IconUrl" type="xs:string" />
            <xs:element name="Humidity" type="xs:float" />
            <xs:element name="Barometer" type="xs:float" />
```

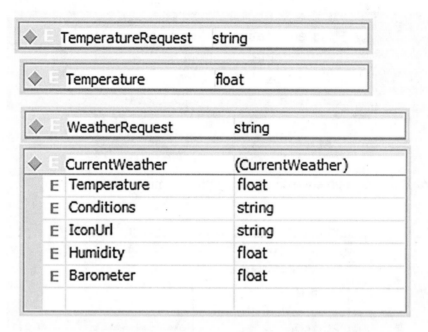

◆	TemperatureRequest	string

◆	Temperature	float

◆	WeatherRequest	string

◆		CurrentWeather	(CurrentWeather)
	E	Temperature	float
	E	Conditions	string
	E	IconUrl	string
	E	Humidity	float
	E	Barometer	float

Figure 13.6   Using the VS .NET Schema Designer to design Web service messages

```
        </xs:sequence>
      </xs:complexType>
   </xs:element>
</xs:schema>
```

I wanted to keep request and response messages as simple as possible so I tried not to use complex types unless they were really needed. For example, both request messages, TemperatureRequest and WeatherRequest, are simply elements that contain the requested ZipCode directly so they are of type string. This design reduces a request message from the current form in the old weather service (namespaces omitted):

```
<GetTemperature>
      <zipCode>20171</zipCode>
</GetTemperature>
```

to this simpler form in the new service (namespaces omitted):

```
<TemperatureRequest>20171</TemperatureRequest>
```

Similarly, the response from GetTemperature is equally simple: an element named Temperature that contains the returned temperature value. However, the response from GetWeather has to be a complex type to carry the weather information. A typical GetWeather response message would look like this:

```
<CurrentWeather xmlns="http://www.learnxmlws.com/WeatherService">
    <Temperature>float</Temperature>
    <Conditions>string</Conditions>
    <IconUrl>string</IconUrl>
    <Humidity>float</Humidity>
    <Barometer>float</Barometer>
</CurrentWeather>
```

Note that these messages do not contain the traditional wrapper elements created by .NET. For example, a straightforward GetTemperature implementation would result in the following request and response messages:

```
<!-- traditional GetTemperature request message -->
<GetTemperature xmlns="http://www.learnxmlws.com/WeatherService">
    <TemperatureRequest>string</TemperatureRequest>
</GetTemperature>

<!-- traditional GetTemperature response message -->
<GetTemperatureResponse
xmlns="http://www.learnxmlws.com/WeatherService">
    <Temperature>float</Temperature>
</GetTemperatureResponse>
```

Clearly this is not what we want. Not only does it add unnecessary wrapper elements, it also creates the impression that this Web service is based on RPC-style design, when in fact I started by designing the messages, not the RPC interface. Let's take a look at how you can implement a .NET Web service that receives and emits the messages described in Listing 13.1.

13.3 Implementing the Service

There are two options for implementing the messages we designed. First, you could create a WSDL document using the messages schemas from Listing 13.1, then run wsdl.exe –server on this WSDL to generate a Web service stub implementation. If you do this, you are essentially defining the interface (the

WSDL) first, and then implementing it—which is exactly what I explained in Chapter 8.

Alternatively, you can code the Web service directly and use a combination of attributes on the service and on each Web method to ensure the emitted WSDL adheres to the message specification in Listing 13.1. In Chapter 8, I covered the interface-based approach, so I will take the second approach here. But if you are comfortable with WSDL, I recommend you try the first approach at least once for this Web service to get a feel for it.

13.3.1 Generating Classes from Complex Types

The first thing we'll do is generate classes that correspond to complex types in service messages. In this example, only the CurrentWeather element has a complex type. To generate a class that corresponds to this type, you run xsd.exe with the /classes option. Since you want to generate a class for one of the elements in the schema (rather than classes for all elements in the schema), you specify the element name and namespace with the /e and /u options, respectively.

```
xsd.exe /classes /e:CurrentWeather /u:http://www.learnxmlws.com/
➥WeatherService  /l:vb WeatherMessages.xsd
```

This generates a class named CurrentWeather in a file named WeatherMessages.vb. I renamed this file to Messages.vb and removed the namespace prefix System.Xml.Serialization from it because this namespace is already imported at the top of the file. The resulting class, in Listing 13.2, contains a public field for each element defined in the complex type. We will use this class to return weather information from the GetWeather operation.

Listing 13.2 A class generated by xsd.exe from the CurrentWeather element schema (VBWSBook\Chapter13\Messages.vb)

```
<XmlTypeAttribute( _
  [Namespace]:="http://www.learnxmlws.com/WeatherService"), _
XmlRootAttribute( _
  [Namespace]:="http://www.learnxmlws.com/WeatherService", _
  IsNullable:=False)> _
Public Class CurrentWeather
    Public Temperature As Single
    Public Conditions As String
```

```
        Public IconUrl As String
        Public Humidity As Single
        Public Barometer As Single
    End Class
```

13.3.2 Writing the Service Code

Now you actually get to write some code. Start by creating a Web service project, then add to it the CurrentWeather class that was previously generated. Then add a Web service named Weather. Open the code view for this Web service and add Import statements for System.Web.Services.Protocols and System.Xml.Serialization namespaces.

This service should ignore SOAPAction as specified in the requirements section; therefore, add to the Web service class a SoapDocumentService attribute and set its RoutingStyle property to SoapServiceRoutingStyle.RequestElement.

By default, there should be a WebService attribute on the Web service class. Modify the namespace property of this attribute to http://www.learnxmlws.com/WeatherService. In this particular example, I chose to add a WebServiceBinding-Attribute and specify the binding's name and namespace as shown in Listing 13.3. I did this because the Web service's binding will be registered with UDDI as a tModel and I want it to have a more descriptive name than the standard "WeatherSoap."

To implement the GetTemperature operation, simply create a function named GetTemperature that takes in a Sring parameter and returns a Single as in Listing 13.3.

Listing 13.3 A Web Service implementing the predefined messages (VBWSBook\Chapter13\Weather.asmx.vb)

```
<SoapDocumentService( _
    RoutingStyle:=SoapServiceRoutingStyle.RequestElement), _
WebService(Namespace:= _
"http://www.learnxmlws.com/WeatherService"), _
WebServiceBindingAttribute("WeatherInterface", _
    "http://www.learnxmlws.com/WeatherService")> _
Public Class Weather
    Inherits System.Web.Services.WebService

    'Note that we don't want to use SoapAction
```

```
'so .NET relies on request element name
'so if we use Bare we must ensure there's only one parameter
'And that parameter name must be unique
<WebMethod(), _
SoapDocumentMethod( _
    Binding:="WeatherInterface", _
    Action:="", _
    ParameterStyle:=SoapParameterStyle.Bare)> _
Public Function GetTemperature( _
    <XmlElement("TemperatureRequest")> _
    ByVal ZipCode As String) _
    As <XmlElement("Temperature")> Single
    Return WeatherInfo.GetTemperatureFromZip(ZipCode)
End Function

<WebMethod(), _
SoapDocumentMethod( _
    Binding:="WeatherInterface", _
    Action:="", _
    ParameterStyle:=SoapParameterStyle.Bare)> _
Public Function GetWeather( _
    <XmlElement("WeatherRequest")> ByVal ZipCode As String) _
        As <XmlElement("CurrentWeather")> CurrentWeather
        Return WeatherInfo.GetWeatherFromZip(ZipCode)
    End Function
End Class
```

In addition to the WebMethod attribute, this function has a SoapDocument-
Method attribute that is used to control various aspects of the operation. The
binding property specifies that this operation is part of the WeatherInterface
binding defined earlier. The Action property specifies that the SOAPAction should
be an empty string. I expected that setting the service's RoutingStyle to Request-
Element would mean the Web service would not require a SOAPAction. But it
turns out that SOAPAction is required, but its value is ignored. The only reason I
set it to an empty string here is to make it clear that the value of SOAPAction
does not matter.

Finally, the ParameterStyle property is set to SoapParameterStyle.Bare,
meaning the ZipCode parameter and the return value are not wrapped in an additional XML element. This setting works with the XmlElement serialization attributes on the ZipCode parameter and the return value to form the correct

request and response message according to the schema in Listing 13.1. As a result, the request element contains only the input parameter as a direct child of the SOAP `<Body>` element. In this case, we want the request message to contain one element named TemperatureRequest; therefore, I add an XmlElement attribute on the ZipCode parameter to set the element name to Temperature-Request. Similarly, the return value is represented as an element contained directly within the response message's `<Body>` element. We want this element to be called Temperature per the schema in Listing 13.1, so I use another XmlElement attribute on the return value to specify Temperature as the element name.

The GetWeather Web method has the same SoapDocumentMethod attribute. This time, the ZipCode parameter is serialized to an element named WeatherRequest and the returned CurrentWeather object is serialized to an element named CurrentWeather.

13.3.3 Getting Weather Information

The National Weather Service (NWS) exposes current weather information via FTP and HTTP (at weather.noaa.gov). To make it easy for you to retrieve Weather information, I created a class named WeatherInfo that uses HTTP to get the weather from NWS's Web site.

To get weather information for a specific location, you must know the weather station id corresponding to that location. Realistically, most people don't know their weather station id; therefore, this service needs a way to translate a U.S. postal zip code to a weather station id. I did some digging and data mining and created a database table that provides this mapping.

Although it has close to 35,000 records, the table does not contain all current zip codes. This should not be a problem since the main purpose of the exercise is to illustrate the process of building Web services by building a live Web service. So don't expect that the Web service built in this chapter will use production-class data.

Returning to Listing 13.3, you'll notice that both GetTemperature and GetWeather rely on the WeatherInfo class to get current weather information. WeatherInfo exposes two shared (static) methods named GetTemperature-FromZip and GetWeatherFromZip. Internally, both methods retrieve complete weather information but GetTemperature returns only the temperature and ignores the rest of the information. You'll find the WeatherInfo class in the file named WeatherInfo.vb.

13.3.4 LogOn and LogOff

To prepare for implementing security, we need to implement two additional Web methods named LogOn and LogOff as shown in Listing 13.4.

Both LogOn and LogOff use shared methods of a class named SessionMgr to do the real work (SessionMgr is part of the security infrastructure built in Chapter 10. See Chapter 10 for more information on the SessionMgr class).

LogOff is an especially interesting method for two reasons. First, it doesn't return any value; therefore, it's a Sub not a Function. Second, when a client calls LogOff, it probably won't be interested in finding out if the LogOff succeeded or not. Consider a client that is being shut down; it might fire off a LogOff request as it is shutting down. The last thing the client needs is to wait for a response to come back. To make things easier for clients, I marked this method as one-way by setting the OneWay property to True. This means the corresponding WSDL operation has an input message but not an output message.

Listing 13.4 Adding LogOn and LogOff methods for authentication (VBWSBook\Chapter13\Weather.asmx.vb)

```
<WebMethod(), _
SoapDocumentMethod( _
 Binding:="WeatherInterface", _
 Action:="", _
 RequestElementName:="LogOnRequest", _
 ResponseElementName:="NewSession")> _
Public Function LogOn(ByVal UserId As String, _
                 ByVal Password As String) _
    As <XmlElement("SessionId")> String
        'implementation coming in a later section
End Function

<WebMethod(), _
SoapDocumentMethod( _
 Binding:="WeatherInterface", _
```

```
OneWay:=True, _
Action:="", _
RequestElementName:="LogOffRequest", _
ParameterStyle:=SoapParameterStyle.Bare)> _
Public Sub LogOff(ByVal SessionId As String)
    'implementation coming in a later section
End Sub
```

13.3.5 The RequestElement-Bare Dilemma

Looking at the LogOn method in Listing 13.4, you'll notice that the Parameter-Style property is missing from the SoapDocumentMethod attribute—hence the default (SoapParameterStyle.Wrapped) applies. This means that parameters are wrapped in a request element and the return value is wrapped in a response element. The reasons why I had to do this are explained in the next few paragraphs.

When you tell .NET to ignore the SOAPAction header (by setting RoutingStyle to RequestElement), you are essentially relying on the request element's name to identify which method should be invoked. So each request must have exactly one element as a direct child of <Body> and that element must have a unique name for each Web method on your service.

If you eliminate the wrapper elements by setting ParameterStyle to Bare, you are saying that serialized method parameters should appear as direct children of <Body>. When you combine both settings (RountingStyle = RequestElement and ParameterStyle = Bare) you end up with an interesting dilemma: Each Web method must have *exactly one parameter* and that parameter must have a unique serialized name among all other Web method parameters. For example, you can't have two methods, GetTemperature and GetWeather, each with a parameter that gets serialized to an element named ZipCode. To see why this makes sense, consider the following request message:

```
<soap:Body>
    <ZipCode
      xmlns="http://www.learnxmlws.com/WeatherService">20171
      </ZipCode>
</soap:Body>
```

Is this a request for the GetTemperature or GetWeather web method? If both methods have one parameter named ZipCode, there's no way to tell which method the client intended to invoke. Therefore, each method must have exactly one parameter and the serialized parameter must have a unique name.

The LogOn method has two parameters: User id and password, so it can't use Bare parameter style and RequestElement routing style together. I can replace the user id and password with a structure or a class that has two public members called UserId and Password and make LogOn accept an object of this class. But that makes it a little less convenient for a .NET client as it would have to instantiate an object, set its members, then pass it to LogOn as opposed to just calling LogOn and passing it the UserId and password directly.

I decided to keep things simple for .NET clients so I chose to use the default ParameterStyle that is wrapped. This is a design decision; there's no absolute right or wrong so your choice may very well be different from mine.

13.4   Authentication and Authorization

At this point, we have the core Web service operations implemented and working. However, there's still a lot of work to be done. We must secure the Web service so that only registered users with the appropriate permissions can access each of the methods. We must also modify the standard, auto-generated, documentation page to inform users that registration is required and to give them a link to the registration page. We also need to implement a usage tracking system so that we can monitor the usage for each user and, possibly, bill for it.

As you can see, a typical Web service requires substantial infrastructure. Instead of building security and usage accounting from scratch, we will simply use the infrastructure SOAP extensions from Chapter 10.

To reuse the infrastructure SOAP extension from Chapter 10, you must add a reference to infrastructure.dll (the assembly that contains the SOAP extensions). Then you add an Import statement for the namespace LearnXm-lWS.Web.Services.Infrastructure as shown in Listing 13.5.

Listing 13.5   Adding SoapHeader attribute to GetTemperature and GetWeather as part of implementing authorization (VBWSBook\Chapter13\ Weather.asmx.vb)

```
Imports System.Web.Services
Imports System.Web.Services.Protocols
```

```
Imports System.Xml.Serialization
Imports LearnXmlWS.Web.Services.Infrastructure
<SoapDocumentService( _
    RoutingStyle:=SoapServiceRoutingStyle.RequestElement), _
WebService(Namespace:= _
"http://www.learnxmlws.com/WeatherService"), _
WebServiceBindingAttribute("WeatherInterface", _
     "http://www.learnxmlws.com/WeatherService")> _
Imports LearnXmlWS.Web.Services.Infrastructure
Public Class Weather
    Inherits System.Web.Services.WebService

    'The session id
    Public sessHdr As SessionHeader
<WebMethod(), _
SoapDocumentMethod( _
    Binding:="WeatherInterface", _
    Action:="", _
    ParameterStyle:=SoapParameterStyle.Bare), _
 SoapHeader("sessHdr", _
   Required:=True, Direction:=SoapHeaderDirection.In)> _
Public Function GetTemperature( _
    <XmlElement("TemperatureRequest")> ByVal ZipCode As String) _
    As <XmlElement("Temperature")> Single
    Return WeatherInfo.GetTemperatureFromZip(ZipCode)
End Function

<WebMethod(), _
SoapDocumentMethod( _
    Binding:="WeatherInterface", _
    Action:="", _
    ParameterStyle:=SoapParameterStyle.Bare), _
SoapSecurity("Weather"), _
SoapHeader("sessHdr", _
   Required:=True, Direction:=SoapHeaderDirection.In)> _
Public Function GetWeather( _
   <XmlElement("WeatherRequest")> ByVal ZipCode As String) _
     As <XmlElement("CurrentWeather")> CurrentWeather
    Return WeatherInfo.GetWeatherFromZip(ZipCode)
End Function
End Class
```

Recall that the security SOAP extension relies on a SOAP header of type SessionHeader. So you need to add a public variable to your Web service class. The variable is sessHdr and its type is SessionHeader as shown in Listing 13.5.

Next, you need to add the SoapHeader attribute to both GetTemperature and GetWeather methods and specify that it is a required attribute and its direction is In. To apply authorization, you need to add the SoapSecurity attribute to each method and pass its constructor the required permission to execute that method. You can make up those permissions as long as they match what's in the UserPermissions database table (see Chapter 10 for more information about the database schema used for authentication and authorization).

13.5 Usage Accounting

Usage accounting can also be implemented by simply applying the usage accounting SOAP extension built in Chapter 10. You do this by adding the Accounting attribute to each method for which you want to track usage accounting. Assuming you already applied the security extension, you don't need to do anything else to apply usage accounting. Listing 13.6 shows the GetTemperature and GetWeather methods with the Accounting attribute added.

Listing 13.6   Applying the security and usage accounting SOAP extensions using attributes (VBWSBook\Chapter13\Weather.asmx.vb)

```
<WebMethod(), _
SoapDocumentMethod( _
    Binding:="WeatherInterface", _
    Action:="", _
    ParameterStyle:=SoapParameterStyle.Bare), _
SoapSecurity("Temperature"), _
SoapHeader("sessHdr", _
    Required:=True, Direction:=SoapHeaderDirection.In), _
Accounting (LogResponse:=True)> _
Public Function GetTemperature( _
    <XmlElement("TemperatureRequest")> ByVal ZipCode As String) _
    As <XmlElement("Temperature")> Single
    Return WeatherInfo.GetTemperatureFromZip(ZipCode)
End Function

<WebMethod(), _
```

```
SoapDocumentMethod( _
    Binding:="WeatherInterface", _
    Action:="", _
    ParameterStyle:=SoapParameterStyle.Bare), _
SoapSecurity("Weather"), _
SoapHeader("sessHdr", _
    Required:=True, Direction:=SoapHeaderDirection.In), _
Accounting(LogResponse:=True)> _
Public Function GetWeather( _
    <XmlElement("WeatherRequest")> ByVal ZipCode As String) _
        As <XmlElement("CurrentWeather")> CurrentWeather
    Return WeatherInfo.GetWeatherFromZip(ZipCode)
End Function
```

13.6   Customizing the Documentation Page

When a user uses a browser to navigate to the Web service end point (for example, weather.asmx) he or she will get a standard help page that lists the Web service's methods. This help page is generated by the file DefaultWsdl-HelpGenerator.aspx. We need to customize this page to inform the user that this service requires registration and to give him or her a link to the registration page.

The name of the default help page is specified in machine.config in the section called WebServices:

```
<wsdlHelpGenerator href="DefaultWsdlHelpGenerator.aspx"/>
```

To customize the generated documentation pages, make a copy of this .aspx file and do your customization in this copy. Then edit the machine.config file and specify the name of your copy instead of DefaultWsdlHelpGenerator.aspx. Alternatively, if you want the custom page to be used for a specific vroot, add the following to the `<system.web>` section in the vroot's web.config file.

```
<webServices>
    <wsdlHelpGenerator href="YourCustomPage.aspx"/>
</webServices>
```

The default page contains a large chunk of server-side script that inspects your Web service class to retrieve information such as the list of Web methods and example SOAP request and response for each method. After this script comes the HTML used to display this information. If you want to customize the page's look, you'll want to customize this HTML. For example, I created a page called CustomHelpGenerator.aspx that informs users about the registration requirement to use this Web service. The custom help page is shown in Figure 13.7. Note that the same header is displayed for the method listing page as well as for each method test page.

13.7 A VB 6 Client

To test the Web service, I decided to build a VB 6 client with the SOAP Toolkit's low level API. The project includes a form and a class module that acts as the Web service proxy. Listing 13.7 shows the pertinent parts of the class module's code (the entire class is in the file WeatherClient.cls).

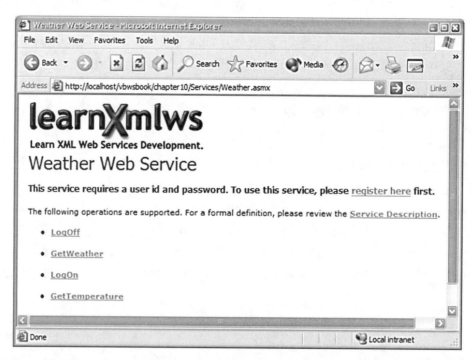

Figure 13.7   A custom help page notifying users that registration is required. Note that the registration link should point to a user registration Web form.

Listing 13.7 Implementing a VB 6 client using the SOAP Toolkit (VBWSClientCode\Chapter13\VB6Client\WeatherClient.cls)

```vb
Option Explicit
Private m_SessionHeader As String
Private m_SessionId As String
Private Const SERVICE_URL = "http://vbwsserver/vbwsbook/
➡Chapter13/Weather.asmx"
'Private Const SERVICE_URL = _
"http://www.learnxmlws.com/weather/Weather.asmx"
Private m_Connector As SoapConnector30
Private m_UseProxy As Boolean
Public ProxyServer As String
Public ProxyPort As Integer
Private Function SendMessage(ByVal header As String, _
            ByVal body As String, _
            Optional ByVal IsOneWay As Boolean = False) _
               As MSXML2.IXMLDOMElement
    On Error GoTo eh
      If m_Connector Is Nothing Then
          ConnectToService
      End If
      m_Connector.BeginMessage

      Dim Serializer As SoapSerializer30
      Set Serializer = New SoapSerializer30
      Serializer.Init m_Connector.InputStream
      'write the SOAP message
      Serializer.StartEnvelope
      If Len(header) > 0 Then
          Serializer.StartHeader
          Serializer.WriteXml header
          Serializer.EndHeader
      End If
      Serializer.StartBody
      'write the request document directly
      Serializer.WriteXml body
      Serializer.EndBody
      Serializer.EndEnvelope
      Serializer.Finished
      'send the message
      m_Connector.EndMessage
      If Not IsOneWay Then
          'get the response
```

```
            Dim Rdr As SoapReader30
            Set Rdr = New SoapReader30
            Rdr.Load m_Connector.OutputStream
            If Rdr.Fault Is Nothing Then
                If Rdr.BodyEntries.length > 0 Then
                    Set SendMessage = Rdr.BodyEntries.Item(0)
                End If
            Else
                On Error GoTo 0
                Err.Raise vbObjectError + 200, _
                    "WeatherClient", _
                    "The server returned a Fault: " & Rdr.Fault.Text
            End If
            Set Rdr = Nothing
        End If

        Set Serializer = Nothing

        Exit Function
eh:
    Err.Raise vbObjectError + 100, "WeatherClient", _
            "Error sending SOAP message: " + Err.Description
End Function

Public Sub LogOn(ByVal userid As String, ByVal password As String)
    Dim requestMessage As String
    requestMessage = "<LogOnRequest " & _
        " xmlns='http://www.learnxmlws.com/WeatherService'>" & _
        "<UserId>" & userid & "</UserId>" & _
        "<Password>" & password & _
        "</Password></LogOnRequest>"

    Dim SessionId As IXMLDOMElement
    'get the session id
    Set SessionId = SendMessage("", requestMessage)
    If Not (SessionId Is Nothing) Then
        m_SessionId = RemoveWhiteSpace(SessionId.Text)
        'make the session header for later use
        MakeSessionHeader m_SessionId
    End If
End Sub

Public Function GetWeather(ByVal zipcode As String) _
        As MSXML2.IXMLDOMElement
```

```
        Dim requestMessage As String
        requestMessage = "<WeatherRequest " & _
            "xmlns='http://www.learnxmlws.com/WeatherService'>" & _
            zipcode & "</WeatherRequest>"

        Dim weather As IXMLDOMElement
        Set GetWeather = SendMessage( _
            m_SessionHeader, requestMessage)

End Function

Private Sub ConnectToService()
    Set m_Connector = Nothing
    Set m_Connector = New HttpConnector30
    m_Connector.Property("EndPointURL") = SERVICE_URL
    m_Connector.Property("SoapAction") = ""
    If m_UseProxy Then
        m_Connector.Property("ProxyServer") = Me.ProxyServer
        m_Connector.Property("ProxyPort") = Me.ProxyPort
        m_Connector.Property("UseProxy") = True
    End If
    'establish connection
    m_Connector.Connect
End Sub
```

SendMessage is the core method that is responsible for sending SOAP messages and receiving responses. The code first checks if the member variable m_Connector is nothing. If it is, ConnectToService is called to create a new HttpConnector30, set its properties, and connect to the service. This new connector object is stored in m_Connector for future use.

SendMessage then creates a new SoapSerializer30 object and calls StartEnvelope to begin writing the SOAP envelope. If it's passed to a header string, it gets written out to the request message by first calling Serializer.StartHeader then Serializer.WriteXml and passing it the header string. This assumes that the header string is a well-formed XML fragment that represents the header you want to send.

Next, the body is written in a similar way: First, call StartBody followed by WriteXml to write the body string. When serialization is finished, the message is sent by calling m_Connector.EndMessage.

Then comes a check for the IsOneWay flag to determine if a response needs to be retrieved. This is needed because SendMessage does not read the service's WSDL document so it has no way of knowing if an operation is one-way unless the caller of SendMessage sets the IsOneWay parameter to True.

If the operation is not one-way, SendMessage creates a new SoapReader30 object and uses it to read the output stream. It then uses Rdr.Fault to check for errors and returns the Fault text if there is an error. If no errors are found, it gets the first body entry and returns it. The assumption here is that the returned XML is contained within one element that is a direct child of Body.

Listing 13.7 also shows the LogOn and GetWeather methods (LogOff and GetTemperature are implemented but not shown in this listing). LogOn creates the request message using primitive string concatenation. Instead of string concatenation, you can use the XML Document Object Model (DOM) to form your request messages. You can store template request messages in an XML document on the client and use the DOM API to read a message template from this document and substitute data as needed. The resulting XML is the request message.

After forming the request message, LogOn calls SendMessage to send the requestMessage and get back the response in the form on an XML DOM element. It then uses the Text property to extract the sessionid out of this element and calls RemoveWhiteSpace to remove leading and trailing carriage return, line feed, and space characters. Then it stores this sessionid in the member variable m_SessionId and calls MakeSessionHeader to prepare the SessionId header for future use with GetWeather and GetTemperature.

When GetWeather is called, it forms the WeatherRequest message with the supplied zip code and sends it along with the SessionId header using SendMessage. Then it returns the CurrentWeather information as an XML element.

Listing 13.8 shows the form code that uses this proxy class to retrieve and display weather information.

Listing 13.8   A VB 6 form to invoke the Weather service (VBWSClientCode\Chapter13\VB6Client\Form1.frm)

```
Option Explicit
Private m_Weather As WeatherClient
Private Sub cmdGet_Click()
On Error GoTo eh
    If m_Weather Is Nothing Then
        CreateProxy
    End If
    m_Weather.UseProxy = chkProxy.Value

    Dim cw As MSXML2.IXMLDOMElement
    Set cw = m_Weather.GetWeather(txtZip.Text)
    DisplayData cw
    Exit Sub
eh:
    lblInfo.Caption = Err.Description
End Sub
Private Sub CreateProxy()
    Set m_Weather = New WeatherClient
    m_Weather.ProxyServer = "localhost"
    m_Weather.ProxyPort = 8080
    m_Weather.UseProxy = chkProxy.Value
    m_Weather.LogOn "user01", "password"
End Sub

Private Sub Form_Unload(Cancel As Integer)
    'intentionally ignore errors
    'this is a one-way method
    'and the form is closing
    On Error Resume Next
    If Not (m_Weather Is Nothing) Then
        m_Weather.LogOff
    End If
End Sub
```

When the user clicks Get Weather, the cmdGet_Click code checks if the service proxy, stored in m_Weather has already been created. If it hasn't, CreateProxy is called. CreateProxy instantiates a new WeatherClient object, configures its proxy settings, and calls the LogOn method to obtain a sessionid.

Going back to cmdGet_Click, once the proxy is created, cmdGet_Click calls its GetWeather method, passing it the user-entered zip code. Then it captures the returned XML element and passes it to DisplayData, which uses the DOM to extract and display weather information. The result is shown in Figure 13.8.

13.8 Leveraging UDDI

In order to provide some recovery facility, I registered the Weather service with production UDDI registry to enable clients to implement the UDDI invocation pattern (see Chapter 11). To register with UDDI, I saved the service's WSDL, edited it, and removed the implementation part (the <service> element). I saved the resulting WSDL document at http://www.learnxmlws.com/weather/weatherinterface.wsdl. I already had a business entity registered with UDDI so all I had to do was register a new tModel and then register the service itself. The resulting service key is C6DDD2FB-593B-452A-A225-C6A930EFCDE8 and the binding key (which is what you use for the UDDI invocation model) is 400d2ea3-bc66-485d-9594-b3474d801442.

Figure 13.8   Running the VB 6 client

REAL WORLD XML WEB SERVICES

13.8.1   Implementing the Invocation Pattern

I chose to implement the UDDI invocation pattern in a .NET client in order to show you two different clients for the Weather service. Listing 13.9 shows a partial listing of the client code that retrieves and displays weather information. See frmWeather.vb for the complete code.

Listing 13.9   A VB .NET client that uses the UDDI invocation pattern to locate the Web service at runtime (VBWSClientCode\Chapter13\DotNetClient\ frmWeather.vb)

```
Const BINDING_KEY As String = _
  "eb045631-c5bb-4621-b052-830c13b5d7c8"

Private _ws As VBWSSERVER.Weather
Private Sub btnWeather_Click( _
 ByVal sender As System.Object, ByVal e As System.EventArgs) _
     Handles btnWeather.Click
    Dim cw As CurrentWeather
    Try
        cw = GetWeather(txtZip.Text)
    Catch ex As Exception
           If UDDIInvocationPattern.IsRecoverable(ex) Then
               lblStatus.Text = "Checking UDDI ..."
               Me.Refresh()
               If GetCurrentUrl() Then
                   cw = GetWeather(txtZip.Text)
                   lblStatus.Text = ""
               End If
           Else
               MessageBox.Show(ex.Message)
               _ws = Nothing
           End If
    End Try
    If Not (cw Is Nothing) Then
        ShowWeatherInfo(cw)
    End If
End Sub
Private Function GetWeather(ByVal ZipCode) As _
                VBWSSERVER.CurrentWeather
    If _ws Is Nothing Then
        CreateProxy()
    ElseIf chkProxy.Checked Then
        _ws.Proxy = New System.Net.WebProxy( _
```

```
                        "http://localhost:8080", False)
        Else
            _ws.Proxy = Nothing
        End If
        Return _ws.GetWeather(ZipCode)
End Function


Private Sub CreateProxy()
    _ws = New Weather()
    Me.SetProxy()
    Me.DoLogOn()
End Sub
Private Sub SetProxy()
    If chkProxy.Checked Then
        _ws.Proxy = New _
            System.Net.WebProxy("http://localhost:8080", False)
    End If
End Sub
Private Sub DoLogOn()
    'you can change the userid and password here ...
    Dim sess As New SessionHeader()
    sess.SessionId = _ws.LogOn("user01", "password")
    _ws.SessionHeaderValue = sess
End Sub
Private Function GetCurrentUrl()
        Try
            Dim newUrl As String = _
UDDIInvocationPattern.GetCurrentUrl (BINDING_KEY)
            _ws.Url = newUrl
        Catch ex As Exception
        MessageBox.Show( _
"There was an error retrieving the current URL from UDDI." + _
    " Please try again later. " + _
    ex.Message)
            Return False
        End Try
        Me.DoLogOn()
        Return True
End Function
```

```
Private Sub frmWeather_Closing(ByVal sender As Object, _
    ByVal e As System.ComponentModel.CancelEventArgs) _
            Handles MyBase.Closing
    Try
        If Not (_ws Is Nothing) Then
            'call LogOff to end the session
            _ws.LogOff(_ws.SessionHeaderValue.SessionId)
        End If
    Catch ex As Exception
        'ignore the exception
    End Try
End Sub
```

When the user clicks Get Weather, the event handler calls GetWeather, passing it the user-entered zip code. If an exception occurs while getting the weather information, the Catch block checks to see if this is a recoverable error. If so, it calls GetCurrentUrl to get the current Web service end point URL from UDDI. Then it proceeds to call GetWeather again using this new URL. If the exception is non-recoverable, it is reported in a message box. Once weather information is retrieved, ShowWeatherInfo (not shown here) handles displaying it to the user.

The GetWeather function checks if the Web service proxy is created. If it's not, it calls CreateProxy, which instantiates a new Web service proxy, calls Set-Proxy to configure the HTTP proxy, then calls DoLogOn to invoke the Web service's LogOn method. If the Web service proxy was already created, GetWeather sets the HTTP proxy if the user checked the Use Proxy check box. Then it calls the Web service's GetWeather, passing it the ZipCode. When the form is closing, it calls the Web service's LogOff method, catching and ignoring any exceptions that might occur.

You can test this client by first pointing it to the weather Web service on your own server. Then stop your server (for example, by typing iisreset -stop on the command line) and click Get Weather. The client will query UDDI, get the Web service URL (on LearnXmlWS.com), then go on and invoke the service at this location.

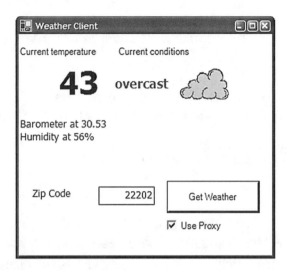

Figure 13.9   Using the VB .NET client. This client implements the UDDI Invocation Pattern to attempt to recover from failures.

13.9   Summary

This chapter is a walkthrough of the Web service development process. The process begins with message design where you create XML Schemas describing the service's input and output messages. Then you use xsd.exe to generate complex types from those schemas as needed. To implement the service itself, you use .NET attributes to shape each operation's messages according to the schema you defined earlier. To implement Web services infrastructure, you use a combination of reusable components and SOAP extensions that can be easily applied to any Web service. Finally, if your Web service is for public use, you can register it with UDDI enabling clients to implement UDDI scenarios such as the invocation pattern.

13.10   Resources

DevelopMentor's .NET Web discussion list: http://discuss.develop.com/dotnet-web.html

Tutorials and resources on LearnXmlws.com.

Appendix A

Data Type Mappings

To read this table, locate the XML Schema type that you want to look up, then read across to find the corresponding SQL Server and .NET data types. Note that some schema types have no direct mapping in SQL Server. To handle these, you need to convert them into a SQL Server supported type. For example, anyURI has no direct mapping in SQL Server; instead you store it as a string (varchar).

There are also some types that have no SQL Server mappings and could potentially lose information if you convert them. For example, unsignedLong is an unsigned 64-bit integer. SQL Server has no support for such types (bigint is a signed 64-bit integer) so you can either convert it to a signed 64-bit integer, which changes the range of allowable values, or you can store it as a string (varchar) and lose the numeric semantics associated with integers.

XML Schema	SQL Server	.NET Framework
anyURI	Same as string	System.Uri
base64Binary	Binary, Varbinary, or Image	System.Byte[ ]
boolean	Bit	System.Boolean
byte	SmallInt	System.SByte
date	DateTime	System.DateTime
dateTime	DateTime	System.DateTime
decimal	Decimal	System.Decimal

XML Schema	SQL Server	.NET Framework
double	Float	System.Double
duration	N/A	System.TimeSpan
ENTITIES	N/A	System.String[ ]
ENTITY	Same as string	System.String
float	Real	System.Single
gDay	N/A	System.DateTime
gMonthDay	N/A	System.DateTime
gYear	N/A	System.DateTime
gYearMonth	N/A	System.DateTime
hexBinary	Binary, Varbinary, or Image	System.Byte[ ]
ID	Same as string	System.String
IDREF	Same as string	System.String
IDREFS	N/A	System.String[ ]
int	Int	System.Int32
integer	BigInt	System.Decimal
language	Same as string	System.String
long	BigInt	System.Int64
Name	Same as string	System.String
NCName	Same as string	System.String
negativeInteger	BigInt	System.Decimal
NMTOKEN	Same as string	System.String
NMTOKENS	Same as string	System.String[ ]
nonNegativeInteger	BigInt	System.Decimal
nonPositiveInteger	BigInt	System.Decimal
normalizedString	Same as string	System.String
NOTATION	Same as string	System.String

XML Schema	SQL Server	.NET Framework
positiveInteger	BigInt	System.Decimal
QName	Same as string	System.Xml.XmlQualifiedName
short	SmallInt	System.Int16
string	Varchar, Text, NVarChar, or NText	System.String
time	N/A	System.DateTime
timePeriod	N/A	System.DateTime
token	Same as string	System.String
unsignedByte	TinyInt	System.Byte
unsignedInt	BigInt	System.UInt32
unsignedLong	N/A	System.UInt64
unsignedShort	Int	System.UInt16

Appendix B

.NET Web Services Tips and Tricks

Scott Guthrie started a tradition of having a chapter or appendix titled "Tips and Tricks" in ASP.NET-related books. Following this tradition, I decided to write a similar appendix for this book. The tips you'll find here are recommendations or best practices that, if used, will serve you well in the long term. Of course, things are never black and white, so don't consider these recommendations the ten commandments of Web services; just reconsider if you are not following them.

B.1   Use Document/Literal SOAP Messages for Data Exchange

RPC/encoded format caught on very quickly because it didn't rely on XML Schemas, which were not standard at the time that SOAP 1.0 was released. Now schemas *are* standard and most vendors support them. Document/literal messages rely on an XML Schema that defines the message format so you can design elaborate messages that use the full power of XML Schema. Such elaborate schemas are usually required when you are exchanging business data across applications or businesses.

The good news is that by default, ASP.NET Web services use document/ literal messages unless you explicitly configure them to use one of the other two supported formats (RPC/encoded or RPC/literal). See Chapters 3 and 4 for details about the difference between RPC/encoded and document/literal formats.

B.2   Design Messages Not Methods

This tip comes naturally after you adopt the previous one. Web services are concerned with messaging and exchanging data between applications. Today, the best way to provide a formal, machine-readable description of this data is to use XML Schema. When building a Web service, start by designing your messages. How do you want the request and response messages to look? You can use VS .NET's Schema Designer to do most of the work. You can also take this formal description and show it to developers who will program against your Web service to get their buy-in. Then start building your Web service based on the final schema design. This decoupling of message design from implementation (methods) allows you to change the implementation later and preserve the same interface. See Chapter 13 for an example of this process.

B.3   Use an HTTP Proxy Tool for Troubleshooting

You can't always troubleshoot a Web service or a Web service client by stepping through the code. In many cases, especially those that have to do with interoperability, you need to see the SOAP messages to determine what is going on. The easiest way to do this is to use an HTTP proxy tool such as ProxyTrace (www.pocketsoap.com). With a tool like this you can easily capture the request and response and inspect them for problems. See Chapter 6 for details on using ProxyTrace.

B.4   Use Output and Data Caching

Many of the Web services you'll build, at least initially, will expose data to clients. You can cache returned data in memory to reduce the number of hits on your back-end data source (the database). Naturally, the rule of "nothing comes for free" applies here so whether you use output or data caching you need to buy lots of RAM for your server.

B.5   Don't Use HTTP Cookies

Although ASP.NET lets you use sessions per Web method, you should think hard before you decide to do this. Using ASP.NET sessions relies on HTTP cookies (cookieless sessions do not work with Web services), which means you are tying your session handling to HTTP. That's fine for now, but long term I think this is a mistake. HTTP is not perfect and it forces many limitations on the Web services platform (for example, no callbacks). This means you should expect alternate transports to emerge with higher capabilities and lots of cool, useful features. If, in the future, you decide to expose the same Web service over another trans-port, (for example, Message Queuing), you have to figure out session manage-ment all over again. Generally speaking, try not to rely on HTTP-specific features.

B.6   Use SOAP Headers for Session Management

SOAP headers can be used to communicate cookies much like HTTP cookies. You can build your own sessions using SOAP headers which are transport-independent (they work just as well over SMTP as HTTP). See Chapters 5 and 6 for details on using SOAP headers and Chapter 13 for an example implementing sessions with SOAP headers.

B.7   Use RequestElement Routing

Normally SOAPAction is used to route request messages to the appropriate methods. This has many problems, not the least of which is its reliance on HTTP. For the reasons explained in Chapter 6, avoid using SOAPAction if you can. By default, ASP.NET Web services rely on SOAPAction. You can change that by add-ing a SoapDocumentServiceAttribute attribute to the Web service class and set-ting its RoutingStyle property to SoapServiceRoutingStyle.RequestElement. See Chapter 6 for more details on the RoutingStyle property.

B.8   Use One-Way Operations

SOAP defines client-to-service communications in terms of messages. If you are using document-style messages, nothing says that every request must have a response message. In fact, WSDL defines a one-way operation as one that has a request message and no response message. This can be a very powerful design pattern for submitting requests or notifying services without requiring a re-sponse. A client sends a request and receives an empty HTTP response as soon as the request reaches your Web method. Of course you lose the ability to return data and error information, but there are some scenarios where this still makes sense. See Chapter 6 for details on implementing one-way operations and Chapter 13 for an example service with a one-way operation.

B.9 Don't Implement Properties on Web Services

Properties don't belong on Web services. Sure, you can implement a property procedure and store the data in the ASP.NET session instead of a private variable. But just because you can doesn't mean you should. It's appalling to see literature with examples of implementing properties on Web services. Web services are all about exchanging documents based on messaging—not properties. Get over properties, and design stateless, message-oriented Web services.

B.10 Use Distributed Transactions Only If You Need Them

It's very easy to use distributed transactions (also known as Enterprise Services, COM+, and DTC transactions) within a Web method. Simply set the WebMethodAttribute's TransactionOption property to RequiresNew and you're set. This is another example of "just because you can doesn't mean you should." Please understand that distributed transactions are designed for specific scenarios and are not intended to replace TSQL or ADO.NET transactions. Each has its role and the scenarios where each makes sense. See Chapter 6 for a discussion of when distributed transactions make sense and a link to an MSDN article that compares the performance of the three transaction control mechanisms.

B.11 Don't Re-Invent the Wheel

I've seen far too many examples showing developers how to encrypt SOAP messages between client and service. To me, this is exactly like reinventing the wheel. All such examples rely on hand-crafted encryption code using the .NET framework's cryptography classes. The main argument for using this approach versus SSL (the wheel) is that SSL causes a performance hit. Intuitively, I think that if you are going to do your own encryption, either it won't be as cryptographically strong as SSL or it will be just as computationally expensive. If you are really concerned about SSL's performance, you can take advantage of hardware SSL accelerators available from several vendors. The point is: Someone has already built encryption/decryption infrastructure for you at the transport level and has optimized it as much as possible. Why would you want to reinvent that wheel?

Strategically, you should avoid plumbing whenever possible because vendors such as Microsoft are likely to implement such plumbing for you in the future. For example, the WS-Security specification addresses how XML Encryption can be used for end-to-end message privacy. If you create your own encryption routines now, you're likely to throw them away when WS-Security implementations become available.

Index

A

fractionDigits facet, `<restriction>` element (XSD), 32

G

Global elements, complex types, 34
GLUE (The Mind Electric), SOAP implementation testing, 494

H

Handling errors, SOAP
  basics, 116–117
  `<detail>` element (SOAP), 117, 118–119
  `<faultCode>` element (SOAP), 117, 118–119
  `<faultString>` element (SOAP), 117
  high level APIs, 201–202
Handling SOAP binary data
  attachments, 122–124
  Base64 encoding/decoding, 121–122
  sending URLs where clients retrieve data, 124–126
Headers (SOAP)
  authorization extensions, 387
  extending SOAP, 119–121
    bindings with WSDL, 153–155
  IHeaderHandler interface
    exposing services, 215, 216–218
    invoking services, 218–221
  .NET Web services
    defining classes, 273–274
    unknown headers, accessing, 279–282
    unknown headers, using DidUnderstand property, 282–284
    using in services, 274–276
    using proxy classes, 276–279
High level APIs (SOAP Toolkit), 185–186
  from classic ASP pages, 203–204
  error handling, 201–202
  exposing Web services, 188–199
  invoking Web services, 199–201
  serialization/deserialization
    alternative with XML as native data format, 212–215
    basics, 205–206
    custom type mappers, 212
    generic type mappers, 206–210

UDT type mappers, 210–211
troubleshooting with Trace Utility, 202–203
HTTP
  binding and WSDL, 179–183
  and distributed applications, 2
  interoperability problems, 483
  invoking .NET Web services with proxies, 244–247
  and SOAP, 85–87
  SOAP messaging, 95–96
Hypertext Transfer Protocol. *See* HTTP

I

IBM's APPC (Advanced Program to Program Communication), 2
identifierBag schema (UDDI), 441
Identifiers (UDDI), identifierBag schema, 441
IHeaderHandler interface (SOAP)
  Web services
    exposing, 215, 216–218
    invoking, 218–221
IIS (Internet Information Server), role in Web services, 6
`<import>` element (WSDL), 173, 176–177
Importing WSDL elements, 173
  bindings, 174–175
  messages, 174–175
  portTypes, 174–175
  separating elements, 174
Internet-based Web service interfaces
  changing namespaces, 312–315
  defining, 294–301
  implementing, 301–306
    multiple interfaces, 306–309
    multiple interfaces, steps, 309–312
    at runtime, 320–321
  programming against interfaces by generating proxies, 315–319
Internet Information Server (IIS), role in Web services, 6
Internet protocol stack, 86
Interop
  definition, 481–482
  distributed applications, 2
  efforts
    SOAP-Builders forum, 485–486
    testing techniques, 486–487

Interop *(continued)*
    problems
        basics, 482–483
        HTTP, 483
        SOAP, 484–485
        WSDL, 484
Interoperability. *See* Interop
Invocation patterns (UDDI), 415, 416
`<invoice>` element (XSD), 58, 59
    overriding serializing, 78
ISAPI listeners, SOAP Toolkit Web services, 190
    advanced settings, 232
    basics, 229–231
`<item>` element (XSD), 38
IXMLDOMNodeList, result of invoking
        complexTypeServer, 212–215

J–K

Java, Apache SOAP for Java clients and alternate
        tools, 494
Key-based relationships, *versus* foreign-key and
        primary-key in relational databases, 57,
        59–61
`<key>` element (XSD), 59
keyedReference elements (UDDI), 439–441
`<keyref>` element (XSD), 59, 61

L

`length` facet, `<restriction>` element (XSD),
    32
Low level APIs (SOAP Toolkit), 186, 221
    Web services
        exposing, 221–225
        invoking, 226–229

M

`maxExclusive` facet, `<restriction>` element
    (XSD), 32
`maxInclusive` facet, `<restriction>` element
    (XSD), 32
`maxLength` facet, `<restriction>` element
    (XSD), 30, 32
`maxOccurs` attribute, `<quantity>` element
    (XSD), 29–30
    restrictions on global element declarations, 34

Messaging (SOAP), 6–7
    capturing messages, 96–97
    contents, 88–90
    document/encoded, 91–93
    document/literal, 91–93
        basics, 93–95
    message part (WSDL), 132–133
    .NET Web services support, 6–7
    RPC/encoded, 91–93
    RPC/literal, 91–93
    versus RPC, 6–7
    SOAP over HTTP, 95–96
    Web services
        client-side, 102–103
        example, 97–101
Metering (usage accounting), SOAP extensions,
        542–543
    basics, 391–395
    client example, 396–397
    ThreadPool object, 395–396
Microsoft SOAP Toolkit. *See* SOAP Toolkit
MIME binding, WSDL, 183–184
`minExclusive` facet, `<restriction>` element
    (XSD), 32
`minInclusive` facet, `<restriction>` element
    (XSD), 32
`minLength` facet, `<restriction>` element
    (XSD), 32
`minOccurs` attribute, `<quantity>` element
    (XSD), 29–30
    restrictions on global element declarations, 34
Model groups, complex types, 34
MSXML 4.0 parser, 49–50, 51, 97, 102

N

NAICS (North American Industry Classification
        System), 440
Namespaces (XML)
    default changes in .NET Web services, 255–257
    .NET SDK and UDDI, 474–475
    and XSD
        basics, 39–42
        in instance XML documents, 42–43
        XSD types, 43–46
Naming collisions, XSD and XML namespaces
    basics, 39–42
    in instance XML documents, 42–43

V

W